WRITING
SOCIAL
HISTORY

WRITING SOCIAL HISTORY

SUMIT SARKAR

OXFORD
UNIVERSITY PRESS

Oxford University Press is a department of the University of Oxford.
It furthers the University's objective of excellence in research, scholarship,
and education by publishing worldwide. Oxford is a registered trademark of
Oxford University Press in the UK and in certain other countries

Published in India by
Oxford University Press
YMCA Library Building, 1 Jai Singh Road, New Delhi 110001, India

First published 1997
Oxford India Paperbacks 1998
Thirteenth impression 2013

ISBN-13: 978-0-19-564633-7
ISBN-10: 0-19-564633-9

Typeset in Garamond TTF
by Excellent Laser Typesetters, Pitampura, Delhi 110 034
Printed in India by Anvi Composers, New Delhi 110 063

To Aditya

Preface

The essays in this volume were written at various times since 1986, mostly between 1991 and 1996. Two of them, Chapters 4 and 8, are reprints with minor modifications. The others are being published for the first time, though parts of them have had earlier incarnations as seminar papers or articles. Details of past publication appear at the end of the Preface.

The unity these essays have come to acquire is largely on account of their composition amidst the pressures and stimuli of a decade of massive change: the transformations in Indian life signified by the destruction of the Babri Masjid and lower-caste affirmations, and, on a world scale, the collapse of the Soviet Union, the apparently irresistible advance of new forms of global capitalism, and what often seems to be a general displacement of the politics of class by that of ethnic or religious identity. Within my own discipline the historiographical tradition that has attracted me most — namely the radical social history of the 1960s and 1970s associated with flexible patterns of Marxian thinking and visions of more democratic and humane forms of socialism, epitomized best perhaps by E.P. Thompson — has come under formidable attack. The evident shift from social history to forms of cultural studies largely abstracted from 'material' contexts, and the accompanying displacement of Marxism, whether orthodox or revisionist, by a variety of postmodernistic (and postcolonial) moods, appear to many today to be both inevitable and salutary. There is also an occasional opposite tendency towards nostalgic evocations of the lost verities of Marxist dogma and bureaucratic socialist regimes.

The essays that follow should make clear my unhappiness with both these trajectories. Part I seeks to develop an argument about the new orthodoxy of colonial discourse analysis via essays on the changing social contexts of modern Indian history-writing, the extent and forms of relevance today of Thompsonian social history, and a critique of *Subaltern Studies*. I find Saidian moods generally unhelpful for understanding colonial middle-class culture, and a hindrance in the exploration of areas which current developments make increasingly crucial: notably, studies of gender and subordinate castes. At the same time, there are elements of great value in the 'linguistic turn' and the self-reflexivities they can stimulate among historians. An unproblematized return or adherence to old patterns and styles of historical writing is neither possible nor desirable.

Part II moves from critique towards the probing of alternatives, through specific research. The essay on the elder Thompson apart — chronologically the earliest, which I am reprinting with a new Postscript — the focus is on late-nineteenth and early-twentieth-century Bengal. The colonial middle class, I have argued, should not be treated as a homogenized bloc, as both 'renaissance' historiography and its latter-day critics have tended to treat it. The trajectory of this middle class was not determined, again, entirely by English education — no matter whether its impact be seen as worthy inspiration or disastrous cultural conquest. There is need to give due weight also to other institutional innovations, all of them replete, like education itself, with multiple implications: print-culture and the vernacular public space it helped to create, open to small but growing numbers of women and upwardly-mobile lower-caste men; clock-time; and office-work *(chakri)* under foreign bosses in mercantile firms and government departments. Studies of Calcutta and of the modulations of Kaliyuga myths in late-nineteenth-century urban and village settings lead up to the two long essays on Vidyasagar and Ramakrishna — to my mind, the core of this book. The first tries to look at the forms and contexts of Vidyasagar's initiatives concerning education and gender in what are perhaps somewhat novel ways. The second attempts, through a textual study of the *Kathamrita*, a social history of the religious world of Ramakrishna. The concluding essay is a preliminary stocktaking of some work I have recently started on the discourses and manifestations of caste in late-colonial Bengal.

Many ideas in the book have evolved through discussions with my Delhi University students, and I would like to thank them for helping to keep teaching still a pleasure, and, for me, inseparable from research. Among the very many who have helped, through criticisms, comments, suggestions, and sometimes by simply being there, helping to maintain spaces of meaningful, free discussion through difficult times, I must mention particularly Aijaz Ahmed, G. Arunima, Rajeev Bhargava, Akeel Bilgrami, Mahmood Mamdani,

Dilip Menon, Nivedita Menon, Gautam Navlakha, Kumkum Sangari, and Achin Vanaik. Neeladri Bhattacharya's comments and suggestions for rearrangement proved enormously helpful at the moment of going to press. I am grateful to Rukun Advani for the great interest he has taken, and for valuable editorial corrections. Stimulating discussions with Pradip Datta have been part of our family's life for years, and it will be evident that I have benefited in exceptional ways from his pioneering research on communal formations in early-twentieth-century Bengal.

Tanika, as always, has been my severest critic and greatest inspiration. Without her, there would have been no book.

The responsibility for errors and inadequacies must remain mine alone.

This book is for Aditya, who has helped in many more ways than he knows.

An early version of 'The Many Worlds of Indian History' was presented at the International Congress of Historians, Madrid, August 1990, and published in Italian in *Storia della Historiographia*, 19, 1991. More recently, parts of it went into my talk on 'Indian History: The State of the Art', at the School of Social Sciences, Jawaharlal Nehru University, in November 1995. I am very grateful for the criticisms and comments made there.

'The Relevance of E.P. Thompson' had its origins in my article, 'E.P. Thompson', published, shortly after Thompson's death, in *Economic and Political Weekly* (xxviii 39, 25 September 1993), and in two presentations at memorial meetings in Delhi University and the India International Centre, September–October 1993.

Earlier versions of 'The Decline of the Subaltern in Subaltern Studies' were presented at seminars on E.P. Thompson at the Max Planck Institut für Geschichte, Göttingen (June 1994) and History Workshop, London (July 1994), and subsequently at the Sociology Department, Delhi University (December 1994). I have benefited greatly from comments and criticisms, particularly at the Delhi presentation.

'Edward Thompson and India: *The Other Side of the Medal*' is being reprinted, with slight modifications and a new Postscript, from my Afterword to a new edition of Edward Thompson's *The Other Side of the Medal*, ed. Mulk Raj Anand (New Delhi, Sterling, 1989).

'The City Imagined: Calcutta of the Nineteenth and Early

Twentieth Centuries' includes material from my 'Calcutta and the Bengal Renaissance' in Sukanta Chaudhuri, ed., *Calcutta: The Living City* (Delhi, Oxford University Press, 1990), and 'Calcutta in the Early Years of the Twentieth Century' in J. Racine, ed., *Calcutta 1905-1971: Au coeur des créations et des révoltes du siecle* (Paris, Editions Autrement, 1997, in French).

A version of 'Renaissance and Kaliyuga: Time, Myth and History in Colonial Bengal' was presented at the International Round Table of Historians and Anthropologists at Bellagio, August 1989, and has been accepted for publication in Gerald Sider and Gavin Smith, eds, *Between History and Histories: Making Silences and Commemorations* (Toronto University, forthcoming).

'Vidyasagar and Brahmanical Society' is a modified version of two lectures given at Vidyasagar University (Midnapur, West Bengal) in December 1996.

'Kaliyuga, Chakri and Bhakti: Ramakrishna and His Times' is being reprinted, with minor changes, from *Economic and Political Weekly*, 18 July 1992. Another version has been published as *An Exploration of the Ramakrishna-Vivekananda Tradition* in the series *Socio-Religious Movements and Cultural Networks in Indian Civilisation: Occasional Paper I* (Shimla, Indian Institute of Advanced Study, 1993).

Versions of parts of 'Identity and Difference: Caste in the Formation of Ideologies of Nationalism and Hindutva' have been presented in seminars at the universities of Pennsylvania (Philadelphia, February 1994), Melbourne (October 1994), and Chicago (May 1995) and published as 'Indian Nationalism and the Politics of Hindutva' in David Ludden, ed., *Making India Hindu* (Delhi, OUP, 1996).

Contents

Preface vii

PART ONE

1 The Many Worlds of Indian History 1

2 The Relevance of E.P. Thompson 50

3 The Decline of the Subaltern in *Subaltern Studies* 82

PART TWO

4 Edward Thompson and India: *The Other Side of the Medal* 109

5 The City Imagined: Calcutta of the Nineteenth and Early Twentieth Centuries 159

6 Renaissance and Kaliyuga: Time, Myth and History in Colonial Bengal 186

7 Vidyasagar and Brahmanical Society 216

8 Kaliyuga, Chakri and Bhakti: Ramakrishna and His Times 282

9 Identity and Difference: Caste in the Formation of the Ideologies of Nationalism and Hindutva 358

PART ONE

1

The Many Worlds of Indian History

Introspection about their own location in society has not been too common among Indian historians. Our historiographical essays tend to become bibliographies, surveys of trends or movements within the academic guild. They turn around debates about assumptions, methods, ideological positions. Through these, historians get pigeon-holed into slots: Neo-colonial, Nationalist, Communal, Marxist, Subaltern. The existence of not one but many levels of historical awareness attracts much less attention. But outside the world of metropolitan centres of learning and research there are provincial universities and colleges, schoolteachers, an immensely varied student population, and, beyond these, vast numbers more or less untouched by formal courses, yet with notions about history and remembrances of things past, the nature and origins of which it could be interesting to explore. What is neglected is the whole question of the conditions of production and reception of academic knowledge, its relationships with different kinds of common sense.[1] We lack, in other words, a social history of historiography.

This problem of levels has become exceptionally acute in India in recent years, with the growth of right-wing Hindu communal forces, and the multiple responses to the Mandal proposals for affirmative action in favour of 'backward' castes. In very different

1 Which, as Gramsci reminded us, must be understood as a 'collective noun', and as 'a product of history and a part of the historical process. . . . "Common sense" is the folklore of philosophy, and is always halfway between folklore properly speaking and the philosophy, science and economics of the specialists.' Antonio Gramsci, *Selections from the Prison Notebooks*, ed. Quentin Hoare and Geoffrey Nowell Smith (New York, 1971), pp. 325-6.

ways, both these sets of developments have in effect projected views of Indian history at variance with what generally holds sway in today's high-academic circles. More specifically, I have in mind the debate around the Ramjanmabhumi issue, where well-established academic knowledge has had to confront, not too effectively, one kind of organized and largely manufactured common sense. Secular historians refuted, with ample data and unimpeachable logic, the justifications put forward by the Hindu Right, for its eventually successful campaign to demolish a four-hundred-year-old masjid at Ayodhya. They undeniably had the better of the intellectual — and human — argument. Yet for a decisive year or two the views of the leading historians of the country, most notably scholars at the Centre for Historical Studies, Jawaharlal Nehru University, had less impact than pamphlets of the order of *Ramjanmabhumi ka Rakta-ranjita Itihas* (Bloody History of the Birthplace of Ram). This, however, was very far from being a simple triumph of age-old popular faith over the alienated rationalism of secular intellectuals. Viswa Hindu Parishad (VHP) pamphlets, and audio and video cassettes, systematically combined an ultimate appeal to faith with a battery of their own kind of historical facts: quotations from (real or spurious) documents, a certain amount of evidence fielded by archaeologists of some stature, a parade of alleged facts and dates about precisely seventy-six battles fought by Hindus to liberate the birthplace of Ram from the evil 'descendants of Babar'. 'Faith' was deployed as the final weapon usually only when such 'historical' arguments were seen to be in danger of total refutation.[2]

What this VHP quest for historical facticity revealed was that history of one kind or another has come to occupy a position of exceptional importance in a variety of Indian discourses, but that in the moulding of many such histories the best scholars often have a very limited role. Historical consciousness, even when fairly organized, systematic, and far from spontaneous, evidently cannot be equated with the thinking of professional historians alone, still less with that of its highest echelons. Both the importance of history and its multiple levels require further probing.

Some 'presentist' explanations, relating to the conditions of

[2] For analysis of the 'historical' literature of the Ramjanmabhumi movement, see Neeladri Bhattacharya, 'Myth, History and the Politics of Ramjanmabhumi', in S. Gopal (ed.), *Anatomy of a Confrontation* (New Delhi, 1991), and Pradip Kumar Datta, 'VHP's Ram: The Hindutva Movement in Ayodhya', in G. Pandey (ed.), *Hindus and Others* (New Delhi, 1993).

production and dissemination of historical awareness in today's India, are fairly obvious, and helpful — up to a point. The leading members of the historians' guild write and teach mainly in English for easy inter-regional and international communication. The majority of universities and colleges, however, have switched over to Hindi or regional languages, translations are far from abundant, and the historical common sense of the bulk of students and teachers is determined much more by textbooks of very poor quality, or media influences. After independence, history, and particularly narratives of the 'freedom struggle' or the 'national movement', became a major means of legitimizing ruling groups in the postcolonial nation-state through claims of continuity with a glorious past. A very eclectic range of 'national heroes' therefore had to be projected as knights in shining armour, abstracted from real-life contradictions and contextual pressures. Through the media and the majority of schools, the message that has been constantly broadcast is that history is valuable because it stimulates pride in one's country. The other meaning of history, in these days of 'objective' tests and proliferating quiz culture, is of random facts and dates that have to be efficiently memorized. Patriotism and quiz culture combine to ensure a very low priority, in the bulk of history-teaching, to techniques of critical evaluation of narratives about the past and the development of questioning attitudes. History, in other words, tends to become hagiography, and this opens the way towards giving hagiography the present-day status and aura of history. Sometimes the links with current chauvinistic developments are even more direct, most notably through the enormously popular state television screening of the *Ramayana*, just before the Ayodhya movement got into its stride. The epic heroes were presented there as national figures, and Ram returned to Ayodhya in triumph amidst wildly anachronistic twentieth-century slogans of 'Long Live Mother India'.

But a merely presentist explanation will not take us very far. The centrality of history today, as well as its markedly multi-level features, are not universal or natural phenomena. They are evidently related to the ways in which history came to be taught, written, and exceptionally valorized under colonial and then postcolonial conditions. My essay, then, will have to go back to the nineteenth century, when specifically modern ways of thinking about history are generally supposed to have begun in India. My own area of competence, as well as the early location of colonial power and cultural influence, justify a primary focus on Bengal material.

There is a second reason, too, why a retrospect, at once historiographical and social-historical, is relevant for my argument, and once again the polemics around Ramjanmabhumi provide a point of entry. The importance given to apparently scientific history, complete with facts, dates and evidence, as well as the central assumption of Hindus and Muslims as homogenized blocs existing fundamentally unchanged across a thousand years, expose the 'tradition' deployed by the Sangh Parivar as overwhelmingly invented, moulded by colonial and postcolonial conditions and influences. No great effort is required to recognize it to be as 'modern' as its secular-rationalistic Other. Our glance back at colonial Indian historiography will incidentally confirm that the 'history' used by the Ramjanmabhumi movement was not any spontaneous welling-up of folk or popular memories, but made up of bits and pieces from the academic wisdom of an earlier generation of nationalist historians, as orchestrated by a very modern political machine. A generalized critique of post-Enlightenment modernity and Orientalizing colonial discourse, therefore, might seem to offer an effective ground for the rebuttal of Hindutva's claims to indigenous authenticity. More generally, the moods stimulated by Edward Said's *Orientalism* which have been transplanted to South Asia by Partha Chatterjee and the later volumes of *Subaltern Studies* have provided for many intellectuals an overall framework that combines the virtues of apparent radicalism with a satisfactory distance from the Marxism of yesteryear, now widely assumed to be finally and deservedly dead.

Many of the essays in this volume express my sense of disquiet with this current turn in South Asian scholarship. Very briefly, at this point: what had started as an understandable dissatisfaction with the economistic reductionisms of much 'official' Marxism is now contributing to another kind of narrowing of horizons, one that conflates colonial exploitation with Western cultural domination. Colonial discourse analysis abstracts itself, except in the most general terms, from histories of production and social relationships. A 'culturalism' now further attenuated into readings of isolable texts has become, after the presumed demise of Marxism, extremely nervous of all 'material' histories: the spectre of economic reductionism looms everywhere. Colonial-Western cultural hegemony, secondly, tends to get homogenized, abstracted from internal tensions, and presented as all-pervasive, virtually irresistible within its own domain — those touched by it become capable of only 'derivative discourses'. A total rupture then has to be presumed between pre-colonial and colonial, and a temptation sometimes develops to make the former a world of attractive *ur*-traditions, of innocence confronting Western power–knowledge.[3] A more fundamental methodological problem is the abandonment in practice of any quest for immanent critique through the elision of possibilities of mutually conflicting groups taking over and using in diverse, partially- autonomous ways, elements from dominant structures and discourses. What is ignored, in other words, is precisely that which had been central to Marxist analysis: the dialectical search for contradictions within structures. If modern power is total and irresistible within its own domain, autonomy or resistance can be located only in grounds outside its reach: in a 'community-consciousness' that is pre-colonial or somehow untainted by post-Enlightenment power–knowledge, or in fleeting, random moments of fragmentary resistance. These become the only valid counterpoints against the ultimate repository of that power–knowledge – the colonial or postcolonial 'nation-state'. We have moved, then, from perspectives in which relationships between capitalist imperialism and multiple strands within anti-colonial movements had constituted the basic framework, to one where the post-Enlightenment modern state is counterposed to community. Questions of exploitation and power have been collapsed into a unitary vision of the modern bureaucratic state as the sole source of oppression.

These caveats, summarized in a telegraphic manner, represent some of the problems I have been encountering in my own thinking and research, and I intend to elaborate them in specific historical contexts, as, hopefully, invitation to dialogue rather than confrontational polemic. An exploration of colonial and postcolonial historical consciousness, vital for understanding today's many worlds of history, can be useful also as the first of these contexts. A framework grounded in the assumption of pervasive colonial cultural domination has naturally paid considerable attention to the development of 'modern' attitudes towards history, and in fact this provides at first sight exceptionally

---

[3] The 'derivative discourse' argument was elaborated by Partha Chatterjee in *Nationalist Thought and the Colonial World: A Derivative Discourse?* (Delhi, 1986). In a seminal text published three years before, Ashis Nandy had sought to 'justify and defend the innocence which confronted modern Western colonialism and its various psychological offshoots in India.' *The Intimate Enemy* (Delhi, 1983), p. ix.

suitable material for a colonial discourse approach.[4] I hope to show that the assumptions I have just catalogued tend to be restrictive, even when deployed on such a favourable site. In part, then, I will have to go over already familiar material, but hopefully making new points and sometimes arguing the case for fundamental departures. Three temporal cross-sections appear particularly relevant: the apparently total early-nineteenth-century rupture with which 'modern' Indian historiography began; late-nineteenth and early twentieth-century crystallizations of 'nationalist' and 'communalist' historical assumptions and methods; and today's predicaments.

II

Pre-colonial India, with its very long traditions of written culture, produced numerous texts of recognizable historical intent or value: Puranic king-lists, dynastic chronicles, histories of castes and religious sects, biographies of holy men, genealogies of prominent families. As elsewhere, there were evident links between the quantum of such texts or documents and levels of organized, bureaucratic power. Thus, ancient Indian historiography, not surprisingly, never attained the stature of that of China with its unique bureaucratic continuity, and historical accounts became much more numerous under the Delhi sultanate and the Mughal empire. (Islam, with its single Hizrat era, also brought in a new chronological certitude.)

Yet it remains undeniable that the impact and imposition of Western historiographical models through English education and British Indian scholarship created a widespread sense of a *tabula rasa*. Pre-colonial texts, since then, have always figured as 'sources' to be evaluated by modern Western canons, not as methodological influences. In 1958 a competent survey of history-writing in nineteenth and early twentieth-century Bengal could assume that 'we had to start from scratch'.[5]

A convenient and much-used initial benchmark for examining this rupture is provided by Mrityunjoy Vidyalankar's *Rajabali*

---

[4] Ranajit Guha, *An Indian Historiography of India: A Nineteenth-Century Agenda and Its Implications* (Calcutta, 1988); Partha Chatterji, *The Nation and Its Fragments: Colonial and Post-Colonial Histories* (Princeton and Delhi, 1994), Chapters IV, V.

[5] B.P. Mukherji, *History*, in a collection entitled, significantly, for my argument, *Studies in the Bengal Renaissance*, ed. A. Gupta (Calcutta, 1958).

(Chronicle of Kings, Serampur, 1808).[6] Its author was an orthodox Brahman commissioned by the British authorities to write the first overall historical survey in Bengali prose, to serve as a language text for Company officials being trained at Fort William College. The text began by expounding, in a manner totally unselfconscious and free of defensive apologetics, the standard Brahmanical concept of time as cyclical, with Satya, Treta, Dwapar and Kaliyuga endlessly succeeding each other. The moral trajectory across the four-yuga cycle was always imagined as inevitably retrogressive, and the present (invariably, in these texts, the Kaliyuga) was the worst of times, characterized by overmighty Shudras and insubordinate women. Time, in other words, was never abstract, empty duration: it was relevant primarily for moral qualities assumed to be inseparable from its cyclical phases. The principal role of the yuga-cycle in Brahmanical discourses, from the *Mahabharata* down to Mrityunjoy, was to suggest through dystopia the indispensability of right caste and gender hierarchy. The two have been necessarily imagined as interdependent, for purity of caste lineage is vitally related to male control over the reproductive capacities of women, ensured through marriage, within the permitted boundaries.

For the rest, *Rajabali* was a compendium of king-lists, many of them soon to be discarded as mythical by modern historians. The striking feature, for anyone trained in Indian history in the ways that became standard from around the 1820s, is really a notable absence. Mrityunjoy displayed no awareness at all of any breaks between 'Hindu', 'Muslim', and 'British' periods, but remained content with awarding good or bad marks to kings with a fine indifference to religious identities. The recurrent criteria, incidentally, for immoral behaviour are *strayinata* (subordination to women) and *nimakharami* (being 'untrue to one's salt', i.e. violating obligations of loyalty and obedience, and thus implicitly weakening proper hierarchical relationships). The link with standard Kaliyuga notions of disorder is fairly obvious.

As in the bulk of pre-colonial history-writing, the predominant note in *Rajabali* was didactic, with exploration of the uniqueness of historical situations less important than teaching obedience and morality through archetypes. A ninth-century Jaina text had described *'Itihasa'* (history) as 'a very desirable subject . . . it prescribes *dharma* [right conduct]', and even Kalhana, much praised by modern

6 It has been used in that way recently by both Ranajit Guha, and Partha Chatterjee, op. cit.

historians for his unusually critical treatment of sources and striving for objectivity, claimed that his *Rajatarangini* would be 'useful for kings as a stimulant or a sedative, like a physic, according to time and place.'[7]

The contrasts with histories that English-educated Indians started writing after around the mid nineteenth century are obvious enough. British rule brought with it clocks and a notion of time as linear, abstract, measurable in entirely non-qualitative units, an independent framework within which events happen.[8] The other major change was the imposition of the ancient/medieval/modern schema which had become standard in the post-Renaissance West. James Mill transplanted this into India by dividing the subcontinent's history into Hindu, Muslim and British periods. By the time of Nilmoni Basak's *Bharatbarsher Itihas* (History of India, Calcutta, 1857), which may serve as our second benchmark, the yuga cycle is mentioned only in a brief, defensive preface, after which the author quickly passes on to a periodization that distinguished the 'Age of Hindu Empires' from 'Muslim Kingdoms'.

Yet I think it is important to resist bland, homogenized presentations, both of pre-colonial notions of time and history as well as of the colonial rupture. It is now generally recognized that the cyclical/linear binary is not absolute, for duration, or sequentiality, is common to both.[9] High-Hindu cyclical time, for

[7] R.C. Majumdar, *Ideas of History in Sanskrit Literature*, in C.H. Phillips (ed.), *Historians of India, Pakistan, and Ceylon* (London, 1961), p. 21.

[8] I have found very helpful Moishe Postone's recent suggestion that a concrete/abstract distinction is more relevant than the conventional cyclical/linear binary. Elaborating a suggestion of E.P. Thompson ('Time, Work-Discipline and Industrial Capitalism', *Past and Present*, 38, 1967), Postone argues that the concrete time of a pre-capitalist societies 'was not an autonomous category, independent of events, it could be determined qualitatively, as good or bad, sacred or profane.' It 'is characterized less by its direction than the fact that it is a dependent variable.' Moishe Postone, *Time, Labour and Social Domination: A Reinterpretation of Marx's Critical Theory* (Cambridge, 1993), pp. 200–16, *passim*.

[9] Combinations of the two have been noticed in places and times as far apart as present-day Bali and pre-colonial Yucutan. Balinese notions of duration exhibit features of both cyclicity and linearity. The *Chilam Balam* texts of Yucutan described endless cycles marked out by specific moral qualities, but the Mayans also had chronicles of ruling dynasties which were entirely linear. L.E.A. Howe, 'The Social Determination of Knowledge: Maurice Bloch and Balinese Time', *Man*, New Series, 19, 1981; Nancy M. Farriss, 'Remembering the Future, Anticipating the Past: History, Time and Cosmology among the Maya of Yucutan', *Comparative Studies in Society and History*, 29, iii, July 1987.

instance, encompassed an element of linearity, for within a *maha-yuga* the successive downward movement of Satya through Treta and Dwapar to Kali was taken to be irreversible. The polarity between concrete and abstract time is perhaps more fundamental, but here again further distinctions within both might become necessary. Thus, generalizations of the order attempted by Mircea Eliade about a 'myth of the eternal return', supposedly characteristic of an undifferentiated 'Hindu' world or even of 'traditional civilization',[10] really rest upon an unproven assumption of homogeneity. That we know little — virtually nothing, in fact — of notions about time among pre-colonial peasants or lower-caste people is surely no ground for assuming that they must have invariably internalized the highly Brahmanical and hierarchized values which are inseparable from formulations of the four-yuga cycle that have come down to us. One needs to be open, rather, to the possibility of work or task-oriented times, which could vary greatly in precision according to specific requirements. The *purohit* and astrologer needed a precise fix on certain 'time points' to determine auspicious ritual moments or make predictions.[11] Rural labour processes, in contrast, demanded little more than a grasp over general seasonal and daily rhythms.

Even at more philosophical or speculative levels, some scholars feel that Brahmanical texts indicate the presence of not one but several layers in pre-Islamic Indian notions of time. Raymondo Panikkar, for instance, refers to a tradition called Kalavada where time is placed above all gods and identified with images of death as supreme leveller of all distinctions, human and even divine. He considers this to have been 'a widely-held popular view, belonging probably to the less Brahmanic stratum of Indian tradition'.[12]

[10] Mircea Eliade, *The Myth of the Eternal Return* (Paris, 1949, trans., London, 1955), Chapters I, II, IV.

[11] The concrete time of medieval European monasteries, Postone points out, had its own, specific notion of time-discipline, through 'a series of time points, which marked when various activities were to be done.' This, however, is quite distinct from capitalist forms of time-discipline, where 'commensurable, interchangeable, and invariable' time-units become 'the *measure* of activity.' Once again, it is the concrete/abstract distinction which is crucial. Postone, pp. 203, 209.

[12] Raymondo Panikkar, 'Time and History in the Tradition of India: Kala and Karma', in L. Gardet, et al. (ed.), *Cultures and Time* (Paris, 1976). The *Mahabharata*, interestingly, associates this view with Bali, a demon (Asura) chief defeated by Indra, the king of the gods: 'In Time's course many thousands of

Orthodox Brahmanical denunciations of Kalavada often associated it with materialism, *nastika* views, and an epistemological position called *pratyakshyavada*, according to which sense impressions constituted the sole criterion of valid knowledge or proof.[13] Such views were lumped together in dominant philosophical discourse as the tradition of Lokayata, said to have been founded by Carvaka. (One, evidently pejorative, meaning of Lokayata, incidentally, is 'that which was prevalent among the common people'.) Quite remarkably, Mrityunjoy's *Rajabali* at one point interrupts its placid chronicle of kings with a two-page diatribe against nastika views which once again associated the extreme empiricism of pratyakshyavada with Kalavada: 'like trees in a mighty forest, the world appears and disappears by itself, subject only to time.'[14]

Kaliyuga, we are always told, will end in an apocalyptic manner, with universal destruction (*yuga-pralay*), or, alternatively, the coming of Kalki-avatar (the last incarnation of the high-god Vishnu), after which another identical cycle will commence. In yet another interesting shift or variation, however, the apocalypse, and in some ways the entire framework of four-yuga cycles, seems to have become somewhat downgraded over time. Yuga-pralay was pushed far out into the future, and so in practical terms the key message became one of enduring the inevitable evils of 432,000 years of Kaliyuga through tightened-up rules of caste and patriarchal discipline. The endless cycles themselves came to be considered part of the world of *maya* (illusion, or, more exactly, inferior order of reality) in the increasingly dominant philosophy of Vedanta.[15]

Indras and deities have been swept off yuga after yuga. . . . Time has no master . . . wealth, comforts, rank, prosperity, all fall a prey to time . . . All things that proudly raise their heads high are destined to fall down.' *Mahabharata*, English translation by Pratap C. Roy, ed. Hiralal Haldar (12 vols, Calcutta, n.d.), vol. IX, pp. 140–56.

[13] *Nastika*, often taken today as the equivalent of an atheistic position, meant more precisely in Indian philosophical traditions the denial that revealed texts (*sruti*, i.e. the *Vedas*) have the status of valid proof (*pramana*) in philosophical arguments. The extreme empiricism of pratakshyavada entailed such a denial, and could lead also to the rejection of belief in gods or the immortality of souls. Debiprasada Chattopadhyay, *Lokayata: A Study in Ancient Indian Materialism* (New Delhi, 1959, 1978), Chapter I. Surendranath Dasgupta, *A History of Indian Philosophy*, vol. III (London, 1961), pp. 512–50.

[14] Mrityunjoy Vidyalankar, *Rajabali* (Serampur, 1808; Calcutta, 1905), pp. 11–13. Mrityunjoy attributed the origin of these views to an Asura king.

[15] For a more detailed account of Kaliyuga and its variations, see Chapter 8 below.

The relevant points, in considering the importance of these varied notions of time for perceptions of history, are that none of the alternative frameworks hindered the construction of narratives about the past connected to specific purposes, such as the glorification of dynasties, families or religious traditions; but neither did they require, or stimulate, a sense of overall social process or interest in its possible causes.[16] The central high-Hindu ideal was the individual breaking out of the bondage of *karma* (endless rebirth, in which merits and sins accumulated in previous lives rigidly determined one's status in life, and therefore one's *dharma*, in the sense of appropriate rituals and duties). Unlike Christianity or Islam, with their notions of a day of judgement common to all, the idea of salvation here was not community-based, and so the conception of universal causality implicit, in a way, in the doctrine of karma, applied only to individuals. It did not lead to any interest in the causes of aggregate phenomena. The yuga framework did involve a sense of a moral texture common to an era, but then its lineaments and causes were already known: being fore-ordained, divinely determined, or related to the quality of kings — i.e. to the *lila* (game, or play), as it was said, of time, gods or kings. The purpose of history remained, therefore, a combination of royal propaganda and the teaching of. dharma with examples, and its place in education, we shall see, seems to have been negligible or non-existent.

Historical texts became much more abundant under the Delhi sultanate, the Mughals, and their successor states, but it is doubtful whether there was a fundamental break with regard to the aims and presuppositions of history-writing. The Persian narratives are often impressive in the careful attention they pay to specific — usually military-administrative — events, and even to their secular, 'secondary' causes. Yet the overall aim remained, as earlier, a combination of exalting the rulers with religious and moral teaching via examples. 'Interest concentrated on how far a man conformed to an ideal prototype, not how far he diverged.'[17] The dominant Islamic conception of time as 'piecemeal vision of . . . a sequence of instants . . . which are the signs and spaces of God's intervention' also did

---

[16] Pre-colonial histories, Ranajit Guha has argued, consequently tended to be 'made up of discrete moments, recovered synchronically as the occasion required.' Ranajit Guha, *An Indian Historiography of India: A Nineteenth Century Agenda and Its Implications* (Calcutta, 1988).

[17] P. Hardy, *Historians of Medieval India* (London, 1960, 1966), pp. 113, 118.

not encourage, on the whole, any total view of history as diachronic social process.[18]

We may now be in a better position to evaluate the precise extent and lineaments of the 'break' brought about in the ways of constructing the past by colonial rule and English education. In the making of British Indian historiography, and 'colonial knowledge' in general, an important dimension of genuine curiosity and excitement, as a vast and varied subcontinent was opened up to the Western gaze, went along with fairly obvious links with the logic of colonial power. The British, as utterly alien rulers, needed to know something about the traditions and 'prejudices' of their subjects; extraction of revenue, dispensation of justice, and maintenance of order all demanded knowledge of past administrative practices; meticulous enquiry into possible causes became standard practice after every rebellion. The power-knowledge theme is very self-consciously present in much official writing: Risley's *Tribes and Castes of Bengal* (1891), for instance, claimed that an ethnographic recording of the customs of people was 'as necessary an incident of good administration as a cadastral survey of the land and a record of rights of its tenants.'[19]

Notions of time, now assumed to be linear and abstract (i.e. no longer primarily perceived in terms of moral quality, as Kaliyuga had been), methods of collecting data and assessing its reliability, and, above all, levels of efficiency in the processes of accumulating knowledge had altered dramatically through the incursion of the post-Enlightenment West with its novel and expanding resources of bureaucratic power; less so, possibly, the basic motivations of more effective governance and legitimation of authority, which may not have seemed very novel to, say, Abul Fazl. Power-knowledge far antedates the modern West, as Umberto Eco so delightfully reminds us in his *The Name of the Rose,* set in a medieval monastic library where control over dangerous knowledge is defended through murder.

What *was* new was the unprecedented importance and reach that history quickly acquired in colonial times. History became the principal instrument for inculcating the stereotypical dichotomy between the backward, immobile Orient as contrasted with the dynamic, Christian and/or scientific West, thus simultaneously buttressing British self-confidence and reminding Indians of their lowly place in the world's scheme of things. Foreign rule, conversely, soon

---

[18] L. Gardet, p. 201.

[19] H.H. Risley, *Tribes and Castes of Bengal: Ethnographic Glossary*, vol. I (Calcutta, 1891, 1981), p. vii.

provoked a search for sustenance in past glories, real or imagined, as well as efforts to use history to probe the causes of present-day misfortunes. History thus came to acquire a new centrality in the concerns of the Indian intelligentsia, for it became a principal 'way of talking about the collective self, and bringing it into existence.'[20]

This much is well known, and hardly in need of restatement. Very much less explored, but perhaps more significant, is the vastly extended *reach* of history. While the transition from manuscript to print obviously enlarged the potential readership of history books, the subject itself came to acquire a totally new position in structures of formal education. These structures themselves simultaneously became more crucial, for the links between formal education and respectable jobs, professions, and careers were now tighter than ever before. It was no longer possible, for instance, under colonial 'law and order' for military adventurers to carve out kingdoms for themselves, while recruitment to administrative posts became dependent on examinations. It had been possible for an Akbar to remain virtually illiterate: not so for the meanest colonial Indian official or clerk. The restriction of alternative opportunities (of independent business enterprise, for instance, particularly in Bengal, with its overwhelming colonial economic presence) further enhanced the centrality of formal 'liberal' education. This became indispensable for a self-consciously 'middle-class' existence, one which combined the material and cultural resources for entering high schools and colleges with a need for income from jobs or professions. Such need was less acute for the really big zamindars or businessmen, and impossible to satisfy for the vast majority of peasants.

The place of history in the new educational system thus needs some explication. Derozio, we know, taught History to Hindu College students, and is said to have inspired 'Young Bengal' through 'examples from ancient history of the love of justice, patriotism, philosophy and self-abnegation.'[21] But surprisingly little is known about the mundane details of college courses and texts, and there is a need to explore the patterns of change and continuity involved in the displacement of traditional *pathshalas*, *tols* and *madrasas* by the

[20] Sudipta Kaviraj, *The Unhappy Consciousness: Bankimchandra Chattopadhyay and the Formation of Nationalist Discourse in India* (Delhi, 1995), p. 108.

[21] Pyarichand Mitra, *Biographical Sketch of David Hare* (Calcutta, 1877), p. 27, quoted in my 'Complexities of Young Bengal', *Nineteenth Century Studies*, October, 1973; reprinted in Sumit Sarkar, *A Critique of Colonial India* (Calcutta, 1985), pp. 20-1.

modern classroom ordering of space, time, and methods of teaching.[22] The new interest in Western education stimulated by colonial discourse analysis remains content, far too often, with yet another critique of Macaulay's Minute.

For elementary education, however, Kazi Shahidullah's *Pathshalas into Schools* does provide some illuminating details, based on a diligent study of the surveys of Francis Buchanan and William Adam. The traditional pathshala had concentrated on providing an eminently practical training in language, arithmetic and accountancy, while the few written texts (manuscripts) were of a religious, moral, or grammatical kind: history of any sort seems to have been conspicuously absent. The early Bengali printed textbooks provided free to pathshalas by the School Book Society from 1817 onwards, in contrast, 'covered a variety of subjects like History, Geography and Astronomy'. The publications of the Serampur missionaries meant for schools, similarly, included *Dig Darshan*, 'a miscellaneous collection of Truths and Facts covering history, science and ethics', and *Historical Anecdotes* took its place next to *Aesop's Fables* as reading lessons 'illustrative of justice, fidelity, probity and humanity'. To take a final example, the hundred-odd vernacular village schools set up in some Bengal districts by Hardinge's orders in 1844 were to have a curriculum of 'vernacular reading, writing, arithmetic, geography, and history of India and Bengal.'[23] The missionary juxtaposition of Aesop with historical anecdotes is an important indication that history of one sort or another was now being given an exalted place in general education, even outside its position as a distinct subject. The pattern continues, and quite emphatically so: school textbooks for teaching Hindi today, for instance, tend to contain an enormous amount of crude 'historical' tales for inculcating a patriotism often difficult to disentangle from Hindu-communal assumptions and values.

History, then, acquired a new and vast pedagogical and intellectual domain in the nineteenth century. Content-wise, however, it would be misleading to assume a simple, unambiguous or complete rupture, a leap from 'myth' to positivistic 'objectivity'. In fact the assumption

[22] Work like Barbara Metcalf's study of the transition from madrasa to the Deoband seminary (*Islamic Revival in British India: Deoband, 1860-1900*, Princeton, 1982) needs to be followed up. See now, however, the useful collection of essays, Nigel Crook (ed.), *The Transmission of Knowledge in South Asia* (Delhi, OUP, 1996).

[23] Kazi Shahidullah, *Pathshalas into Schools* (Calcutta, 1987), pp. 15, 25, 29, 33.

so often made that the culture imposed through Western education was always rationalist and invariably dominated by 'post-Enlightenment' values seems in need of some questioning. An earlier historiography had hailed such rationalism as harbinger of a Bengal (sometimes Indian) 'renaissance' or 'awakening'. The critique of colonial discourse which today has largely displaced that old consensus inverts the value judgement but otherwise maintains a basic continuity through its assertion of a total rupture.[24] There was nothing particularly rational (or secular), surely, about the oft-repeated formula of British rule in India being an act of divine providence. Again, the missionaries used modern Western science to undermine the 'superstitions' of the Hindus, but their overall aim was conversion to another, not noticeably more rational, religion. Here I must add that I find Dipesh Chakrabarty's assertion in a recent article — that 'missionaries did not perceive much contradiction between 'rationalism and the precepts of Christianity' — difficult to understand. Chakrabarty refers in particular to Alexander Duff, and cites M.A. Laird (1972) as the source for his reading of the Scottish missionary.[25] Duff's own *India and India Missions* (Edinburgh, 1839), in striking contrast, recounts how much effort he had had to make to persuade the pupils of Derozio to accept the Reformation as their model in place of 'the terrible issue of French illumination and reform in the last century', and how happy he was when Krishnamohan Banerji's conversion to Christianity indicated that 'avowed atheism' was on the decline.[26]

The myth of Kaliyuga vanished quickly from formal Indian historical writings or textbooks, but it continued to enjoy a vigorous if interestingly modulated life in other texts and contexts right down to the early twentieth century. Kaliyuga, I have argued elsewhere, became a whole language for expressing resentments about the new discipline of time being imposed under colonial rule in clerical office-work *(chakri)*. It thus provides an important entry point into

[24] A similar continuity is noticeable in the focus, in 'renaissance' and 'Saidian' writing alike, on the high literati alone. For elaborations of this argument, as well as some efforts at developing an alternative approach, see Chapters 5 and 6.

[25] Dipesh Chakrabarty, 'Radical Histories and the Question of Enlightenment Rationalism: Some Recent Critiques of Subaltern Studies', *Economic and Political Weekly*, xxx, 14, 8 April 1995, p. 752.

[26] Alexander Duff, *India and India Missions* (Edinburgh, 1839), pp. 629, 667, cited in my 'Complexities of Young Bengal', *Critique of Colonial India*, pp. 20, 26.

a level of colonial middle-class life largely ignored so far by historians.[27] A recent thesis has emphasized the intertwining of what, by strict Enlightenment-rationalist standards, should have been dismissed as myth, with positivistic facticity in much nineteenth-century Bengal history writing. Nilmoni Basak may have been embarrassed by notions of cyclical time, but his *Nabanari* (4th ed., Calcutta, 1865) could still lump together two historical with seven mythical or legendary figures in biographies of exemplary women.[28] And Sudipta Kaviraj has drawn our attention to the combination of 'real' and 'imaginary' histories in the writings of major late-nineteenth-century figures such as Bankimchandra and Romeshchandra Dutt. Dutt, India's pioneer economic historian, was also the author of historical romances about Rajputs and Marathas, while Bankimchandra made several attempts to reconstruct bits and pieces of Bengal's past on the basis of carefully sifted evidence. Bankim, Kaviraj suggests, came to feel that 'the rational discourse of fact-gathering' could provide inadequate grounds for the kind of itihasa that 'Bengalis' needed if they were to become 'men', or in order to constitute themselves into a collective self: hence there was a shift in Bankim's later writings to the 'mythic discourse' of the historical novel.[29]

This collective self, however, was for Bankim almost invariably Hindu, and pitted usually against Muslims, in language that sometimes turns downright abusive. This is a feature that Kaviraj seems disinclined to probe, but it does seem to suggest a high degree of the internalization of the tripartite schema in its most anti-Muslim form.[30] The far-reaching impact of James Mill's periodization of

[27] See Chapter 6, 'Renaissance and Kaliyuga: Time, Myth and History in Colonial Bengal', and Chapter 8, 'Kaliyuga, Chakri and Bhakti: Ramakrishna and His Times'.

[28] Indira Chowdhury Sengupta, 'Colonialism and Cultural Identity: The Making of a Hindu Discourse', Chapter II (unpublished thesis, School of Oriental and African Studies, London University, 1993). I am very grateful to Ms Sengupta for allowing me to read her thesis.

[29] Kaviraj, pp. 124, 131.

[30] Unlike many of his contemporaries, however, Bankim did not accept an idealized, golden-age view of the ancient 'Hindu' period, and went so far as to suggest that the conditions of the Shudras might have been worse in independent Aryan India than under British rule. Paradoxically, this recognition of discordances within the Hindu fold seems to have stimulated his passionate search in the 1880s for an imaginary history of Hindu war against an externalized Muslim Other. See the critical, yet nuanced, discussion of Bankimchandra in Tanika Sarkar, 'Bankimchandra and the Impossibility of a Political Agenda', *Oxford Literary Review*, XVI, 1–2, 1994.

Indian history provides at first sight a particularly telling instance of a 'derivative discourse' which lives on even today in many Indian textbooks and syllabi, inadequately concealed by a nomenclatural change ('medieval' in place of 'Muslim', but still beginning from the establishment of the Delhi sultanate). That the implications of this have often been communal is equally obvious. Even at its most innocuous, the translation of ancient and medieval into Hindu and Muslim assumed the existence of homogenized entities, supposedly unified by religion, as the basic building blocks of all precolonial history. In addition the stigma, commonly attached to the middle term in the ancient/medieval/modern schema evolved in post-Renaissance Europe, deepened when the British transplanted it into India. Islam had been the great enemy of Christendom, the British had displaced Mughal emperors, the 1857 revolt and the Wahabi movement seemed to indicate Muslims to be on the whole more dangerous than the Hindus, and meanwhile Orientalist scholarship claimed to have discovered a glorious 'classical' age of early Hinduism (which was embodied in a language generically related to Greek and Latin). Many of the central propositions of mainstream nationalism and Hindu communalism (and, with values inverted, of its Muslim alter ego) can thus be shown to have originated in colonial discursive patterns.

But how much, really, do such origins explain? Marc Bloch warned historians many years ago of the 'idol of origins', the tendency to assume that 'a beginning . . . is a complete explanation.'[31] If histories written within the Saidian mould homogenize, they also often tend to impose closures by suggesting ready answers to issues that could have developed into interesting inquiries. Even in cases where the derivation is undoubted, we need to ask further questions as to what is (and sometimes is not) being accepted or internalized, by precisely which groups, and why. Western critiques of the conditions of Hindu women acquired an early resonance in Bengali middle-class circles: much less so the equally trenchant attacks on caste and high-caste oppression. The tripartite schema and the related myth of centuries of Muslim tyranny were very quickly taken over, but not the fairly common missionary or utilitarian denunciation of all Indian culture which was embodied, in its most notorious form, in Macaulay.

An incidental reference in Rajat Kanta Rãy's recent account (in Bengali) of politics and society around 1757 can provide an example

---

31 Marc Bloch, *The Historian's Craft* (1954; Manchester, 1963), pp. 29-35.

of the kind of inquiry that has remained foreclosed,[32] both in the earlier 'Bengal Renaissance' historiography and in its current Said-inspired inversions.[33] Rajiblochan Mukhopadhyay's *Maharaja Krish-nachandra Raysva Charitra* (1805), the second biographical work that we have in Bengali prose, contains a very early example of the Muslim tyranny myth that would become near-ubiquitous in so much nineteenth-century Bengali Hindu writing. Rajiblochan's hero Krishnachandra, the powerful zamindar of Krishnanagar (Nadia district), is shown to be taking a leading part in a conspiracy of Hindu zamindars, court officials, financiers and Mir Jafar to seek the aid of the English in overthrowing Nawab Sirajuddoula. A clearly formulated desire to end 'Yavana' misrule is attributed to the Hindu plotters (who, curiously, are described as openly display-ing their anti-Muslim motivations in front of Mir Jafar). As Rajat Kanta Ray points out, more contemporary texts, whether in Persian or English, or the odd Bengali village poems referring to Plassey, are totally silent about any such self-consciously Hindu conspiracy to overthrow Muslim tyranny (as distinct from the misrule of a particular nawab).[34] Rajiblochan's text, interestingly, precedes the organized spread of English education, and for that matter Mill's tripartite schema of Indian history. It combines adulation for the Krishnanagar Raj family with flattery of the English as liberators from Muslim misrule, and seems to demand location in a milieu of high-caste Hindu literati transiting from zamindari to Company patronage. Rajiblochan had a family connection with the Krish-nanagar Raj, and had then been recruited, along with other Nadia pandits, by William Carey to work for the Bengali printing press set up by Baptist missionaries at Serampur — from where he followed his master to Fort William College, established by Wellesley in 1800.[35] It may not be irrelevant to note that Maharaja Krishna-chandra is remembered as a very major patron of orthodox Brah-manical culture, and that his power base was in a region (Nadia) notorious in the eighteenth century and beyond for its multitude of heterodox lower-caste sects: Kartabhaja, Sahebdhani, Balarami, and many others.[36] It is tempting to suggest a link, therefore,

[32] Rajat Kanta Ray, *Palasir Sharayantra o Sekaler Samaj* (Calcutta, 1994).

[33] See below, Chapter 6, for a discussion of the 'renaissance' debate.

[34] Ibid., pp. 183-7 and *passim*.

[35] Brojendranath Banerji, 'Fort William Colleger Pandit', pp. 28-9, in *Sahitya-Sadhak-Caritmala*, I (Calcutta, 1942).

[36] Sudhir Chakrabarti, *Sahebdhani Sampraday Tader Gan* (Calcutta, 1985).

between the easy acceptance of some key aspects of Anglo-Indian historiography, projecting the British as saviours of Hindus from earlier Muslim misrule, and possible late-eighteenth and nineteenth-century efforts at reasserting high-caste power. These came to be closely associated with the eventually more secure zamindari and tenure-holdings of post-Cornwallis Bengal, and the new importance of the 'liberal' professions — entry to which became restricted to the products of bhadralok-dominated higher education. For such a strata — privileged, benefiting in many ways from foreign rule, yet increasingly aware of a humiliating colonial dependency — the thought that British rule was a great improvement on 'medieval Muslim tyranny' could provide considerable solace as well as a safe and distant site for locating a largely imaginary history of Hindu prowess against — not British, but Muslim — invaders.

That colonial history, developed primarily to sustain and ratify British rule, quickly became the ground for contradictory and limited yet powerful assertions of patriotism is a well known and quite undeniable feature of nineteenth-century Bengali intellectual history. Yet some minutiae of dating and language indicate that it still puts the framework of derivative discourse under some strain. Partha Chatterjee feels impelled to add the phrase 'curiously enough' to the fact that 'the new Indian literati, while it enthusiastically embraced the modern rational principles of European historiography, did not accept the history of India as it was written by British historians'.[37] Ranajit Guha pushes the moment of autonomous assertion forward to Bankimchandra's historical essays of the late 1870s and early 1880s. Chatterjee, through a survey of school textbooks, brings it back to the 1860s. Neither mention the plenitude of very similar material in the proceedings of the Derozian Society for Acquisition of General Knowledge (1838–43), i.e. emerging precisely from a group often accused of being, quintessentially, denationalized Anglicists, who in Guha's framework should have displayed 'unquestioning servility to the ruling power'.[38] Pyarichand Mitra's *State of Hindoostan under the Hindus*, for instance, combined warm references to the 'Xattries' (Kshatriyas) as 'great warriors', akin to 'the Rajpoots and Marhatas who are but their descendants', with much celebration of ancient Hindu cultural glory. Such Hindu nationalistic themes had been inserted, it goes without saying, into the general tripartite

[37] Partha Chatterjee, *The Nation and Its Fragments* (Princeton, 1993; Delhi, 1994), p. 88.
[38] Ranajit Guha, pp. 17–18.

framework of ancient Hindu glory/medieval Muslim tyranny and decline/ modern reawakening, and other contributors to the SAGK proceedings extended the formula to conditions of women and the history of the Bengali language.[39] A decade later Nilmoni Basak, who had also been a member of that Derozian society,[40] likewise accepted without question Mill's periodization, but then launched into a bitter attack on British writings on Indian history for denigrating Hindu achievements. A trend-setting feature of Basak's *Bharatvarsher Itihas* was the effort to shift the focus within the 'Hindu' period from politics to culture and religion. Relegating to a closing section the 'brief description' of Hindu kingdoms — difficult to reconstruct, full of fables, without a firm chronology — Basak embarked upon an enthusiastic account of theories of statecraft and law, religion, literature and science, even Hindu colonies and cultural influences allegedly in places as far distant as Bali and Peru.[41]

These are matters of detail, relevant only for their symptomatic value: far more crucial are the constraints and closures late-Subalternism is imposing through its key assumption of statism as the root of all evil in modernity. The corollary often drawn is that modern history-writing is necessarily state-centred: it is either narrowly political in subject matter, or looks at other processes from the point of view of the making or unmaking of states. Several recent essays by Gyanendra Pandey, in particular, assume almost as a matter of course that all post-Enlightenment historiography has been the 'grand narrative' of the nation-state — till, presumably, the present moment of liberation achieved through the contemplation of 'fragments'.[42] For Partha Chatterjee, similarly, the important thing about late-nineteenth-century Bengali history textbooks is that in them 'history had become merely the struggle for power'. 'Hindu nationalism', it seems, is unacceptable for Chatterjee (and Pandey)

---

[39] Pyarichand Mitra, *State of Hindoostan under the Hindoos*; Maheshchandra Deb, *A Sketch of the Condition of Hindoo Women*; Udaychandra Addya, *Bangla Bhasha Uttamrupe Shikshakaraner Abashyakata*, in Gautam Chattopadhyay, *Awakening in Bengal in Early Nineteenth Century: Selected Documents*, vol. I (Calcutta, 1965), pp. 94, 131, 156, 178–80, and Appendix, i–ii.

[40] See the list of members of the SAGK in Chattopadhyay, pp. lxiv–v.

[41] Basak, Preface, and Chapters 2–7. Mrityunjoy's text in contrast had been entirely about kings.

[42] Gyanendra Pandey, 'In Defence of the Fragment: Writing about Hindu-Muslim Riots in India Today', *Economic and Political Weekly*, Annual Number, 1991, and 'The Prose of Otherness', in *Subaltern Studies VIII* (Delhi, 1995).

in large part because 'like other modern ideologies, it allows for a central role of the state in the modernization of society — in this sense, the framework of its reasoning is entirely secular.'[43] This position is close to that of Ashis Nandy, who has been critiquing Hindutva for a number of years now from a consistently anti-secular standpoint.

I have many differences with such assertions, which I intend to elaborate in several of the essays that follow. For the moment, my concern is only with the homogenizing silences they impose on colonial Indian, and specifically Bengal, historiography. For, a striking feature of much late-nineteenth and early-twentieth century Bengali history-writing and thinking about the past was precisely its persistent critique of state-centred, merely political, histories. This was a critique, further, that at times deployed arguments uncannily close to some in common use today, for central to it was the assumption that statism was a principal instrument of modern Western cultural domination. Such recurrence appears both significant and worthy of exploration.

The valorization of culture over narratives of kings and wars in Pyarichand Mitra or Nilmoni Basak had been a response to the paucity, at that time, of firm, chronologically grounded data about the ancient or 'Hindu' period, which was consequently then in some danger of being dismissed by British scholars as having no history — in the sense of worthwhile past politics. An absence of information about dynasties and wars had become much less of a problem by the late-nineteenth and early-twentieth century, and yet it was then, and most notably in and around the Swadeshi years, that *samaj* (society, community) came to be regularly counterposed to *rashtra* or *rajshakti* (state, the political domain). The real history of India, it was repeatedly asserted, was located in the first, not the second, for samaj embodied the distinctive qualities peculiar to the genius, culture and religion of the Indian people.

In moves — the theoretical lineages of which go back to Herder — romantic nationalisms in many parts of the world have often identified value and authenticity with difference, with what is supposedly distinctive and unique to a particular language, culture, or history. A politics of identity grounded in the recognition of such difference has thus been repeatedly counterposed to that of equal dignity and universal rights — to borrow the terms of a

[43] Chatterjee, *Nation*, pp. 91, 110.

seminal recent analysis by Charles Taylor.[44] The specific contexts for its flowering in late-colonial Bengal still require investigation, but there certainly were connections with what, many years ago, I had described as a 'constructive swadeshi' trend during the movement against the Partition of Bengal. This valorized autonomous self-help efforts in indigenous enterprise, education and village organization over the politics of both 'Moderate' and 'Extremist' varieties, and was embodied most notably in the writings and activities of Rabindranath Tagore and Satish Mukherji (editor of *Dawn*, founder of the Dawn Society, and key figure in the national education movement of the Swadeshi years).[45]

The appeal of the state/society disjunction at this specific historical conjuncture was clearly related to intelligentsia disillusionment both with 'improvement' under colonial hegemony and initiative, and the possibilities of oppositional politics of what had widely come to be termed the 'mendicant' kind — a dual loss of faith that was not always accompanied by enthusiasm about the new politics of the extremist or terrorist varieties. Certain structural features of colonial rule also provided a basis for the conceptualization of samaj as autonomous from rashtra, and identifiable in the main with religious community rather than territorial nationhood. Census classification and enumeration helped to consolidate community boundaries defined in terms of religion and caste, while colonial justice made personal and family laws into distinct religious domains within which textualized norms of high-caste or ashraf social behaviour were sought to be universalized in unprecedented ways.[46] In census and

[44] Charles Taylor, 'The Politics of Recognition', in Amy Gutman (ed.), *Multiculturalism* (Princeton, 1994).

[45] Sumit Sarkar, *Swadeshi Movement in Bengal, 1903–1908* (New Delhi, 1973), Chapter II, and passim.

[46] Warren Hastings laid down in 1772 that 'inheritance, marriage, caste and other religious usages or institutions' were to be administered in different ways to Hindus and Muslims, according to the 'Shaster' and Islamic jurisprudence respectively: pandits and ulema were therefore appointed to aid British Indian courts in a system which continued till 1864. In form, this was a continuation of Mughal practice which had been marked by a similar duality in Diwani, as distinct from Nizamat, adalats, where Muslim criminal law prevailed. 'But by far the greater part of litigation was never brought before Muslim officials, but was settled by recourse to traditional methods of resolving disputes, which differed according to the caste, the status in society, and the locality of the parties.' J.D.M. Derrett, *Religion, Law, and the State in India* (London, 1968), pp. 229, 233. For a specific instance of the legal homogenization brought about under British

law alike, 'colonial knowledge', it needs to be added, was not just a Western superimposition: such an interpretation gravely underestimates the extent and significance of inputs from relatively privileged Indian groups with autonomous interests and inclinations.[47]

The focus upon samaj as counterposed to politics could acquire alternative stresses, logically distinct even though quite often intermingled within the same activity or text. One strand was clearly populist, and manifested itself through appeals to the urban bhadralok to re-establish links with rural life. Concrete efforts in that direction included village reconstruction initiatives, attempts to promote elementary education and cottage crafts (as distinct from Swadeshi textile mills or an alternative, Calcutta-based 'national' university), and the gathering-together of invaluable collections of folk literature, songs and fairy tales.[48] Yet samaj was simultaneously all too often conceptualized in Hindu, high-caste gentry, and paternalist terms, and these were the nuances that the term itself tended to carry over from earlier usages.[49]

Both tendencies can be seen at work in extensions of constructive swadeshi moods into historical retrospects. An initial consequence of the valorization of samaj as actual or potential site of autonomy

---

rule, in this case actually restricting the rights of lower-caste women even while implementing an undoubtedly progressive legislation, see Lucy Carroll, 'Law, Custom and Statutory Social Reform: The Hindu Widows' Remarriage Act of 1856', in J. Krishnamurti (ed.), *Women in Colonial India* (Delhi, 1989).

[47] The Bengal Census Report of 1901 provides a concrete example of such an input in a crucial area. E.A. Gait interpreted Census Commissioner H.H. Risley's instruction to classify castes in each region 'by social precedence as recognized by native public opinion' to mean that 'the decision must rest with enlightened public opinion and not with public opinion generally.' But 'enlightened opinion would inevitably mean the views of highly educated Hindus, i.e. overwhelmingly of upper-caste men. Not surprisingly, the vast majority of claims for higher status by subordinate castes were summarily rejected by the Bengal Census Report. *Census (India)*, 1901, Volume I.1, p. 538; *Census (Bengal)*, 1901, vol. VI, pt I, pp. 354, 378–84.

[48] Two striking examples would be Dakshinaranjan Mitra Majumdar's *Thakumar Jhuli* (Grandma's Tales, published in 1907), and Dineshchandra Sen's discovery of the Mymensingh folk ballads. For an account of the many dimensions of constructive swadeshi, see *Swadeshi Movement in Bengal*, Chapters 2, 3, 4, and 10.

[49] The Bengali word *samaj* referred to collectivities or gatherings of particular castes (in the sense of *jatis*, and more particularly, sub-divisions of the latter) or religious sects (e.g. Brahmo 'Samaj') before its late-nineteenth-early-twentieth-century extension to signify also more wide-ranging notions of society or community.

was a fairly remarkable and precocious interest in social and cultural history: very different, really, from the supposed British colonial prototype, for it developed precisely around the time when the turn towards professionalized accuracy on the Ranke model was making such themes disreputable in Western academic scholarship. The two main areas of original research were ancient Indian culture and religion and, in Bengal particularly in the wake of the Swadeshi upsurge, regional and local histories as well as extremely important surveys of the development of Bengali language and literature. Here, pioneering use was made of vernacular literary texts, oral folk traditions, artistic works, and a very wide range of cultural artefacts. To take one remarkable instance: Dineshchandra Sen's *Brihat Banga*, published in 1935 as the fruit of two decades of labour, began with a declaration that 'the social, artistic and religious evolution of a civilization does have some relationship with political history, but the connection is not necessarily always close or vital.' A later chapter argued that wanderings among the common people, and studying their patterns of life, crafts and traditions, could often reveal more about true history than poring over inscriptions or written texts. It went on to illustrate this proposition through inferences teased out from peasant ways of learning measurements and predicting the weather, folksongs, and the material culture of boatmaking, house-construction, the weaving of quilts, and the preparation of sweets. For Sen, it appears at times, the true repositories of Bengal's culture have been plebeian, low-caste people bound up with everyday material production, not the Brahman bearers of high Sanskrit learning. The weakening of that high-culture-bearing strata under Pathan rule is presented, most uncharacteristically, as a boon which opened the way for the development of the Bengali language.[50]

If Sen's populism, probably inspired by one kind of reading of Vaishnava traditions, represented an effort at a kind of peoples' history, there was also the slightly later and much more carefully crafted initiative of Niharranjan Ray (*Bangalir Itihas*, Calcutta, 1949). This attempted a veritable total history of pre-thirteenth-century Bengal, with sections on ecology, economic conditions, land relations, caste and class structures, statecraft, religion, culture, and everyday life. Ray, too, had spent years wandering through Bengal's countryside, but as a Left-nationalist activist, and his work reveals signs of Marxian influence.

[50] Dineshchandra Sen, *Brihat Banga*, 2v (Calcutta, 1935; repr., 1993), pp. v, 895–946.

It must be added immediately, however, that Niharranjan Ray and even Dineshchandra Sen were hardly typical of the bulk of writings built around the rashtra/samaj dichotomy. A local history like Jogendranath Gupta's *Bikrampurer Itihas* (Calcutta, 1909) would be a much more representative example. Gupta enumerated in great and loving detail the past and present achievements of the Bengali Hindu bhadralok in what was one of its classic heartlands. No one would guess from reading his book that more than half the population of the region he was writing about were Muslims, or that, among the Hindus, Namashudras considerably outnumbered the Brahmans, Baidyas and Kayasthas combined. The bhadralok history of Bikrampur was emphatically not about people like them.[51] As Niharranjan Ray pointed out in the Introduction to his *Bangalir Itihas*, 'samaj' had generally been understood 'in a very narrow manner', excluding the plebeian strata, even by those who had grasped what Ray reiterated as the key feature of pre-colonial Indian life: its centring around 'samaj', not 'rashtra'.[52]

Partha Chatterjee's detailed account of writings about history in colonial Bengal does make fleeting reference to a trend in early nationalist historiography which 'denied the centrality of the state in the life of the nation'. The general framework he has adopted leads him to locate 'the principal difficulty with this view, which has many affinities with the later politics of Gandhism', in 'its inherent vulnerability to the overwhelming sway of the modern state.'[53] Other kinds of vulnerabilities, of the sort implicit in the silences of Gupta's history of Bikrampur, appear more obvious and vital to me, at least so far as Bengal historiography is concerned. The clearest evidence for them comes from more general or programmatic statements about history conceived in terms of the state/society disjunction, made during the Swadeshi years by Rabindranath Tagore and Satish Mukherji.

Rabindranath wrote often about history between 1901 and 1912,

51 For some details of Gupta's book, as well as census data about the religious and caste composition of the Bikrampur region, see my 'Kalki-avatar of Bikrampur: A Village Scandal in Early Twentieth Century Bengal', in Ranajit Guha (ed.), *Subaltern Studies VI* (Delhi, 1989).

52 Niharranjan Ray, *Bangalir Itihas: Adiparba*, vol. I (Calcutta, 1949, 1980), pp. 2, 5.

53 The reference extends over two paragraphs in a forty-page analysis of 'The Nation and Its Pasts', and 'Histories and Nations', in *The Nation and Its Fragments*, pp. 76–115.

and these essays provide rich indications of a mind grappling with a rashtra/samaj framework, and then in important ways going beyond it through an auto-critique of some of his own earlier assumptions: a complicated and contradictory process that attained abiding literary form through *Gora* (serialized between 1907 and 1909). *Bharatvarsher Itihas* (1902), probably the best known of Rabindranath's historical essays, used an interesting language that pressed the politics/culture divide towards a Muslim/Hindu dichotomy which is never explicitly avowed in the text. Thus the narrative of wars and invasions, proclaimed by Tagore at the beginning of this article to be no more than a bad dream — not genuine, valuable, history — is immediately defined by him to have extended 'from Mahmud's invasions to the imperial boasts of Lord Curzon'. 'In the darkness caused by the storm and thunder of Mughal and Pathan, our ancient temples had to cover their heads, while the marbled, ornate tombs of the mistresses of Sultans soared to kiss the stars.' The general denigration of statecraft, it seems, does not extend to the wars and conquests of a Samudragupta, while the exaltation of culture quickly slips into a firmly Hindu mould.[54]

In *Nababarsha* and *Brahman*, two other 1902 essays published a few months before *Bharatvarsher Itihas*, Rabindranath spelled out what was then his notion of ideal Hindu samaj, in terms explicitly, even aggressively Brahmanical and patriarchal. (A combination that seems almost inseparable: we may recall the conflation of over-mighty Shudras and disorderly wives in the dystopia of Kaliyuga.) Inequality is inevitable in all human societies, he argued, but India has given appropriate respect to 'low and high, women and men'.[55] He counterposed the entire society of gentlefolk *(bhadrasampraday)* who should be given *dwija* (twice-born) status, to those considered 'Shudras', in ancient India as well as today — 'Santals, Bhils, Kols, bands of sweepers' — for in a proper samaj 'neck and shoulders must not be lowered to the level of the ground.' 'We want to become *dwijas*, not *feringhees*', whereas today there was the danger of all Brahmans degenerating into 'a vast society of tired clerks worn out by excessive work.'[56] And, still on the theme of the necessary inequality of

---

[54] *Bharatvarsher Itihas* (Bhadra 1309/1902), *Rabindra Rachanabali*, vol. IV (Calcutta, 1940, 1975), pp. 377, 379.

[55] *Nababarsha* (Baisakh 1309/1902), ibid., p. 373.

[56] *Brahman* (Asar 1309/1902), ibid., pp. 395, 401–2. I find this counterpositioning of proper hierarchy to the miseries of contemporary clerical life, where 'the Brahman has to work with lowered head in the office of the *sahib*'

humankind, Rabindranath in his *Nababarsha* essay attacked the 'modern wife' who, in imitation of the West, feels ashamed of 'serving' her husband and children. In the Indian tradition, however, 'sweeping the floor, bringing water, preparing food, eating after everyone else . . . considering even husbands without any exceptional qualities akin to gods' have been rightly taken to be the hallmarks of the 'grihalakshmi', the embodiment of true feminine grace and beauty.[57]

Rabindranath, as is well known, soon moved away from most of these positions. The Hindu–Muslim riots in East Bengal in 1906-7, and the failure of the Swadeshi movement to enthuse the bulk of the peasantry, set him thinking about the problematic features of the samaj he had briefly idealized. Tagore, after about 1907, developed a powerful and consistent anti-communal critique, and by 1909 was condemning the samaj based on hierarchized caste difference as a 'gigantic system of cold-blooded repression'.[58] The repudiation of gender inequality was, perhaps less sharp or consistent, but still a short story like *Streer Patra* (1914) stands in utter and total contrast to the passage I have just quoted.

For a more consistent elaboration of the implications of a Hindu communitarian ideology grounded in hierarchy we need to turn to Satish Mukherji and his *Dawn*. Mukherji's 'The Question of Caste' (*Dawn*, August 1903) proclaimed axiomatically 'that in all ages and by virtue of a law of nature, there shall be inequalities and distinctions between man and man.' He reminded those who objected to caste as being hereditary that property, too, descended 'from father to son'. Admittedly, an element of flexibility enabling some promotions or demotions on the basis of merit was advisable to allow 'proper placement and chance of transfer': but this necessarily presupposed 'a group who can make the needed choices'. The Brahmans, Mukherji concluded, have the best qualifications and traditional expertise for this job of guardianship. Thus a mildly reformist criticism of caste was neatly co-opted into a defence of

---

(p. 393) extremely significant, and will be discussing its significance in Chapters 6 and 8. Late-nineteenth-century modulations of the Kaliyuga myth, we shall see, are important primarily as an entry point into representations of this clerical world.

[57] Ibid., p. 374.

[58] Letter to Myron Phelps, 4 January 1909, reprinted in *Modern Review*, August 1910. For more details about the change in Rabindranath's views after 1907, see my *Swadeshi Movement in Bengal*, pp. 62, 82-91.

Brahmanical order. Only through caste hierarchy, *Dawn* editorials and articles repeatedly proclaimed, could 'progress' be reconciled with 'order' or 'stability'. The editorial for the November 1900 issue, for instance, urged the need to understand the specific 'laws' of India's 'social evolution'. It admitted the need to overcome 'the present *inertia* of Indian society in many matters in respect of which its hands are free, e.g., social, educational, religious and industrial', but emphasized that this should be done only through pursuing 'a course that is consistent with *stability*'.[59] The language reminds us that Satish Mukherji had some connections with a Positivist group in late-nineteenth-century Bengal which had inflected the doctrines of Comte in a highly conservative, Brahmanical direction. As so often, caste and gender hierarchy were seen as interdependent, and in March 1903 *Dawn* gave great prominence to the views of the 'eminent Hindu Positivist, the late Jogendrachandra Ghosh, Zemindar', that India's progress 'must be securely based on continuance of the traditional family system.'[60] The Bengal Positivists, I will argue in a subsequent chapter, provide an illuminating case study of the ways in which specific aspects of colonial structures and discourses (legal recognition of a sphere of community-based personal law, and fragments of Comtean theory) were used as resources to reaffirm Brahmanical hegemony.[61]

Dawn regularly counterposed Brahmanical and patriarchal order against the incessant competition and 'gospel of enjoyment' of the West. It related the craze for increasing 'consumption per head' to the 'undue importance attached to the *doctrine of rights*', as manifested, in its opinion, notably in the advance of democracy in Victorian England.[62] Its very first issue emphasized the need for India 'to steer clear of the Labour Problem of Christendom'.[63] The anti-capitalistic note is quite striking, but so is the precise angle of attack as revealed

59 Italics in original. 'Indian Social Evolution and Reform' (*Dawn*, November 1900). See also 'Principles of Social Order: The Statical Aspect' (Editorial, *Dawn*, March 1900) which reiterated that 'all progress is built on Order and — is delusive, and even mischievous, when it is not built on order . . .'.

60 For a more detailed discussion of this Positivist-cum-Brahmanical inflection of the *rashtra/samaj*, see Chapter 9. The pioneering, and still the most detailed study of Comte's Bengali disciples is Geraldine Forbes, *Positivism in Bengal* (Calcutta, 1975).

61 Chapter 9.

62 'Social Movements Round a Centre' (anon., *Dawn*, August 1897).

63 'The Situation in India: A Problem and an Illustration' (anon., *Dawn*, March 1897).

by the kind of (totally inegalitarian) samaj or community being posited against it. And here, it has to be added, the anticipations in *Dawn* of some very contemporary trends become really startling. An article entitled *Western Ideal of Nationalism* (unsigned, but probably by Satish Mukherji) in *Dawn*, June 1911, contrasted the 'Western' notion of 'political nationalism', focussed upon the 'development of men's activities as *members of a state*', with the Hindu ideal of community based on regulated, hierarchized difference. The unity sought by Hindu society was not something 'homogeneous', but based on *dharmashastras* that laid down differentiated 'standards of righteous conduct adapted to various and varying . . . classes and divisions of people'. Unity came also from 'allegiance to the framers of these Laws, who form a distinct spiritual order. . . .' Western 'political nationalism', in contrast, sought 'a homogeneous political existence' through 'a suppression of all diversity'. Mukherji traced its origins back to 'France during the Revolutionary epoch of the eighteenth century', and in particular to 'the French Encyclopaedists . . . who in the name of equality and fraternity had preached a *jehad* against all that men and nations held sacred.' Such ideas, the article implied, had been imposed on India by Bentham and Mill, with a minor modification that substituted utility for the 'goddess of Reason'. Large parts of this essay, one is tempted to comment, could walk into a contemporary anti-'Orientalist' collection with a minimum of editorial updating: they counterpose, in remarkably clear language, an ideal of cultural difference premised on internal hierarchy against notions of universal rights which are felt to be homogenizing.

But of course the argument was anything but purely indigenous or traditional: even a cursory glance through the issues of *Dawn* indicates a striking degree of derivation from that other, more insidious kind of Orientalism that patronizes and praises, instead of denouncing, an equally essentialized Orient. A Cambridge don, Oscar Browning, was quoted with great approval for his statement that his Indian visit had taught him 'to tolerate *purdah*, and to have an admiration for caste',[64] while many of the strongest assertions of patriarchal values come from the pens of Annie Besant and Sister Nivedita.[65]

[64] *Dawn*, July 1903.

[65] Thus Annie Besant argued in an article entitled 'The Education of Hindu Youth' (*Dawn*, June 1897) that passing the matriculation examination was useless for Indian girls, who should be trained rather in 'devotion and piety'. Any imitation of the West with respect to the education of women could 'break up

Assertions of values that otherwise would have been considered
socially retrogressive are quite often explained or even justified today
as valid responses to the all-pervasive colonial authority and interference. It therefore becomes important to note that the *Dawn* variety
of 'constructive swadeshi' was not conspicuously anti-colonial, so far
as politics was concerned. Indeed, the politics/society disjunction in
this case permitted at times a rather remarkable degree of loyalism.
In February 1898 *Dawn* justified Satish Mukherji's Bhagavat Chatuspathi (a 'Hindu Boarding Religious Institution' to train students
'under a system of Hindu discipline') in part on the grounds that
'in this way alone could we live happily amongst our rulers, and
setting an example of lofty character repay them tenfold the debt
which we owe them for the era of uninterrupted peace and tranquil-
lity which India had not enjoyed for many and many a day until
she came by the dispensation of an All-wise Providence under British
overlordship.' That was 1898: thirteen years later, after the storms
of Swadeshi had come and gone, Satish Mukherji was hailing the
'transcendental importance' of the visit of the King-Emperor, and
arranging to present George V with a full set of the copies of his
Dawn.[66] The important point that seems to emerge is that the
refurbishing, or invention, of ideologies of Brahmanical hegemony
and patriarchy under colonial rule did not necessarily flow from
anti-colonial impulses alone: more internal compulsions and power
relations also deserve attention.

I have been emphasizing a precocious, if in many ways problem-ridden, thrust towards social history. A qualification that needs
to be made at this point is that such tendencies had developed

---

the family system, drive the women out in the world to earn their living, make
them competitors with men . . . .' An earlier essay by Besant on Hindu women
(1894), which *Dawn* reprinted in October 1901, had extolled the charms of
chaste widowhood. It admitted that Hindu ideals of womanhood could have
no place in the West, but pleaded, in a classic statement of one kind of
Orientalism: 'Leave the Hindu woman untouched by Western thought, and do
not destroy a type just because it is unique . . . We have women enough, who
are brilliantly intellectual and competent: let us leave unmarried the one type
which is the incarnation of spiritual beauty.' Nivedita, too, was full of admiration for the 'nun-like qualities' of the Hindu widow, and felt that 'there are
few great relationships in human life like that between a Hindu man and his
mother.' (*Dawn*, May 1903.)

66 'The Imperial Visit' (*Dawn*, December 1911). For the presentation of *Dawn*
to George V, see Haridas and Uma Mukherji, *Origins of the National Education
Movement* (Calcutta, 1957), p. 249.

primarily outside the world of the professional Indian historian, which in any case took quite some time to constitute itself. University departments began systematic research in history rather late, as they had been primarily examining-cum-teaching bodies till the early twentieth century, and an all-India organization of the historical profession (the Indian History Congress) was floated only in the 1930s. As had happened in the West a generation or two earlier, the turn to the Ranke model of academic precision and strictly archive-based history placed a heavy premium on political-military-administrative narratives. The tone was set by the major British Indian surveys: Vincent Smith's *Oxford History of India* (1919) and the Cambridge History series published during the inter-war years, while among Indian historians Jadunath Sarkar emerged as the most respected and influential scholar through his predominantly political works on the Mughal empire and the Maratha kingdoms.[67] A state-oriented Indian history had thus come to dominate academia now, largely displacing social-cultural interests[68] — without however fundamentally modifying many of the underlying premises of that other kind of work. Thus the more abundant and precise data that had now become available about the ancient (or 'Hindu') period led to dynastic histories marked often by an uncritical preference for alleged periods of 'imperial unity', particularly the Guptas, Asoka Maurya remaining a bit suspect because of his Buddhist affiliations. Imperial unity, however, ceased to be such a plus point if the rulers happened to be Muslims, for, as in nineteenth-century historical novels, the wars of sections of Rajputs, Marathas, and Sikhs with centralizing Muslim rulers were generally given the status of national struggles. Another revealing discrepancy consisted in a variation across time of the degree of attention professional historians were prepared to give to social-cultural matters. Ancient Indian civilization and culture still attracted a lot of attention in syllabi and research alike, quite often in highly apologetic, even revivalist forms. Similar themes were much less studied or taught for the 'Muslim' period, except by a few firmly

[67] Jadunath Sarkar, however, had the imagination, flexibility and grace to hail Niharranjan Ray's book as a landmark in what he declared would be increasingly recognized as the 'highest' kind of history: social history. See his preface to the first edition of *Bangalir Itihas*, p. x.

[68] In Bengali-language works, too, the new political focus was exemplified in Ramaprasad Chanda's *Gaur Rajmala* (Rajshahi, 1912) and Rakhaldas Bando-padhyay's *Banglar Itihas* (Calcutta, 1914).

anti-communal nationalist historians who tried to highlight 'syn-cretic' Bhakti-Sufi movements and foregrounded Akbar against Aurangzeb.[69]

One curious feature of history-writing about the 'modern' or colonial period prior to the 1950s needs some emphasis. Nationalist historiography developed on sites some distance from what, on logical grounds, should have been its proper location: the rich and growing traditions of contemporary anti-colonial movements. There was virtually no professional research on such themes (or on 1857) till some years after independence, and the history of colonial India consequently remained very much a narrative of viceroys, Afghan or Burmese wars, and administrative and 'constitutional' reforms. Home Department files or private papers for recent years were largely inaccessible, most academic historians worked in govern-ment-controlled or financed institutions, and with the rise of mass nationalism (as well as revolutionary terrorism and Left formations) the factor of censorship (and, more often, self-censorship) had probably become much more important than in the more placid late nineteenth century. Even the critique of British Indian economic policies worked out by Moderate Congress intellectuals like Naoroji or R.C. Dutt seldom entered standard history textbooks: certainly I cannot recall such themes in my college courses, a decade after 1947. The social-historical impulse also tended to wither away for the colonial period, with the major exception of the middle class studying its own cultural origins in an increasingly self-adulatory manner through the renaissance myth. Caste and religion in colonial times were probably felt to be divisive themes, from the perspectives of countrywide unity and anti-British struggle.

Through silences and stresses alike, the bulk of late-colonial Indian professional historiography came to have a tilt that was strongly Hindu, as well as North Indian. The alternatives that sometimes emerged within that same milieu were based on simple inversions of mainstream assumptions, and hence did not mark any qualitative break. Thus there were occasional writings which glorified Muslim rulers, eras of pan-Islamic grandeur, and powerful Southern or regional dynasties, in equally uncritical ways. What remained fairly ubiquitous were views from the top: whether North-ern, Southern, or regional, Brahmanical/high caste or *ashraf*. By far

---

[69] An obvious example is Tarachand, *Influence of Islam on Indian Culture* (1922; reprinted Allahabad, 1963).

the most influential model, of course, was that of a fundamentally harmonious 'Indian' civilization and culture, all too often implicitly identified with 'Hindu' traditions of alleged catholicity, with an underlying Brahmanical or high-caste slant. In a simultaneous move, the sting was sought to be removed from inconvenient questions of gender oppression by postulating a Vedic or ancient golden age of learned and respected women subsequently shattered by foreign, usually Muslim, intrusions.[70]

There were some signs of an inversion of a more fundamental kind. In Maharashtra and Tamilnadu, in the wake of powerful lower-caste movements, alternative versions of history were constructed which stood the theory of the assimilative spread of 'Aryan' civilization on its head, and projected a counter-myth of Northern-Brahmanical foreign conquest and tyranny over the indigenous 'bahujan samaj' of intermediate and low castes. The Shivaji projected in Jyotirao Phule's ballad about him in 1869 was primarily a Kunbi-Maratha folk hero distinguished by concern for peasants, while *Ghulamgiri* (1873) dismissed 'fictions' about his 'freeing the motherland from *Mlecchas* and protecting Brahmans and cows' as 'false religious patriotism'.[71] In the 1920s, the Chamars of Punjab would use the recent discovery of Harappan civilization to develop a similar anti-Brahmanical Aryan rhetoric.[72] Even in Bengal, much less known for its caste politics, the thrust towards bhadralok-dominated social and regional histories of the Swadeshi and post-Swadeshi years actually coincided with a quite independent stream

[70] Traces of this myth can be seen already in a paper on the conditions of Indian women presented to the Derozian Society for Acquisition of General Knowledge (Maheshchandra Deb, *A Sketch of the Condition of Hindu Women*, reprinted in Gautam Chattopadhyay). It attained the status of a historical commonplace through Altekar's *The Position of Women in Hindu Civilisation* (1938). Two excellent recent critiques are Uma Chakrabarti, 'Whatever Happened to the Vedic Dasi? Orientalism, Nationalism, and a Script for the Past', in Kumkum Sangari and Sudesh Vaid (eds), *Recasting Women: Essays in Colonial History* (New Delhi, 1989), and Kumkum Roy, '"Where Women are Worshipped, there the Gods Rejoice": The Mirage of the Ancestress of the Hindu Woman', in Tanika Sarkar and Urvashi Butalia (eds), *Women and the Hindu Right* (New Delhi, 1995).

[71] Rosalind O'Hanlon, *Caste, Conflict and Ideology* (Cambridge, 1985), Chapter 10; *Collected Works of Mahatma Jyotirao Phule, Volume I (Slavery)* (Bombay, 1991), p. 26.

[72] Mark Juergensmeyer, *Religion as Social Vision: The Movement against Untouchability in Twentieth-Century Punjab* (California, 1982).

of tracts. These expressed lower-caste grievances and aspirations, and constituted for them, sometimes, imagined pasts built out of selective appropriations from elite myths and histories. Thus the Rajbansi claim to Kshatriya status could be buttressed through the Brahmanical myth of the destruction of Kshatriyas by Parashuram,[73] while the metrical biography of the founder of the Matua sect which had laid the foundations of the Namashudra movement in Faridpur laid claim to the anti-caste heritage of the Buddha (and Kabir) a generation before Ambedkar.[74] Alternative historiographies like these have been generally, and symptomatically, ignored by academic scholarship. Today they seem on the point of becoming a formidable force, as an opportunist BJP–BSP (Hindu upper-caste and trader with Dalit, lower caste) alliance in Uttar Pradesh breaks down partly through Dalit insistence on celebrating, precisely in the state where Ayodhya is located, an anti-Brahman leader of far-off Tamilnadu who had publicly burned pictures of Ram on Madras beach in 1956.[75] Implicit here is a very different way of imagining, not only the subcontinent's pasts, but perspectives of national unity or integration.

III

I have been emphasizing the differences within late-colonial Indian historical thinking, in particular a contrast between social-historical impulses mainly generated outside the formal historical profession, and statecraft-oriented narratives written from within its confines. Certain features common to both appear equally significant, however, when looked at from today's perspectives, and in terms of their conditions of production and dissemination. These demarcate the late-colonial situation quite sharply from the many historical worlds of today, and consequently offer a vantage point for a brief review of contemporary opportunities and predicaments.

There were two notable absences. The Asiatic Society and the

[73] The ancestors of the Rajbansis, it was claimed, were Kshatriyas who had taken refuge in the wilds of North Bengal to escape the wrath of Parashuram, and had subsequently forgotten their high-caste origin and customs. Harakishore Adhikari, *Rajbansi Kulapradip* (Calcutta, 1908).

[74] Tarakchandra Sarkar, *Sri Sri Harililamrita* (P.O. Olpur, Faridpur, 1916). For a more detailed discussion of such alternative constructions, see Chapter 9.

[75] For details about Periyar's burning of images of Ram, as well as his other violent attacks on the Ramayana, see Paula Richman, 'E.V. Ramaswami's Reading of the Ramayana', in Paula Richman (ed.), *Many Ramayanas: The Diversity of a Narrative Tradition in South Asia* (Delhi, 1994).

Anthropological Survey apart, official funding for pure research, detached from pedagogy, hardly existed, and there was very little of today's accelerating globalization which has made trips abroad for degrees, research or seminars an important part of the more prestigious kinds of academic life. Opportunities for any kind of higher education were more restricted and therefore even more class-cum-caste defined than today, given the far fewer universities and colleges. Within this smaller educated community, however, the hierarchical divisions between research/teaching, university departments/undergraduate colleges/schools, metropolitan/provincial universities seem to have been somewhat less sharp. Repositories of books, manuscripts, art objects and cultural artefacts were often built up by autodidacts, gentlemen with access to local resources and antiquarian interests but little formal academic training: a zamindar, lawyer or schoolteacher could sometimes contribute as much or more as a university professor. For Bengal, one thinks immediately of the Bangiya Sahitya Parishad, many local libraries, and the Varendra Research Society, the latter located in a small North Bengal district town (Rajshahi) yet enjoying at one time an academic prestige which it would be difficult for any non-metropolitan centre to emulate today. Another example of this relative absence of internal hierarchization within a smaller educated elite is provided by the career of Sir Jadunath Sarkar (1870–1958). A Rajshahi zamindar's son, Jadunath's formal degrees were in English, and till retirement he combined research with the teaching of History, together sometimes with English and Bengali, mainly to undergraduate students (at Ripon, Metropolitan and Presidency Colleges in Calcutta, followed by Patna and Cuttack, and then briefly at the Benaras Hindu University). Jadunath became internationally renowned but never went abroad.[76]

Late-colonial histories, then, were generally written by teachers for students or general readers. Very many of the topmost professional scholars also produced textbooks, and most of them published original works both in English and in indigenous languages. There was therefore much less of a gap than is evident now between the best and the worst or even average histories. But it would be dangerous to romanticize: inadequate funding for full-time research, confinement within national or regional parameters in the absence of opportunities for wider contacts, the restrictive aspects of a

[76] Biographical data taken from S.P. Sen (ed.), *Dictionary of National Biography*, vol. IV (Calcutta, 1974).

nationalist paradigm shot through with unstated class and high-caste assumptions (quite often sliding into communalist attitudes), all exerted a price. The 'best' scholarship of those times, with rare exceptions, appears unacceptably limited, parochial and unselfquestioning today.

Post-independence historiographical developments, in contrast, have been marked by a dialectic which simultaneously enhanced standards vastly at elite levels, while paying far too little attention to histories being taught to the majority of college and school students as well as diffused through other means among the general public. Advanced historical research has come to have as its intended audience one's academic peer-group, research students of the best universities, and, increasingly, international conferences. Meanwhile the now very seriously dated historiography of a past generation has kept on getting reproduced and disseminated, in diluted and crude forms, at other, inferiorized and neglected levels. Thus has come to be constituted a 'common-sense' — using that term in the most negative of Gramsci's several different formulations[77] — open to appropriation and orchestration by organizations such as the Sangh Parivar.

There has certainly been a qualitative transformation in the work of the leading practitioners since the 1950s, bound up with very significant shifts in basic approaches and choice of research questions. In ancient and medieval Indian historiography, where the changes have been most obvious, work from the late 1950s has focussed on themes like 'social formations',[78] debates about the existence and nature of Indian feudalism, or the possibilities of

[77] Gramsci, who always made clear that for him there could never be 'just one common sense', quite often emphasized its 'fragmentary, incoherent, and inconsequential' aspects, as a kind of bricollage of residues from the high cultures and 'prejudices from all past phases of history . . . ' But it could also include elements evolving from below, as it were, from shared experiences in labour and in social relations, with an embryonic oppositional potential. Assertions of lower-caste identities through imagined histories have obviously no intrinsic superiority in sheer academic terms over dominant-caste constructions, but they do seem to include elements of common-sense of the latter kind. Antonio Gramsci, *Selections from Prison Notebooks*, ed. Quentin Hoare and Geoffrey N. Smith (New York, 1971), pp. 323-7, 419-25. See also the helpful comments of E.P. Thompson, *Customs in Common* (London, 1991, 1993), pp. 10-11.

[78] The major breakthrough, of course, was D.D. Kosambi's *An Introduction to the Study of Indian History* (Bombay, 1956).

capitalistic developments in pre-colonial times. Inscriptions and land grants have been probed, no longer primarily for information about kings, dynasties or conquests, but for the inferences that could be teased out from them on broader socio-economic relationships and questions of state formation. Impressive detailed studies of medieval agrarian, artisanal or commercial structures have similarly taken the place of old-fashioned dynastic and military histories.

Ranke, then, has been displaced in considerable measure by Marx. The specific direction of this change owes much to the overall conjuncture of the 1950s and 1960s, marked by a strong and apparently growing Left presence in Indian political and intellectual life. Mere enhancement in research opportunities obviously cannot explain it, nor was it just a question of wider international contacts. It was not mainstream British or American historiography, not even writings on South Asian themes, but a journal like *Past and Present*, the 'transition debate', and the work of historians like Hill, Hobsbawm and Thompson – often sought to be marginalized by academic establishments in the West – that appeared most stimulating to Indian scholars exploring new ways of looking at history.

The new history had been iconoclastic in the 1960s; today, in leading universities as well as in the Indian History Congress (though hardly elsewhere), it has been functioning as a kind of establishment for almost a generation. This provokes, nowadays, a certain legitimate impatience about the occasionally simplified and restrictive nature of its applications of Marxism, and attempts at more wholesale repudiation are not unlikely, given the context of the collapse of socialist regimes and the sharp Right turn in recent world and Indian politics. It is important, therefore, to retain a sense of the sheer distance that separates the post-Kosambi or post-Irfan Habib historical world from what had preceded it, even while developing the qualities of self-criticism vital for any living tradition of radical historiography.

An aspect of this 'shift in the paradigm',[79] one which has not been much emphasized but is particularly relevant for my present argument, is the rupture with a conventional nationalist historiography which, when transposed into ancient or medieval times, all too often had become indistinguishable from communalism. To cite only a few obvious instances: the casualties of the transformation

[79] Romila Thapar has used this phrase to describe the impact of Kosambi: 'The Contribution of D.D. Kosambi to Indology', in Romila Thapar, *Interpreting Early India* (Delhi, 1992).

in ancient Indian history-writing include not only the 'Gupta Golden Age', but the basic premise of a distinctive and once-glorious Aryan 'race',[80] taken over from Orientalist scholarship and made into a central plank of much nationalist-communalist ideology. The work on the Shudras pioneered by R.S. Sharma helped to expose the seamy, exploitative undersides of ancient Indian civilization, while after the massive research of the 'Aligarh School' the counterposing of a 'good' against a 'bad' Muslim king, an Akbar against an Aurangzeb, is no longer felt to be a necessary task for secular-minded medieval historians. Themes like technological change, surplus-appropriation, and peasant resistance have come to be considered far more significant, and tolerance or intolerance are seen as determined not by the personal catholicity or bigotry of rulers but primarily by material, especially political, pressures and relationships. In paranthesis, it needs to be noted that there are the seeds of a problem here, in a kind of absolute valorization of the economic and political-administrative over the religious, cultural, or social. As in the sometimes reductionist interpretations of culture in the ancient period, there are obvious connections with simplified notions of Marxism in which consciousness figures as merely ephiphenomenal to the 'material base'. But interesting also are the ways in which certain earlier patterns are being reproduced. Social history of a kind had received considerable attention from nationalist intellectuals working on the 'Hindu' period, but very much less so for the 'Muslim' or 'British' centuries. That, more or less, seems to have remained its fate even after the 1960s. Caste, for instance, can hardly ever be avoided in studies of ancient Indian history, whereas it is only very recently that it has started to figure significantly in historical works on the colonial era.

Modern Indian history has actually had a somewhat different trajectory, for here nationalist historiography really came into its own and occupied its 'proper', anti-colonial domain only from the 1950s and 1960s. Political inhibition was increasingly replaced by state encouragement, access to late-colonial archives became easy with the introduction of a thirty-year rule, and the 'national movement' — all-India, regional, even district-level — became the favourite topic of research in the history departments of India's proliferating universities. The second major area of advance was in economic history, once again at first within a broad colonial/anti-colonial paradigm.

[80] Romila Thapar, 'Ideology and the Interpretation of Early Indian History', in ibid.

This enriched through more sophisticated tools and empirical detail the basic critique of colonial policies and structures that had been initiated by the first generation of nationalist economists and developed by Marxists like R.P. Dutt.

As the example of economic history indicates, there was considerable scope in modern Indian history for a kind of Left nationalist-Marxist consensus, a rough counterpart perhaps in historiography to the Nehruvian consensus which, at least in retrospect, seems to have characterized middle-class Indian intellectual life during those decades. A basic framework grounded in anti-colonial nationalism appeared all the more urgent in view of attacks from what, with some justice, were identified as neo-colonialist positions, instances, it was feared, of the empire striking back. One recalls the polemics against the efforts of what is popularly known as the Cambridge School to reduce anti-colonial nationalism to mere factional politicking; the debate around deindustrialization provoked by a revisionist essay by Morris David Morris; and the sharp reactions generated by the second volume of the *Cambridge Economic History of India*.

An unintended consequence of this continued and indeed enhanced domination of the nationalist paradigm in historiography pertaining to colonial India has been yet another subordination of the social by the political or economic. The nineteenth-century prehistory of the nationalist middle-class intelligentsia, construed in terms of a narrative of education and social reform leading up to patriotism, received considerable attention: yet Jyotiba Phule, symptomatically, had to wait for his first sophisticated historical study till Gail Omvedt's book in 1976.[81] Lower-caste protest had often developed antagonistic relationships with mainstream anti-colonial nationalism, and the penalty extracted was its frequent characterization as 'collaborative', 'divisive', or 'sectional'. Straightforward anti-colonial narratives could be constructed fairly easily out of political and economic developments: the social, inevitably constituted in large part also by 'internal' tensions, presented more intractable material for a nationalist historiography committed to a saga of a basically united people. Openly communal histories could contribute even less, for the central assumption of homogenized, unchanging, and inevitably conflicting religious identities effectively blocked meaningful social-historical exploration. A critique of mainstream nationalism for its many 'betrayals' was mounted

[81] Gail Omvedt, *Cultural Revolt in a Colonial Society: The Non-Brahman Movement in Western India, 1873 to 1930* (Bombay, 1976).

at times, it is true, by Left studies of class struggles of workers and peasants. But once again socio-cultural dimensions tended to get marginalized, as simplified Leninist frameworks gave priority to a combination of economic pressures and 'external' organization, and tended often to get lost in debates on the correctness or otherwise of party strategies.

The would-be social historian of modern India had perforce often to turn for guidance to social anthropologists. But that too has been a domain full of problems, where conservative attitudes have often blended with structural-functionalist premises to produce an abundance of bland, tension-denuded categories. Thus all kinds of caste mobility, including radical protest, have been grouped together under one label, 'Sanskritization', indicative primarily of the most assimilative kind of change. A parallel instance would be the 'jajmani system', where elements of mutuality in relations between the Brahman ritual expert and the householder have been extended to the rather different transactions of peasants and artisans, even landholders and agricultural labourers.

That the standard anti-colonial nationalist model, at least in its more totalizing, unmediated versions, can be constrictive is indicated by the fact that much interesting and stimulating recent work has been taking place outside, or in a tangential relationship to, its boundaries. Take for example the notable growth areas of economic history, and studies, often over the long-term, of the grossly neglected South. The framework of abrupt and cataclysmic late-eighteenth and early-nineteenth-century economic decline that still works fairly well for some regions of early colonial penetration (most notably, Bengal) does appear somewhat less helpful, for other areas. (A work like Chris Bayly's *Rulers, Townsmen and Bazaars*,[82] however controversial at times, cannot be dismissed as simply neo-colonialist.) The rapidly growing genre of environmental or ecological history, to take a second example, often has to work with scales of time that need not coincide with conventional periodizations. Parts of the South, again, seem to have had patterns and rhythms of their own: looking outwards commercially towards and across the Indian Ocean rather than inland, and marked in the inter-War years more by lower-caste assertions (and in some regions by Left movements) than mainstream Gandhian nationalism or Congress and League politics.

[82] C.A. Bayly, *Rulers, Townsmen and Bazaars: North Indian Society in the Age of British Expansion, 1770–1870* (Cambridge, 1983; rpt. Delhi, 1993).

There developed, in the 1970s and early 1980s, a conjuncture during which conventional nationalist and Left-nationalist premises seemed on the point of more direct challenge, even decisive over-throw. As in the 1950s, a changed overall context was crucial. Its constituent elements included the (slightly delayed) academic fall-out from worldwide moods of radical optimism characteristic of the 1960s and early 1970s, and the rise within India of a variety of extreme-Left tendencies which combined disillusionment with organ-ized Marxist parties with hopes of an impending peasant revolution. As the prospects of radical change withered, there was a proliferation of volunteer groups engaged in constructive work at the grassroots, while women's movements with self-consciously feminist perspectives emerged as a novel and permanent element in the Indian scene. Meanwhile, lower-caste protests were gathering strength, forcing, after the Mandal flare-up in the mid-nineties, considerable rethinking among Left activists who had for long underestimated its auton-omous appeal. History-writing was modified in this changed con-juncture in two more or less parallel but largely unconnected ways: the sudden popularity of 'histories from below' (early *Subaltern Studies*, of course, but also quite a lot of work outside and sometimes preceding it),[83] and a quantum leap, virtually from scratch, in women's studies, increasingly informed by feminist approaches.

The first wave of Indian feminist scholarship — original, powerful, but nowadays largely neglected or forgotten — questioned the trium-phal narrative of unilinear advance in the 'status of women' through male-initiated nineteenth-century social reform, followed by women's participation in Gandhian, revolutionary-terrorist or Left-led move-ments. More nuanced and ambiguous patterns were suggested, em-phasizing the contradictions of reform and the ways in which nation-alism could have displaced the women's question and recuperated patriarchal ideologies and structures, even while opening up public spaces for women, and there were interesting efforts to relate shifting gender relations to detailed studies of socio-economic processes.[84]

---

[83] I attempted a survey-cum-analysis of the early moves towards histories from below in *Popular Movements and Middle-Class Leadership in Late Colonial India* (Deuskar Lecture, given at the Centre for Studies in Social Sciences, Calcutta, 1982; published Calcutta, 1983); see particularly p. 74, fn. 3. Like my *Modern India 1885-1947* (Delhi, 1983), I had drafted this lecture before reading *Subaltern Studies I* (Delhi, 1982).

[84] I owe this assessment of early feminist historiography to Tanika Sarkar — 'Women's Histories and Feminist Writings in India: A Review and A Caution'

Meanwhile, there was a spate of research publications on tribal, peasant and labour movements, as well as a few pioneering, sympathetic studies of lower-caste initiatives in large part independent of, or even hostile to, mainstream nationalism. The generalizations that emerged from some of this work were not dissimilar at times to those being worked out independently by historians of women. An inverse relationship was suggested between moments of popular, specifically peasant, autonomy, and Gandhian nationalism in its more organized forms and phases. *Subaltern Studies*, in particular, began with a programmatic statement simultaneously critiquing the elitism of both colonialist and nationalist historiographies.[85] The habit of looking at history solely from the top downwards, in terms of leaders mobilizing the masses through ideals, charisma, or manipulation, it was cogently argued, has often coincided with economistic assumptions: both had combined, even in Left historiography, to obstruct efforts at studying the consciousness and culture of subaltern groups.

I have argued later in this volume that the possibilities that had opened up a decade or so back, the chances of a social-historical breakthrough, have today become restricted once again, and that this, too, has happened in contexts both worldwide and specific to India.[86] For the moment I will merely suggest a connection between such closures and a paradoxical kind of nationalist recuperation associated with critiques of colonial discourse, particularly in the dominant strand within today's *Subaltern Studies*. Paradoxical, both in terms of the starting point of that project, and because the critique of official, state-centred nationalism has not been given up. But a two-fold displacement has occurred: from colonial domination to Western cultural conquest; and from subaltern, usually peasant, consciousness (often marked by the centrality of religion, but not detached from questions of class, exploitation, and power) to affirmations of community consciousness in effect *defined* by religion and abstracted from indigenous power relations (other than

---

(Plenary Session Address, Seventh Berkshire Conference, Chapel Hill, North Carolina, June 1996), forthcoming. A fine example of this earlier work is J. Krishnamurti (ed.), *Women in Colonial India: Essays on Survival, Work and the State* (Delhi, 1989), consisting of essays published several years earlier in the *Indian Social and Economic History Review*.

[85] Ranajit Guha, 'On Some Aspects of the Historiography of Colonial India', in Guha (ed.), *Subaltern Studies I* (Delhi, 1982).

[86] See Chapter 3 below.

those embodied in that alleged quintessence of post-Enlightenment rationality, the bureaucratic nation-state). The adoption of the single criterion of subordination or otherwise to modern Western power-knowledge is not too distant, surely, from the familiar digits of cultural nationalism. And the related tendency to valorize all assertions of indigenous community values is likely to inhibit sympathetic explorations of a vast range of initiatives by or on behalf of subordinated groups: women, lower-castes, Left-led peasant and workers movements, all of which have selectively appropriated elements from Western ideologies. Later chapters will provide instances of how such inhibitory pressures are already at work, even in the writings of scholars with undeniably radical values.[87] Histories from below have ceased to be in vogue, being displaced by a focus on colonial or elite discourses, and feminist studies of the nineteenth century often dwell obsessively on the limitations of West-inspired reform initiatives.

A clarification may be needed at this point. I am far from suggesting any rupture with basically anti-colonial parameters in writing the history of colonial India. Colonial exploitation and domination of course constituted the central set of relationships during these centuries. In so far as its cultural manifestations have been highly productive of undifferentiated illusions of progress, modernity or reason, the critique of colonial discourse does have its uses — though more perhaps in the West, and in English Literature circles, than in the specifically historical world of South Asia, where many of its findings sound rather familiar. There remains a need to recognize nuances and mediations, variations in the extent of colonial cultural or other domination across times, regions, social spaces, and the possibility of earlier tensions (around caste and gender, notably) being reproduced in ways no doubt conditioned by the colonial presence, but not uniquely determined by it. The traditional, or-thodox-Marxist way of looking at the colonial world in terms of a series of class-determined oppositions to an alliance between imperialism and a subordinated feudalism rightly appears problem-ridden, stilted, and reductionist today. But it did provide some space

---

[87] A major example would be certain significant silences in Partha Chatterjee's comprehensive recent work, *The Nation and Its Fragments: Colonial and Post-Colonial Histories* (Delhi, 1994). Chatterjee's subsequent article, 'Secularism and Toleration', *Economic and Political Weekly*, XXIX, 28, 9 July 1994, is the clearest embodiment so far of the slide from subaltern through peasant to religious community. For a more detailed discussion, see Chapter 3.

for distinguishing between varieties of nationalism in terms of their social perspectives and composition. A glance back at the pages of a journal like *Dawn* suggests that we are today in some danger of unwittingly reproducing the assumptions and values of a particularly narrow and elitist cultural nationalism. What is required, perhaps, is some equivalent of the 'doubled' (or better, multiple) vision socialist-feminist historians have been struggling to attain. Gender in capitalist societies cannot be understood in total separation from class: it has repeatedly proved disastrous to collapse the one into the other.[88]

Much more is at stake here than merely academic historiography. I have argued elsewhere that the shift towards criteria of indigenous 'authenticity' and 'community' can constitute, however unwittingly, certain dangerous common discursive spaces, for already some of the more sophisticated ideologues of Hindutva have started using similar categories and arguments.[89] My glance back at non-statist, samaj-oriented patriotic histories should raise some doubts also about the strategy, often advocated nowadays in the spate of writings about communalism (provoked by recent developments), of postulating traditional catholicities against the homogenizations being projected by Hindutva or Muslim fundamentalist groups: 'authentic community-consciousness', so to say, against 'communalisms' ultimately attributable to colonial discourses.[90] A journal like *Dawn*, for instance, carefully kept away from the communal numbers game that had begun in Bengal soon after the decline of the Swadeshi movement,[91] argued that homogenization was contrary to the true spirit of Hinduism and an offshoot of Western cultural domination, and yet quite aggressively asserted high-caste, patriarchal values.

---

[88] Joan Kelly, 'The Doubled Vision of Feminist Theory', in Judith Newton, Mary Ryan and Judith Walkowitz (eds), *Sex and Class in Women's History* (London, History Workshop Series, 1983).

[89] Sumit Sarkar, 'The Anti-Secularist Critique of Hindutva: Problem of A Shared Discursive Space', in *Germinal: Journal of Department of Germanic and Romance Studies*, Delhi University, vol. I, 1994. See also Chapter 3.

[90] That, roughly, seems to be Gyanendra Pandey's argument in *The Construction of Communalism in Colonial North India* (Delhi, 1990).

[91] See the pioneering discussion of this theme in P.K. Datta, ' "Dying Hindus": Production of Hindu Communal Common-Sense in Early 20th Century Bengal', *Economic and Political Weekly*, 20 June 1993. *Dawn* seems to have carefully side-stepped the question of the alleged decline of Hindu numbers in Bengal as compared to Muslims, raised by U.N. Mukherji in 1909: see the unsigned essay 'Who are Hindus and Who are Not', in *Dawn*, January, February, June 1911.

Such assertions were actually more blatant at times in catholic, non-communal texts that were not primarily engaged in efforts to build Hindu unity against the Christian or Muslim Other. Projects for such unity, in partial contrast, on occasion seemed to demand assimilative caste reform: U.N. Mukherji, once again, provides an excellent Bengal example.[92] The emergence, already around the Swadeshi years and on a vastly enhanced scale today, of alternative lower-caste histories and conceptions of solidarities makes the reiteration of indigenous, undifferentiated community-values highly problematic. Their concordance with contemporary feminist values would be as difficult.

Much of the appeal of late *Subaltern Studies*, as well as some of the criticisms it has evoked, flow from its apparent affinities with aspects of postmodernism — or more precisely perhaps with what has come to be called postcoloniality. These include the centrality of anti-Enlightenment rhetoric, the oscillation between 'community' and 'fragment', and an occasional toying with moods of epistemological uncertainty. Postmodernisms in recent years have swung sharply between what can amount to affirmations of identity-politics (as counterposed to the allegedly homogenizing politics of universal and equal rights going back to the Enlightenment), and celebrations of hybridization, of identities disintegrating as globalization intensifies.[93] I have argued in another chapter that I find the one pole as unacceptable as the other, particularly in post-Ramjanmabhumi India, but also that the parallels with postmodernism, whether drawn in admiration or as critique, I believe to be based in large part on misrecognitions.[94] Rhetoric against other people's metaphysical totalities apart, there has been very little, really, in late *Subaltern Studies* of reflexive, self-doubting moods and methodological disquiet raised by the problematizations of language in recent years. This to me is a matter of some regret, for such reflexivity can have considerable value. It has helped to make an increasing number of historians far more self-aware and questioning about the representations they use

[92] See Chapter 9 for some elaboration of this argument.

[93] For two recent critiques of this 'tendency . . . to waver constantly between the opposing polarities of cultural differentialism and cultural hybridity', see Aijaz Ahmad, 'The Politics of Literary Post-Coloniality', from which I have taken the quoted passage (*Race and Class*, 36, iii, January–March 1995), and Terry Eagleton, 'Where do Post-Modernists Come From?', *Monthly Review*, 47, iii, July–August 1995.

[94] See Chapter 3.

as their 'sources', the categories they employ, and the rhetoric implicit in their writings, and much fine work is being done nowadays dancing, as it were, at the edges of relativism.

Yet it is difficult to deny that a complete surrender to relativistic positions tends to become self-contradictory, being far easier to apply to other people's positions than to one's own. Paradoxically, it can also become a kind of soft option: if all statements are really on the same level, what matters is presentation, display, command over up-to-date style, not the toil of hard research or genuine auto-critique. Charles Taylor has argued recently that extreme subjectivism ignores the fundamentally dialogic nature of human life, language and knowledge, its development, always, through interaction and exchange.[95] A dialogical imagination, further, need not necessarily abstract from power relations, though that has happened at times in some readings of Mikhail Bakhtin. What it necessarily emphasizes are the non-monologic, social, conditions of production of consciousness. The effort to develop a social history of historical awareness acquires, then, an added significance. It can point towards ways of recognition of the reflexive turn that do not have to succumb to complete subjectivism.

I have argued implicitly throughout this essay that an exploration of the social conditions of production of history cannot afford to remain a merely intellectual project. It needs to become part of wider and far more difficult efforts to change these conditions. The paradox of postcolonial front-ranking historiography has been that the affirmation of socially radical values and approaches (unimaginable for old masters like Jadunath Sarkar or R.C. Majumdar, for instance) has been accompanied by more, rather than less, elitism in structures of historical production and dissemination. Late *Subaltern Studies*, as the first Indian historiographical trend to achieve an international prestige largely prior to, and in excess of, its reputation within India, is peculiarly open to a critique in terms of its 'politics of location'. But of course elitism operates within academic structures inside the country too, and at many different levels. Residence, or even language — writing in Hindi or other indigenous languages rather than in English — will not automatically eliminate hierarchies.

The marginalization of the JNU historians' manifesto was a reminder that there has been relatively little sustained or effective attempt to spread the methods, findings, and values of even the

---

[95] Charles Taylor, 'The Politics of Recognition'.

more India-rooted, post-1950s Left-nationalist historiography beyond 'higher' academic circles. The spread-effects of History Congress sessions, the possibly more effective state-level conferences conducted through regional languages, sporadic translation efforts, and occasional refresher courses, remain fairly limited, and the possibilities of democratic dialogue often get further restricted, even within these limits, by the prevalence of hierarchized structures and attitudes. And it is surely symptomatic that the high degree of interest in Western Marxist and radical historiographies has never been extended to include efforts to learn from 'history workshop' experiments. In Britain, Germany and some other Western countries, these have sought to go beyond the academic guild through extra-mural adult and workers' education initiatives. They have encouraged workers and other ordinary folk to write or speak about their experiences and memories, and tried to form groups of local 'barefoot historians'.[96] In India, however, with the important and honourable exception of gender studies, which has offered considerable opportunities at times for fruitful interaction between activists and academics, research and teaching tend to remain highly hierarchized even among Left intellectuals.

The contrasting experiences of two efforts at preparing school textbooks can serve in conclusion as indicators of problems — and possibilities. In the schools where they have been in use, the National Council of Education, Research and Training (NCERT) textbooks commissioned in the mid-1970s from front-ranking (and mostly Delhi-based) historians have certainly helped to eliminate the blatant communal bias at the level of prescribed texts (through not necessarily from actual teaching),[97] and outdated histories have been displaced to some extent by the findings and approaches of post-independence research. But their impact has been reduced by over-

---

[96] It is seldom remembered that E.P. Thompson's *Making of the English Working Class* originated as lectures to adult education classes for Yorkshire workers. The *History Workshop Journal* contains abundant information about extra-guild initiatives, emerging from British New Left and socialist-feminist movements. For the less known but important West German developments in the 1980s, see Alf Ludtke's Introduction to Ludtke (ed.), *The History of Everyday Life* (Frankfurt, 1989; Eng. trans., Princeton, 1995), and Geoff Eley, 'Labour History, Social History, Alltagsgeschichte: Experience, Culture and the Politics of the Everyday — A New Direction for German Social History?', *Journal of Modern History*, 61, June 1989.

[97] RSS-run schools in Delhi often use NCERT textbooks, no doubt interpreting them in their own way.

burdened syllabi, bureaucratic management, and a concentration on providing 'correct' factual information and interpretation rather than imaginative pedagogical presentations. The texts were written by university scholars with little possibility of contact with secondary education: inputs through discussions with schoolteachers, difficult to organize for such a centralized, Delhi-based project, seem to have been minimal.

A decade or so later, the Eklavya volunteer group was able to work out much more interesting and innovative history texts and teaching methods through sustained grassroots work in the not particularly propitious atmosphere of Hoshangabad's small town and village schools in Madhya Pradesh. There were consultations with metropolitan historians (the initiators of the history textbooks project were themselves JNU graduates), but also repeated rounds of discussions with local schoolteachers. Eklavya history texts contain less factual detail than the NCERT books: combined with constant attention to teaching methods, they do seem geared towards much more classroom discussion and creative assimilation.[98] Eklavya recently organized a teaching-cum-research seminar of Madhya Pradesh college teachers, and has had plans for collecting historical material through its far-flung and socially diverse local contacts. Money of course remains a very major constraint, for Eklavya, unlike most NGOs today, has so far kept away from all international funding agencies.

Such experiences are a reminder that what is needed is not just more effective channels of communication through which high academic wisdom can be disseminated downwards, but efforts to democratize also the production of historical knowledge, to work towards a new kind of historical culture. There is a need to pioneer ways of developing interaction among researchers, teachers, and activists drawn from, or working among, diverse social strata. On

[98] The ancient Indian history textbook, to take a specific example, includes a number of stories, some taken from the Jatakas and other texts, others invented. A story set in a hunting-foodgathering community is followed by questions as to what its members would do if hunters fail to find game. Initial responses, I was told, often suggest going to the market, or, more commonly, borrowing from the mahajan. Further classroom discussions can then highlight what is and is not possible in a particular historical situation, thus introducing basic notions about the logic of a social formation far more imaginatively and effectively than any formal definition. Incidentally, I recall being amazed by the level of animated discussion in an Eklavya village class — admittedly in one of their best schools.

a long-term scale, collaborative research works and textbooks could emerge, enriched by multiple social and pedagogical experiences, and based on a mutual reformulation of perspectives.

I know this will sound hopelessly utopian, and particularly so because any suggestion for moving beyond the professional guild tends to get equated with some form of 'going to the people', which is then dismissed as unrealistic for the vast majority of academics. What I am suggesting as beginnings are far more modest things. There seems no reason, for instance, why participants at the many seminars that are constantly being held in cities like Delhi should not include at least some schoolteachers. The hierarchical divisions between scholars at research institutes, university teachers, and those working in undergraduate colleges are visibly deepening: surely something should be done to reduce these barriers. One way could be informal discussion groups — inevitably middle class, perhaps, but still including people other than academics: for history, surely, is a subject in which intelligent interest does not demand great professional knowledge. I can recall some groups like these, one of them consisting of trade union activists, as well as dedicated efforts to bring out a historical journal in the vernacular, from the Calcutta of my youth, and no doubt there have been many such instances elsewhere. Small beginnings: but surely we can agree that the many worlds of Indian history must not be allowed to fly totally apart, as the social base of producers and intended audiences of front-ranking South Asian scholarship narrows, even while reaching out towards global horizons.

2

The Relevance of
E.P. Thompson

The passing of Edward Thompson in August 1993 was deeply mourned. There were memorial meetings in many parts of the world, seminars and international conferences, and warm tributes even from many who had little sympathy with his combination of radical Marxian social history and political commitment of an exceptionally passionate and activist kind. Thompson's connections with India were close,[1] and his address at the Trivandrum session of the Indian History Congress (1976) provided a major stimulus to 'histories from below', and social-historical research and teaching in general, in this country.[2] Edward and Dorothy, fellow-historians and comrades, had gathered together over the years a wide and diverse circle of Indian friends, and for many it was, and will remain, a personal bereavement.

Yet, notwithstanding tributes and sincere admiration, there is a widespread feeling, amounting sometimes to an academic 'common sense', that the moment of Thompsonian social history now definitively belongs to the past, along with the other enthusiasms and soaring radical hopes of the 1960s and 1970s. Thus the *Economic History Review* felt obliged to locate *Customs in Common* (1991) as 'part of a romantic, empathetic, historical tradition which is no longer useful', having become outmoded 'in the eyes of current

[1] He was the son of another Edward Thompson, an ex-Methodist missionary who developed a lifelong commitment to Indian liberal nationalist causes, wrote a scathing exposure of British atrocities during 1857, and became a friend of Jawaharlal Nehru. (For a discussion of the elder Thompson, see Chapter 4.) E.P. Thompson inherited a deep interest in matters Indian and came to India twice, in 1976–7 and briefly, as peace activist, in the mid 1980s.

[2] The address was subsequently published, as 'Folklore, Anthropology and Social History', in *Indian Historical Review*, III, 2, 1977.

students . . . [in] the ideological and research climate of the Thatcher years.'[3] In similar vein, Gyan Prakash, a recent entrant into the *Subaltern Studies* group, dismissed aspects of the earlier work of that collective — in the formation of which Thompson, and British Marxist history-writing in general, had been a major input — as 'the familiar "history from below" approach.'[4] To the best of my knowledge, Thompson's posthumous study of Blake, *Witness Against The Beast* (New York/Cambridge, 1993), still awaits a major review. And the recent omission of 'socialist' from the subtitle of *History Workshop Journal* will seem to many to be yet another sign of our changed times.

Thompson's historical work had been integrally bound up with generous dreams of alternative, democratic and humane forms of socialism. After 1989–91, amidst the worldwide triumphalism of free-market ideology, such prospects might appear totally chimerical. The disastrous fall-outs from the collapse of the Soviet Union, conversely, also stimulate among some an uncritical nostalgia for the lost verities of orthodox Marxism and bureaucratic socialist regimes.

The stature and quality of Thompson the historian is unlikely to be ever seriously disputed. The relevance of his work for a changed political and intellectual world is a different question that needs exploration. It will be my argument in this essay that such relevance continues, in some ways more than ever before, and that many of the moves away from 'Thompsonian' social history have been simplistic and retrogressive.[5] At the same time, what is required is not blind adherence, far less impossible efforts at imitation, but critical engagement and extension through debate of an extraordinarily rich heritage.

II

The question of the continued relevance of Thompson is bound up with that of the theoretical significance of his work, and thus extends beyond the undeniable importance of his specific contributions to English labour history and eighteenth-century studies. Here there has existed ground for serious misunderstandings, for Thompson's

[3] Pat Hudson, reviewing E.P. Thompson's *Customs in Common* (London, 1991) in *Economic History Review*, Second Series, XLVI, 4, 1993.

[4] Gyan Prakash, 'Writing Post-Orientalist Histories of the Third World: Perspectives from Indian Historiography', *Comparative Studies in Society and History*, 32, 1990.

[5] See Chapter 3 for an elaboration of this argument in the specific context of *Subaltern Studies* historiography.

overtly theoretical passages tend to be brief, often excessively polemical, and not free of inconsistencies, while the sheer brilliance and
lucidity of his narrative style conceal for many the theoretical
self-awareness behind the grand rhetorical flow. There are no short-
cuts to Thompson, for theory to him was not a signboard or outer
cover, detachable from the labour of going through a massive, if
also eminently readable, corpus. Yet a close reading of his work does
reveal considerable originality (as well as relevance for contemporary
debates) in the handling of a whole series of categories vital for
social-historical analysis. For the purposes of this essay, it will be
helpful to concentrate on four: culture, class, state, and community.

In 1955, while still an active member of the British Communist
Party, Thompson published the first edition of his *William Morris*.[6]
A massive book originally running to more than nine hundred
pages, this has attracted relatively few readers. It is not difficult
today, however, to find embedded within this virtual rediscovery
of a most unusual revolutionary socialist many of the basic contours
of Thompson's entire political and historical praxis. From Morris,
romantic poet, Pre-Raphaelite artist and designer, and socialist
activist, Thompson found sustenance for his own developing vision
of socialism — a vision that remained irreconcilably hostile to the
claims of the capitalist market economy, but rejected the bureaucratized structures of both Stalinism and social democracy. More
profoundly, as he described it in an interview given many years
later to the *Radical History Review*, the problem lay in

the degeneration of the theoretical vocabulary of mainstream orthodox
Marxism — the impoverishment of its sensibility . . . the extrusion (if you
like) of that whole area of imaginative passion that informs the later
writings of William Morris. . . . The injury that advanced industrial capitalism did, and that the market society did, was to define human relations
as being primarily economic. Marx . . . proposed revolutionary-economic
man as the answer to exploited-economic man. But it is also implicit,
particularly in the early Marx, that the injury is in defining man as
'economic' at all.[7]

Thompson's biography of Morris therefore emphasized the importance of the ethical-cultural dimensions of the socialist ideal,
and spoke of the need for the education of desire. By 1991, writing
the introduction to his *Customs in Common*, Thompson was linking

---

6 A revised and somewhat shorter edition came out in 1977.

7 MARHO, *Visions of History* (Manchester University Press, 1983), pp. 21-2.

up these themes with contemporary environmental concerns, the ways in which 'economic man, whether in classically avaricious capitalist form or in the form of the rebellious economic man of the orthodox Marxist tradition, could bring about 'ecological catastrophe'. The alternative lay in the decomposition of 'both capitalist and state communist needs and expectations', 'human nature . . . made over in a new form', a world 'in which material satisfactions remain stable (if more equally distributed) and only cultural satisfactions enlarge, and in which expectations level out into a customary steady state.'[8] Hopes utopian, perhaps, and yet relevant most profoundly to our times.

Through *The Making of the English Working Class* (1963), a true classic that has inspired and provoked generations of labour and social historians across the world, Thompson was able to ground his repudiation of economistic versions of Marxism upon a largely novel analysis of problems of class, class consciousness and culture, backed up by a superbly presented wealth of empirical detail. He rejected the persistent tendency among many Marxists to make class into a fixed thing, to reify it into merely a set of people who had a determinate connection with a particular kind of production-relations. From this usually followed an abstract reading-off of what class-consciousness ought to be at a given stage of development: if, as has happened much more often than not, practical experiences did not live up to theoretical hopes, various forms of substitutist vanguardism tended to take over. There could also be that 'enormous condescension of posterity'[9] for movements that had not made the grade in terms of today's standards of ideology or achievement: teleological frameworks, in other words. But Thompson was quick to point out also that Marxists have had no monopoly over economism. He built a simultaneous rejection of conventionally anti-Marxist 'modernization' theories into the structure of his work, giving it a dimension·that has often been forgotten by his radical critics. Reification of class and class consciousness made empirical refutations of Marxism easy; simultaneously, class reduced into a measurable entity tended to rob the wretched of the earth from the possibilities of agency or creative initiative. This dialectic of structure and agency, with the balance tilted usually towards the

---

[8] E.P. Thompson, *Customs in Common* (London, 1991, 1993), p. 15.

[9] Thompson's justly famous and endlessly quoted phrase: *The Making of the English Working Class* (New York, 1963), p. 12.

second term — people living in conditions and amidst presuppositions inherited from the past, and so not of their choice, but still
striving to make their own history — remained central to Thompson's writing and politics throughout.

Thompson irreversibly transformed the whole field of labour
history, which, before his work, had tended to consist either of
narrowly economistic debates about rising or falling living standards
of workers, or of studies of trade union or socialist organizations.
The new focus on the immensely varied experiences of toilers, both
within and outside workplaces, has now become standard historiographical common sense. The continued centrality of Thompson's
work in this respect is seldom questioned: the problem might consist,
rather, in simplified and distorted understandings of what the
transition from narrowly economic or political to broader cultural
concerns had really meant for its inaugurator.

Most bright and ambitious postgraduate and research scholars
today would know that teleology and economic determinism are 'bad'
things — from which an increasing number seem to be developing a
most unfortunate contempt or boredom with things thought to be
merely economic or pertaining to organized political movements.
Thompson has been hailed, and often debunked, as the founder of
some kind of culturalism. What such assessments, applications and
critiques have generally lacked is Thompson's uncanny capacity for
grasping any concept or method in the full range of its possibilities
— and limits. Thus *The Making* is actually steeped in economic history,
and nowhere in his writings is culture abstracted either from material
conditions, or from relationships of power. Some of the richest
chapters of his *magnum opus* deal precisely with organized, radical or
socialistic political groups. Thompson repeatedly called for dialogues
with anthropology, but at the same time admitted that this would
be a difficult, though necessary, process for historians, for the mainstream of that discipline often tended to ignore historical specificities
and elide questions of power.[10] He summed up his own distinctive
position at the beginning of *Customs in Common*, stating that popular
or plebeian culture needed to become 'a more concrete and usable
concept, no longer situated in the thin air of "meanings, attitudes
and values", but located within a particular equilibrium of social
relations, a working environment of exploitation and resistance to

<hr>

[10] 'Folklore, Anthropology and Social History', in *Indian Historical Review*,
III, 2, 1977.

exploitation, of relations of power which are masked by the rituals of paternalism and deference.'[11]

In history-writing at least, however, Thompson argued, the economy could not be allowed to remain at the level of abstractions, governed by inexorable, purely 'objective' laws, as 'bases' precisely separable from 'superstructures'. That, he had come to feel by the 1960s and 1970s, had only been an analogy, one among several and not the most helpful, used by Marx to convey much more complex and nuanced ideas.[12] In Thompson, economic relationships and categories constantly get translated into everyday life, the market ceases to remain an abstraction and becomes poor people haggling over prices at shops and fairs, and sometimes struggling to enforce norms of subsistence vital for their survival through collective action. Class, too is what happens, sometimes, and in ever-shifting forms, in actual human relationships: it cannot be grasped, or at least used in actual historical reconstruction, as a finished or isolable entity. 'The finest-meshed sociological net cannot give us a pure specimen of class, any more than it can give us one of deference or of love. The relationship must always be embodied in real people and in a real context. . . . We cannot have love without lovers, nor deference without squires and labourers.'[13]

The 'Moral Economy' essay apart, Thompson's writings on eighteenth-century English history have evoked less general interest than *The Making*: a pity, for they are sometimes more outstanding examples of the historian's craft than even that classic, and considerably refine and elaborate his theoretical positions.[14] Certainly

---

[11] *Customs in Common*, p. 7.

[12] In his 'The Peculiarities of the English', Thompson argued that the base-superstructure model 'inherits a dialectic that is right, but the particular mechanical metaphor through which it is expressed is wrong. This metaphor from constructional engineering . . . must in any case be inadequate to describe the flux of conflict, the dialectic of a changing social process.' Reprinted in *The Poverty of Theory and Other Essays* (London, 1978), p. 79. See also Thompson, 'Folklore', and the further elaboration of the argument in course of the polemic against Althusser, *Poverty of Theory*, pp. 349-52. A similar critique was being developed around the same time, but with greater theoretical precision, by Raymond Williams: see particularly the chapters entitled 'Base and Super-structure' and 'Determination' in his *Marxism and Literature* (Oxford, 1977). In general, Williams with his conceptions of cultural materialism has been the Marxian thinker closest to Thompson.

[13] *The Making*, p. 9.

[14] These include his third book, *Whigs and Hunters* (London: Allen Lane, 1975), and a whole series of essays, among them 'Time, Work-Discipline and Industrial

this is so with regard to class, for in eighteenth-century England (as indeed in all epochs prior to the Industrial Revolution), Thompson was entering an era in which the language of class was not 'present in the evidence itself . . . not available within people's own cognitive systems'. Social conflicts were fought out in terms of 'estates', 'ranks', or 'orders'.[15]

Thompson's wrestling with the problems posed by a society not yet fully transformed by capitalism obviously have a very high degree of relevance for historians working on eras of Indian history prior to the most recent. Class analysis, if applied to such situations in a manner identical with what might be appropriate to a developed capitalist society, would evidently produce the reifications Thompson had been attacking throughout — as has happened, one might add, in quite a lot of Indian Marxist historiography. Class would figure as something purely 'objective', constituted mechanically by production relations, while evidence about actual patterns of consciousness (commonly in terms of religion, local community, caste, etc.) would be treated condescendingly as illusory or 'false'. The Althusserian way of avoiding such reductionism did not appeal to him either, for he seems to have felt that in effect it was an attempt to have the best of both worlds, by combining abstract ideological-political purity with practical eclecticism. It preserved a fairly dogmatic notion of mode of production as base, but only as a kind of distant horizon, removed from the world of everyday experience and historical specificities through the devices of relative autonomy and determination in a last instance whose lonely hour would never strike. The other logical alternative so common today — evacuating totally the ground of class, certainly for pre-capitalist societies and perhaps everywhere — remained alien to Thompson, who preferred to go on searching for historically specific connections between social being

---

Capitalism', *Past and Present*, 1967; 'Moral Economy of the English Crowd in the Eighteenth Century', *Past and Present*, 1971; 'Patrician Society, Plebeian Culture', *Journal of Social History*, Summer 1974, and 'Eighteenth Century English Society: Class-Struggle without Class?', *Social History*, May 1978 — to cite only four of the most outstanding. Geoff Eley's article apart, however, the eighteenth-century work is sparsely analysed even in what is perhaps the best collection of essays on Thompson to have come out so far, namely Harvey J. Kaye and Keith McClelland (eds), *E.P. Thompson: Critical Perspectives* (Polity, 1990). See however the recent review by Peter King, 'Edward Thompson's Contribution to Eighteenth Century Studies: The Patrician-Plebeian Model Reexamined', *Social History*, May 1996.

15 'Eighteenth-century English Society'.

and social consciousness. He never gave up his belief that class, used in subtle, mediated ways, remained a helpful tool for understanding the pressures and constraints flowing from property relationships. But relationships, he had already argued in his *Making*, precede identity,[16] and in his eighteenth-century studies he elaborated this theme through the deliberately paradoxical formulation of 'class struggle without class'.[17] What he preferred to call a 'plebeian' culture was not defined by class, 'in the sense that one can speak of a working-class culture', but it was still impossible to understand its emergence in the 'field of force' constituted by gentry–plebeian relationships without employing 'the concept of the dialectical antagonisms, adjustments, and (sometimes) reconciliations, of class. I am therefore employing the terminology of class conflict while resisting the attribution of identity to *a* class.'[18]

English history between the Glorious Revolution and the 1770s, before Thompson entered it, had seemed a placid, stable, and rather dull interlude between centuries obviously marked by dramatic changes. It was assumed to have been an age dominated without question by aristocrats and gentlemen, engaged in dignified party-politics or (in the Namierite version) factional squabbles, but in both versions with subordinates firmly tied to them through relationships of paternalism and deference. Violence was relegated to the domain of a distinct 'criminal' sub-culture, and the evidence about occasional plebeian riots, usually over high prices, was interpreted as mere outbursts of an unthinking mob, reacting spontaneously to economic pressures. It was, and in dominant part remains, what Thompson in one of his last essays described as a historiography of the 'bland leading the bland.'[19]

Working in collaboration with a group of young research scholars at Warwick University — a very rare opportunity for him — Thompson helped to constitute a new eighteenth-century, at once more brutal and far more open in its possibilities than the conventional models. There was the collectively produced and edited *Albion's Fatal Tree*,[20]

16 'We cannot have two distinct classes, each with an independent being, and then bring them into relationship with each other.' *The Making*, p. 9.

17 'Eighteenth-century English Society'.

18 *Customs in Common*, pp. 72–3.

19 'Patricians and Plebs', in *Customs in Common*, p. 18.

20 Douglas Hay, Peter Linebaugh, John G. Rule, E.P. Thompson and Cal Winslow (eds), *Albion's Fatal Tree: Crime and Society in Eighteenth-Century England* (London: Allen Lane, 1975).

consisting of pioneering studies of law, crime and society. Through detailed analysis of the making of the Black Act of 1723 to protect royal forests from hungry poachers in the interests of the Whig oligarchy, Thompson's own *Whigs and Hunters* exposed, as never before, the horrors of class domination and state violence in an era not marked by any major upheaval, and previously assumed to have been peaceful, stable, and gentlemanly. *Whigs and Hunters*, along with a series of pathbreaking essays, illumined in meticulous detail the interrelations between a developing agrarian capitalism and transformations in English law, ruling ideologies, and state structures through the eighteenth century.

There was no lack, then, in Thompson's eighteenth-century work of an emphasis on power. And yet controls and domination could never become absolute, for there were also important elements of a rebellious popular culture, rooted in local communities that fought back through their own interpretations of traditions and customs. In the context of much historiography operating today with apparently similar categories ('popular culture', 'subaltern', 'tradition', 'community consciousness', etc.), it is important to note how careful Thompson was to specify, to particularize. Such rebelliousness, to him, was far from being some kind of universal trait of pre-industrial popular culture. It was bound up with concrete historical developments in England at a particular time. The English Revolution, despite failure and compromise, had weakened the authority of the official church, and simultaneously made the gentry suspicious of over-efficient bureaucracies and armies. Things, therefore, were rather different from the absolutist consolidation in some other parts of Europe, notably France. In England, crimes legally punishable with death multiplied in the eighteenth century in tandem with the tightening-up of conceptions of private property — but the number of actual executions did not rise in anything like the same proportion. The law was an instrument of terror, but it was also a theatre where hegemony had to be periodically re-enacted. In its interstices developed a plebeian counter-theatre of insubordination and defiance. And so, as Thompson brilliantly revealed through his writings on the eighteenth century, the bland categories of ruling class and conventional historical and anthropological discourses needed to be given 'a new dialectical ambivalence'. 'An "act of giving" must be seen, simultaneously, as an "act of getting", a social consensus as class hegemony, social control (very often) as class control.'[21] Deference, the term so

---

[21] 'Folklore, Anthropology and Social History'.

often used in, and about, eighteenth-century England, Thompson pointed out in another essay, could be at times 'one part necessary self-preservation, one part the calculated extraction of whatever could be extracted.'[22] 'The same man who touches his forelock to the squire by day — and who goes down to history as an example of deference — may kill his sheep, snare his pheasants or poison his dogs at night.'[23] The dialectic has to operate the other way too: *Whigs and Hunters*, a scathing exposure of the inequities and hypocrisies of the eighteenth-century legal system, therefore ends with an extraordinarily subtle and important section on the post-seventeenth-century British rule of law as an instrument of ruling class coercion-cum-hegemony, but also open to occasional appropriation by subordinated groups. Rulers, Thompson reminds us, could become prisoners of their own rhetoric. 'If this rhetoric was a mask, it was a mask which John Wilkes was to borrow', and later, Gandhi and Nehru, in mass anti-colonial struggles.[24] Neat, and hence often homogenized, binary opposites found no place in Thompson's rich tapestry of historical reconstruction.

This seems an appropriate place to touch upon what has been a recurrent criticism of Thompson: that he was a rank empiricist disdainful of theory. Some of his more sweeping statements, eloquent but potentially misleading, have certainly contributed to this impression, as for instance the passage I have cited with approval about lovers and deferential labourers.[25] But Thompson's is not really an empiricist position that claims to reject all theory, and he used general concepts and theoretical schema all the time, including ones (notably, flexible readings of Marxism) that Karl Popper, for instance, would certainly have condemned as totalizing, holistic and historicist. In *Poverty of Theory* he distinguished carefully between empirical procedures and controls, and empiricism as an (untenable) philosophical position, and tried to develop a simultaneous polemic against Althusser and Popper.[26] What Thompson did remain exceptionally aware of was the need to specify and contextualize the usages or applications of theoretical schema. And he felt also that some

---

[22] 'Eighteenth-century English Society'.

[23] *Customs in Common*, p. 66.

[24] *Whigs and Hunters*, pp. 264, 266.

[25] We obviously cannot do without general, abstract terms like 'love' or 'deference', even if every specific instance escapes their 'net' — otherwise there will be only an infinite multitude of particulars, making analysis, indeed any communication, impossible.

[26] *The Poverty of Theory*, p. 224, and *passim*.

abstractions (including some versions of Marxism) could be more prone to the dangers of homogenization than others, particularly those which failed to take sufficient cognizance of possibilities of internal, dialectical tension.

By the late 1970s, intellectual moods in the West were changing in directions opposed to Thompson's values and methods. In retrospect, the violent attack on Althusser (*Poverty of Theory*, 1978), felt even by many admirers to have been excessively polemical and not entirely fair, makes more sense within this wider scenario.[27] Althusser was just one indicator, and not perhaps the best choice of target. Althusserian Marxism had a notable, and quite often fruitful, impact on literary criticism, interdisciplinary cultural studies, feminist theories, and anthropology, but it never became much of a force in mainstream historical writing. The emphasis on structural determinants in place of agency, on history as a 'process without a subject', when detached from Althusser's own Marxist faith, did however contribute to an obsessive conviction in the all-pervading and irresistible nature of power relations. The year 1978 saw also the publication of Edward Said's *Orientalism*, and Robert Muchembled's influential analysis of the 'conquest' of once-autonomous French popular culture through successful acculturations by absolutist state, Counter-Reformation Church, and eventually Enlightenment rationality.[28] These were works written quite outside the realms of Althusserian Marxism, but perhaps an overall context was being set by the final collapse of hopes of radical transformation through autonomous popular action, once aroused by Vietnam, May 1968, and the Prague Spring. In studies of crime and law, too, where Foucault had become the dominant influence, the focus was now on confinement and the near-irresistible disciplinary regimes of modern bureaucracies. The realm of popular freedom tended to be thrust back into a romanticized pre-modern (or pre-colonial, in Third World contexts), and/or located in brief moments of carnivalesque license. Power and resistance were thus detached from each other, absolutized into impenetrable binaries, and increasingly abstracted from specificities of historical context.

---

[27] Things were worsened by Thompson's intemperate attack on critics like Stuart Hall and Richard Johnson at the History Workshop session in Oxford in December 1979. See Raphael Samuel's editorial comment in Samuel (ed.), *People's History and Socialist Theory* (London, 1981), pp. 376-8.

[28] Robert Muchembled, *Culture populaire et culture des élites dans la France moderne (XVe-XVIIIe siecle)* (Paris, 1978).

Attempts to search for possible 'material' connections or contexts stood *ipso facto* condemned as economistic.[29]

For a decade after 1979 Thompson found no time for methodological debates or the pursuit of the historian's craft. In a world on the brink of nuclear catastrophe, he concentrated all his energies in efforts to build new and effective instruments for mass mobilization, and not on abstract debates about structure and agency. When he returned to academic work in the late 1980s, it was with a body made frail and exhausted by years of endless campaigns.

The achievements of the few years that remained will be a source for both joy and sorrow. Like Raymond Williams, the British socialist intellectual with whom comparison has always seemed most appropriate, Thompson died at the height of his creative powers, leaving much unfinished — including, it seems, a book about Wordsworth.

Customs in Common (1991) has already figured often in these pages. It does not consist mainly of reprints, as an unwary reader skimming through its contents page might think: nearly all the essays are either new or thoroughly revised. Old themes have absorbed and grown on experiences of the intervening years, both political and academic. Thus 'Moral Economy Reviewed', written in the midst of worldwide hosannas to the wonders of the free market, actually sharpens Thompson's lifelong critique of capitalism, while avoiding at the same time, perhaps more carefully than before, the romanticizing of the pre-modern. The implicit moral economy of the food rioters, Thompson points out, was not anti-market in any absolute sense. Rather, 'the crowd's preferred model was precisely the "open market" in which the petty producers freely competed, rather than the closed market when large dealers conducted private bargains over samples in the back parlours of inns.' The distinction, in other words, is between the relative mutuality of small commodity production and exchange, and capitalistic takeover. Thompson here has stayed close to the insights of classic Marxism, with its powerful critique of the frequent ideological elisions between these two conceptions of the market, and the consequent mystification: 'It may even seem that it is the "market system" which has "produced" the nation's wealth — perhaps "the market" grew all that grain?'[30]

Other essays in the volume develop themes pioneered in the Warwick years: the lineaments of a part-rebellious plebeian culture,

29 For an analysis of broadly similar developments more recently in Indian historiography, see Chapter 3.

30 *Customs in Common*, p. 305.

the complex interfaces of customary and formal law as integrally bound up with the nitty-gritty of everyday agrarian production. There is need to note also the illuminating theoretical discussion of cultural hegemony in which Thompson — while fully acknowledging the power and relevance of that concept in analysis of the limits of what is possible, the inhibitions upon the growth of alternative horizons and expectations — still rejects interpretations of Gramsci which equate hegemony with 'an all-embracing domination upon the ruled.' He points to two specific limits, operative at least in eighteenth-century England. Hegemonic culture remained open to multiple plebeian appropriations, it did not 'entail any acceptance by the poor of the gentry's paternalism upon the gentry's own terms or in their approved self-image.' And such hegemony was not all-embracing, could not extend everywhere, did not prevent plebeians 'from defending their own modes of work and leisure, and forming their own rituals, their own satisfactions and view of life.'[31] Both qualifications, I feel, may be relevant for studies of colonial India, currently under the sway of assumptions of seamless acculturation of the intelligentsia by colonial discourses.

Thompson had inherited from his father a lifelong special interest in India. It is fitting,· therefore, that Thompson's one book on a (partly) non-English theme, which happened also to be the last he was able to see in print, was *Alien Homage* (1993), based on his father's correspondence with Rabindranath Tagore. This is a quiet, almost excessively modest work, quite unlike his other writings: but then Thompson for once was writing about a country and culture about which he knew himself to be largely ignorant. Thompson, till the end of his days, remained very different from a growing number of academics today who stride confidently across countries, continents and centuries, armed with simple talismans of theory.

If *Alien Homage* is a somewhat minor work, the posthumous *Witness Against The Beast* is something quite different — Thompson at his finest. Through detailed research into the ideas, activities and lineages of obscure sects, Thompson in the first part of this study of Blake looks for possible links between radical antinomian movements during the English Revolution and the upsurge of artisanal militancy during the 1790s: the lost connections, in other words, between the milieus explored in Christopher Hill's *World Turned Upside Down* and his own *Making*. At times Thompson's

---

[31] Ibid., pp. 85-7.

presentation of the story of this search has the excitement and interest of a detective story, as when he tracks down the last Muggletonian and finds a rich collection of documents about that sect — with which, just possibly, Blake's family may have had some connections — in apple-boxes in his storeroom. Then comes a superb analysis of some of Blake's poems, notably of 'London', combining textual close reading with location in specific historical contexts. In more general terms, Thompson is exploring through Blake a difficult, ambiguous, and partial coming together of submerged antinomian traditions, rooted in dissident readings of Christianity and therefore steeped in Biblical exegesis and imagery — and the Jacobinical, Painite radicalism of the 1790s, a product broadly of the Enlightenment, in outlook rationalist, deistic and utilitarian. Through this exploration emerge, implicitly, Thompson's own mature views about Enlightenment rationalism and humanism: the nodal point of the contemporary changes in intellectual climate that have tended in the minds of many to make Thompson himself seem a figure of the past.

III

My essay so far might appear to be in danger of becoming one more celebration of Thompson. There are ample reasons for such celebration, but this by itself will not do justice to the problem with which I began: why Thompsonian social history appears dated and somewhat irrelevant to many today, and how far such a rejection is appropriate. An explanation in terms of contextual changes alone, like the fading away of hopes of radical transformation through popular initiatives, is helpful only upto a point, for it remains too external, and therefore reductive, to be entirely satisfactory.

Thompson's historical and political work had been a crucial, constitutive, element of the dissident Marxist New Left of the late 1950s and 1960s, which had responded to the international socialist crisis of 1956 by searching for alternative, democratic and humane forms of socialism free of Stalinist bureaucratic deformation, terror, economistic dogma, and amoral pragmatism: 'socialism with a human face', as Dubcek described it in 1968. 'Humanism', and 'actual' or 'lived' experience had become key terms in this quest, and Thompson in particular sometimes elevated 'experience' into a kind of master key that as a 'junction-concept' could somehow unproblematically link together social being with social consciousness, structure with process and agency.[32] Precisely these terms, however, came under sustained critique, initially within a limited Parisian intellectual mileu from the early 1960s, but then with very wide-ranging consequences, building up into what has come to be called 'anti-humanism'.[33] Basically, the 'man' of European humanism was felt to be irremediably white and male, complicit with, indeed perhaps inseparable from, both colonial and patriarchal structures. Such charges resonated with the rise of feminist movements and theories in the West from the 1970s, as well as with many features characteristic of the new era of resurgent neo-colonialism and racism. Problems of non-white immigration, race and ethnic identity were becoming central elements in the everyday life of the West, while there was a simultaneous rise to unprecedented prominence of expatriate Third World intellectuals resident in metropolitan countries. Marxist class analysis, even of the refined kinds developed in the 1960s and 1970s by Thompson and others, appeared to many to be too restrictive, unable to comprehend problems of gender and ethnicity except in ultimately reductive terms. Meanwhile, in moves bound up with the linguistic turn in the social sciences, any un-problematized valorization of 'experience' became suspect. For surely experience, in any but the most inchoate form, could not be independent of language and culture, and hence was bound to be

32 'For experience is exactly what makes the junction between culture and not-culture, lying half within social being, half within social consciousness.' E.P. Thompson, 'The Politics of Theory', in Raphael Samuel (ed.), *People's History and Socialist Theory*, p. 405. As even his sharpest critics generally admit, Thompson's practical, historical handling of the experiences of determinate social groups has been nuanced, rich, indeed often exemplary. Statements like the above, however, remain philosophically dubious, and do little justice to the complexity of the author's own historical reconstructions, See, for some pertinent comments, Stuart Hall's intervention in the same volume, entitled 'In defence of theory'.

33 In a recent, highly sympathetic, account of these developments, Robert Young locates the beginnings of the change in Paris' intellectual climate in Lévi-Strauss' critique of the existential Marxism of Sartre in *The Savage Mind* (1962), Sartre's own preface to Fanon's *The Wretched of the Earth*, and, generally, the shock of the Algerian war. See *White Mythologies: Writing History and the West* (Routledge, London/New York, 1990), pp. 41-7, 119-26, and *passim*. I have found Young useful despite — sometimes precisely because of — my own extreme disagreements with him. He is totally dismissive of the Thompsonian tradition, and indeed of virtually all research-based Marxist history-writing. Such dismissal allows him to assume that all Marxist approaches to history are necessarily totalizing and teleological.

moulded by dominant ideologies. Much of Thompsonian social history, in this changed milieu, seemed tainted by the sins of Eurocentrism and gender-blindness, philosophically naive and hopelessly dated by the linguistic turn, and guilty of complicity with liberal humanism and rationalism — for which the Enlightenment has become today the convenient, if homogenizing, polemical shorthand.

The Eurocentric charge that came to be levelled against Western and eventually all Marxism could appear to be particularly damaging for a social history the foundation text of which had deliberately confined itself to the making of the 'English' working class, written moreover by a historian who subsequently spoke with some pride about the 'peculiarities' of the English. Hobsbawm apart, the great masters of British Marxian historiography have admittedly written little on Empire. It needs to be emphasized that there was a real absence here, a space that could consequently be filled, following Said's *Orientalism*, by colonial discourse analysis. I have argued elsewhere, however, that this new intellectual mood, widespread today in those limited circles in the West that still wish to be recognized as radical, has been marred by displacements of its own, and is characterized by specific procedures of silencing.[34] There is, for instance, a remarkable absence of reference to the long history of critiques of imperialism and colonialism developed in the main within European Marxism: a silencing, dare one add, in particular of Lenin. Certainly such critiques were often economistically reductive, and are in need of quite fundamental updating and revision. But what is happening instead is a closing-off of many potential queries, as discussion gets virtually confined to themes of race and culture, firmly abstracted (generalities apart) from class and production. It is tempting to suggest some broad correlations at this point with the lived experiences of migrant intellectuals for whom racial discrimination and questions of cultural or ethnic identity tend to have greater immediacy than class.

[34] For elaborations of this argument, see my 'Orientalism Revisited: Saidian Frameworks in the Writing of Modern Indian History', *Oxford Literary Review*, XVI, 1-2, 1994; 'A Marxian Social History Beyond the Foucaultian Turn: Peter Linebaugh's *The London Hanged*', *Economic and Political Weekly*, XXX, 30, 29 July 1995; and Chapter 3 of this book. See also Arif Dirlik, 'The Postcolonial Aura: Third World Criticism in the Age of Global Capitalism', *Critical Inquiry*, 20, ii, Winter 1994, for an excellent critique of recent ideological expressions of the new status of migrant Third World intellectuals who 'have arrived in First World academe' as epitomized in the development of theories of 'postcoloniality'.

This is ground largely untrodden by Thompson,[35] but not perhaps resistant to extended and modified versions of the social-historical approaches he had pioneered. Striking confirmation here has come recently from Peter Linebaugh, Thompson's student and colleague of the Warwick days, whose *The London Hanged* makes crime and punishment in London the entry point for a study of the eighteenth-century Atlantic economy 'from below'.[36] Along with the work of Marcus Rediker,[37] Linebaugh opens up for social history the deep-sea world of ships and sailors which linked 'the handicrafts of India to the plantation in America to manufactures and putting-out in London.' Linebaugh emphasizes that 'the ship was not only the means of communication among continents, it was the first place where working people from the continents communicated.' As a by-product of the centrality of the slave trade to the eighteenth-century Atlantic economy, a substantial population of slave and ex-slave Afro-Americans emerged in the metropolis of that economy, London, and some of them Linebaugh discovers to have been active in well-known instances of popular and artisanal protest that have been viewed so far through 'English' prisms alone.[38] Reading Line-baugh, one is tempted to speculate whether the popular — and quite

---

[35] It is only fair, however, to recall his 'apology' at the beginning of *The Making of the English Working Class*, explaining the restrictive term 'English' (to the exclusion, he says, of Scottish and Welsh) as flowing 'not out of chauvinism but out of respect. It is because class is a cultural as much as an economic formation that I have been cautious as to generalizing beyond English experi-ence' (p. 13). *Customs in Common* does try to make considerable use of non-European material, in a manner still very rare among Western historians who have not specialized in Third World studies (see particularly 'The Moral Economy Reviewed', and 'Custom, Law and Common Right'). I have already commented on the refreshing diffidence of *Alien Homage*, so different from quite a lot of critiques of colonial discourse which, through imposition of questions, assumptions, and restrictive agendas basically formulated in response to metropolitan conditions, seem at times to be unconsciously constituting a new form of the Orientalism they denounce.

[36] Peter Linebaugh, *The London Hanged: Crime and Civil Society in the Eighteenth-Century* (Harmondsworth: Penguin, 1991, 1993).

[37] Marcus Rediker, *Between the Devil and the Deep Blue Sea* (Cambridge, 1987).

[38] Two out of the six men tried for leading the attack on Newgate prison during the Gordon Riots of 1780 were Afro-Americans, and the ex-slave Olaudah Equiano was active in the early 1790s, helping the radical English artisan Thomas Hardy organise the London Corresponding Society — a detail that Thompson does not mention in the chapter on that Society with which his *Making* begins. Linebaugh, pp. 348–56, 415–16.

often working-class — racism of the late nineteenth century and beyond could not have been in part an ideology that developed as a counter to incipient alternative solidarities across racial divides. There does seem to be a need to go beyond the fairly widespread assumption today of Western racism as a virtually transhistorical constant.[39] The point has a relevance that goes beyond the purely academic or historical, for globalization today is creating a much more internationalized labour force in the metropolitan countries, amidst conditions of a white racism that is often sought to be countered purely through forging ethnic or religious solidarities of specific immigrant groups.

Linebaugh's book does not mention Said, but his fully selfconscious and masterly dialectical transcendence of Foucault once again illuminates both the power of an analysis clearly still rooted in Thompson, and the need to go beyond the master. He maintains the Thompson tradition of emphasizing the possibilities of plebeian resistance, against Foucaultian tendencies that make 'the rulers of government and society seem all-powerful.'[40] But this is not a simple rejection, for Foucault's central theme of growing disciplinary authority and interest in the 'micro-physics' of power is very much also Linebaugh's concern. The major difference is that *The London Hanged* explores the connections between many of the changes noted by Foucault and specific processes of labour, profit, and class-struggle — and this not through any reiteration of an abstract or generalized base–superstructure formula, but a brilliantly original series of detailed histories of a number of London-centred trades. Linebaugh thus extends to urban crafts and manufactures Thompson's theme of erosion of traditional rights and perquisites of toilers through the development of absolute property rights. His framework is able to relate this progressive criminalization of the customary appropriations of the poor through the tightening-up of property laws, penal codes, and police-bureaucratic authority, with 'rational' technological innovations and the transition to factory production: for both processes were intimately bound up with changing forms of the capitalist

[39] There are passages in Said that seem to suggest a continuity going back to Aeschylus. See, in interesting contrast, the distinction made by the socialist-feminist historian Catherine Hall between 'cultural' and 'biological' racism in the context of the 1830s anti-slavery agitation and the 1860s debate between Carlyle and John Stuart Mill about British atrocities in Jamaica: *White, Male and Middle Class: Explorations in Feminism and History* (Oxford: Polity, 1992).

[40] Linebaugh, p. 4.

extraction of surplus. The end-results were the modern state and the factory, the latter defined, strikingly, as 'a place where the principles of production and punishment can be united. . . . '[41] Particularly impressive is Linebaugh's unravelling of the contextual underpinnings of Bentham's Panopticon, which Foucault had made central to the argument of his *Discipline and Punish*. Through a study of Bentham's private papers, Linebaugh is able to establish that the idea had actually originated with Samuel Bentham, brother of the Utilitarian philosopher, from out of attempts to instil discipline and efficiency in the naval dockyard he was helping to construct on the Black Sea for Catherine the Great's favourite *Potemkin*. Subsequently, in 1795, the British government appointed Samuel Inspector-General of Naval Works at a critical moment in Britain's war against Revolutionary France, and at a site where capitalist innovation and the vital interests of the British state intertwined in inseparable ways.[42]

Gender is the other great area of virtual silence in the bulk of Thompson's work, an absence which I find less excusable and more troubling. It cannot be denied that women were no more than marginal in his narrative of the formation of the English working class, and while Thompson did occasionally try to make amends in his later writings,[43] gender on the whole still remained additive rather than a central, transformative category of his historical analysis. Yet Catherine Hall has described *The Making* as the 'text on which many feminist historians cut their teeth'.[44] Relations between Thompsonian social history and feminist historiography — particularly of the socialist-feminist kind which has flourished in Britain around the *History Workshop* — have been complicated, as inspiration and irritant, at once productive and fraught with tension. Thompson extended labour history far beyond the conventional, public, and predominantly male domains of wages, unions, and strikes, and his entire work repeatedly touched upon, indeed often pioneered, themes and methods that have become central to feminist scholarship and thinking. The relationship therefore was always deeply paradoxical: many feminist scholars have said that it was the combination in the *Making* of a neglect

[41] Ibid., p. 285.

[42] Linebaugh, Chapter XI.

[43] Particularly in the two essays on moral economy, and the studies of sale of wives and rough music in *Customs in Common*. 'Rough Music' also contains an interesting discussion of the concept of patriarchy: ibid., pp. 499–505.

[44] *White, Male and Middle Class*, p. 9.

of gender dimensions, with the elaboration of tools and concepts clearly very relevant for exploring the greater part of those 'hidden from history', that set them off on their distinct but not unrelated paths.

Feminist theory and history-writing have been on the whole far more original and transformative than critiques of colonial discourse.[45] Its trajectories, at the same time, have increasingly moved away from the radical social history of the 1960s and 1970s, making a recuperation-cum-extension of Thompson in ways similar, say, to Linebaugh's, no longer entirely satisfactory.[46] The initial focus on the recovery of women's history, of patriarchal oppression and the forgotten importance of women in moments of popular resistance, could still be considered as extension, a belated and necessary gendering of narratives of class.[47] But already feminists found it difficult to share Thompson's summary dismissals of Althusser and

[45] It is necessary to add immediately, however, that feminists of non-white origin have helped to transform Western feminism in crucial ways. As Catherine Hall has emphasized, 'The most sustained *political* critique of essentialism . . . was developed by black women. "Difference" became an issue for Western feminism because of the challenge to ethnocentrism, to the assumption that one group of women could speak for another. That challenge, coterminous with the development of critiques both of the unified subject and the possibility of fixed meanings being attached to the categories "man" or "woman", has contributed to the necessity for feminist historians to assess our practices, uncomfortable though this may be.' 'Feminism and Feminist Theory,' in Catherine Hall, *White, Male and Middle Class*, p. 25.

[46] It may not be irrelevant to note that Linebaugh's handling of gender inequality and oppression within plebeian communities is quite unsatisfactory, more so indeed than in some of Thompson's later writings. A brief discussion of gender relations at the end of the chapter on sailors as a picaresque proletariat contains, for instance, the curious phrase 'the work of his hands and the labour of her body', *London Hanged*, p. 152.

[47] Thus Sally Alexander recalls that for her and other British socialist-feminists in the 1970s, the initial 'point was to write women into the history of the working class' — and thus expand 'a narrative of historical materialism whose subject was class and whose determining relationships were those of production or property.' Sally Alexander, *Becoming A Woman, and Other Essays in 19th and 20th Century Feminist History* (London: Virago, 1994), Introduction, pp. xi–xii. Impressive instances of such work include Alexander's own 'Women's Work in Nineteenth-Century London: A Study of the Years 1820-60s' (1976; reprinted in ibid.), Barbara Taylor's *Eve and the New Jerusalem: Socialism and Feminism in the Nineteenth-Century* (London: Virago, 1983), and Leonore Davidoff and Catherine Hall, *Family Fortunes: Men and Women of the English Middle Class, 1780-1850* (London/Chicago, 1987).

'French' theory. Althusserian concepts like ideological interpellation, and Foucault's theorization of the multiplicity of sites of power, appeared helpful particularly as feminists moved into the more difficult terrain of exploration of the times, far more common than visible nonconformity, of women's compliance, apparently willing submission, and even occasional enthusiastic participation in movements consolidating patriarchy.[48]

Feminism necessarily has to insist on the historical presence of subjectivities other than class. Today even the socialist-feminist Sally Alexander feels impelled to write that 'the temporalities of class and mode of production are only some of the many composite times which make up the present – and that history has no Subject.'[49] Some, like Alexander herself, have been exploring the possibilities of psychoanalysis, of Freud read through Lacan, in the search for a 'subjective history through image, symbol and language.'[50] Others, like many US radical-feminists who emerged from a background of academic literary studies rather than history and New Left activism, have gone more into deconstruction, a more extreme 'decentring' of subjecthood through the endless play of signifiers in language. Feminism, in more general terms, has clearly shared in, and contributed to, contemporary postmodernistic critiques of undeniably male-centred 'Enlightenment' reason, modernity, and liberal humanism. One notable instance would be feminist re-readings of the French Revolution, which have revealed the crucial role of Jacobin radicalism in the suppression of incipient women's movements, and the deliberate exclusion of women from the new public spaces being created by the Revolution in the name of the equal rights of 'man'.[51]

---

[48] Fascism in Germany and Italy, some contemporary developments in the United States, and the Hindu Right today in India, would be obvious examples that have stimulated a lot of research and rethinking. See, for instance, Claudia Koonz, *Mothers in the Fatherland: Women, the Family and Nazi Politics* (London: Methuen, 1988), and Tanika Sarkar and Urvashi Butalia (eds), *Women and the Hindu Right* (Delhi, 1995).

[49] Sally Alexander, *Becoming A Woman*, Introduction, p. xii.

[50] Sally Alexander, 'Feminist History and Psychoanalysis' (1990; reprinted in her *Becoming A Woman*), p. 225.

[51] Joan B. Landes, *Women and the Public Sphere in the Age of the French Revolution* (Ithaca: Cornell University Press, 1988); Darline Gay Levy and Harriet B. Applewhite, 'Women and Militant Citizenship in Revolutionary Paris', in Sara E. Melzer and Leslie W. Rabine (eds), *Rebel Daughters: Women and the French Revolution* (New York/Oxford: OUP, 1992).

And yet signs are not lacking that the marriage between feminism and postmodernism might turn out to be as unhappy as the earlier one with Marxism. The postmodern celebration of the disintegration of identities and wholesale rejections of Enlightenment humanism do not always mesh with feminist perspectives. For feminism needs to valorize the possibilities of women's agency, and sometimes might seek the extension, rather than the theoretical undermining, of notions of individualized rights from which women, like other subordinated groups, have often been excluded. Modernity to them might appear unfinished, in need of renovation and extension, rather than total rejection. In a recent important article, Patricia Waugh has characterized postmodern *fin-de-siècle* moods as 'nihilism produced by nostalgia'. The nostalgic moment tends to be located in a lost sense of community, and this in turn often gets intermingled with a highly idealized notion of femininity that has little to do with actual women or feminist political practice.[52] But it is difficult to get nostalgic about realms where you have been subordinated or excluded from, and so the 'community' that many (mostly male) radical intellectuals have often too easily valorized can provoke contrary or ambiguous responses from more gendered perspectives. Feminism therefore, Waugh argues, 'cannot repudiate entirely the framework of Enlightened modernity without perhaps fatally undermining itself as an emancipatory politics.' It needs to 'posit some belief in the notion of effective human agency, the necessity for historical continuity in formulating identity and a belief in historical progress.' She finds Habermas' nuanced evaluations of the Enlightenment more helpful for feminism than the wholesale rejections common today.[53] Significantly, some recent feminist empirical research on late-eighteenth-century France seems to be moving in directions that are broadly similar. Feminists, they conclude, have to relate to the Enlightenment and the French Revolution as 'rebel

---

52 Patricia Waugh, *Stalemates? Feminists, Post-Modernists and Unfinished Issues in Modern Aesthetics*, in Philip Rice and Patricia Waugh (eds), *Modern Literary Theory: A Reader* (London, etc., 1989, 1992), pp. 341, 346, 348. Waugh's critique sometimes seems almost uncannily appropriate for some tendencies within recent *Subaltern Studies*: see my discussion of Dipesh Chakrabarty in Chapter III.

53 Waugh cites approvingly Habermas' statement 'that modernity is not exhausted, simply unfinished'. Feminism, while necessarily critical of Habermas' own quite evident gender-blindness, needs to work towards a not-dissimilar understanding which would neither 'simply repeat the Enlightenment concept of modernity nor repudiate it in an embrace of anarchic dispersal.' Waugh, pp. 353, 355.

daughters'.[54] I intend to argue in conclusion that here there are possibilities of a confluence with Thompson's own dialectical modes of understanding of bourgeois radical/romantic traditions.

If colonial discourse analysis can afford to ignore Thompson (as it explores themes virtually untouched by him), and feminist history has had conflictual but productive relations with his work, calls for direct repudiations and total rupture have been voiced mainly by scholars, influenced by the linguistic turn, working in areas close to his central concerns — above all, nineteenth-century British labour history. Historians like Gareth Stedman Jones and Patrick Joyce have been arguing for some years that Thompsonian social history remains in the ultimate analysis a refined variety of economistic reductionism, for it still postulates some kind of connection between objective class existence and class consciousness, and ignores the constitutive role of inherited structures of language. Thus Stedman Jones feels Chartism to have been less a product of emerging working-class interests than the continuation of eighteenth-century radical discourses which ranged all 'producers' against parasitic aristocrats, and Joyce is able to find little of authentic class language even in industrialized late-nineteenth-century Britain.[55] Thompson in the late 1970s had been criticized by intellectuals influenced by Althusser for being a 'culturalist'.[56] Paradoxically, he is now under attack for persistent

---

[54] 'While women have been excluded historically from the universality of human rights, this discourse of universal rights and freedoms alone provides the ground upon which we can pursue our feminist critiques and thereby continue to claim equality and freedom . . . we can proceed only by pulling out from under us the ground on which we stand.' Melzer and Rabine, *Rebel Daughters*, p. 10.

[55] Gareth Stedman Jones, *Languages of Class: Studies in English Working-Class History* (Cambridge, 1983); Patrick Joyce, *Visions of the People: Industrial England and the Question of Class 1848-1918* (Cambridge, 1991). For a sophisticated and balanced critique of Thompson which goes part of the way in a similar direction, see William H. Sewell, Jr, 'How Classes are Made: Reflections on E.P. Thompson's Theory of Working-Class Formation', in Harvey J. Kaye and Keith McClelland (eds), *E.P. Thompson: Critical Perspectives*.

[56] A particularly intemperate example of that critique was Richard Johnson, 'Edward Thompson, Eugene Genovese, and Socialist-Humanist History', which insisted upon the need 'to submit the best historical practices to an Althusserian critique', and found 'a necessarily anti-theoretical tendency in culturalism, a tendency to prefer "experience" to "theory".' *History Workshop Journal*, n. 6 (Autumn 1978). The essay is a reminder that Thompson had no monopoly over polemical violence. Such a hectoring tone, incidentally, surfaces quite often nowadays in some postmodernistic critiques of history. Thus Geoff Eley and

adherence to materialist social history and a modernist grand narrative of class, which many today would like to see replaced totally by 'culture' and the deconstructive play of language.

An intense and fruitful debate has been going on in recent years in the pages of *Social History* about the continued relevance, after the linguistic turn, of the 'Thompsonian' moment of the 1960s and 1970s.[57] On the whole, that legacy is proving rather difficult to repudiate in entirety. It seems clear that the cultural-cum-linguistic turn can at times produce determinisms of its own as disabling as those of orthodox Marxism.[58] The excessive claims to originality often characteristic of postmodernist writing are being challenged. Several commentators on the recent work of Stedman Jones and

---

Keith Nield speak of the 'theoretical *hauteur*' of Patrick Joyce (referring to the latter's 'The end of social history?', in *Social History*, 20, i, January 1995), a 'peremptory, exhortatory . . . apocalyptic tone. . . . Historians *must* do this, they *cannot ignore* that, they had better get their act together.' It should be noted, however, that Eley and Nield are simultaneously critical of the 'methodological conservatism' that leads some historians to dismiss all postmodernism without a proper understanding or discussion. Geoff Eley and Keith Nield, 'Starting-over: The present, the postmodern, and the moment of social history', *Social History*, 20, iii, October 1995.

[57] Important contributions include D. Mayfield, 'Language and Social History', *Social History*, October 1991; David Mayfield and Susan Thorne, 'Social History and its Discontents: Gareth Stedman Jones and the Politics of Language', ibid., May 1992; Jon Lawrence and Miles Taylor, 'The Poverty of Protest', and Patrick Joyce, 'The Imaginary Discontents of Social History: A Note of Response to Mayfield and Thorne, and Lawrence and Taylor', ibid., January 1993; Mayfield and Thorne, 'Reply to "The Poverty of Protest" and "The Imaginary Discontents" ', ibid., May 1993; James Vernon, 'Who's Afraid of the Linguistic Turn? The Politics of Social History and its Discontents', ibid., January 1994; Neville Kirk, 'History, Language, Ideas, and Postmodernism: A Materialist View', ibid., May 1994; Patrick Joyce, 'The End of Social History?', ibid., January 1995; Geoff Eley and Keith Nield, 'Starting Over: The Present, the Postmodern, and the Moment of Social History', ibid., October 1995; and Marc W. Steinberg, 'Culturally Speaking: Finding a Commons between Post-structuralism and the Thompsonian Perspective', ibid., May 1996.

[58] Interestingly, feminist scholarship about the French Revolution is encountering similar difficulties: 'a body of recent scholarship interprets revolutionary political opportunities and outcomes for women as largely predetermined by . . . gendered political discourse and by the male-dominated hegemonies it supported and reflected. Our documentation of women's involvement . . . suggests the need for a more complexly nuanced reading than these cultural determinisms encourage.' Darling Gay Levy and Harriet B. Applewhite, 'Women and Militant Citizenship in Revolutionary Paris', in *Rebel Daughters*, p. 86.

Joyce note that their accounts come surprisingly close to conventional intellectual history: 'For all their warnings on the indeterminacy of meaning, their own readings of "political" language often ineluctably slide into assumptions of transparency.'[59] Eley and Nield have reminded us that the atmosphere sometimes sought to be evoked in today's anti-Marxist polemic of a struggle against an establishment is remarkably out of place, while the critiques themselves often follow the time-honoured strategy of refutation through simplistic reduction.[60] And the 'essentialist' charge is sometimes rebounding on its makers. In his actual historical practice, it has been pointed out, Thompson with his emphasis upon shifting relations and contexts and rejection of class as fixed identity or object was often more anti-essentialist than his present-day critics. Mayfield and Thorne even discover a hidden affinity with Derrida: more plausibly, Steinberg wants to explore the possibility of some common ground between Thompsonian perspectives and the dialogism of Bakhtin and Voloshinov, which had prioritized language-use over structure, and emphasized its connections with social contexts.[61]

Suggestions for an expansion of the legacy of radical social history through bringing it into dialogical relationships with other intellectual currents are obviously of greater interest and importance than mere polemical exchanges. In two valuable recent essays, Geoff Eley has explored the possibilities of such interanimation between Thompsonian social history and Habermas' analysis of the emergence of the 'bourgeois public sphere' in eighteenth- and nineteenth-

[59] Geoff Eley, 'Edward Thompson, Social History and Political Culture: The Making of a Working-Class Public, 1780-1850', in McClelland and Kaye, pp. 26-7; and Marc W. Steinberg. I have argued elsewhere that it will not be unfair to make a similar comment about some recent *Subaltern Studies* work, particularly that of Partha Chatterji: see Chapter III.

[60] Such evocation misremembers 'how embattled and maligned the presence of marxism in academic history has actually been', even in pre-Thatcherite Britain. Eley and Nield (October 1995). Steinberg (May 1996) argues that the failure of Joyce to discover class in Victorian Britain is because he has 'been looking for class language and consciousness in most unlikely forms — a working-class language *distinct from* the processes of hegemony and struggle.' He finds a parallel here with the sociologist failure to find class about which Thompson had commented at the beginning of his *Making*. At a very different, philosophical, level, Robert Young's *White Mythologies* follows a similar strategy by identifying all Marxist historical thinking with Lukacs, Sartre and Althusser, to the virtual exclusion, or summary dismissal, of the entire work of professional Marxist historians.

[61] Mayfield and Thorne (1992); Steinberg (1996).

century Britain, France, and Germany.[62] The terminology of the 'making' of 'class-consciousness', Eley feels, has a thrust at variance with the overall tenor of Thompson's work, for it tends to carry with it Lukacsian connotations of necessary and progressive working-class unification — an ascribed norm towards which history will ultimately move. This causes difficulties, for in England 'making' seemed to have been succeeded by a long era of 'unmaking', after the collapse of Chartism. More crucially, the language encourages an insufficiently problematized passage from the evidence of affirmations of class among an articulate radical minority (mainly skilled artisans in Thompson's period, rather than factory workers or unskilled and casual labour), to assumptions of emergent selfconsciousness of an entire class. *The Making* has indeed been often criticized for not giving adequate weight to recurrent disunity and sectionalism, as well as of course to gender distinctions. Eley argues that a more helpful framework could be worked out through deploying the concept of a working-class or proletarian public, which may be unified only in part, and that intermittently and under specific circumstances and political initiatives, but which may still be articulated in more long-term ways through distinctive communicational networks, forms of sociability and solidarity, cultural norms, organizations, movements, and ideals.[63] Thompson's later work on the eighteenth century could then be used to illuminate the ruptures, as well as the continuities, between the characteristics of that earlier plebeian space, and the evidence for

[62] The reference, of course, is to Jurgen Habermas' classic work, translated into English only recently: *The Structural Transformation of the Public Sphere: An Inquiry into a Category of Bourgeois Society* (1962; trans. Oxford: Polity Press, 1989). The book is limited, as the Preface makes clear, 'to the structure and function of the *liberal* model of the bourgeois public sphere', but it does make a passing reference to the emergence (and suppression) of alternative 'plebeian' publics. Geoff Eley, 'Edward Thompson, Social History and Political Culture: The Making of a Working-Class Public', in Kaye and McClelland; and Eley, 'Nations, Publics, and Political Cultures: Placing Habermas in the Nineteenth-Century', in Craig Calhoun, ed., *Habermas and the Public Sphere* (Cambridge, Mass., MIT Press, 1993). I have found these essays by Eley very helpful in formulating this part of my paper. The second article, significantly, also explores possible common grounds between Thompsonian social history, the early Habermas, Gramscian concepts of civil society and hegemony (some readings of which Thompson found very helpful, as has been mentioned already), and developments in feminism (where Habermas has been perhaps even weaker than Thompson).

[63] Eley (1990), in Kaye and McCleland, pp. 27–35.

such a working-class 'presence' by the 1820s or 1830s. The signs of this transition would include the displacement of 'riot, revelry and rough music' by pamphlets, petitions, orderly demonstrations, trade unions and other forms of modern democratic politics.[64]

Even the most spirited of defences of the Thompsonian moment generally recognize now that in some important respects today's practices of history need to be different. For the impact on historical writing of the diverse currents and pressures loosely tied together under the rubric of postmodernism have not been entirely negative, despite the sweeping nature of some of the current attacks on the historian's craft as irremediably white, male, complicit with the 'modern' state, and tainted with the sins of 'Enlightenment rationalism' or 'positivism'. Among the potential benefits one could cite a heightened self-reflexivity, an enhanced awareness of the assumptions and rhetorical strategies implicit in one's own writing. The problematization of representations coming about through the linguistic turn has also had profoundly ambiguous consequences. A total rupture between representation and what it seems to represent, pushed to the point of complete relativism, can indeed become what one recent critic has rudely described as a 'luxury of endless deferral', available only 'to those who play with themselves in the abstract realm of *langue*.'[65] But there are indications also that a certain disjunction can help to produce some very insightful history. Thus Sara Maza's analysis of the texts generated by courtroom scandals in late-eighteenth-century France owes much of its strength to her refusal to assume immediate, reflexive connections with social tensions that quite often have been considered to exist independently of representations. This, with Maza, does not involve any denial of the reality of social antagonisms, but it does imply an emphasis upon the 'reciprocity between social "structures" and "ideologies", or between "reality" and its "representations", a belief that the one cannot exist without the other.'[66]

What needs to be resisted, however, is the slide towards new forms of reductionism — linguistic or cultural, in place of economic — and the not infrequent efforts at erasure of all other kinds of history, the calls for total repudiation, above all, of a Marxism presented in polemic as totally 'undifferentiated, "past" in some irretrievable and

---

[64] Eley (1993), in Calhoun, p. 328.

[65] See Marc W. Steinberg.

[66] Sara Maza, *Private Lives and Public Affairs: The Causes Celebres of Pre-Revolutionary France* (California, 1993), p. 67, and *passim*.

unlamented manner.'[67] Such erasure is disabling, for it is clear that the interanimations we have been considering would often be of mutual benefit and empowerment.

Enlightenment rationalism can provide an excellent example, and one that has become implicit already through the preceding discussion of Thompson, feminist history, and Habermas. Thompsonian history could be a corrective to the tendencies in *Structural Transformation* towards some idealization of the early, liberal-bourgeois phase of modernity and the public sphere, as contrasted to later degeneration into instrumental rationality and mass consumerist culture. Habermas, writing in 1962, was of course also largely unaware of alternative kinds of emancipatory impulses emerging from popular radical traditions: themes the study of which became the life-work of Christopher Hill and Thompson. More generally, the current stereotype of Marxism as being just one more by-blow of Enlightenment rationalism forgets that the major part of Marx's intellectual energies was devoted, precisely, to the critique of that quintessentially Enlightenment product, classical political economy. And it hardly needs restatement that Thompson was uncompromisingly hostile to 'rationalisms' grounded in the unrestricted pursuit of enlightened self-interest by property owners. He was worried that Marxist theory and practice at times showed signs of becoming complicit with such confinement of human needs and satisfactions to the logic of the market. Thompson's rejection of even the 'rebellious economic man' of the then 'actually existing' socialist regimes led him into a life-long interest and empathy with possible alternative resources to be found, perhaps, in romantic critiques of industrialized modernity and rationalist individualism: a quest that began with William Morris and ended with William Blake.

And yet there is a fundamental difference. Thompson refused the stark, homogenized polarity of 'modern' and 'pre-modern', whether evaluated as progress, as by yesterday's modernization theorists, or retrogressive, as in much postmodernism today. He was able to sustain that refusal because of his consistent insight into contradictions, the 'undersides', as he had once described them, of every concept, institution, or process.[68] Despite the empathy with

---

67 Eley and Nield. As this article points out, the denial of the existence of 'many Marxisms' is part of a strategy to brand all Marxian thought and practice, as somehow complicit with Stalinism — an erasure of a complex history in which, repeatedly, 'exactly a distance from the Soviet Union . . . was the point.'

68 *Customs in Common*, p. 72.

which he approached the traces of eighteenth-century plebeian culture — village customs, community norms, notions of time, even the sale of wives and rough music — Thompson on the whole remained free of nostalgia (traditionally conservative, now at times, I am afraid, postmodernist) for 'the world we have lost.'[69] Moral economy for him did not flow from any bland, undifferentiated, conflict-free community tradition. The norms of the plebeian crowd were based on selective appropriation and autonomous use of the paternalism of the gentry and the state, and enforcement through popular initiative and violence clearly went beyond ruling-class notions of right and proper behaviour.

Thompson's sense of discrimination is at its highest and most brilliant in his posthumous *Witness Against The Beast*. Through Blake's poetry Thompson explored the (partial) confluence in the 1790s of dissident religious traditions and antinomian heresies, survivals from the mid-seventeenth-century moment of 'the world turned upside down' — and secular, rationalistic, Jacobinical and deist influences. What he does in effect is to deconstruct both, and simultaneously seek to relate them in the subtlest possible ways with social contexts (by beginning with Blake's specific ways of reading, for instance, derived from his position as an 'autodidact' far removed from formal university training). Blake, he argues, was rooted in a milieu of London artisans and tradesmen, who through their relative occupational independence could at times afford to be less deferential than many of their social betters. The antinomian 'counter-Enlightenment' he embodied was opposed equally to the learned Reason of Newton or Locke, the non-conformism of respectable middling folk, and conservative church establishments where 'Priests in black gowns were walking their rounds,/ And binding with briars my joys and

---

[69] The partial exceptions, predictably, are often related to gender: there are passages particularly in the 'Sale of Wives' chapter of *Customs in Common* which leave one uncomfortable. But note also the important qualifying note on which the book ends: 'Because law belongs to people, and is not alienated, or delegated, it is not thereby made necessarily more "nice" and tolerant, more cosy and folksy. It is only as nice and as tolerant as the prejudices and norms of the folk allow. . . . For some of its [rough music's] victims, the coming of a distanced (if alienated) Law and a bureaucratized police must have been felt as a liberation from the tyranny of one's "own"' (pp. 530–1). The entire passage appears enormously relevant for current South Asian debates, where the modern state is so often simply counterposed to community, and the considerable evidence of subordinated groups (notably, lower castes and women) at times using colonial structures and discourses as resources tends to get ignored.

desires.'[70] If Blake's denunciation of 'the Reason of the Seed of the Serpent' is read

as a simple opposition between reason and unreason (or blind faith) then this is self-convicted irrationalism. But if we consider the *actual* assumptions of the 'Age of Reason' then the antinomian stance acquires a new force, even a rationality. For it struck very precisely at critical positions of the hegemonic culture, the common sense of the ruling groups. . . .[71]

It is in his grasp of dialectics — not of course as totalizing laws of development, but as an openness to the possibility of tensions and contradiction in the heart of all processes — I would like to argue, that there resides Thompson's abiding strength, the source of his continuing intellectual relevance: a relevance that is much needed in the context of recent South Asian historiography.[72]

IV

But Thompson remains important not just as an academic historian. Perhaps the most remarkable thing about him was the way he could combine, throughout his life, passionate political commitment and activism with the highest standards of professional rigour and originality, each feeding into the other, and both communicated through superb prose, meticulously-wrought arguments, and carefully accumulated material. He was very far removed from the stereotype of the basically ivory-tower — even if at times academically Marxist — professional scholar. Academic establishments acknowledged this uniqueness in their own way: arguably the finest British historian of his generation, Thompson was never offered an university Chair or formal honours in Britain.

While an active member of the Communist Party of Great Britain, Thompson helped to set up what proved to be the extraordinarily fertile Marxist Historians Group. Fellow members included Christopher Hill, Eric Hobsbawm and Rodney Hilton, and the group became the seedbed of the now very famous historical journal *Past and Present*. Along with very many of its most dedicated cadres, Thompson resigned from the Party when it failed to condemn the

70 William Blake, 'The Garden of Love', in *Songs of Innocence and Experience*.
71 *Witness Against the Beast: William Blake and the Moral Law* (New York/ Cambridge, 1993), p. 110.
72 See Chapter 3.

Soviet intervention in Hungary in 1956. But his commitment to radical causes only deepened, and could now take on wider, more imaginative dimensions. One of the founding fathers of the New Left in Britain after 1956, Thompson as activist will of course be remembered most for his absolutely outstanding role in peace and anti-nuclear movements: the Campaign for Nuclear Disarmament in the late 1950s and 1960s, and the European Nuclear Disarmament campaigns during the second Cold War of the 1980s which for some years became a powerful mass movement. The END had tried to combine the struggle to remove missiles from Europe with broad programmes of democratic transformation within both power blocs. It was hardly its fault that the ossified and bureaucratic regimes of 'actually existing socialism' obstructed and delayed reforms till it became too late, and so the eventual collapse of 1989-91 shattered, for the time being, also the generous dreams of alternative, democratic and humane forms of socialism. Thompson had been warning of such dangers right from 1956.

One can hope, perhaps, that the failure is not for all time, for the needs persist, more urgent than ever. Capitalism at its moment of greatest global triumph is proving singularly incapable of tackling its own problems of recession, unemployment, massive poverty, and racism even in its metropolitan heartlands. Less than five years after the 'Fall', ex-Communist groups have been registering major electoral gains in Russia and most parts of Eastern Europe, as well as in Italy, and it is equally significant that the renewal is taking place through organizations that usually emphasize a rupture with the Stalinist-Brezhnevite past. And, still on the note of continued relevance, the terms of the current debate in India around the Comprehensive Test Ban Treaty (CTBT) bring back certain memories for those familiar with Thompson's anti-nuclear activities. The major part of Indian public opinion, including the organized Left, seems to accept very readily the argument that national security and honour can be preserved only by retaining the nuclear option. The CND and the END, and for a brief while even the British Labour Party, had stood for unilateral disarmament even at moments of acute bipolar conflict. Advocates of such disarmament had dared to be unpatriotic enough to reject the standard militaristic, Tory and Cold War argument that national interest and prestige demanded national bombs.

The abiding quality of Thompson's work, the presence within it of exhilarating possibilities even in the last years of failing health, underlines how much he gave to the cause of world peace when, for ten long years he imposed upon himself a virtual break from the domain where he was the master. That, as nothing else, brings home the compulsive force of his political commitment.

What Thompson, writing about his father's Indophile activities, once described as the 'chores of solidarity' must have been at times tedious and irritating.[73] But on the whole he had the rare ability to make historical research and politics interanimate each other, and the resulting tension was profoundly productive. The *Making of the English Working Class* originated from trade union and adult education classes in Yorkshire,[74] and Thompson's historical insights flowed into what could otherwise have remained the most ephemeral of political pamphleteering.

Let me end with a passage from a now seldom remembered political article, written in honour of a British miners' strike: not the heroic failure of 1984, but the one in 1972 which helped to throw out a Tory government and is therefore relegated to obscurity by media silence:

The pits of Ballingry and of much of West Fife have now closed down. And we had supposed, poor fools that we are, that all that heroic and intelligent history, all that 200 years of inconceivable stubbornness and courage, was quite dead. But out of this history has come this moment of illumination; we stir uneasily as, once again, there are men in our streets shouting 'One and All'. It is a moment of cultural transmission, as the pent-up energies of the dead flow back into the living. We shall burn that history for many years, as we have burnt the black forests which for generations they have raised. For the future historian it will seem that this week of darkness in February 1972 was an incandescence.[75]

Perhaps a bit of the incandescence that was Thompson's whole life may help to light our paths, too, in these difficult times.

---

[73] E.P. Thompson, 'The Nehru Tradition', in *Writing by Candlelight* (London: Merlin Press, 1980), p. 140. On a personal note, I recall how irritated Thompson became when I tactlessly asked him, at Worcester in May 1985, about the progress of his *Customs in Common*. 'Don't ask me that, it makes me very angry.'

[74] Radical history-writing in Britain has often had this interesting and impressive connection with socially-oriented adult education: 'Feminist history in Britain began in the WEA [Workers' Education Association] and Extra-Mural Departments.' Sally Alexander, p. vii. Things, unfortunately, have been very different in India so far.

[75] 'A Special Case', in *Writing by Candlelight*, p. 76.

3

The Decline of the Subaltern in *Subaltern Studies*[*]

M y title may sound provocative, but at one level it is no more than description, with no necessarily pejorative implications. A quick count indicates that all fourteen essays in *Subaltern Studies I* and *II* had been about underprivileged groups in Indian society — peasants, tribals, and in one instance workers. The corresponding figure for Volumes *VII* and *VIII* is, at most, four out of twelve.[1] Guha's preface and introductory essay in the first volume had been full of references to 'subaltern classes', evocations of Gramsci, and the use of much Marxian terminology. Today, the dominant thrust within the project — or at least the one that gets most attention — is focussed on critiques of Western-colonial power-knowledge, with non-Western 'community consciousness' as its valorized alternative. Also emerging is a tendency to define such communities principally in terms of religious identities.

Change within a project which is now well over a decade old is entirely understandable and even welcome, though one could have hoped for some internal analysis of the shifting meanings of the core term 'subaltern' and why it has been thought necessary to retain it despite a very different discursive context. What makes the shifts within *Subaltern Studies* worthy of close attention are their association

[*] I have benefited greatly from the comments and criticisms of Aijaz Ahmad, Pradip Kumar Datta, Mahmud Mamdani and Tanika Sarkar.

[1] I am excluding from my count the two chapters in volume VIII about Ranajit Guha and his writings. Out of the four, one is by Terence Ranger about Africa, a second (Saurabh Dube) from outside the editorial group — which leaves us with David Hardiman on the Dangs, and Ranajit Guha himself on nationalist mobilization/disciplining of subaltern strata through 'social boycott'.

with changes in academic (and political) moods that have had a virtually global range.

Subaltern Studies emerged in the early 1980s in a dissident-Left milieu, where sharp criticism of orthodox Marxist practice and theory was still combined with the retention of a broad socialist and Marxian horizon. There were obvious affinities with the radical-populist moods of the 1960s and 1970s, and specifically with efforts to write 'histories from below'. The common ground lay in a combination of enthusiastic response to popular, usually peasant, rebellions, with growing disillusionment about organized Left parties, received versions of orthodox Marxist ideology, and the bureaucratic state structures of 'actually existing socialism'. In India, specifically, there were the embers of abortive Maoist armed struggle in the countryside, the spectacle of one of the two major Communist Parties supporting an authoritarian regime that was close to the Soviet Union, and then the hopes briefly aroused by the post-Emergency electoral rout of Indira Gandhi. Among historiographical influences, that of British Marxian social history was probably the most significant. Hill, Hobsbawm and Thompson were much admired by the younger scholars, and Thompson in particular had a significant impact when he visited India in the winter of 1976-7 and addressed a session of the Indian History Congress.[2] Ranajit Guha seems to have often used 'subaltern' somewhat in the way Thompson deployed the term 'plebeian' in his writings on eighteenth-century England. In the largely pre-capitalist conditions of colonial India, class formation was likely to have remained inchoate. 'Subaltern' would be of help in avoiding the pitfalls of economic reductionism, while at the same time retaining a necessary emphasis on domination and exploitation.[3] The radical, Thompsonian, social history of the 1970s, despite assertions to the contrary which are made sometimes nowadays for

[2] The paper he presented at that session was published by the journal of the Indian Council of Historical Research: 'Folklore, Anthropology, and Social History', *Indian Historical Review* (1977).

[3] Guha's *Elementary Aspects of Peasant Insurgency in Colonial India* (Delhi, 1983) frequently cited Thompson with approval, and the references, significantly were to *Whigs and Hunters* and the essay in *Albion's Fatal Tree*. In 1985, a defence by Dipesh Chakrabarty of the project against criticism in *Social Scientist*, some of it from orthodox Marxist standpoints, pleaded for greater openness to 'alternative varieties of Marxism' and rejected the base–superstructure metaphor in terms reminiscent of Thompson. 'Invitation to a Dialogue', in Guha (ed.), *Subaltern Studies IV* (Delhi, 1985), pp. 369, 373. See also Partha Chatterjee, 'Modes of Power: Some Clarifications', in *Social Scientist* 141, February 1985.

polemical purposes, never really became respectable in the eyes of Western academic establishments. It is not surprising, therefore, that the early *Subaltern Studies* volumes, along with Guha's *Elementary Aspects of Peasant Insurgency in Colonial India* (1983), were largely ignored in the West, while they attracted widespread interest and debate in Left-leaning intellectual circles in India.[4]

Things have changed much since then, and today a transformed *Subaltern Studies* owes much of its prestige to the acclaim it is receiving from that part of the Western academic postmodernistic counter-establishment which is interested in colonial and postcolonial matters. Its success is fairly obviously related to an ability to move with the times. With the withering of hopes of radical transformation through popular initiative, conceptions of seamless, all-pervasive, virtually irresistible power–knowledge have tended to displace the evocation of moments of resistance central to the histories from below of the 1960s and 1970s. Domination is conceptualized overwhelmingly in cultural, discursive terms, as the power–knowledge of the post-Enlightenment West. If at all seen as embodied concretely in institutions, it tends to get identified uniquely with the modern bureaucratic nation-state: further search for specific socio-economic interconnections is felt to be unnecessarily economistic, redolent of traces of a now finally defeated Marxism, and hence disreputable. 'Enlightenment rationalism' thus becomes the central polemical target, and Marxism stands condemned as one more variety of Eurocentrism. Radical, Left-wing social history, in other words, has been collapsed into cultural studies and critiques of colonial discourse, and we have moved from Thompson to Foucault and, even more, Said.

The evolution has been recently summed up by Dipesh Chakrabarty as a shift from the attempt 'to write "better" Marxist histories' to an understanding that 'a critique of this nature could hardly afford to ignore the problem of universalism/Eurocentrism that was

---

[4] Thus the October 1984 issue of *Social Scientist*, a journal with CPI(M) affiliations, published a collective review essay on *Subaltern Studies II* written by a group of young scholars of Delhi University. A similar review of volumes III and IV came out in the same journal in March 1988. Guha and his colleagues, in significant contrast, were ignored by *Modern Asian Studies* till Rosalind O'Hanlon's 'Recovering the Subject: Subaltern Studies and Histories of Resistance in Colonial South Asia' (22, i, 1988), and the footnotes in this article clearly demonstrate that the initial debate around the project had been entirely within South Asia. Western discussion and acclaim has proliferated since then: within India, in contrast, there has been a largely derivative adulation, but nothing remotely resembling the critical engagement of the early years.

inherent in Marxist (or for that matter liberal) thought itself.' His article goes on to explain the changes within *Subaltern Studies* primarily in terms of 'the interest that Gayatri Spivak and, following her, Edward Said and others took in the project.'[5] Going against the views of my ex-colleagues in the *Subaltern Studies* editorial team, I intend to argue that the trajectory that has been outlined with considerable precision and frankness by Chakrabarty has been debilitating in both academic and political terms. Explanations in terms of adaptations to changed circumstances or outside intellectual influences alone are, however, never fully adequate. I would like to attempt a less 'external' reading, through a focus on certain conceptual ambiguities and implicit tensions within the project from the beginning.

II

The achievements of the early years of *Subaltern Studies* in terms of widening horizons and concrete historical research need to be rescued, perhaps, from the enormous condescension of recent adherents like Gyan Prakash, who dismisses such work as 'the familiar "history from below" approach'.[6] (It is difficult to resist at this point the retort that postmodernistic moods are today not only 'familiar' but academically respectable and advantageous in ways that would have been inconceivable for radical social historians in the 1970s.) The early essays of Ranajit Guha in *Subaltern Studies* located the origins of the new initiative in an effort to 'rectify the elitist bias', often accompanied by economistic assumptions, common to much colonialist, 'bourgeois-nationalist' and conventional-Marxist readings of modern Indian history.[7] Thus it was argued with considerable justice by Guha and other contributors that anti-colonial movements had been explained far too often in terms of a combination of economic pressures and mobilization from the top by leaders portrayed as manipulative in colonial,

5 Dipesh Chakrabarty, 'Marx after Marxism: Subaltern Histories and the Question of Difference', in *Polygraph* 6/7, 1993.

6 Gyan Prakash, 'Writing Post-Orientalist Histories of the Third World: Perspectives from Indian Historiography', *Comparative Studies in Society and History*, 32, 1990.

7 Ranajit Guha, 'Preface', and 'On Some Aspects of the Historiography of Colonial India', in Guha (ed.), *Subaltern Studies I* (Delhi, 1982). The quoted phrases are from pp. vii and 1. A more explicit critique of orthodox Marxist historiography was made by Guha in the second volume (Delhi, 1983), in his 'The Prose of Counterinsurgency'.

and as idealistic or charismatic in nationalist, historiography. Studies of peasant and labour movements, similarly, had concentrated on economic conditions and Left organizational and ideological lineages. The new trend would seek to explore the neglected dimension of popular or subaltern autonomy in action, consciousness and culture.

Subaltern Studies from its beginnings was felt by many, with some justice, to be somewhat too dismissive about predecessors and contemporaries working on not entirely dissimilar lines,[8] and the claims of setting up a new 'paradigm' were certainly over-flamboyant. Yet a new theoretical — or at least polemical — clarity was added to ongoing efforts at exploring histories from below, along with much empirical work at once solid and exciting. Thus Ranajit Guha's analysis of specific themes and movements — the role of rumour, the interrelationships and distinctions between crime and insurgency, or aspects of the Santal rebellion and the 1857 upheaval, to cite a few stray examples — were appreciated by many who could not accept the overall framework of *Elementary Aspects*. The publications of the *Subaltern Studies* group, within, outside, and in some cases before the constitution of the project, helped to significantly modify the historiography of anti-colonial nationalism through a common initial emphasis on 'pressures from below'. One thinks, for instance, of David Hardiman's pioneering exploration of the peasant nationalists of Gujarat through his meticulous collection of village-level data, Gyanendra Pandey's argument about an inverse relationship between the strength of local Congress organization and peasant militancy in Uttar Pradesh, and Shahid Amin's analysis of rumours concerning Gandhi's miracle-working powers as an entry point into the processes of an autonomous popular appropriation of messages from nationalist leaders.[9] Reinterpretations of mainstream nationalism apart,

[8] One could think, for instance, of some of the essays in Ravinder Kumar's *Essays on Gandhian Politics* (Oxford, 1971) influenced by Rudé, or Majid Siddiqi's *Agrarian Unrest in North India: The United Provinces 1918-22* (New Delhi, 1978). In my *Popular Movements and Middle-Class Leadership in Late Colonial India: Problems and Perspectives of a 'History from Below'* (Calcutta, 1983), drafted before the publication of the first volume of *Subaltern Studies*, I attempted a catalogue of available research material relevant for such studies (fn. 3, p. 74). And the critique, central to much early *Subaltern Studies*, of nationalist leaders and organizations often restraining militant mass initiatives, had been quite common in some kinds of Marxist writing, most notably in R.P. Dutt's *India Today* (Bombay, 1947).

[9] David Hardiman, *Peasant Nationalists of Gujarat: Kheda District, 1917-34* (Delhi, 1981); Gyanendra Pandey, *Ascendancy of the Congress in Uttar Pradesh 1926-34* (Delhi, 1978); Shahid Amin, 'Gandhi as Mahatma: Gorakhpur District,

there were also important studies of tribal movements and cults, Dipesh Chakrabarty's stimulating, if controversial, essays on Bengal labour history, and efforts to enter areas more 'difficult' for radical historians such as mass communalism, or peasant submissiveness to landlords.[10]

Once the initial excitement had worn away, however, work of this kind could seem repetitive, conveying an impression of a purely empiricist adding of details to confirm the fairly simple initial hypothesis about subaltern autonomy in one area or form after another. The attraction felt for the alternative, apparently more theoretical, thrust also present within *Subaltern Studies* from its beginnings is therefore understandable. This had its origins in Guha's attempt to use some of the language and methods of Lévi-Straussian structuralism to unravel what *Elementary Aspects* claimed was an underlying structure of peasant insurgent consciousness, extending across more than a century of colonial rule and over considerable variations of physical and social space. Guha still confined his generalizations to Indian peasants under colonialism, and sought to preserve some linkages with patterns of state-landlord-moneylender exploitation. Partha Chatterjee's first two essays in *Subaltern Studies* introduced a much more general category of 'peasant communal consciousness', inaugurating thereby what has subsequently become a crucial shift from 'subaltern' through 'peasant' to 'community'. The essays simultaneously expanded the notion of 'autonomy' into a categorical disjunction between two 'domains' of politics and 'power' — elite and subaltern. Chatterjee claimed that 'when a community acts collectively

---

Eastern UP, 1921-2', *Subaltern Studies III* (Delhi, 1984). My *Modern India, 1885-1947* (Delhi, 1983), written before I joined the *Subaltern Studies* group, tried to introduce a 'history from below' perspective while attempting an overall survey.

[10] David Arnold, 'Rebellious Hillmen: The Gudem-Rampa Risings, 1839-1924', *Subaltern Studies I* (Delhi, 1982); David Hardiman, 'Adivasi Assertion in South Gujarat: The Devi Movement of 1922-3', *Subaltern Studies III* (Delhi, 1984), subsequently enlarged into his fascinating *The Coming of the Devi* (Delhi, 1987); Tanika Sarkar, 'Jitu Santal's Movement in Malda, 1924-32: A Study in Tribal Protest', *Subaltern Studies IV* (Delhi, 1985); Dipesh Chakrabarty, 'Conditions for Knowledge of Working-Class Conditions: Employers, Government and the Jute-Workers of Calcutta, 1890-1940', *Subaltern Studies II* (Delhi, 1983) and 'Trade Unions in a Hierarchical Culture: The Jute Workers of Calcutta, 1920-50', *Subaltern Studies III*; Gyanendra Pandey, 'Rallying Round the Cow: Sectarian Strife in the Bhojpur Region, c. 1888-1917', *Subaltern Studies II*; Gautam Bhadra, 'The Mentality of Subalternity: Kantanama or Rajdharma', *Subaltern Studies VI* (Delhi, 1989).

the fundamental political characteristics are the same everywhere', and achieved an equally breathtaking, unmediated leap from some very general comments in Marx's *Grundrisse* about community in pre-capitalist social formations to Bengal peasant life in the 1920s.[11]

In the name of theory, then, a tendency emerged towards essentializing the categories of 'subaltern' and 'autonomy', in the sense of assigning to them more or less absolute, fixed, decontextualized meanings and qualities. That there had been such elements of 'essentialism', 'teleology' and epistemological naivete in the quest for the subaltern subject has naturally not escaped the notice of recent postmodernistically inclined admirers. They tend, however, to blame such aberrations on Marxist residues which now, happily, have been largely overcome.[12] What is conveniently forgotten is that the problems do not disappear through a simple substitution of 'class' by 'subaltern' or 'community'. Reifying tendencies can be actually strengthened by the associated detachment from socio-economic contexts and determinants out of a mortal fear of economic reductionism. The handling of the new concepts, further, may remain equally naive. The intervention of Gayatri Chakravorty Spivak,[13] we shall see, has not changed things much in this respect for the bulk of later *Subaltern Studies* work, except in purely verbal terms.

The more essentialist aspects of the early *Subaltern Studies* actually indicated moves away from the Marxian worlds of Thompson and Gramsci. Reification of a subaltern or community identity is open to precisely the kind of objections that Thompson had levelled in the famous opening pages of his *Making of the English Working Class* against much conventional Marxist handling of class: objections that paradoxically contributed to the initial *Subaltern Studies* rejection of the rigidities of economistic class analysis. It is true that Thompson's own handling of the notion of community has been critiqued at times for being insufficiently attentive to 'internal' variations:[14] the contrast in this respect with the ultimate trajectory

11 Partha Chatterjee, 'Agrarian Relations and Communalism in Bengal, 1926–35' and 'More on Modes of Power and the Peasantry', *Subaltern Studies I, II.* My quotation is from the first essay, p. 35.

12 See, particularly, Gyan Prakash, as well as a more nuanced and less dogmatically certain review article by Rosalind O'Hanlon, 'Recovering the Subject: Subaltern Studies and Histories of Resistance in Colonial South Asia', *Modern Asian Studies,* 22, i, 1988.

13 'Subaltern Studies: Deconstructing Historiography', *Subaltern Studies IV* (Delhi, 1985).

14 See, for instance, Suzanne Desan, 'Crowds, Community and Ritual in the

of *Subaltern Studies* still seems undeniable. Through deliberately paradoxical formulations like 'class struggle without class', Thompson had sought to combine the continued quest for collectivities of protest and transformation with a rejection of fixed, reified identities.[15] He refused to surrender totally the ground of class, and so the rejection of the base–superstructure analogy did not lead him to any 'culturalism'. Thompson, it needs to be emphasized, never gave up the attempt to situate plebeian culture 'within a particular equilibrium of social relations, a working environment of exploitation and resistance to exploitation . . . its proper material mode.'[16] What he possessed in abundant measure was an uncanny ability to hold together in creative, dialectical tension dimensions that have often flowed apart elsewhere.

It would be relevant in this context to look also at Gramsci's six-point 'methodological criteria' for the 'history of the subaltern classes', referred to by Guha with much admiration in the very first page of *Subaltern Studies I* as a model unattainable but worth striving for:

1. the objective formation of the subaltern social groups, by the developments and transformations occurring in the sphere of economic production . . . 2. their active or passive affiliation to the dominant political formations, their attempts to influence the programmes of these formations in order to press claims of their own . . . 3. the birth of new parties of the dominant groups, intended to conserve the assent of the subaltern groups and to maintain control over them; 4. the formations which the subaltern groups themselves produce, in order to press claims of a limited and partial character; 5. those new formations which assert the autonomy of the subaltern groups, but within the old framework; 6. those formations which assert the integral autonomy . . . etc.[17]

Subaltern 'social groups' are emphatically not unrelated to 'the sphere of economic production', it will be noticed — and the

---

Work of E.P. Thompson and Natalie Davis', in Lynn Hunt (ed.), *The New Cultural History* (California, 1989). I owe this reference to Dr Hans Medick.

[15] E.P. Thompson, 'Eighteenth-Century English Society: Class-Struggle Without Class?', *Social History*, III, 2, May 1978.

[16] E.P. Thompson, *Customs in Common* (London, 1993), p. 7. It is this methodological imperative to contextualize within specific social relations and material modes that has been progressively eliminated, we shall see, from the dominant strand within late *Subaltern Studies*.

[17] Antonio Gramsci, 'Notes on Italian History', in Hoare and Smith (eds), *Selections from Prison Notebooks* (New York, 1971), p. 52.

indication is clear even in such a brief outline of an enormous range of possible meanings of 'autonomy'. Above all, the emphasis, throughout, is not on distinct domains of politics, but interpenetration, mutual (though obviously unequal) conditioning, and, implicitly, common roots in a specific social formation. Otherwise the subaltern would logically always remain subaltern, except in the unlikely event of a literal inversion which, too, would not really transform society: perspectives that Gramsci the revolutionary could hardly be expected to endorse.

Chatterjee's terminology of distinct elite and subaltern domains was initially felt by many in the *Subaltern Studies* group to be little more than a strong way of asserting the basic need to search for traces of subaltern autonomy. (I notice, for instance, that I had quite inconsistently slipped into the same language even while arguing in my *Subaltern Studies III* essay against over-rigid application of binary categories.[18]) The logical, if at first perhaps unnoticed and unintended, consequences have been really far-reaching. The separation of domination and autonomy tended to make absolute and homogenize both within their separate domains, and represented a crucial move away from efforts to develop immanent critiques of structures that have been the strength of Marxian dialectical approaches.[19] Domination construed as irresistible could render autonomy illusory. Alternatively, the latter had to be located in pre-colonial or premodern spaces untouched by power, or sought for in fleeting, fragmentary moments alone. Late *Subaltern Studies* in practice has oscillated around precisely these three positions, of 'derivative discourse', indigenous 'community', and 'fragments'.

A bifurcation of the worlds of domination and autonomy, I

[18] 'The Conditions and Nature of Subaltern Militancy: Bengal from Swadeshi to Non-Cooperation, *c.* 1905-22', in Guha (ed.), *Subaltern Studies III* (Delhi, 1984), pp. 273-6.

[19] For a powerful, if also highly 'revisionistic', exposition of the strength of Marxism as immanent critique, see Moishe Postone, *Time, Labor, and Social Domination: A Reinterpretation of Marx's Critical Theory* (Cambridge, 1993, 1995). The effort, on the other hand, to make resistance totally external to power can attain really curious levels, at times. See for instance Gyan Prakash's assertion that 'we cannot thematise Indian history in terms of the development of capitalism and simultaneously contest capitalism's homogenization of the contemporary world.' 'Postcolonial Criticism and Indian Historiography', *Social Text* 31/32, 1992. How does one contest something, I wonder, without talking about it? The best critique of such positions that I have seen is Arif Dirlik, 'The Postcolonial Aura', *Critical Inquiry*, 20, ii, Winter 1994.

have argued elsewhere, became characteristic of several otherwise unconnected spheres of intellectual enquiry in the political conjuncture of the late-1970s and 1980s: the 'acculturation thesis' about early modern French popular culture, Foucault's studies of modern power-knowledge, Said's critique of Orientalism.[20] Not surprisingly, the similar disjunction that was occasionally made in early *Subaltern Studies*[21] provided the initial point of insertion of Said, through an article, and then a very influential book, by Partha Chatterjee.[22] Said's views regarding the overwhelming nature of post-Enlightenment colonial power-knowledge was applied to the colonized intelligentsia, who were thus virtually robbed of agency and held to have been capable of only 'derivative discourses'. Beyond it lay the domain of community consciousness, still associated, though rather vaguely now, with the peasantry, but embodied somehow in the figure of Gandhi, who was declared to have been uniquely free of the taint of Enlightenment rationalism, prior to his partial appropriation by the Nehruvian 'moment of arrival'. Both poles of the power relationship tend to get homogenized in this argument, which has become extremely influential. Colonial cultural domination, stripped of all complexities and variations, faces an indigenous

[20] In studies of early modern French popular culture, notably, much early 1970s *Annales* scholarship assumed an autonomous popular level manifested in distinct texts, forms, and practices. With the growing influence of Foucault, and Robert Muchembled's *Culture populaire et culture des elites dans la France moderne* (Paris, 1978), published, significantly perhaps, in the same year as Said, *Orientalism*, there was a shift towards frameworks of successful conquest of once-uncontaminated popular culture through the cumulative impact of Counter-Reformation Church, absolute monarchy, and Enlightenment rationalism. The more fruitful historical works, however, have on the whole operated with a model of multiple appropriations rather than distinct levels: see particularly Roger Chartier's critique of Muchembled's acculturation thesis in his *Cultural Uses of Print in Early Modern France* (Princeton, 1987), Introduction. I have elaborated these points in my 'Popular Culture, Community, Power: Three Studies of Modern Indian Social History', *Studies in History*, 8, ii, n.s., 1992, pp. 311-13, and 'Orientalism Revisited: Saidian Moods in the Writing of Modern Indian History', *Oxford Literary Review*, XVI, 1-2, 1994.

[21] Ranajit Guha's programmatic essay in *Subaltern Studies I* had also described 'the *politics of the people*' as 'parallel to the domain of elite politics — an *autonomous* domain, for it neither originated from elite politics nor did its existence depend on the latter' (p. 4).

[22] 'Gandhi and the Critique of Civil Society', *Subaltern Studies III* (Delhi, 1984), followed by *Nationalist Thought in the Colonial World: A Derivative Discourse?* (Delhi, 1986).

domain eroded of internal tensions and conflicts.[23] The possibility of pre-colonial forms of domination, however modified, persisting through colonialism, helping to mediate colonial authority in vital ways, maybe even functioning autonomously at times — for all of which there is ample evidence — is simply ignored.[24] Colonial rule is assumed to have brought about an absolute rupture: the colonized subject is taken to have been literally constituted by colonialism alone.[25] And so Gandhi's assumed location 'outside the thematic of post-Enlightenment thought' can be described as one 'which could have been adopted by any member of the traditional intelligentsia in India', and then simultaneously identified as having 'an inherently [sic] "peasant-communal" character.' The differences between the 'traditional intelligentsia', overwhelmingly upper-caste (or elite Muslim) and male, and bound up with structures of landlord and bureaucratic domination, and peasant-communal consciousness, are apparently of no importance whatsoever: caste, class, and gender divides have ceased to matter.[26]

There are elements of a rich paradox in this shift of binaries from elite/subaltern to colonial/indigenous community or Western/Third-World cultural nationalist. A project that had started with a trenchant attack on elite nationalist historiography had now chosen as its hero the principal iconic figure of official Indian nationalism, and its most influential text after *Elementary Aspects* was built entirely around the (partial) study of just three indisputably elite figures, Bankimchandra, Gandhi, and Nehru. The passage to near-nationalist positions may have been facilitated, incidentally, by an unnoticed drift implicit even in Guha's initial formulation of the project in *Subaltern Studies I*. The 'historiography of colonial India' somehow slides quickly into that of Indian nationalism: the fundamental lacuna is described as the failure 'to acknowledge the contribution made by the people *on their own* to the making and development of this nationalism', and the central problematic ultimately becomes *'the historic failure of the nation to come into its own.'*[27]

23 For a more detailed critique of Chatterjee's *Nationalist Thought*, see my 'Orientalism Revisited'.

24 For a more extensive discussion, see Chapter 1.

25 For an effective critique of this *tabula rasa* approach, see Aijaz Ahmad, *In Theory: Classes, Nations, Literatures* (London, 1992; Delhi, 1993), Chapters III, V.

26 *Nationalist Thought*, p. 100; see also *Subaltern Studies III*, p. 176.

27 Ranajit Guha, 'On Some Aspects of the Historiography of Colonial India', *Subaltern Studies I*, pp. 2–3, 7.

With *Nationalist Thought*, followed in 1987 by the publication in the United States of *Selected Subaltern Studies*, with a foreword by Edward Said and an editorial note by Gayatri Chakravorty Spivak, subaltern historiography was launched on a successful international, and more specifically metropolitan and US-academic, career. The intellectual formation of which its currently most prominent practitioners are now part, Aijaz Ahmad argues, has gone through two phases: Third-World cultural nationalism, followed by postmodernistic valorizations of 'fragments'.[28] For *Subaltern Studies*, however, located by its subject matter in a country that has been a postcolonial nation-state for more than four decades, an oppositional stance towards existing forms of nationalism has been felt to be necessary from the beginning. The situation was rather different from that facing a member of a Palestinian diaspora still in quest of independent nationhood. This opposition was reconciled with the Saidian framework through the assumption that the postcolonial nation-state was no more than a continuation of the original, Western, Enlightenment project imposed through colonial discourse. The mark of late *Subaltern Studies* therefore became not a succession of phases, but the counterposing of reified notions of 'community' or 'fragment', alternatively or sometimes in unison, against this highly generalized category of the 'modern' nation-state as the embodiment of Western cultural domination. The original separation of the domains of power and autonomy culminates here in an oscillation between the 'rhetorical absolutism' of structure and the 'fragmented fetishism' of the subject — to apply to it the perceptive comments of Perry Anderson, a decade ago, about the consequences of uncritically applying the linguistic model to historiography.[29]

It might be interesting to take a glance at this point at the glimmerings of an alternative approach that had appeared briefly within *Subaltern Studies* but was soon virtually forgotten. I am thinking, particularly, of Ranajit Guha's seldom-referred-to article 'Chandra's Death' — along with, perhaps, an essay of mine about a very unusual village scandal, and Gyanendra Pandey's exploration

[28] Aijaz Ahmad, Chapter V, and *passim*.
[29] Perry Anderson, *In the Tracks of Historical Materialism* (London, 1983), p. 55. Very relevant also are his comments about the general trajectory from structuralism to poststructuralism: 'a total initial determinism ends in the reinstatement of absolute final contingency, in mimicry of the duality of *langue* and *parole*.'

of local memory through a small-town gentry chronicle and a diary kept by a weaver.[30] 'Fragment' and 'community' were important for these essays, but in ways utterly different from what has now become the dominant mode within *Subaltern Studies*. Hindsight indicates some affinities, rather, with the kind of micro-history analysed recently by Carlo Ginzburg, marked by an 'insistence on context, exactly the opposite of the isolated contemplation of the fragmentary' advocated by postmodernism. This is a micro-history which has become anti-positivistic in its awareness of the constructed nature of all evidence and categories, but which nevertheless does not plunge into complete scepticism and relativism. 'Chandra's Death' and 'Kalki-Avatar' tried to explore general connections — of caste, patriarchy, class, colonial rule — through 'the small drama and fine detail of social existence' and sought to avoid the appearance of impersonality and abstraction often conveyed by pure macro-history. Their starting point was what Italian historians nowadays call the 'exceptional-normal':[31] a local event that had interrupted the everyday only for a brief moment, but had been unusual enough to leave some traces. And the 'community' that was unravelled, particularly through Guha's moving study of the death (through enforced abortion after an illicit affair) of a low-caste woman, was one of conflict and brutal exploitation, of power relations 'sited at a depth within the indigenous society, well beyond the reach of the disciplinary arm of the colonial state.' These are dimensions that have often been concealed, Guha noted, through a blending of 'indigenous feudal ideology . . . with colonial anthropology.'[32] Not just colonial anthropology but Guha's own brainchild, one is tempted to add, sometimes

---

[30] Ranajit Guha, 'Chandra's Death', *Subaltern Studies V* (Delhi, 1987); Sumit Sarkar, 'The Kalki-Avatar of Bikrampur: A Village Scandal in Early Twentieth Century Bengal', *Subaltern Studies VI* (Delhi, 1989); Gyanendra Pandey, ' "Encounters and Calamities": The History of a North Indian Qasba in the Nineteenth-Century', *Subaltern Studies III* (Delhi, 1984). 'Chandra Death' has been warmly praised by Aijaz Ahmad in *In Theory*, but this is unlikely to enhance its reputation with the bulk of present-day admirers of *Subaltern Studies*.

[31] Carlo Ginzburg, 'Microhistory: Two or Three Things That I Know about It', *Critical Inquiry*, 29, Autumn 1993. I have benefited also from Hans Medick's unpublished paper on a similar theme: 'Weaving and Surviving at Laichingen 1650-1900: Micro-History as History and as Research Experience'. I am grateful to Professor Ginzburg and Professor Medick for sending me copies of their papers.

[32] The quotations from 'Chandra's Death' are from *Subaltern Studies V*, pp. 138, 144, 155.

carries on that good work nowadays: with the result that essays in late *Subaltern Studies* which implicitly take a different stance tend to get relatively little attention.[33]

But there was no theorization on the basis of such micro-study, nothing of the kind being attempted nowadays by some Italian and German scholars to develop micro-history into a cogent methodological alternative to both positivism and postmodernism. And there was the further fact that this was emphatically not the kind of South Asian history that could win easy acclaim in the West, for its reading demanded, if not prior knowledge, at least the readiness to try to grasp unfamiliar and dense material, thick descriptions which were not at the same time exotic. One does get the strong impression that the majority among even the fairly small section of the Western intelligentsia interested in the Third World prefers its material conveniently packaged nowadays, without too much detail or complexity. (Totally different standards would be expected in mainstream work on any branch, say, of European history.) Packaged, moreover, in a particular way, fitted into the slots of anti-Western cultural nationalism (one recalls Frederic Jameson's assertion that 'all third world texts are necessarily . . . *national allegories*'[34]) and/or poststructuralist play with fragments. The West, it seems, to borrow from Said, is still engaged in producing its Orient through selective appropriation and essentialist stereotyping: Orientalism flourishes at the heart of today's anti-Orientalist tirade.

Partha Chatterjee's *The Nation and Its Fragments* epitomizes the latest phase of *Subaltern Studies* at its most lucid and comprehensive.[35] A new binary has been introduced, 'material'/ 'spiritual' (or 'world'/

[33] I am thinking particularly about the very substantial and impressive ongoing work of David Hardiman, of which the latest example is *Feeding the Baniya: Peasants and Usurers in Western India* (Delhi, 1996), which seldom gets due recognition. But even Ranajit Guha's 'Discipline and Mobilize', in Chatterjee and Pandey (eds), *Subaltern Studies VII* (Delhi, 1992), far more critical of Gandhian nationalism than usual nowadays, based on a premise of 'indigenous' as well as 'alien' moments of dominance in colonial India, and emphasizing 'the power exercised by the indigenous elite over the subaltern amongst the subject population itself' — seems to have attracted little attention.

[34] Frederic Jameson, 'Third World Literature in the Era of Multi-national Capital', *Social Text*, Fall 1986. For a powerful critique, see Aijaz Ahmad, *In Theory*, Chapter III.

[35] Partha Chatterjee, *The Nation and Its Fragments: Colonial and Postcolonial Histories* (Princeton, 1993; Delhi, 1994).

'home'[36]), probably to take care of the criticism that the earlier 'derivative discourse' thesis had deprived the colonized subject of all autonomy or agency. Through such a bifurcation, we are told, nationalists kept or created as their own an autonomous world of literature, art, education, domesticity, and above all, it appears, religion. They were surrendering in effect to the West, meanwhile, on the 'material' plane: for the efforts to eradicate 'colonial difference' (e.g. unequal treatment of Indians in law courts, with respect to civil rights, and in politics generally) actually meant progressive absorption into the Western colonial project of building the modern nation-state — a project inevitably left incomplete by colonialism, but realized by Indian nationalists. Here is paradox indeed, for all commonsensically promising or effective ways of fighting colonial domination (mass political struggle, for instance, or even economic self-help) have become signs of surrender.

Further implications of this suspicion about indigenous ventures into the 'external' or 'material' domain become evident in the principles of selection followed in the chapters about the nation and 'its' women and subordinate castes. For Chatterjee, women's initiative or autonomy in the nationalist era apparently found expression only inside the home, or at best in autobiographies, while evidence for lower-caste protest against Brahmanical hegemony is located solely in the interesting, but extremely marginal, world of heterodox religious sects. He remains silent about the active role of women in virtually every kind of politics, as well as in specific women's associations, from at least the 1920s. Within the home, Chatterjee focuses much more closely on how women preserved pre-colonial modes of being and resistance, echoing standard nationalist concerns. There is not much interest in how women struggled with a patriarchal domination that was, after all, overwhelmingly indigenous in its structures. Even more surprisingly, the book tells the reader nothing about the powerful anti-caste movements associated with Phule, Periyar, or Ambedkar. No book can be expected to cover everything, but silences of this magnitude are dangerous in a work that appears on the surface comprehensive enough to serve as a standard introduction to colonial India for non-specialists and newcomers, particularly abroad.

---

[36] I have no space here to comment on this curious equation of the 'spiritual' with home, domesticity and femininity. How, one wonders, did highly patriarchal religious traditions like Hinduism and Islam manage such an identification?

The new binary elaborated in *The Nation* is not just a description of nationalist ideology, in which case it could have had a certain, though much exaggerated, relevance. The pattern of stresses and silences indicates a high degree of authorial acceptance. And yet the material/spiritual, West/East divide is of course almost classically Orientalist, much-loved in particular by the most conservative elements in Indian society in both colonial and postcolonial times.[37] Chatterji remains vague about 'the new idea of womanhood in the era of nationalism', the 'battle' for which, he tells us, 'unlike the women's movements in nineteenth- and twentieth-century Europe and America', 'was waged in the home . . . outside the arena of political agitation.'[38] His editorial colleague Dipesh Chakrabarty has recently been much more explicit. Chakrabarty has discovered in nineteenth-century Bengali valorizations of *kula* and *grihalaksmi* (roughly, extended lineage and bounteous wife) 'an irreducible category of "beauty" . . . ways of talking about formations of pleasure, emotions and ideas of good life that associated themselves with models of non-autonomous, non-bourgeois, and non-secular personhood.' All this, despite the admitted 'cruelties of the patriarchal order' entailed by such terms, 'their undeniable phallocentrism'.[39] Beauty, pleasure, the good life . . . *for whom*, it is surely legitimate to ask.

Chatterjee's new book ends on the metahistorical note of a 'struggle between community and capital'. His notion of community, as earlier, is bound up somehow with peasant consciousness, which, we are told, is 'at the opposite pole to a bourgeois consciousness'. (Significantly, this work on what, after all, is now a fairly developed capitalist country by Third World standards, has no space at all for the nation and its capitalists, or workers.) A pattern similar to that just noticed with respect to gender now manifests itself. The Indian peasant community, Chatterjee admits, was never egalitarian, for 'a fifth or more of the population, belonging to the lowest castes, have never had any recognized rights in land.' No matter, however: this profoundly inegalitarian community can still be valorized, for its 'unity . . . nevertheless established by

---

37 For some data about a near-perfect fit between early-twentieth-century cultural nationalism in Bengal and the current argument, see Chapter 1.

38 Chatterjee, *The Nation*, p. 133.

39 Dipesh Chakrabarty, 'The Difference-Deferral of a Colonial Modernity: Public Debates on Domesticity in British Bengal', in *Subaltern Studies VIII* (Delhi, 1994), pp. 83-5.

recognizing the rights of subsistence of all sections of the population, albeit a differential right entailing differential duties and
privileges.' One is almost tempted to recall the standard idealizations
of caste as harmonious, even if hierarchical. The Narodniks had
tried to read back into the *mir* their own indisputably egalitarian
and socialist ideals: Chatterjee's rejection of such 'populist idealization of the peasantry' has led him back to a Slavophile position.[40]

Late *Subaltern Studies* here comes close to positions of neo-
traditionalist anti-modernism, notably advocated with great clarity
and vigour for a number of years by Ashis Nandy.[41] A significant
section of the intelligentsia has been attracted by such appeals
to an earlier, pre-colonial or pre-modern catholicity of inchoate,
pluralistic traditions, particularly in the context of the rise in
India today of powerful religious-chauvinist forces claiming to
represent definitively organized communities with fixed boundaries
— trends that culminated in the destruction of the Babri Masjid
and the communal carnage of 1992–3. Right-wing Hindutva can
then be condemned precisely for being 'modern', a construct of
late- and postcolonial times, the product of Western, colonial
power–knowledge and its classificatory strategies like census enumeration.[42] It may be denounced even for being, in some paradoxical
way, 'secular', and the entire argument then gets bound up with
condemnations of secular rationalism as the ultimate villain.
Secularism, inexorably associated with the interventionist modern
state, is inherently intolerant, argued Nandy in 1990. To him,
it is as unacceptable as Hindutva, a movement which typifies
'religion-as-ideology', imbricated in 'non-religious, usually political
or socio-economic, interests.' Toleration, conversely, has to be
'anti-secular', and must seek to ground itself on pre-modern
'religion-as-faith' . . . which Nandy defines as 'definitionally non-
monolithic and operationally plural'.[43]

What regularly happens in such arguments is a simultaneous

---

[40] Ibid., pp. 166–7, 238.

[41] See, for instance, the declaration of intent at the beginning of Nandy's
The Intimate Enemy (Delhi, 1983) 'to justify and defend the *innocence* [my italics]
which confronted Western colonialism' (p. ix).

[42] Gyanendra Pandey attempted to apply this Saidian framework to the study
of early-twentieth-century communalism in his *The Construction of Communalism
in Colonial North India* (Delhi, 1990).

[43] Ashis Nandy, 'The Politics of Secularism and the Recovery of Religious
Tolerance', in Veena Das (ed.), *Mirrors of Violence: Communities, Riots and Survivors
in South Asia* (Delhi, 1990).

narrowing and widening of the term secularism, its deliberate use as a wildly free-floating signifier. It becomes a polemical target which is both single and conveniently multivalent. Secularism, in the first place, gets equated with aggressive anti-religious scepticism, virtually atheism, through an unique identification with the Enlightenment (itself vastly simplified and homogenized). Yet in twentieth-century India systematic anti-religious polemic, far less activity, has been extremely rare, even on the part of dedicated Leftists and other non-believers. Being secular in the Indian context has meant, primarily and quite often solely, being non- or anti-communal — which is why Mahatma Gandhi had no particular problem with it. 'The Indian version of secularism', Rajeev Bhargava has recently reminded us, 'was consolidated in the aftermath of Partition, where Hindu–Muslim sectarian violence killed off over half a million people': sad and strange, really, that such reminders have become necessary.[44] Even in Europe, the roots of secularism go back some 200 years beyond the Enlightenment, for elements of it emerged in the wake of another epoch of 'communal' violence, the religious wars of the Reformation era. The earliest advocates of a 'secular' separation of church from state were not rationalist freethinkers, but sixteenth-century Anabaptists passionately devoted to their own brand of Christianity who believed any kind of compulsory state religion to be contrary to true faith.

The anti-secular position can retain its plausibility only through an enormous widening of the term's meaning, so that secularism can be made to bear the burden of guilt for all the manifold and indisputable misdeeds and crimes of the 'modern nation-state': 'the new forms of man-made violence unleashed by post-seventeenth century Europe in the name of Enlightenment values . . . the Third Reich, the Gulag, the two World Wars, and the threat of nuclear annihilation.'[45] The logical leap here is really quite startling: Hitler and Stalin were no doubt secular, but was secularism, per se, the ground for Nazi or Stalinist terror, considering that so many of their victims (notably, in both cases, the Communists) were also atheists? Must secularism be held responsible every time a murder is committed by an unbeliever?

A recent article by Partha Chatterjee reiterates Nandy's position,

---

[44] Rajeev Bhargava, 'Giving Secularism Its Due', *Economic and Political Weekly*, 9 July 1994.

[45] Nandy, 'The Politics of Secularism', in Das, p. 90.

with one very significant difference.[46] The essay is a reminder of
the almost inevitably slippery nature of the category of community.
Sought to be applied to an immediate, contemporary context,
romanticizations of pre-modern 'fuzzy' identities seem to be in
some danger of getting displaced by an even more troubling
'realistic' reconciliation or accommodation with the present.[47] Community, in this article, becomes an 'it', with firm boundaries and
putative representative structures: most startlingly, only communities
determined by religion appear now to be worthy of consideration.
Realism for Chatterjee now suggests that religious toleration and
state non-interference should be allowed to expand into legislative
autonomy for distinct religious communities: 'Toleration here would
require one to accept that there will be political contexts where a
group could insist on its right not to give reasons for doing things
differently provided it explains itself adequately in its own chosen
forum. . . . What this will mean in institutional terms are processes
through which each religious group will publicly seek and obtain
from its members consent for its practices insofar as those practices
have regulative power over the members.'[48]

This, to be sure, is in the specific context of the current motivated
and majoritarian BJP campaign for imposing an uniform civil code
through an unilateral abrogation of Muslim personal law. Chatterjee's
argument has a certain superficial similarity with many other positions which express concern today over any imposed uniformity. It
remains a world removed, however, from the proposals being put
forward by some women's organizations and secular groups for
mobilizing initially around demands for specific reforms in distinct
personal laws. Such mobilization is definitely not intended to remain
confined within discrete community walls, but seeks to highlight
unjust gender inequalities within all communities. The Hindutva

[46] Partha Chatterjee, 'Secularism and Toleration', *Economic and Political Weekly*, 9 July 1994. For a more detailed discussion of both Nandy (1990) and
Chatterjee (1994), see my 'The Anti-Secularist Critique of Hindutva: Problem
of A Shared Discursive Space', *Germinal*/Journal of Department of Germanic
and Romance Studies (Delhi University, 1994), vol. I.

[47] Chatterjee takes over Nandy's secularism/toleration disjunction, but gives
it a very 'presentist' twist, explicitly stating in a footnote that he is drawing
out the implications of this position in terms of 'political possibilities within
the domain of the modern state institutions as they now exist in India.' Ibid.,
fn. 2, pp. 1776–7.

[48] Ibid., p. 1775.

campaign demanding uniformity in the name of national integration, it has been argued, 'deliberately ignores the crucial aspect of "uniformity" within communities, i.e. between men and women.'[49] Chatterjee's logic, in contrast, unfortunately seems broad enough to be eminently appropriable, say, by the VHP claiming to speak on behalf of all 'Hindus', or fundamentalists in Bangladesh persecuting a dissenter like Taslima Nasreen. For at its heart lies the assumption that all really dangerous or meaningful forms of power are located uniquely in the modern state, whereas power within communities matters very much less. Despite the deployment of Foucaultian 'governmentality' in the article, this is a position that I find irreconcilable with the major thrust of Foucault's arguments, which have been original and disturbing precisely through their search for multiple locations of power and their insistence that forms of resistance also normally develop into alternative sites of domination.

These, however, cannot but be uncomfortable positions for intellectuals who remain deeply anti-communal and in some sense radical. *Subaltern* historiography in general has faced considerable difficulties in tackling this phenomenon of a communal violence that is both popular and impossible to endorse. There is the further problem that the Hindu Right often attacks the secular, liberal nation-state as a Western importation, precisely the burden of much late-*Subaltern* argument: suggesting affinities that are, hopefully, still distasteful, yet difficult to repudiate within the parameters of an anti-Enlightenment discourse grounded in notions of community.[50] In two recent articles by Gyanendra Pandey, communal violence consequently becomes the appropriate site for the unfolding of that other pole of late-*Subaltern* thinking, built around the notion of the 'fragment', and seeking to valorize it against epistemologically uncertain and politically oppressive 'grand narratives'.[51] Epistemological uncertainty becomes the

[49] Resolution entitled 'Equal Rights, Equal Laws', adopted by a national convention organized by the All India Democratic Women's Association (New Delhi, 9-10 December 1995).

[50] In May 1994, for instance, the RSS ideologue S. Gurumurti described the Ayodhya movement as 'perhaps the first major symptom of social assertion over a Westernized and alienated state apparatus' that has imposed secularism and other 'foreign ideologies on the country, provoking a growing feeling of nativeness.' 'State and Society', in *Seminar 417* (May 1994). An article by Uma Bharati in the same issue entitled 'Social Justice' condemned any labelling of 'Hindutva [as] a Brahmanical and exploitative order' as 'the distorted view that followers of Macaulay hold.'

[51] Gyanendra Pandey, 'In Defence of the Fragment: Writing about Hindu-

ground for rejecting all efforts at causal explanation, or even contextual analysis. (Such uncertainties, it may be noticed, have never been allowed to obstruct sweeping generalizations about Enlightenment rationalism, derivative discourses, or community consciousness.) The polemical thrust can then be directed once again principally against secular intellectuals who have tried to relate communal riots to socio-economic and political contexts. Such efforts, invariably branded as economistic, allegedly leave 'little room for the emotions of people, for feelings and perceptions' through their emphasis upon 'land and property'.[52] That people can never get emotional about 'land and property' is surely a startling discovery. Even a distinction, drawn in the context of the terrifying riots of 1946-7 and simplistically represented by Pandey as one made between 'good' and 'bad' subaltern violence, is apparently unacceptable.[53] Pandey cannot stop here, for he remains an anti-communal intellectual: but the framework he has adopted leaves space for nothing more than agonized contemplation of 'violence' and 'pain' as 'fragments', perception of which is implicitly assumed to be direct and certain. But 'fragment', etymologically, is either part of a bigger whole or a whole by itself: one cannot avoid the dangers of homogenization that easily. It remains unnoticed, further, that valorization of the certainty of knowledge of particulars has been a classically positivistic position, well expounded many years ago, for instance, by Karl Popper in his *Poverty of Historicism*.[54]

But violence and pain, detached from specificities of context, become in effect abstract universals, 'violence' in general. The essays end with rhetorical questions about how historians can represent pain, how difficult or impossible it is to do so. One is irresistibly reminded of Thompson's devastating comment in his last book about the fatuity of many statements about 'the human condition', which take us 'only a little way, and a great deal less far than is

---

Muslim Riots in India Today', *Economic and Political Weekly*, Annual Number, 1991, and 'The Prose of Otherness', *Subaltern Studies VIII*.

52 'In Defence of the Fragment', p. 566.

53 'The Prose of Otherness', *Subaltern Studies VIII*, referring to an old article of mine entitled 'Popular Movements, National Leadership, and The Coming of Freedom with Partition', in D.N. Panigrahi (ed.), *Economy, Society and Politics in Modern India* (New Delhi, 1985).

54 Relevant here would be Frederic Jameson's recent caustic comments about 'the latter-day transmogrification of these . . . quite unphilosophical empirical and anti-systemic positivist attitudes and opinions into heroic forms of resistance to metaphysics and Utopian tyranny.' 'Actually Existing Marxism', *Polygraph 6/7*, p. 184.

sometimes knowingly implied. For "the human condition", unless further qualified and disclosed, is nothing but a kind of metaphysical full stop' — or: 'worse — a bundle of solecisms about mortality and defeated aspiration.'[55]

III

Let me try to sum up my disagreements with late *Subaltern Studies*, which flow from a compound of academic and political misgivings.

Two sets of misrecognitions have obscured the presence in *Subaltern Studies* of a high degree of redundancy, the tendency to reiterate the already said. Both follow from a novelty of situation: *Subaltern Studies* does happen to be the first Indian historiographical school whose reputation has come to be evaluated primarily in terms of audience response in the West. For many Indian readers, particularly those getting interested in postmodernist trends for the first time, the sense of being 'with it' strongly conveyed by *Subaltern Studies* appears far more important than any possible insubstantiality of empirical content. Yet some eclectic borrowings or verbal similarities apart, the claim (or ascription) of being postmodern is largely spurious, in whichever sense we might want to deploy that ambiguous and selfconsciously polysemic term. Texts are still being read here in a flat and obvious manner, as straightforward indicators of authorial intention. There have been few attempts to juxtapose representations of diverse kinds in unexpected ways, or selfconscious efforts to think out or experiment with new forms of narrativization. Partha Chatterjee's *Nationalist Thought*, to cite one notable instance, reads very much like a conventional history of ideas, based on a succession of great thinkers. One of the thinkers, Bankimchandra, happens to have been the first major Bengali novelist: his imaginative prose, inexplicably, is totally ignored. Again, much of the potential richness of the *Ramakrishna-Kathamrita* explored as a text gets lost, I feel, if it is virtually reduced to a 'source of new strategies of survival and resistance' of a colonized middle-class assumed to be living in extreme dread of its foreign rulers — a class moreover conceptualized in excessively homogenized terms.[56] Problems like

---

[55] E.P. Thompson, *Witness Against the Beast: William Blake and the Moral Law* (Cambridge, 1993), p. 188.

[56] Partha Chatterjee, 'A Religion of Urban Domesticity: Sri Ramakrishna and the Calcutta Middle Class', in Chatterjee and Pandey (eds), *Subaltern Studies VII* (Delhi, 1992), and Chatterji, *The Nation*, Chapter III. The clerical ambience

these are not basically products of lack of authorial competence or quality. They emerge from restrictive analytical frameworks, as *Subaltern Studies* swings from a rather simple emphasis on subaltern autonomy to an even more simplistic thesis of Western colonial cultural domination.[57]

A reiteration of the already said: for it needs to be emphasized that the bulk of the history written by modern Indian historians has been nationalist and anti-colonial in content, at times obsessively so. Criticism of Western cultural domination is likewise nothing particularly novel. The empirical underpinning for the bulk of *Subaltern* cultural criticism has come in fact from work done in Calcutta some twenty years back, which had effectively demolished the excessive adulation of nineteenth-century English-educated intellectuals and reformers through an emphasis upon the limits imposed on them by their colonial context.[58]

Here the second kind of misrecognition comes in, for in the Western context there is a certain, though much exaggerated, novelty and radicalism in the Saidian exposure of the colonial complicity of much European scholarship and literature. Such blindness has

---

Ramakrishna's early audience and often of his conversations with them, for instance, has been totally missed. For another kind of effort to explore the *Kathamrita* — one which in its author's opinion tried to go much beyond the mere 'biographical question of Ramakrishna in relation to the middle class of Bengal' (*The Nation*, p. 36), see my 'Kaliyuga, Chakri, and Bhakti: Ramakrishna and His Times', *Economic and Political Weekly*, 18 July 1992; reprinted with minor changes as Chapter 8 within this book.

57 Shahid Amin's finely crafted *Event, Metaphor, Memory: Chauri Chaura 1922-92* (Delhi, 1995) might be taken to constitute a partial exception, within a basically early-*Subaltern* framework. But the latter often seems too narrow to adequately comprehend the richness of material, while far more has been achieved elsewhere in the innovative handling of representations: as stray examples, one could mention Stephen Greenblatt, *Renaissance Self-Fashioning: From More to Shakespeare* (Chicago, 1980); Marina Warner, *Joan of Arc* (London, 1981); and Sarah Maza, *Private Lives and Public Affairs: The Causes Celebres of Pre-Revolutionary France* (Calcutta, 1993).

58 Partha Chatterjee fully acknowledged this debt, in his 'The Fruits of Macaulay's Poison-Tree', in Ashok Mitra (ed.), *The Truth Unites* (Calcutta, 1985). For a sampling of the early-1970s critique of the Bengal Renaissance, see the essays of Asok Sen, Barun De and Sumit Sarkar in V.C. Joshi (eds), *Rammohan Roy and the Process of Modernization in India* (Delhi, 1975); Asok Sen, *Iswarchandra Vidyasagar and His Elusive Milestones* (Calcutta, 1977); and Sumit Sarkar, 'The Complexities of Young Bengal', a 1973 essay, reprinted in my *Critique of Colonial India* (Calcutta, 1985).

been most obvious in the discipline of literary studies, in the West as well as in the ex-colonial world, and it is not surprising that radically inclined intellectuals working in this area have been particularly enthusiastic in their response to late *Subaltern Studies.* There had been some real absences, too, even in the best of Western Marxist or radical historiography, inadequacies that came to be felt more deeply in the new era of vastly intensified globalization, socialist collapse, resurgent neo-colonialism and racism, and the rise to unprecedented prominence of expatriate Third World intellectuals located, or seeking location in, Western universities. Hobsbawm apart, the great masters of British Marxist historiography have admittedly written little on Empire, and the charge of Eurocentrism could appear particularly damaging for a social history the foundation-text of which had deliberately confined itself to the making of the 'English' working class.

Yet the exposure of one instance after another of collusion with colonial power-knowledge can soon become predictable and tedious. Thompson has a quiet but telling aside about this in his *Alien Homage,*[59] while his posthumous book on Blake should induce some rethinking about uncritical denunciations of the Enlightenment as a bloc that have been so much in vogue in recent years. With its superb combination of textual close reading and historical analysis, *Witness Against the Beast* reminds us of the need for socially nuanced and differentiated conceptions of Enlightenment and 'counter-Enlightenment' that go far beyond homogenized praise or rejection. And meanwhile very interesting new work is emerging. Peter Linebaugh, for instance, has recently explored ways of integrating global, colonial dimensions and themes of Foucaultian power-knowledge within a framework that is clearly Thompsonian-Marxian in inspiration, and yet goes considerably beyond the parameters of the social history of the 1960s and 1970s.[60]

[59] Commenting on William Radice's statement that the elder Thompson had been 'limited by his missionary and British imperial background', E.P. Thompson comments: 'These stereotypes are limiting also, and are calculated to elicit predictable responses from a public as confined within the preconceptions of the "contemporary" as that of the 1920s. . . . The limits must be noted . . . but what may merit our attention more may be what lies outside those limits or confounds those expectations.' *Alien Homage: Edward Thompson and Rabindranath Tagore* (Delhi, 1993), pp. 2-3.

[60] Peter Linebaugh, *The London Hanged: Crime and Civil Society in the Eighteenth Century* (Harmondsworth: Penguin, 1991, 1993). For an elaboration of my

In South Asian historiography, however, the inflated reputation of late *Subaltern Studies* has encouraged a virtual folding back of all history into the single problematic of Western colonial cultural domination. This imposes a series of closures and silences, and threatens to simultaneously feed into shallow forms of retrogressive indigenism. An impression has spread among interested non-specialists that there is little worth reading in modern Indian history prior to *Subaltern Studies*, or outside it, today. Not that very considerable and significant new work is not going on along other lines: but this tends to get less attention than it deserves. One could cite major advances in economic history, and pioneering work in environmental studies, for instance, as well as research on law and penal administration that is creatively aware of Foucault but tends to ignore, or go beyond, strict Saidian–Subaltern parameters. Such work does not usually begin with assuming a total or uniform pre-colonial/colonial disjunction.[61] Another example would be the shift in the dominant tone of feminist history. There had been interesting developments in the new field of gender studies in the 1970s and early 1980s, posing important questions about women and nationalism and relating gender to shifting material conditions. The colonial discourse framework threatens to marginalize much of this earlier work. A simple binary of Westernized surrender/indigenist resistance will necessarily have major difficulties in finding space for sensitive studies of movements for women's rights, or of lower-caste protest: for quite often such initiatives did try to utilize aspects of colonial administration and ideas as resources.

And finally there are the political implications. The spread of assumptions and values associated with late *Subaltern Studies* can have certain disabling consequences for sections of intellectuals still subjectively radical. This is so particularly because India — unlike many parts of the West, perhaps — is still a country where major political battles are engaged in by large numbers of people: where, in other words, depoliticization has not yet given a certain limited relevance to theories of sporadic initiative by individuals or small groups

---

argument with respect to such possibilities, see my 'A Marxian Social History Beyond the Foucaultian Turn: Peter Linebaugh's "The London Hanged"', *Economic and Political Weekly*, xxx, 30, 29 July 1995.

[61] I am thinking particularly of the ongoing work of Sumit Guha on the Maharashtrian *longue durée*, and of Radhika Singha's *Despotism of Law* (forthcoming from OUP, New Delhi), on legal practices in early-colonial India.

glorying in their imposed marginality. The organized, Marxist Left in India remains one of the biggest existing anywhere in the world today, while very recently the forces of predominantly high-caste Hindutva have been halted in some areas by a lower-caste upthrust drawing on earlier traditions of anti-hierarchical protest. *Subaltern Studies*, symptomatically, has ignored histories of the Left and of organized anti-caste movements throughout, and the line between past and present-day neglect can be fairly porous. Movements of a more innovatory kind have also emerged in recent years: organizations to defend civil and democratic rights, numerous feminist groups, massive ecological protests like the Narmada Bachao Andolan, and very new and imaginative forms of trade union activity (the Chattisgarh Mukti Morcha arising out of a miners union, one or two efforts at co-operative workers' control in the context of recession and structural readjustment). A 'social reform' issue like child-marriage had been the preserve of highly educated, 'Westernized', upper-caste male reformers in the nineteenth century: today Bhanwari, a woman of low-caste origin in an obscure Rajasthan village, has been campaigning against that practice in Rajput households, in face of rape, ostracism, and a gross miscarriage of justice. Any meaningful understanding of or identification with such developments is undercut by two kinds of emphasis quite central to late *Subaltern Studies*. Culturalism rejects the importance of class and class struggle, while notions of civil, democratic, feminist and liberal individual rights — many of them indubitably derived from certain Enlightenment traditions — get delegitimized by a repudiation of the Enlightenment as a bloc.

All such efforts need, and have often obtained, significant inputs from an intelligentsia which still includes many people with radical interests and commitments. This intelligentsia, however, is one constituent of a wider middle-class formation, upwardly mobile sections of which today are being sucked into globalizing processes that promise material consumerist dividends at the price of dependency. A binary combination of 'material' advancement and 'spiritual' autonomy through surrogate forms of cultural or religious nationalism is not at all uncommon for such groups. Hindutva, with its notable appeal in recent years among metropolitan elites and non-resident Indians, embodies this combination at its most aggressive. The political inclinations of the *Subaltern* scholars and the bulk of their readership are certainly very different, but some of their work nowadays seems to be unwittingly feeding into softer versions of not entirely dissimilar moods. Words like 'secular', 'rational', or 'progressive' have become terms of ridicule, and if 'resistance' (of whatever undifferentiative kind) can still be valorized, movements seeking transformation get suspected of teleology.[62] The decisive shift in critical registers from capitalist and colonial exploitation to Enlightenment rationality, from multinationals to Macaulay, has opened the way for a vague nostalgia that identifies the authentic with the indigenous, and locates both in the pasts of an ever-receding community, or a present than can consist of fragments alone. Through an enshrinement of sentimentality,[63] a subcontinent with its manifold, concrete contradictions and problems becomes a kind of dream of childhood, of a *grihalakshmi* presiding over a home happy and beautiful, by some alchemy, in the midst of all its patriarchy.

Let me end with a last, specific example. There is one chapter in Chatterjee's *Nation* which, for once, deals with an economic theme. This is a critique of the bureaucratic rationalism of Nehruvian planning: not unjustified in parts, though there has been no lack of such critiques, many of them much better informed and more effective. What is significant, however, is Chatterjee's total silence on the wholesale abandonment of that strategy in recent years under Western pressure. There is not a word, in a book published in 1993, about that other rationality of the 'free' market, derived at least as much from the Enlightenment as its socialistic alternatives, which is being imposed worldwide today by the World Bank, the I.M.F., and multinational firms. The claim, elsewhere in the book, to an 'adversarial' relationship 'to the dominant structures of scholarship and politics' resounds oddly in the midst of this silence.[64]

---

62 I am indebted for this resistance/transformation contrast to an illuminating oral presentation in Delhi recently by Madhavan Palat on the relevance of Marxist historiography today. He used these terms to indicate a vital contrast between Marxian and other strands of social history.

63 I owe this phrase to Pradip Kumar Datta. Such a shift in registers, it needs to be added, has become a cardinal feature of much postcolonial theory. See Arif Dirlik's pertinent comments on the dangers of reducing anti-colonial criticism to the elimination of its 'ideological and cultural legacy' alone: ' . . . by fixing its gaze on the past it in fact avoids confronting the present.' Dirlik, p. 343.

64 *The Nation and Its Fragments*, Chapter 10, and p. 156.

PART TWO

4

Edward Thompson and India: *The Other Side of the Medal**

For history students of my generation, acquaintance with Edward Thompson began — and often ended — with the *Rise and Fulfilment of British Rule in India*, the textbook he had co-authored with G.T. Garratt in 1934. Thirty years have gone by, but I can still recall the excitement and pleasure of an undergraduate discovering a British historian who could expose with such frankness, wit and anger the underside of England's 'work in India': the 'shaking of the pagoda tree' under Clive and Hastings; the 'celebrated backward charge over their own infantry . . . artillery and wagon lines' by the Company cavalry at Chilianwala, led by a superannuated general, who could not mount his horse without assistance,[1] the detailed account of British atrocities during the Mutiny, which contrasted sharply with the presentation of 1857 even in the standard Indian textbook of those days — Majumdar, Roychaudhuri and Datta's *Advanced History of India*.[2] The closing chapters of *Rise and Fulfilment*, like the title itself, produced, however, a sense of ambiguity and anticlimax, with their all too brief references to Gandhian mass movements and focus upon constitutional reforms.[3]

* This is a very slightly modified version of an essay published as the Afterword to a new edition of Edward Thompson's *The Other Side of the Medal*, ed. Mulk Raj Anand (Sterling, New Delhi, 1989).

[1] Edward Thompson and G.T. Garratt, *Rise and Fulfilment of British Rule in India* (1934; reprinted, Allahabad, 1976), pp. 383–4.

[2] The *Advanced History*, first published in 1946, balanced a passing reference to Nicholson's notorious call 'for the flaying-alive, impalement, or burning' of the Delhi mutineers with praise for the alleged 'clemency' of Canning.

[3] The last two chapters, dealing with the 1920s and early 1930s, were entitled 'Dyarchy in Operation' and 'Progress by Conference'.

Not many students read Thompson and Garratt today: a pity, in some ways, but research has obviously dated much of it. Edward Thompson might even be remembered more as the father of another Edward, distinguished historian and peace activist, while students of literature might occasionally meet him as the first English biographer of Rabindranath and a minor, though not uninteresting, novelist and poet.

The Other Side of the Medal, Thompson's first and sensational bid at something like an inversion of established British Indian historiography, has not been too easy to get hold of for several decades. It was published in October 1925, by the Hogarth Press of Leonard and Virginia Woolf, and was reprinted in December 1926 and in an American edition in 1927. No reprints since then, so far as I know, and near-oblivion, except for occasional references in research publications on 1857.[4] A new edition of this major iconoclastic text which appeared in 1989, was thus welcome, particularly in the context of the vogue for popular Raj novels and studies, marked by nostalgia and sentimental melancholy about departed grandeur.

Stereotypes about 1857, in terms of a basic dichotomy between Christian manly heroism and pagan Indian bestiality, entered early and deep into British consciousness. In a review of *The Other Side of the Medal*, K.M. Panikkar described the British martyrdom/Indian atrocities syndrome as 'almost a religion' for the English, 'with its temples, shrines, and places of pilgrimage', and Thompson himself recalled in 1931 'the spell under which I made my own pilgrimage to the Well at Cawnpore and the Lucknow Residency'.[5] The same images were sought to be instilled into Indian minds through school and college textbooks, Anglo-Indian journals, and novels like Flora Annie Steel's bestseller *On the Face of the Waters* (1896), which portrayed the rebellion of 1857 as an 'aimless and meaningless explosion, a reversion to barbarism, a contest between the forces of light and powers of darkness'.[6] Few Indians dared to write openly about the

[4] See f.n. 22.

[5] *The Hindu* (Madras) — February 1926; *Spectator*, 4 July 1931. Press cuttings from reviews of *The Other Side of the Medal*, along with offprints of some of Thompson's own review articles, form part of the collection of his private papers, preserved by his son, Edward P. Thompson. (Henceforward referred to as Thompson Papers.) I am deeply grateful to E.P. Thompson for giving me access to this collection, for taking the trouble of mailing part of this very rich material to me in India, and above all for his extremely stimulating criticism of my first draft.

[6] Benita Parry, *Delusions and Discoveries: Studies on India in the British Imagination, 1880-1930* (London, 1972), p. 119.

'other side' of 1857: Savarkar's *The Indian War of Independence* (1909)
remained banned for a long time, while among academics the silence
continued virtually down to 1947.

What broke the spell for Thompson was clearly the Jallianwallabagh massacre and the blatant justification of Dyer by a substantial
section of the British and Anglo-Indian public, together with the
nationalist upsurge of 1919-22. The first chapter of *The Other Side
of the Medal*, entitled 'Indian Irreconcilability', grapples with the
problem of the spread of 'actual hatred of the British name' far
beyond upper-caste politicians: 'the discontent with our rule is
growing universal'.[7] Thompson's answer is simple, probably simplistic: the memories of the bloody suppression of the Mutiny among
Indians, aggravated by the fact that 'one side has succeeded in
imposing its version of events on the whole world . . .'[8] From 'Bihar
to the Border the Mutiny lives', Thompson declares, 'an unavenged
and unappeased ghost'.[9]

The core of *The Other Side of the Medal* consequently became a
devastating exposure of British atrocities during the 1857 rebellion.
There was little problem in finding evidence, for those engaged in
suppressing the rebellion were often only too eager to boast about
their accomplishments in a spate of published letters, journals, and
books, inspired by a mood summed up in the memorable lines of
the Anglo-Indian poetaster Martin Tupper:

> Destroy those traitor legions, hang every pariah hound,
> And hunt them down to death, in all hills and cities round.[10]

The few who, like the *Times* correspondent W.B. Russell and
(occasionally, and not too effectively) Canning, protested against the
blood-bath added their quota of information. Data about British
atrocities found considerable space in the early standard works on
the Mutiny by historians like Kaye and Montgomery Martin. A
certain coyness crept in, however, with the rise of an English-educated
Indian public opinion, and the second generation of Mutiny historians typified by G.W. Forrest (1904-10) or T. Rice Edward Holmes
(1913) preferred to keep quiet about counterinsurgency exploits while
carrying on the work of erecting Nana Saheb into a worthy successor

---

[7] *The Other Side of the Medal* (first edition, London, 1925), p. 25.
[8] Ibid., p. 26.
[9] Ibid., pp. 86, 30.
[10] Cited from *Calcutta Review* (1858) in S.B. Chaudhuri, *English Historical
Writings on the Indian Mutiny, 1857-59* (Calcutta, 1979), p. 259.

of Sirajuddoulah: precisely the syndrome that provoked Thompson's protest.

Thompson's book is not based on original archival research, but the evidence he marshalled and superbly presented in the sixty pages of his second chapter is telling enough. He tells us about the public blowing from guns of forty prisoners at Peshawar ordered by John Lawrence, quotes from Roberts' cheerful letters to his sister, 'darling Harriet' ('When a prisoner is brought in, I am the first to call out to have him hanged'),[11] and refers to Nicholson's demand for 'excruciating tortures' and Russell's indignant exposure of some of the methods employed: 'sewing Mohammedans in pig-skins, smearing them with pork-fat before execution, and burning their bodies, and forcing Hindus to defile themselves . . .'[12] Neill's column marching on Cawnpore burnt village women and children on a large scale, and Kaye had the honesty to note that this probably had a lot to do with the *later* massacre associated with Nana Saheb.[13] Thompson's 'necessary sanitary work'[14] of exposure continues with accounts of wholesale massacres of civilians after each capture of a rebel stronghold, and attains its point of maximum horror with long extracts from Amritsar Deputy Commissioner Frederick Cooper's *The Crisis in the Punjab* (1858). Forty-five prisoners, shut up in a small room in a police station, were found dead ('Unconsciously, the tragedy of Holwell's Black Hole had been re-enacted'), 237 were shot without any nonsense of court-martial, and the bodies were thrown by village sweepers into a well. Cooper saw in his action 'the manifest and wondrous interposition of Almighty God in the cause of Christianity' — 'There is a well at Cawnpore; but there is also one at Ujnalla.' Thompson adds the pertinent comment: 'I see no reason why he should be denied the immortality he craved so earnestly. Let his name be remembered with Nana Sahib's.'[15]

The concluding part of Thompson's book ('Shadows of the Mutiny') makes the point that such bouts of ferocity did not end with the suppression of the Rebellion of 1857. They had a tendency to recur, with periodic British panic: the blowing of Kuka prisoners

11 *The Other Side of the Medal*, pp. 50-1.

12 Ibid., pp. 44, 48.

13 Ibid., p. 80.

14 Thompson's own — slightly apologetic — phrase in a letter to *Spectator*, 25 July 1931, defending his review of Sir George McMunn's *Indian Mutiny in Perspective* (Thompson Papers).

15 *The Other Side of the Medal*, pp. 62-3, 66.

from guns by Cowan in 1872, Roberts at Kabul in 1879, and of course Jallianwallabagh. On each occasion what made the provocation to Indian feelings worse, according to Thompson, were the later justifications and indeed eulogies. Forsythe, the superior officer who approved of Cowan's measures, was knighted, Roberts became a household hero, a purse of £ 30,000 was raised for Dyer, while Mutiny 'heroes' like Nicholson, Neill, Havelock and Hodson became virtual cult figures through a multitude of hagiographic works. As Thompson remarks caustically, such biographies have tended to forget that these men 'had other activities' during the Mutiny than 'singing hymns and receiving devout and worshipping affection from their soldiers'.[16] 'Devilish cruelty on both sides', Thompson adds, have been characteristic of slave rebellions the world over: 'It is our glorification of the Mutiny that is exceptional, not its brutality.'[17] 'Is it not possible that here is a fire of smouldering bitterness which owes nothing to "Panditji's stoking"?'[18]

'I haven't heard a dog bark in defence of the established accounts of the Mutiny. They are finished', claimed Thompson in a letter dated December 1925.[19] A bit over-optimistic perhaps, considering that in July 1931 Thompson would be writing a bitter review of yet another 'jaunty defence of the darker side of our record', marked by the constant use of 'the language of sport for the chase of enemies to the gallows':[20] yet significant changes did take place in Mutiny historiography. They had started before Thompson's book, but it is not at all unlikely that *The Other Side of the Medal* hastened the

---

16 Ibid., p. 101.

17 Ibid., pp. 36, 120.

18 Ibid., p. 120. The 'Panditji' refers to the stereotype of the alleged Brahman instigator of Indian discontent, as used in a book which provoked Thompson considerably: Al Carthill's (Calcroft–Kennedy, ICS) *The Lost Dominion* (London, 1924). 'I published the Medal, because (i) Al Carthill and the absurd praise of the Tory press made me angry . . . the last straw, in a long process of accumulation of incendiary mind-stuff. . . .' Thompson to S.K. Ratcliffe, 15 December 1925 (Thompson Papers).

19 Thompson to S.K. Ratcliffe, 15 December 1925, Ratcliffe had acquired a somewhat Indophile reputation as editor of the Calcutta *Statesman* in the early years of the century, but his letter to Thompson (14 December 1925) to which this was the reply showed him rather worried about Indian nationalists 'making the most of the ammunition which, as you realized, you could not help supplying them with'.

20 Thompson's review of McMunn's *Indian Mutiny in Perspective*, in *Spectator*, 4 July 1931 (Thompson Papers).

process: 1857 lost its central place in Anglo-Indian historiography after Forrest and Holmes, and the relatively few later works tended to have a narrowly military focus. On the Indian side, in contrast, Savarkar proved to be the harbinger of a flood of studies and debates, particularly during the centenary year.

Indian nationalist literature incorporated the fact of British atrocities, used it occasionally for its exposure value, but seldom gave it centrality. Even the aggressively polemical work of Savarkar was much more concerned with proving that 1857 was a genuine and organized 'war of independence', with attempting, in other words, a teleological link between the Rebellion and the later 'modern' national movement. The great debate of the late 1950s, it will be recalled, was about the 'popular' and 'national' character of 1857.[21] It tended to degenerate into a fight over labels which probably delayed for some time more sophisticated research. Later research — by Eric Stokes, for instance — sought to shift the focus to regional or local studies of social composition of rebels and the variety of tensions leading up to the uprising of 1857.

The central concern of *The Other Side of the Medal* has thus been marginalized by later historiography. R.C. Majumdar in 1957 did include a section on what he called 'the other side of the shield' which acknowledged a debt to Thompson; S.B. Chaudhuri's survey in 1979 of English historical writings on the Mutiny was frankly — indeed unfairly — dismissive.[22] The *Other Side* does contain a few passages which can strengthen the argument that 'the movement was popular, a real war for independence' rather than a 'merely . . . military mutiny',[23] but evidence for this was already voluminous in the pages of Kaye, and the reader interested in such problems can anyway turn today to numerous collections of published sources, like the massive Uttar Pradesh *History of the Freedom Movement* volumes. More significant and thought-provoking is the emphasis upon the persistence of Mutiny memories: the fascinating story, for instance, which Thompson cites from a very anti-Indian missionary account of how

[21] The major protagonists in the debate were R.C. Majumdar, with his iconoclastic *The Sepoy Mutiny and the Revolt of 1857* (Calcutta, 1957), S.N. Sen's officially sponsored history and S.B. Chaudhuri's studies of 'civil disturbances' during the Mutiny.

[22] R.C. Majumdar, Book II, pp. 93-115. S.B. Chaudhuri, *English Historical Writings* makes only a passing reference to Thompson, criticizing him for his allegedly unfair comments about T.R. Holmes.

[23] *The Other Side of the Medal*, pp. 30-2, 107.

Indian Christian pupils, asked to write an essay on the Mutiny, all sent in sheets of blank paper in 'a silent, unanimous and unapologetic refusal to perform the task'.[24] The theme has been sadly neglected so far in conventional historiography, for which nationalism begins with the educated middle class founding the Congress. The vogue for the study of subaltern perceptions might well find such hints worthy of greater attention.

I would suggest, however, that the real interest of *The Other Side of the Medal* lies in a different direction: as a significant text that embodies liberal British perceptions about colonial India during the inter-war years. And a very rich text it is, provided we read it for the tensions, ambiguities and silences which underlie its surface smoothness of polemic. For what emerges is a contradictory, indeed tortured, sensibility.

Like a number of writers of what Greenberger in his study of the literature of imperialism has labelled the 'Era of Doubt',[25] Thompson is contemptuous of the earlier stereotype of 'the strong, silent, "God's Englishman" . . . that the Indian loves', whose 'words are few but pregnant . . . the brief, warning snort of the rhinoceros before he charges through the jungle at his photographer'. He is equally scathing about the favourite counterpoint of 'the martial races – good, easy-going fellows, such as the Sikhs and jolly little Gurkhas . . . the "trusty servants" of countless thrilling boys stories.'[26] Yet the educated babu remains to him a profoundly unattractive figure – 'It would be difficult to libel the miserable being whom our Western system of education, manipulated by incompetent and often grossly dishonest Indians, has evolved.' The 'Indian extremist press' is marked by 'utter irrelevances and reckless unfairness',[27] constitutional government has been 'enlarged . . . generously (as we thought . . . not without reason)',[28] and 'The average British official, whatever his faults, is keen on doing his job – to use the mystic phrase with which we cover up a multitude of merits as well as sins. . . . He is honestly

---

[24] Ibid., p. 120, quoting from H. Fitchett's *The Tale of the Great Mutiny*. Reverend Fitchett was a Methodist missionary whose book is described by Thompson as 'perhaps the most contemptible of all histories of the Mutiny. . . .' Ibid., p. 136.

[25] Allen J. Greenberger, *The British Image of India: A Study in the Literature of Imperialism, 1880-1960* (London, 1969).

[26] *The Other Side of the Medal*, pp. 16-17.

[27] Ibid., pp. 18-19.

[28] Ibid., p. 10.

out to do the best he can for the people under his charge.'[29] The focus on British atrocities as the root cause of Indian discontent is itself deeply self-limiting. An Indian reviewer of the book was quick to point out that such atrocities were 'as nothing to the long-drawn out agonies of a whole nation of 247 million people, exposed daily to starvation, disease, ignorance and lifelong misery.'[30]

Thompson could not have been unaware that his book would help Indian nationalist propaganda, but, as we shall see, this to him was — at least in 1925 — a disturbing and uncomfortable necessity. *The Other Side of the Medal* was explicitly directed towards a British audience, and written in the hope 'that it will change the attitude of every Englishman who reads it to the end'.[31] The precise contours of the hoped for 'change' are spelled out by Thompson in the following crucial passage:

> There is no commoner word on Indian lips today than *atonement*. England, they say, has never made atonement; and she must do it before we can be friends. The word in their minds is the Sanskrit *prayashchitta*, usually translated *atonement*; but its meaning is rather a *gesture*. It is not larger measures of self-government for which they are longing, it is the magnanimous gesture of a great nation. . . .[32]

Significant here, and obviously so, is the dubious transfer of Thompson's own assumptions to the Indians, a substantial and growing proportion of whom had become interested by the 1920s in 'larger measures of self-government', or even independence — and not in any atonement or 'magnanimous gesture' from their rulers. Very significant, too, is the centrality of the deeply Christian concept of atonement in Thompson during these years, just as it is in C.F. Andrews, another ex-missionary friend of India. The nuances and variations within 'atonement' may repay some close attention. Atonement could mean a quick absolution from sin through ritual or gesture, and there are some hints of this in *The Other Side of the Medal*: 'to many who have read my pages, after the first shock of horror and shame must have come relief . . . '; through atonement might also come an 'understanding . . . friendship and forgiveness' between Englishmen and Indians.[33] The welcome extended to Thompson's book

29 Ibid., p. 23.

30 B. Shiva Rao, in Lansbury's *London Weekly*, 19 December 1925 (Thompson Papers).

31 *The Other Side of the Medal*, p. 5 (Preface to First Edition).

32 Ibid., pp. 131-2.

33 Ibid., pp. 132-3.

by notoriously anti-Indian journals like the *Civil and Military Gazette* (Lahore) and the *Pioneer* (Allahabad), expressing 'gratification that the book had been written at last and by an Englishman',[34] fits fairly well into such a framework. Yet atonement, modelled ultimately on Christ dying on the Cross for the sins of humanity, could also imply an incomparably deeper catharsis and sacrifice. In Thompson the quest for reconciliation through atonement led in the end to an involvement in Indian causes much more profound than the somewhat gestural quality of *The Other Side of the Medal*.

Prayashchitta in Hinduism, it may be added, is by no means entirely synonymous with atonement, and Thompson knew enough of Indian traditions to be aware of the differences. It usually implies ritual purification rather than profound inner change ('its meaning is rather a *gesture* . . . '). The whole passage, with its uneasy slides and oscillations, itself suggests an acute discomfort, betraying the lack of complete grasp over a problem too difficult to be contained by the categories atonement/prayashchitta, and yet possible to tackle through such terms alone. Thompson, it may be suggested, is reaching in such passages the outer limits of liberal discourse, and his ambiguities are interesting and moving precisely because of the honesty with which he exposes the crisis of his liberal concern in the colonial situation.[35]

The nuances of atonement are associated also with variations in the specifics of Christian faith and practice, which may range from satisfaction with externals of ritual or dogma to an *imitatio Christi:* agonized self-doubts, tortured quests for inner piety and moral self-transformation. It is not irrelevant, therefore, to note that already in 1925 Thompson's relations with received Christianity were shot through with contradictions and ambiguities. What horrified him above all in British Mutiny accounts was the combination of piety and cruelty, the Christian inspiration and justification for ruthless terror. Thompson dwells almost obsessively on the 'incredible' piety and self-righteousness of men like John Lawrence, calculating in language borrowed from the Prayer Book the pros and cons of killing all, or most, or some of 120 helpless prisoners — 'on full reflection, I would not put them all to death.'[36] Clergymen, together with their wives or widows, emerge from his pages as the most bloodthirsty of

---

[34] Letter of Edward Thompson to *Saturday Review*, 21 May 1927 (Thompson Papers).
[35] I owe this point to Pradip Dutta.
[36] *The Other Side of the Medal*, pp. 33–4.

all, and Thompson reserves his severest comment on Mutiny historians for W.H. Fitchett, a Methodist missionary. The central chapter of *The Other Side of the Medal* ends with a quotation from G.W. Forrest's closing 'unctuous paragraph': 'Justice was done, mercy shown to all who were not guilty of deliberate murder, the land cleansed of blood' — to which Thompson appends perhaps the angriest passage in a very angry book: 'One might throw the lists open to the literature of the whole world, and still not find a more superb example of smug effrontery.'[37]

The Preface to the second edition of *The Other Side of the Medal* recalls that many 'Christian leaders in England' had been critical of its publication; support, however, had come, as the Preface to the first edition had put it, from 'some of the names most honoured in contemporary literature'. Publication by Leonard and Virginia Woolf's Hogarth Press — which since its foundation in 1917 had helped to launch authors of the stature of Katherine Mansfield, T.S. Eliot, Virginia Woolf, Clive Bell and Roger Fry, and which effectively introduced Freudian thought into England through its 1924 agreement with the International Psycho–Analytical Library[38] — was in fact another paradox. The lower-middle-class Methodist background from which Thompson came would be a world removed ordinarily from the social and literary avant garde represented by the Bloomsbury group. Yet *The Other Side of the Medal* came out just a year after *A Passage to India*. Several reviewers noted the coincidence and even drew certain parallels.[39] Affinities can be noticed, perhaps, between Thompson's plea for improved personal relations and E.M. Forster's philosophy, pithily expressed by 'only connect'.

An explanation of such ambiguities and paradoxes demands situating *The Other Side of the Medal* within the broader context of Thompson's life and writings.

---

[37] Ibid., p. 93.

[38] Leonard Woolf, *Downhill All the Way: An Autobiography of the Years 1919-1937* (London, Hogarth Press, 1967), pp. 64-5, 164-8.

[39] 'A reasoned and analytical statement of what Mr Forster has said imaginatively and individually in his *Passage to India*' was the comment made by the *New Leader* (London) about *The Other Side of the Medal* (4 December 1925). *The Boston Evening Transcript* of 12 June 1926 noted that there was a 'very general willingness to listen to criticism of British rule in India' after that 'strange and eloquent novel', *Passage to India* (Thompson Papers).

II

Not much has been written about Edward Thompson, apart from the brief and rather unsatisfactory entry (by H.M. Margoliouth) in the *Dictionary of National Biography*[40] and an interesting chapter in Benita Parry's *Delusions and Discoveries*.[41] A substantial part of his voluminous publications (sixty-two items in the Bodleian catalogue, according to the *DNB* notice) are difficult to trace in India today. The novels and essays that I have been able to see, however, together with a very incomplete survey of his private papers, do permit a tentative exploration of the life and evolving sensibilities of Thompson·as missionary teacher, poet, historian, novelist and political commentator and activist.

Edward John Thompson (1886-1946) was born of Wesleyan Methodist missionary parents working in South India. His father, the Reverend John Moses, had been the son of a farmer. The family returned to England in 1892, and the death of the father two years later caused considerable financial distress, with the widow and her six children living in conditions of genteel poverty at Stockport and then at Walthamstow. From Kingswood School (then open only to sons of Wesleyan ministers) Edward could have got a university scholarship, but had to earn money instead as a bank clerk in London (1902-7), five miserable years, 'an iron band around a growing tree', as his wife Theodosia described it in her biographical notes for Margoliouth. Together with his friend George Lowther, Edward had become interested in reading and writing poetry and drama, though the Methodist background 'kept them at first from any perception of the modern tides in the literature of their day'. They read William Watson and Kipling's *Just So* stories, but 'nothing of Wells or Shaw or Bennett'. Both Edward and Lowther, in fact, 'were . . . oppressed with a sense almost of wrongdoing in taking pleasure in reading or writing poetry' and the 'most important problem of their lives at first' was how 'to reconcile their passion for poetry with their passion for (Methodist) religion'. Two novels of Thompson written much later, *Introducing the Arnisons* (1935) and *John Arnison* (1939), would be largely autobiographical, with one significant modification: 'There

---

[40] *Dictionary of National Biography, 1941-1950* (OUP, 1959), pp. 879-90. The Thompson Papers contain a long correspondence between H.M. Margoliouth and Thompson's wife, Theodosia, indicating that the latter was very critical in several important respects of the *DNB* entry.

[41] Benita Parry, Chapter v.

were, unfortunately, no such people as Hugh and Thomas, the "pagans", socialistically minded. They were invented to provide an escape from the Ministry. . . .'[42] The tension with inherited Christianity would in some sense persist throughout, and just possibly enter into the brilliant and angry chapter Edward Thompson's son would write one day on the 'moral machinery' of Methodism in *The Making of the English Working Class*.[43]

In 1907 Thompson left the bank to join Richmond College, another Wesleyan foundation. He was ordained in 1910 and went off to join the Wesleyan education mission at Bankura, in the western part of Bengal. Here he served till 1923 (except for work as army chaplain in Mesopotamia during the war) as Principal of the High School, English teacher at Bankura Christian College, and eventually (1920-3) Acting Principal of the College. Theodosia explains this course of events as 'perhaps . . . not so much a religious "call" as an attempt to escape from the constricting life he had known in England'.

'When I was a young man', Thompson wrote many years later, 'the loveliness of India held me, I think few Englishmen know the jungle as well as I do . . . I know its sunsets, I know its dawns, I have loved its rains.'[44] He developed the habit of going out on long cycling trips through the jungle and uplands of Bankura with his friend Arthur Spencer, who lived forty miles away in a Santal village. Spencer served as a partial prototype of Findlay of his novels *An Indian Day* (1927) and *Farewell to India* (1931). Vivid sketches of the countryside of Bengal came to constitute some of the most memorable passages of his novels with an Indian setting.

In 1911 Thompson started learning Bengali and soon developed a deep interest in Bengali literature. The *DNB* entry claims that

[42] The quotations in this paragraph are from the notes prepared for H.M. Margoliouth by Theodosia Thompson (herself, incidentally, the daughter of an an American Presbyterian missionary in Lebanon) in 1951-2. Unfortunately I have not been able to get hold of copies of the Aarnison novels.

[43] 'From the outset the Wesleyans fell ambiguously between Dissent and the Establishment, and did their utmost to make the worst of both worlds, serving as apologists for an authority in whose eyes they were an object of ridicule or condescension, but never of trust. . . . In his theology, Wesley appears to have dispensed with the best and selected unhesitatingly the worst elements of Puritanism. . . .' E.P. Thompson, *The Making of the English Working Class* (London, 1963, 1980), pp. 385, 398.

[44] Edward Thompson, *Enlist India for Freedom!* (Victor Gollancz, London, August 1940), p. 89.

'he understood Bengali poetry better than any other Englishman', and from 1923 to 1933 he would be teaching Bengali to ICS probationers at Oxford. Acquaintance — and a somewhat uncertain friendship — with Rabindranath Tagore began in 1913, together with closer connections with some of the poet's younger admirers, most notably Prasanta Chandra Mahalanobis, who became a lifelong friend. Other prominent Bengali intellectuals became friends or acquaintances — men of the stature of Brojendranath Seal and Dineshchandra Sen. Thompson brought out two volumes of translations of Bengali religious lyrics, Vaishnava and Sakta (1923), and an admiring, though not uncritical, biography of Rabindranath (1921-6) which hailed him as 'India's greatest poet since Kalidas'. The praise was not fulsome enough, however, to satisfy either Rabindranath or his associates, who had grown accustomed to a far more extravagant language of 'universal poet' and 'Gurudeva' — a product, perhaps, of an inverted inferiority complex bred by colonialism.

Admiration for the natural beauty and literature of Bengal and some personal friendships did not initially involve any noticeable sympathy for Indian political aspirations. 'When I first came out, I was a pukka John Bull. You ask my earliest students' — the Vishnugram missionary college teacher Alden recalls this in *A Farewell to India* (1931), and an Indian friend describes him elsewhere in the novel as 'perpetuating the tradition of paternalism. Graciously interested in the folk and their ways, touched by their poetry.'[45] Such passages are clearly autobiographical, at least in part, while Thompson's early letters from Bankura reveal a quite uninhibited and pejorative use of stereotypes like 'babu' and 'sedition'. What particularly irritated him was the babu showing off his European learning. There is an angry letter about a pupil quoting Latin back at him, and even in his later, much more pro-Indian novels Thompson could not resist occasional crude jokes about Indian students, clerks and magistrates mispronouncing English poetry.[46]

Yet Thompson could be equally caustic about Englishmen mispronouncing Indian words and displaying their colossal ignorance about Indian culture. Katherine Mayo's assertion in her *Mother India*

---

[45] Edward Thompson, *A Farewell to India* (London, 1931), pp. 89, 118.

[46] Thompson Papers; *An Indian Day* (London, 1927), p. 63, *A Farewell to India*, pp. 7-11. Alden and Findlay, the two principal pro-Indian characters in the novels, constantly play the fool at meetings chaired by the Indian civilian Neogyi, whose pompousness makes him an irresistible butt to them.

(1927) that 'little or no current literature exists available or of interest to the masses' in India made him very angry indeed,[47] and from the early 1920s he spent much of his time trying to reduce the dead weight of such ignorance and prejudice through translations of Bengali literature, traditional as well as modern, plays based on Indian tales, and historical works. Terms like 'pukka John Bull' or 'paternalism' hardly indicate the range of complexities here.

The Bankura experience was crucial for Thompson, creating a set of ambiguities and tensions within him which persisted — though with major shifts — throughout his life. The enterprise he was engaged in was inherently contradictory: spreading (in theory) European enlightenment and (hopefully) Christianity in a far-off district town, creating in practice a hybrid babu social grouping which alternated between servility and sedition, ill-paid clerical jobs and nationalist politics. Thompson was equally irritated by his English companions — the small-town European station and its narrow-minded, self-satisfied Methodist missionaries. The petulance and anger provoked by work in such a factory of babuism found vent at times in sallies against Indians who were in fact its more-or-less dependent victims. Thompson could communicate easily with the Indian intellectual elite — Tagore, Sapru, Nehru — but hardly with the rank-and-file cadres of middle-class nationalism, bred often by the educational system which he despised and yet was working for till his departure from India. He loved the Indian countryside, was attracted by the evidence he found of the rich indigenous culture of rural folk[48] — but here the barriers were even more formidable. A letter of February 1913 vividly and frankly recounts the fear so often generated by a British presence among villagers, and the irritation this at times aroused in Thompson himself: 'These peasants, if you ask them the way, stare and then bolt. One man I managed to catch. He worshipped me with hands orthodoxly folded, but told me nothing. Only great grace kept me from biffing him. . . .'[49]

[47] Edward Thompson's review of Katherine Mayo's *Mother India* in *Bookman*, 30 July 1927 (Thompson Papers).

[48] Thus Thompson's introduction to *Bengali Religious Lyrics: Sakta* (London, 1923) noted that Ramprasad's songs could be 'heard from coolies on the road or workers in the paddy-fields', and recalled that in his Bankura class of 40 highschool students, 38 would write down a Ramprasad whereas only 2 knew any song by Rabindranath (p. 19).

[49] Thompson to Canton, 10 February 1913, quoted in Benita Parry, p. 168.

Service as army chaplain in Mesopotamia and Palestine came to Thompson as a welcome interruption from the tedium and isolation of small-town mission work and teaching.[50] The real transition began with Jallianwallabagh, or, more precisely, with the subsequent hysterical whitewashing and eulogizing of Dyer. In a letter to his close friend P.C. Lyon dated 20 July 1920,[51] Thompson gave vent to his deep sense of isolation: 'As for my own countrymen, I am ashamed of them. . . . The women have been the worst . . . what happens to my countrywomen out here?' Yet the Indians remain 'hopeless for confabulation': the *Englishman* is too contemptible for words, but Thompson can see no difference between it and the nationalist *Amrita Bazar Patrika*. He had just made, rather hesitantly, his first direct political intervention, helping to draft a 'missionary manifesto' critical of the Hunter Report which had so alienated Indian public opinion. The letter shows him rather nervous as to whether he had not been 'a fool for butting in' — 'I am held up to reprobation as "unBritish", full of "maudlin sentimentality". . . . At present Andrews and I seem the two most unpopular Englishmen in India.' Lyon's praise for the statement — 'You must consider how it helped the moderate Indian section'[52] — comforted Thompson considerably. By October 1920 he had gone to the other extreme: 'Yes, our manifesto did a most surprising amount of good. I am cock-certain it was the deciding charge in the battle.' Thompson derived equal satisfaction from two assertions he now confidently made: 'Gandhi has lost his battle, just as decidedly as the Dyerites lost theirs.'[53]

Thompson proved a poor prophet. In October 1920 India was on the eve of the massive Non-Cooperation–Khilafat upsurge, while the racist attitudes he had labelled Dyerism were intensified in the early and mid 1920s by the panic followed by partial relief when

[50] 'the isolation and pettiness of the life he had lived all his days — strict Methodism, the Bank, the mission college . . . was broken into by the much more real and human life of the men of his age that he met at the front.' Theodosia Thompson to H.M. Margoliouth, 11 March 1952. Thompson, however, Theodosia adds in the same letter, would have hated 'to have to kill.'

[51] P.C. Lyon had been a top British official in Bengal during the days of the anti-Partition agitation, notorious in nationalist circles for the 'Lyon Circular' threatening disciplinary measures against student activists. Thompson became his friend from 1916 onwards. In 1920, Lyon, now living in Oxford, was fairly critical of the way the Punjab disturbances had been handled: 'surely we managed things better in Bengal?' Lyon to Thompson, 13 June (Thompson Papers).

[52] Lyon to Thompson, 5 October 1920. Ibid.

[53] Thompson to Lyon, 27 October 1920 (Thompson Papers).

Gandhi called off the movement in February 1922. 'At Amritsar strong action had already been taken, bringing relief to thousands of both races. . . . Martial law arrangements are being carried through to admiration . . . bullets not buckshot. . . . Its the only argument for crowds' — declared Maud Diver's hero Lane Desmond in her novel *Far to Seek* (1920).[54] Al Carthill's *The Lost Dominion* (1924) went even further: 'We are here as representatives of Christ and Caesar to maintain this land against Shiva and Khalifa . . . if you agitate, you will be punished; if you preach sedition, you will be imprisoned; if you assassinate, you will be hanged; if you rise, you will be shot down.' Carthill was particularly severe about Indophile 'mugwumps', the British 'sentimentalists and subversives' for whom 'racialism, patriotism, respect for national honour are anathema. . . .'

It was perhaps wrong to say of these extremists that they thought it a sin to kiss a white girl's mouth, and a virtue to kiss a black man's . . . foot. But it is perhaps no exaggeration to say that their humanity never slumbered save when an Englishman was murdered, or an Englishwoman violated by a negro or an Asiatic.[55]

The Other Side of the Medal contains direct references to Maud Diver and Al Carthill.[56] Contemporary experience and Mutiny literature evidently intermingled in Thompson's mind as he started work on his first historical theme. The sequence of cruel deeds justified by a kind of muscular Christianity seemed all but identical in both cases. Before he actually got down to writing about the Mutiny, however, a major change had taken place in Thompson's personal life. In 1923 he resigned from the Bankura Mission, returned to England, and settled down at Oxford as Lecturer in Bengali (1923-33) and then as Oriel College research fellow in Indian history (1936-46).

At one level, the 1923 break may be regarded as a resolution of the Methodism/literature inner conflict which had plagued Thompson from his adolescent days. He could find more time for literature now, becoming, according to Margoliouth, 'the only notable English poet of Indian scenery and of the Mesopotamian and Palestine campaigns' and bringing out *Collected Poems* (1930), *New Recessional*

---

54 Quoted in Greenberger, pp. 94-5, and Benita Parry, p. 91.
55 'Al Carthill', *The Lost Dominion*, 5th impression (London, 1924), pp. 72-3, 88, 236-7.
56 *The Other Side of the Medal*, pp. 114-17.

(1943), and *Hundred Poems* (1944) apart from a number of novels and plays. Yet, as his wife rightly emphasized in her critical comments on Margoliouth's biographical entry, there is a need to recall 'how much time and energy Edward put, rightly or wrongly, into political activity, how divided his energies were', how often 'his political activity . . . took him away from poetry.'[57] For 1923, to Thompson, did not mean a break from Indian concerns, but its reverse; the break was with the narrowness of life in an European mofussil station with its dominant racist assumptions, and the more unimaginative kinds of missionary endeavour.

Thompson's writings on Indian themes after leaving Bankura took several distinct forms, and none of these, considered singly, can give the full measure of the complexity of his shifting attitudes. Direct political interventions — among which it seems appropriate to include *The Other Side of the Medal*, despite its historical form — include *The Reconstruction of India* (1930), *A Letter from India* (1932) and *Enlist India for Freedom* (1940). Then there is the trilogy of novels set in contemporary India: *An Indian Day* (1927), *A Farewell to India* (1931), and *An End of the Hours* (1938) — as well as the lesser known but significant play *Atonement* (1924), dealing directly with Non-Cooperation, in which both Gandhi and Andrews appear under the thinnest of disguises. A third strand reveals Thompson grappling with varied dimensions of Indian culture and religion — studies of Rabindranath, two volumes of translations of Bengali religious lyrics, *Krishnakumari* (1924), *Three Eastern Plays* (1927), *Suttee* (1928), and *Youngest Disciple* (1938), a novel offering an unorthodox version of Buddhism. And finally there were the historical works on British India: the *Rise and Fulfilment* textbook (1934), followed by the *Life of Metcalfe* (1937) and *Making of Indian Princes* (1943), two solid pieces of research which also reveal a growing fascination and empathy with the generation of Metcalfe, Malcolm and Elphinstone.

It is important, I think, to note how often political and religious self-questioning ran together in Thompson's mind.[58] 'Yes, our Christianity was a bad brand', Thompson writes to another liberal Wesleyan missionary on 26 June 1924, defending his decision to go ahead with publishing his *Other Side of the Medal*, despite the 'fear', evidently expressed by his friend, 'of telling

[57] Theodosia Thompson to H.M. Margoliouth, 11 March 1952 (Thompson Papers).

[58] I feel that both Margoliouth's sketch and the much better analysis by Benita Parry miss out on this dimension.

Indians more than they know already and so stirring up more hatred'.

The Punjab Govt. from first to last has been marked by self-righteousness and hardness. . . . You say the chief result, in yr mind, has been a realization of how imperfect our conception of Xty has been. Well, for me it has been an increasingly indignant taking of the Indian side. You & I hitherto have both been v. distinct moderates, and have had little to do with the left wing . . . the Andrews and Kingsley Williamses. But now I'm becoming a left-winger pretty fast, and I feel how patronizing nearly all our propaganda, political and religious and educational, must seem to an Indian. . . .[59]

And again, three years later, in the context of a rejoinder from the historian T. Rice Holmes concerning *The Other Side of the Medal*:

The truth is, India is now the one subject on which there is a body of orthodox doctrine, which every decent person is assumed necessarily to hold. . . . His (Holmes') school seems to be like the Fundamentalists who *have* to support every deed ascribed to the Old Testament Deity; they dare not admit error or imperfection, because they are always thinking of the effect on Indian opinion. I have ceased to care to do good to Indians, except in so far as it is a by-product in the effort to clear my own mind, so far as I can. I think religion has gained by our minds being set free to examine it; and I think our record in India, and Indian history will both gain if we are freed here also. . . .[60]

Atonement is the central theme of the June 1924 letter to E.W. Thompson: 'And why does Andrews keep hammering about the necessity of doing *prayashchitta?* . . . I don't seem to have got home to you how deeply I feel about the matter. It's obsessed me of recent months. I've thought of v. little else. . . . I'd like, as an individual Englishman, to do my bit of *prayashchitta*, if I c'd.' *Atonement* was the title of a play Thompson published in 1924, portraying the small English community of 'Durgapur', 'an up-country town in Bengal' — police superintendent, district judge, missionary college principal, labour recruiting agent, their wives — caught up 'next year — or, possibly, this year' in a mass non-cooperation movement which turns violent, kills a white officer, and is then shot down: 'We've done it now, and it had to be done.

---

[59] Thompson to E.W. Thompson, 26 June 1924. E.P. Thompson told me that this correspondent of his father was not a relative, but served as godfather to the younger Edward (born 1924) (Thompson Papers).

[60] E.J. Thompson's letter to *Saturday Review* (London), 18 June 1927 (ibid.).

Of course there were children.'[61] The links with *The Other Side of the Medal* are obvious enough. Indian violence, embodied in the firebrand Inayat Khan, is related to Mutiny memories in the most direct way possible. Inayat's father had been blown from a gun in 1857: 'You hanged and blew to pieces and burnt, and you called it righteous vengeance. Your books still call it righteous vengeance.'[62] The play, however, ends on a relatively optimistic note. 'England has got to repent for all her injustice. Then there will be peace',[63] declares the ex-missionary Thorpe (clearly modelled on Andrews), who has joined the nationalists. The sentiment is comfortingly echoed by the Gandhi-like figure of the Indian leader Ranade who rebukes the violent elements in his own movement and predicts that the present conflicts will end 'when atonement has been made'.[64] *Atonement* did, however, have other dimensions, not conveyed by its title (nor by Benita Parry's rather dismissive summary),[65] and Thompson had some justification in feeling that it went 'far deeper and wider than the *Medal*'.[66] We will have occasion to look at it once more, along with the Indian trilogy.

Atonement, relevant for Thompson primarily as the constituent of a lifelong quest for human communication across the colonial divide, could be no more than an ambiguous and limited concept to tackle the problem of colonial political oppression. In a letter written soon after the publication of *The Other Side of the Medal*, we find Thompson in a different, much more defensive and less attractive mood. S.K. Ratcliffe, like E.W. Thompson the year before, had expressed concern about the book providing 'ammunition' to extremists.[67] Thompson now agrees that 'publication was a great risk ... the real risk, as you see, is the effect on Indian and American opinion.' He justifies himself partly by the argument that Savarkar was being read secretly anyway by Indians in England and America, and that he had come to know about inflammatory material on 1857 which 'had fallen into the hands of an implacable group in India and were

[61] *Atonement* (London, 1924), p. 82. The comment is being made by Gregory, 'Principal, Baptist Missionary College'.

[62] Inayat Khan, in ibid., p. 107.

[63] Ibid., p. 76.

[64] Ibid., p. 109.

[65] Parry feels that the play has little literary merit, and contents herself with noticing the obvious anticipations of *The Other Side of the Medal* — Benita Parry, pp. 179–80.

[66] Thompson to S.K. Ratcliffe, 15 December 1925 (Thompson Papers).

[67] S.K. Ratcliffe to Thompson, 14 December 1925 (ibid.).

going to be published. I thought it better that an Englishman and a moderate should forestall this.' To Ratcliffe, who was going to the USA, he suggested a series of arguments to block any anti-British use of the book: 'anyone with imagination can understand the desperate savagery of the English trapped in the Mutiny'; 'it was just a wild madness on both sides . . . a repetition is impossible today'; 'Indian propaganda in America is a pretty dishonest thing'; 'many Indians do not want us to clear out as fast as we are doing; it is their self-respect they want back, and lots of them care nothing about political measures'. Thompson in fact appears deeply worried about his new reputation as a radical Indophile. 'The respectable press', he alleges, 'is pretending the book doesn't exist. . . . And so — owing to the silence of the respectable and religious papers — the book is becoming . . . an extremist manifesto.'[68]

The reviews of *The Other Side of the Medal* preserved in Thompson's papers indicate that he was not being entirely fair to the British press. The unimpeachably 'respectable and religious' *Methodist Recorder* (London) welcomed it 'as a necessary making of amends',[69] and the qualified praise of the *Times Literary Supplement* indicates the relative ease with which an intelligent conservatism could accommodate Thompson.

So far we are in general agreement with Mr Thompson: but it seems to us that he exaggerates the degree in which the recollection of the mutiny still affects our relations with Indians. . . . The events of 1919 reawakened those memories: but our emphatic condemnation of the idea of holding India by frightfulness and the steady manner in which political power has been transferred . . . into Indian hands have done much to allay that feeling in soberer minds.[70]

Both reviews had come out before the letter to Ratcliffe: clearly Thompson's doubts came much more from within himself. He had made his grand gesture of atonement and was for the moment at peace with his conscience. A slide back towards more conventional attitudes was perhaps not surprising.

The slide continues through the next round of Thompson's

---

[68] S.K. Ratcliffe, 15 December 1925. The reference to 'inflammatory material', the use of which Thompson the moderate Englishman had pre-empted, is rather puzzling. The data used in *The Other Side of the Medal* were all taken from published books, many quite well known, and Indian nationalists would have had no real problem in getting legitimate access to this literature.

[69] *Methodist Recorder*, 12 November 1925 (Thompson Papers).

[70] *Times Literary Supplement*, 5 November 1925 (ibid.).

political writings about India, from 1927 to 1932. In *The Reconstruction of India* (1930) Dominion Status (not independence) is acknowledged as 'India's right', but is immediately sought to be made conditional on a long 'process of training'. 'Good administration', Thompson argued, was the key need of a

country of 'little people', of peasants and petty industrialists . . . in most cases, when an Indian takes over from a British official, there is loss of efficiency, and . . . this represents a real loss to the common man. I think it would have been better, far better, if Indian self-respect had been so conciliated that Indians would now be willing to let the transference be less hurried than it seems inevitable it must be.

Gestures of 'good faith and intention', he hopes, could still lead to 'an end of all the nonsense of fixing a definite date for everything to be settled', to an extension for some time more of the essential British role of 'service and guidance'.[71]

Thompson met Gandhi in London during the Round Table Conference of 1931 and arranged a meeting for him at his Oxford home with some British politicians.[72] In the early months of 1932, while the second civil disobedience movement was being brutally suppressed, Thompson visited India as the special correspondent of *Manchester Guardian*. The Congress had been driven underground, and Thompson's political contacts with Indians during this visit were mainly with Jayakar, Malaviya, Munje, 'and other cooperating politicians', apart from one rather acrimonious encounter with Mira Behn. *A Letter from India*, which he published after his return, did condemn censorship and arbitrary arrests and plead for renewal of negotiation. But all this was heavily counterbalanced by condemnation of the Congress as 'an insolent and intolerant faction', of its methods as no longer genuinely non-violent,[73] and of picketings as 'an incongruous alliance of bazaar women, ladies just emerged from purdah, and girls between 6 and 10 years of age'. Gandhi at the Round Table Conference emerged as 'a *bunia* in close alliance with other *bunias*' ('Huckster will give the meaning', Thompson added in a footnote), the Hijli jail shooting was justified, and 'if

71 Quotations from *Are Indians Fit for Self-Government*, in Thompson, *The Reconstruction of India* (London, 1930), pp. 260-1, 278.

72 Hugh Tinker, *Ordeal of Love* (Delhi, 1979), p. 251.

73 Thompson's sudden concern for non-violence is interesting. His attitudes at other times (during the World Wars, for instance) show little sympathy for *ahimsa* or pacifism.

ever reprisals were understandable the Chittagong ones were.'[74]
Thompson seemed to have second thoughts even about Jallianwallabagh. On the strength of a dinner-table reminiscence by the
Amritsar Deputy Commissioner, who informed him that Dyer did
not know that there was no way out of the place and had spent
many sleepless nights after the massacre, Thompson now argued
that Jallianwallabagh 'was the scene of a mistake, and not of
calculated brutality'.[75] It may or may not have been an accident
that the title-page of *A Letter from India* gave a long list of
Thompson's books but omitted *The Other Side of the Medal*.

If all this seems to indicate a singular failure of perception and
empathy during a peak point of mass nationalism and British
repression, a return almost to pukka sahib attitudes, a somewhat
different and much more interesting Thompson emerges from the
two novels he published during these years, *An Indian Day* (1927)
and *A Farewell to India* (1931). As Benita Parry has argued, the novels
are shot through with 'doubts and antipathies which run counter
to his formulated ideas'; at times Thompson seems to be 'devaluing'
the pronouncements 'he himself made in his expository writings'.[76]

Ambiguity, as always in Thompson, is one recurrent theme of
these novels. As with Forster, Orwell, and other writers of this 'era
of doubt', his sympathetic Englishmen — Alden, Findlay, Hamar
— are the antithesis of the earlier manly, martial, 'overgrown public
schoolboy' stereotype.[77] *An Indian Day* begins with Hamar, a civilian
transferred for acquitting Indians in a conspiracy case, meeting his
'athletic Philistine opposite' on the train to Vishnugram, a young
soldier who judges mofussil stations by their proximity to 'that
sine qua non of British bliss, things to kill'.[78] There is a savage
description of the typical memsahib, Mrs Nixon, complaining that

[74] Thompson, *A Letter from India* (London, 1932), pp. 17, 21, 38, 40-1.
Political prisoners had been shot down inside jail at Hijli, and at Chittagong
there had been large-scale beating-up of nationalist sympathizers by whites and
Muslims together after a Muslim police officer had been killed by revolutionaries. See Tanika Sarkar, 'Communal Riots in Bengal', in Mushirul Hasan,
ed., *Communal and Pan-Islamic Trends in Colonial India* (December 1981).

[75] *What Happened at Jallianwallabagh*, in ibid., pp. 102-4.

[76] Benita Parry, pp. 186, 191.

[77] Greenberger, pp. 6, 12, 85.

[78] Thompson, *An Indian Day* (London, May 1927), p. 8. The passage brings
to mind Orwell's brilliant exposé of army mentalities: 'Eleven years of it, not
counting the War, and never killed a man. Depressing!' (*Burmese Days*, 1935,
cited in Greenberger, p. 86.)

the Government squandered money on the education of natives 'but left its officials without a stone wall to their compound', and recalling with pleasure how she had once hit with a catapult a servant carrying boiling stew for her.[79] The 'European station . . . chattered and quarrelled, quarrelled and chattered',[80] and Alden and Findlay sought solace through long trips through the jungle and uplands. And yet: 'How repellent and how attractive he was' thought Hamar about the brash young soldier on the train, while Major Henderson, another fellow passenger, 'spoke of Indians . . . as if their presence on the planet distressed him physically', and 'yet . . . bought every book about India . . . patiently went on pilgrimage to even the lesser sights'.[81] The Chief Secretary of the province had the habit of publicly smacking errant Indian *durwans*, but remained 'the fieriest, most generous, best-loved man in India'.[82] The average educated Indian remains extremely unattractive and comic: 'half-baked babus, cringing, insolent, seditious, wholly unprimitive except in their personal habits and sanitation.' Magistrates and clerks misquote and mispronounce the English classics, and the local elections 'ended, as they began, in farce'.[83] Hamar's pro- Indian decision had been based on an abstract sense of justice alone, and, encountering later a group of terrorists caught redhanded, he briefly admits to himself that 'they were doing only what Bruce and William Tell and Washington had done', but goes on to sentence them with a clear conscience: 'As long as the Raj existed, its business was to prevent violence, and its laws had to be enforced.'[84]

The ambiguities lead on to a second, deeper, level: they are sought to be reconciled in Thompson's structure of feeling through the persistent model of unimaginative, aloof, and tactless Englishmen — officials and missionaries alike — selflessly doing their job and efficiently serving the poor: 'administrating the affairs of myriads evenly and firmly — administering them with an utter lack of perception of what was in the minds of a subject populace . . . if you like, doing his magnificent work like a damned fool — but has the world ever seen such glorious damned fools? Has it ever seen such stupidity yoked with such patience, watchfulness, courage,

[79] *An Indian Day*, pp. 22–3.
[80] Ibid., p. 11.
[81] Ibid., pp. 13, 15.
[82] Ibid., p. 10.
[83] Ibid., pp. 11, 63, 92.
[84] Ibid., p. 206.

boundless capacity for work, indifference to pain and discomfort?'[85] The best of missionary work, similarly, lay not in preaching or conversion, but in social service, as Findlay does among the village poor during a famine: 'with these thousands of grown-up babies all around you, you can't be snug at home. . . . He would get his job done, for this is the religion of the English.'[86]

The contradictions and doubts persist, however, for Alden recalls that the Punjab's 'curse from the very first . . . has been, and is, self-righteousness. . . . There are too many folk loose in India who imagine they are God Almighty' — attitudes that had led up to the Mutiny and Amritsar.[87] His Indian friend, Sadhu Jayananda, reminds him that what vexed Indians most were 'your nobly moral aims. The way you have persuaded yourself that the Empire is just a magnificent philanthropic institution, disinterestedly run for the sake of an ungrateful world.'[88] A parallel questioning goes on in the novel, through Findlay, of missionary presuppositions: 'cliches by the bucketful . . . sand, sand, sand.' The Bishop of Burra–Suppur mouths platitudes in his Sunday sermons while 'a gaunt, spectral mob' of beggars moans 'Saheb, saheb' outside the church door. 'There was nothing . . . that so blinds the eyes of the mind as the religious life. John Wesley had said that the world was his parish; and his followers had somehow got it twisted into the notion that the parish should be their world.'[89]

A counterpoint where opposites are reconciled is provided, however, by the forest home of Sadhu Jayananda, where Englishmen (Findlay, Alden and Hamar) and Indians can meet at last as friends. Jayananda, originally Ramsaran Chakravarti, had been educated in England, had joined and then left the ICS, become a leader of the anti-Partition agitation, and then suddenly had left politics to turn *sanyasi* — clear shades of Aurobindo in all this — preaching a message of pantheistic passivity. He assures his English friends: 'you know, we like the individual Englishmen, when he gives us a chance. Gandhi likes him, you know.'[90] Findlay, the missionary who has started questioning the narrowness of conventional Christianity, feels his

85 Ibid., pp. 169-70. The words are Hilda's, the one sympathetic Englishwoman in the novel.
86 Ibid., pp. 198, 233.
87 Ibid., pp. 228-9.
88 Ibid., p. 226.
89 Ibid., pp. 73-4, 138-9, 211.
90 Ibid., pp. 224.

attraction strongly ('Confess, missionary. You'e half a Vedantist') and is torn by the apparent conflict of the religion of job, duty and social service and that of mystic self-surrender. The novel ends on a note of optimism and East-West reconciliation. Racked by a sense of guilt after his wife and daughter die while he is busy with famine relief, Findlay finds mystic consolation in the forest: 'Insensibly the oneness and unity of the world was flinging its comfort about him.'[91] He recalls St Francis' Canticle of All Created Things — 'I thank Thee for my brother the sun' — and is united with the sanyasi: a coming together of Siva and Christ. Meanwhile, as a spring storm breaks over Vishnugram, the Englishmen take shelter in a covered veranda and gossip, but Hamar goes out into the forest to meet and win Hilda, and together they run, hand in hand, 'for the shelter of the temple'.[92]

A hopeful and rather fine ending, though situated, significantly, outside normal society; but the optimism proved shortlived. An atmosphere of brooding fear and gloom hovers around *A Farewell to India* (January 1931). The cast and the locale are the same, but the time is 1929-30, the eve of Civil Disobedience (Thompson is very meticulous about dates in this novel), and Alden finds Indian faces full of 'evasion, dislike, resentment, or often, venomous wrath and hatred. . . . Menace hung over the land like a thundercloud'.[93] Findlay, who has broken away from the mission, still retains a saintly reputation among the poor, and he and Alden remain friends of Jayananda in the forest: 'I have long ago made my peace with you, Alden, and through you and Findlay with your peoples.'[94] But Jayananda himself is threatened and feels outpaced by the times — 'You and I, Alden', said the Sadhu, 'are only onlookers now.'[95] Thompson tries to conflate the threatened Alden-Findlay-Jayananda reconciliation with the problems allegedly faced by Gandhi. Attending a meeting of the Mahatma, Alden recognized that 'Through a human reed, suffering was speaking — not its own, but a nation's. . . . He was troubled, as a man who had loved and honoured this frail human wisp . . . by the undertone of weariness. . . . Behind the speaker were forces of ruin, which he was serving, though aware of them, and anxious to escape them.' 'I wish my people could have

91 Ibid., p. 237.
92 Ibid., p. 244.
93 Thompson, *A Farewell to India* (London, 1931), p. 256.
94 Ibid., p. 240.
95 Ibid., p. 234.

been his friends' and Gandhi's 'eyes, burning in the emaciated face', remind Alden of Findlay.[96]

The threat comes first and most obviously from the revolutionary firebrand Dinabandhu Tarkachudamani, 'out of patience with Gandhi's methods and with all who played with the notion of Dominion Status', who believed that 'the English can be fought down with their own weapons of brutality and murder'. He snubs Alden's talk of 'peaceful partnership' unmercifully. 'Your condescension is your worst insolence of all: . . . Better rivers of blood than a nation with its soul in chains. . . . What sacrifices is England proposing to make? . . . The giving up of booty is not sacrifice. . . . And why . . . is any other than a peaceful solution unthinkable? . . . India has been subjugated by blood, she shall win freedom by blood.'[97] Thompson is certainly at his 'most paradoxical'[98] here, relentlessly doubting his own beliefs and statements, for Alden is 'too appalled and ashamed to say anything', and Findlay tells him that he had 'jawed to Dinabandhu as if we were still in 1925, instead of 1929'.[99]

More interesting, perhaps, is the threat perceived from Indian business groups. The Indian agitation was no longer 'the work of a few half-baked clerks', Jayananda tells his English friends — 'it has drawn in merchants and businessmen who have traffic in every continent. . . . Do you think the new industrialized India is willing to go back to the village and the spinning-wheel? . . . I tell you, Gandhiji has seen something that has frightened him'. . . . 'It has all gone — my dreams and your service. . . .'[100] 'Greed and righteousness' had joined hands, 'big business, especially on the Bombay side' was now backing Gandhi due to the Imperial Preference issue.[101]

There is a deeper level still, fears so deep and dark that Thompson can express them only in clouded and pseudo-mystical language: 'The Ancient Gods were rising from their slumber of decades. . . . I'm beginning to think that there's something elemental in this land, that's in revolt against us . . . bhuts . . . something dull, stupid, brute, malignant, invulnerable, with feet that take hold of

96 Ibid., pp. 144–5.
97 Ibid., pp. 75, 78, 80–1.
98 Benita Parry, p. 191.
99 *A Farewell to India*, p. 82.
100 Ibid., pp. 83, 90–1.
101 Ibid., p. 257.

the very soil. . . .'[102] Some of these passages are occasioned by Hilda's misadventures as benevolent gentlewoman-farmer, trying to improve agriculture by lending high-quality livestock to peasants on a share-cropping basis: the peasants refuse to take on the land offered them, since it had been an old cremation ground. But the incident is surely too trivial to have really occasioned all these fears; nor is Benita Parry's explanation, in terms of a pale imitation of E.M. Forster's Marabar caves, entirely convincing.[103] The peasants never directly appear in the civil disobedience portrayed in *A Farewell to India*, in which students and revolutionaries still occupy the foreground, and yet Thompson, even though writing from a distance, could hardly have been unaware of their crucial importance. The silence seems deliberate, and the fears expressed through deliberately mystified forms — for the greatest threat of all to every type of paternalist self-image was precisely the peasant rising up against the *ma-baap saheb*.

Civilized human relations, achieved precariously across the racial divide in Jayananda's forest home, are thus threatened by a combination of business avarice and elemental plebeian fury — a theme that has associations, incidentally, with a powerful tradition in English literary culture going back to Matthew Arnold's *Culture and Anarchy*, written in the wake of the Hyde Park riots of 1866.[104] In more specific terms, *A Farewell to India* is a significant record — through its hints and silences as much as its direct statements — of a British perception of 1930, compounded out of revolutionary terrorism, student and middle-class unrest, business involvement, and peasant upsurge. Massive peasant involvement, more than anything else, shattered the self-image of the paternalist British official. It challenged the underlying assumptions common to both brands of paternalism; the hard, self-righteous and unimaginative 'Punjab' variety which Thompson had so often attacked, as well as the softer repentant model seeking improved personal relations through atonement which he had been pleading for since Jallianwallabagh.

The resultant emotional and moral crisis could be resolved in two opposite ways, and as usual Thompson seems to straddle both. One reaction was a petulant fury, justifying — or committing — acts

---

[102] Ibid., pp. 96, 117, 119.

[103] Benita Parry, pp. 187, 194.

[104] For a very perceptive analysis, see Raymond Williams, 'A Hundred Years of Culture and Anarchy', in his *Problems of Materialism and Culture* (London, 1980).

of unmitigated repression: Thompson defends the shooting down
of prisoners in jail; an official like Peddie, with an excellent paternalist reputation, hysterically calls for 'more shootings' in the Midnapur countryside in June 1930.[105] Only in terms like these can one
begin to understand the ruthless beating-up of absolutely non-violent
volunteers during the salt satyagraha. Even a total breakdown of the
salt monopoly would not have hurt the colonial government more
than marginally, yet its officials went completely berserk. In *A
Farewell to India*, Hamar is busy working on a commission to codify
repressive legislation, and Alden, now Acting Principal of his college,
tries desperately to maintain discipline through threats of expulsion
while 'an imperious and reckless nationalism ruled the stage jerking
his students back and forth like puppets' . . . 'everyone in India,
British and Indian, seems to have gone hysterical'.[106]

The price of this kind of reaction, however, Thompson realized,
was an intolerable isolation and constant self-doubt. Alden feels that
at Lexington he would have 'fired at the Americans, and then paid
homage to the slain'.[107] 'Intense loneliness' was 'the Englishman's
destiny in India',[108] and at the end of the novel Alden has a major
breakdown and leaves for England. He returns briefly in the final
volume of the trilogy, *An End of the Hours* (1938), a novel dominated
by 'the mood of bereavement, of failure and pierced dreams.'[109]
'Alden's Indian days were all but over, and he knew well that not
even in history would there be a tiny plot left for his name'.[110]

The obverse of this sense of failure, however, is the gradual and
hesitant recognition of the need to go beyond the premises of
paternalism, the slow realization that the English as a ruling caste,
however efficient and/or repentant, could have no place in India,
and that Indians had a right to be free. The significance of the last
decade of Thompson's life lies in the fact that he did come to such
a recognition, becoming, as his son has recalled, 'in his last years,

105 Memorandum from J. Peddie, 13 June 1930, in Government of Bengal
Political FN 430/1930 — cited in my 'The Logic of Gandhian Nationalism,
Civil Disobedience and The Gandhi-Irwin Pact, 1930-31', *Indian Historical
Review*, July 1976.
106 *A Farewell to India*, pp. 42, 273.
107 Ibid., p. 148.
108 Ibid., p. 39.
109 Benita Parry, p. 197. I have not been able to get hold of a copy of this
novel.
110 Quoted in Benita Parry, ibid.

staunchly pro-Congress'.[111] It is this transition which has been largely ignored by Margoliouth's *DNB* entry — about which Thompson's widow complained, rightly, that it would make future readers 'think of Edward as a man who though he considered India ripe for self-government did little about it beyond writing the *The Other Side of the Medal*'[112] — and missed out also in Benita Parry.

The roots of the choice Thompson made in the 1930s go back to some of the writings other than the political essays and novels. It may be a bit dangerous to identify Thompson too completely with Alden, or even Alden-Findlay, for the trilogy conveys little of its author's deep involvement — much more than 'gracious interest' — in Indian history and culture and occasional sympathetic understanding of Indian nationalism.

Atonement, as I have briefly hinted, in some ways went deeper than *An Indian Day* (or certainly *A Farewell to India*), perhaps because it was written before the years of Thompson's partial slide-back into more conventional attitudes after *The Other Side of the Medal*. The setting of the play is similar to that of his Indian novels: evening in a tiny British upcountry outpost in Bengal, a listless tennis party, Mrs Lomax the 'police memsahib' complaining endlessly about Indian servants who 'are trying to cheat us *all* the time, *all* the time' — and wondering why the mission college had failed to produce 'really good Christian servants'.[113] As in *An Indian Day*, again, there is a rather ridiculous Indian district officer, jokes about Indian English, a prototype of Alden in the mission college Principal Gregory, and a kind of impartial flaying of both sides: 'We're all mad, Banerjee — you folk bragging of your spirituality and we of our general nobleness.'[114] The conversation between district judge Walsh, Gregory, and Thorpe in the second act rehearses the dialogue between efficiency/atonement which would be repeated in the novels. But the Indian characters attain a credibility never achieved later by Thompson. There is Inayat Khan, seeking a bloody vengeance for Mutiny wrongs, and his fellow extremist Basantakumar Chatterji, nursing bitter memories of insult and patronizing praise from his

[111] E.P. Thompson, 'The Nehru Tradition', in *Writing by Candlelight* (London, 1980), p. 138.

[112] Theodosia Thompson to H.M. Margoliouth, 11 March 1952 (Thompson Papers).

[113] *Atonement*, pp. 16, 32. Mrs Lomax obviously foreshadows Mrs Nixon of *An Indian Day*.

[114] Ibid., p. 36.

Oxford days: 'When people wanted to be generous to us at Oxford, it was always "How well you Indians learn to speak English".'[115] The local Non-Cooperation leader is Nagendranath Singh, an ex-mission college teacher, while Saratchandra Datta, in some ways the Indian counterpart of Gregory, resigns his college job to join the nationalists, having realized suddenly the mundane motives behind his earlier loyalist self-justifications: 'Yes, I was afraid. I have a family to support, and I should be penniless if I gave up my work. . . . I suddenly saw something. I forgot to keep my eyes shut. Goodbye, Sir.'[116]

The real strength and interest of the play lies in the way Thompson uses the Indian characters, along with Thorpe who has joined them, to point out the problems and inconsistencies of Gregory. Gregory is certainly part-Thompson, but any complete identification of the author with this mission college principal is clearly impossible. He tells Sarat that 'All these years I've been trying to get at what you people really do think and feel. I've read your literature, I've studied your religion'[117] — and he has an abstract sympathy for the patriotism of his students: 'Wouldn't *you* be a nationalist, in their place?'[118] Yet, when the crisis comes with Lomax's murder: 'We're just Englishmen now, and we've got to do our job', Gregory shoots down the mob along with other Englishmen.[119] The prisoner Basanta taunts him, as a missionary using a gun,[120] while throughout the play Nagen mercilessly exposes the flaws in his arguments. Student strikes harm education — 'But you have often said that the education we get is a sham.' Young men should not be asked to disobey their parents — but 'He that loveth father or mother more than Me is not worthy of Me. . . . Were not the earliest Christians called those who had turned the whole world upside down?'[121] British rule has brought 'Peace, abundance, the world's markets' — to which Nagen responds: 'The kingdoms of the world and their lordship. Only fall down and worship me.'[122]

The solution the play offers is at one level a rather easy, even trite, reconciliation. After Inayat Khan's revelation about 1857 and

115 Ibid., p. 99.
116 Ibid., pp. 56-7.
117 Ibid., p. 47.
118 Ibid., p. 20.
119 Ibid., p. 77.
120 Ibid., p. 85.
121 Ibid., pp. 52-3.
122 Ibid., p. 92.

the entry of Ranade–Gandhi, Walsh releases the prisoners and resigns his job, Gregory throws away his gun (and decides to give up shikar), and Ranade wants to shake hands all around. Yet the second and third acts occasionally go much further and attain a level of perception and analysis seldom attained by Thompson elsewhere. The doubts and self-analysis of Thorpe (Andrews) are particularly interesting, for they indicate how atonement can go beyond the limits of paternalism. Thorpe recalls — as something that is *past*, that 'I was proud that I was a missionary. . . . I really was keen on mediating between my own race and Indians. . . . High officials used to consult me. When I went to Simla, I always stayed at Viceregal Lodge. . . .'[123] In those days, 'everything was so simple. There were the Church's sacraments and means of grace. . . . Just a good, straight-ahead motor-road. . . . But . . . I fancy Christ picked His way through swamps and jungles often enough, in Galilee.'[124] The problem was that 'I seemed to take it for granted that I was entitled to talk to Indians as if they were a class I was instructing for confirmation'.[125] The solution Thorpe has found in the play — probably going some way beyond the real-life Andrews — is not mediation but complete identification with Gandhian nationalism, warts and all. Gregory had complained that the Indian cause was just, but its adherents often ignoble: 'venomous, cowardly, lying journalists . . . double-faced pleaders . . . babyish and treacherous students. . . .'[126] Thorpe's reply is one of the best passages in the play:

We never think these words apply to us — 'He that denieth Me'. We imagine a grand, brave figure facing his enemies. . . . But it doesn't happen so. . . . Usually it's negroes singing hymns and chicken-stealing — or it's illiterate and bigoted village Non-Conformists — or rabbit-brained High Church idiots — or envious, half-educated Bengali oafs . . . the treasures in earthen vessels, truly, and the vessels are rarely decently clean.[127]

Such identification implied a political break, not reconciliation through gestures alone: and there are some hints about that, too, in the play, foreshadowing Thompson's last years rather than the

123 Ibid., pp. 69–70.
124 Ibid., p. 71.
125 Ibid., p. 72.
126 Ibid., p. 67.
127 Ibid., p. 75.

novels. 'Heaps of officials are clearing out now', comments Gregory in the last act,[128] and Nagen had earlier predicted that he and Gregory could be colleagues again, but only after independence: 'We do not want to get rid of Englishmen, but only of the English Government.'[129] Walsh wants to 'chuck this governing trade. Why is it you can't stay a gentleman if you once start standing over other people'?[130] And Thorpe points out that whitewashing of atrocities like those of 1857, Amritsar, and the asphyxiation of Moplah prisoners in 1921, . . . can't be avoided, so long as you have one race ruling another'.[131]

Atonement also contains some interesting comments about gender relations and identities, dimensions in which Thompson's trilogy is extremely weak. The racism of the average Englishwoman in India is pitilessly exposed, but there is a hint of a connection here with the boredom and suppressed tensions bred by separate spheres: the men after dinner tell 'manly' shikar stories to each other, the women complain about servants.[132] Thompson's ambiguity about the stereotype of the masculine, evident in the opening chapter of *An Indian Day* (and by implication in the entire efficiency–atonement tension), is extended in the play to partly Westernized Indian males in their relations with Englishmen and their own women. Sarat recalls that Gregory, who could sympathize even with the cult of Kali, was repelled by the stories of Krishna and Radha:

Yet that moves us Bengalis more passionately than any other story . . . we *are* effeminate — yes, there *is* more of the woman than of the man in us — and so we put ourselves — we put the whole nation — in the place of Radha . . . (bitterly). We are fools, and we have fallen long ago in love with the English spirit, which is so hard and masculine and — so contemptuous of us. . . . I begin to see that there is more justice in the world than I thought. We have always refused freedom to our women

128 Ibid., p. 121.
129 Ibid., p. 55.
130 Ibid., p. 88.
131 Ibid., p. 64.
132 Mrs Walsh (sarcastically): 'I wouldn't have them disturbed for our sake. Their conversation is far more enthralling than merely talking to a couple of ladies, . . . They are men, remember. . . . Who started this system of herding us off by ourselves? And what's the idea behind it, now that practically every woman smokes?'
   Mrs Gregory: 'I fancy the idea is that we can exchange notes about our dirzis, while the men make arrangements for the next shoot.' Ibid., pp. 117, 119.

for the very reasons for which it is now being refused to us — because they are emotional, swayed by their passions and loyalties, and cannot be calm and collected.[133]

The references to Gregory reacting to the Krishna–Radha tradition can serve as a bridge to what was, after all, the central Indian concern of Thompson: the problem of personal and cultural communication across the colonial–racial divide. Appreciating Rabindranath was not too difficult, but the introduction to *Bengali Religious Lyrics* (1923), the plays with Indian themes of the mid 1920s, the comments on Katherine Mayo's *Mother India* (1927-8), and *Suttee* (1928) show Thompson grappling with the much greater challenge posed by aspects of Hindu culture which could not but repel his puritanical sensibilities and his conception about right attitudes towards women. His writings reveal considerable awareness of the dangers of falling into the Western ethnocentric trap of complete condemnation — but an awareness, also, that 'orientalist' patronage could hide behind a romantic glorification of the exotic.

The translation of the Sakta lyrics is, perhaps, somewhat bowdlerized, for the introduction declares that the intention was 'not to trouble the reader with a subtle and sometimes dull, occasionally disgusting, significance'.[134] Thompson's comments on Katherine Mayo have been somewhat unfairly summarized by Benita Parry: in fact they make the sharpest possible distinction between what he felt was legitimate and necessary exposure of the abuses of Hinduism (in the first 134 pages of the book) and the wholesale racist-imperialist condemnation of Indians which accompanied it. He does feel that 'Hinduism is beneath contempt in its worship of the male and its sex obsession generally',[135] but added in a later comment that 'It is not sexual indulgence that shocks, it is the subjugation of women.'[136] Nor is Thompson unaware of the mote in the Western critic's eye: Hindus display 'callousness to misery inflicted on animals — but we have our field sports' — and he feels that Miss Mayo 'lost her case when she wove into it a bitter conviction that the White Man's rule is so overwhelmingly good

133 Ibid., p. 48, 50.
134 E.J. Thompson and A.M. Spencer, *Bengali Religious Lyrics: Sakta* (London, 1923), Introduction, pp. 12, 13.
135 Review of *Mother India* in *Bookman*, 30 July 1927.
136 *A Reply to 'Mother India'* — review of Lajpat Rai's *Unhappy India*, in *The Nation and Athenaeum*, 30 June 1928.

for inferior breeds that it is only wickedness that makes them dissatisfied'.[137]

The introduction to the Sakta lyrics made a passing reference to the association of mass immolations of women with the cult of Kali in Chitor,[138] and several of Thompson's plays with Indian motifs, written soon after returning to England — *Krishnakumari* (1924), set in Mewar, *The Queen of Ruin* (1927), *The Clouded Mirror* (1927) — turn on the themes of sati and jauhar. He included a brief 'terminal essay' on sati in his *Three Eastern Plays*, and followed it up next year with a major historical study, *Suttee* (1928),[139] technically a better-researched and more scholarly work than *The Other Side of the Medal*. The Preface to this book traces Thompson's own interest in the subject to 'shame and anger' about occasional European glorification of sati, along with 'amazement' at seeing sati memorials and encountering examples of voluntary and heroic self-sacrifice by women. This dualism is sought to be maintained throughout. Efforts are made to avoid Western attitudes of superiority through recalling the days of Europeans 'witch-burning and religious persecution', of 'our own Smithfield burnings and public hangings'.[140] Thompson was careful to emphasize also that though some misguided Indian patriots might be occasionally provoked by Western abuse to glorify sati, as a whole the Gandhian national movement was 'a cleansing one. . . . It has brought with it the deepest and most radical criticism to which Indians have ever submitted themselves.'[141]

Chapters IV and V ('Reasons for Suttee', and 'Was Suttee Voluntary?') of the book made a notable effort at sympathetic understanding of women's perceptions about sati. It could be, and often was, 'voluntary', but behind the willingness or even enthusiasm lay the weight of cultural tradition, 'the whole tremendous, impalpable weight of familiar tradition and of expectation'.[142] The moral judgement Thompson makes is best conveyed by one of the quotations he gives on the first page, from a comment on Euripides' Alcestis: 'For herself she deserves much admiration, but for men and for

[137] Review in *Bookman*, op. cit.

[138] *Bengali Religious Lyrics: Sakta*, p. 15.

[139] E.J. Thompson, *Suttee: A Historical and Philosophical Enquiry into the Hindu Rite of Widow-Burning* (London, 1928), p. 9.

[140] Ibid., pp. 27, 51, 132.

[141] Ibid., p. 139.

[142] Ibid., p. 51.

society, no!'[143] The problematic 'agency' of women in 'voluntary' sati has once again become very much of a live issue in contemporary India, after the sati episode at Deorala.

Thompson made an attempt to link his analysis of sati with a major theme of his *The Other Side of the Medal* through the argument that the character of the 'Nicholson generation' was partly formed by the experience of the preceding period of 'intensive warfare against violent and cruel crime — *suttee, thuggee*, human sacrifice, etc.' In this context, 'the ruthlessness and spiritual arrogance with which our people confronted the Mutiny, becomes explicable' — though 'I do not believe that to explain is to justify', and the consequences of such 'beneficial ruthlessness' was 'self-satisfaction' and 'isolation from the people of India'. Thompson's imagination was evidently seeking solace in the age of the 'able and generous men . . . before the great annexations and the great rebellion', the generation of Munro, Malcolm, Elphinstone, Tod.[144]

An undated draft of a letter, which from internal evidence seems to be written in the mid 1930s, offers an interesting summary of Thompson's evolution:

Over twenty years ago, I made a rapt pilgrimage of the Mutiny country, my mind full of Nikal Seyn and the Lawrences. It has been a slow long process that has taken me so far from that old attitude; and the last part of it has been the increasing discovery of how immeasurably more attractive the men of the pre-Mutiny time were. Men like Metcalfe, Elphinstone, Jenkins, Graeme Mercer, Tod, Malcolm . . . belonged to a more civilized state in every way, whereas the Mutiny men seem to have read nothing but the Bible, and the Old Testament mostly.[145]

Rethinking about received John Bull attitudes, as always, is accompanied in Thompson by rethinking about aspects of received Christianity. The novel *The Youngest Disciple*, written in 1938, offered a reconciliation between an unorthodox view of Christ and an unorthodox version of Buddhism. In *An End of the Hours*, published in the same year, Alden has fallen into the background, and we seem to be left with Findlay and Jayananda, unorthodox mystics who can hopefully reconcile West and East.

---

[143] Ibid., title page.
[144] Ibid., pp. 135–7.
[145] The xerox copy of this letter, sent to me by E.P. Thompson, contains no date or name of addressee, but the reference to 'over twenty years', and a later mention of the exaltation of Russia by some of the 'youngest poets', would indicate a date around the mid 1930s.

The major part of Thompson's Indian involvement during the last decade of his life, however, took much more directly political forms. Personal contacts, as usual, were very important for Thompson, and one major influence behind the transition to active solidarity with Indian nationalism was a growing friendship with Jawaharlal Nehru through occasional meetings in the mid and late 1930s and a regular correspondence, including many from jail.[146] Some of the earlier letters, now published in Nehru's *A Bunch of Old Letters*, reveal a certain impatience on the part of the Indian leader at Thompson's apparent failure to understand the democratic significance of the Congress as a vast movement of the masses, and a related gross overestimation of the role of the Liberal coterie of Sapru, Shastri, and Jayakar.[147] To some extent, this illusion persisted throughout. Thompson's last public speech on Indian affairs at a meeting organized by the India League in London on Amritsar Day in April 1945 referred to 'Tej Bahadur Sapru and his powerful group',[148] and Thompson's writings till the mid 1930s on the whole reveal little awareness of the importance of democracy in the sense of popular initiatives and movements.

Something of this, too, changed in his last years, in the context of the threat from Fascism — a dimension which must have contributed greatly to his deepening friendship with Nehru. Way back in 1927, Thompson had made a very unpleasant British ex-Secretary of State praise the Italian dictator — 'What we need is the Mussolini touch and we're going to get it.'[149] Spain moved him deeply,[150] and Munich came to him as a tremendous shock. It made Thompson plunge into electoral politics, for possibly the only time in his life, canvassing against a Chamberlain admirer in an Oxford byelection.[151]

[146] Some of these were intercepted by the censors. See *Selected Works of Jawaharlal Nehru*, vols 11-13 (New Delhi, 1978-80).

[147] 'You talk of democracy and regret failure of it in Europe, and yet fail to appreciate the only real democratic organization in India, and you think in terms of handfuls of people at the top imposing their will on others.' Nehru to Thompson, 22 April 1937, quoted in Benita Parry, p. 176.

[148] Typescript sent to me by E.P. Thompson.

[149] *An Indian Day*, p. 187.

[150] 'we are thinking a great deal about Spain, and my close friend and colleague Geoffrey Garratt, as well as other friends, have been there for a long while.' Thompson to Nehru, 3 May 1937, reprinted in *A Bunch of Old Letters* (Bombay, 1958), p. 235.

[151] Edward Thompson, *Enlist India for Freedom!* (London, October 1940), p. 92. Thompson campaigned for A.D. Lindsay, distinguished scholar and

Anti-Fascism and 'peoples war' made him, as we shall see, something of an admirer of the Soviet experiment in his last years. Both his sons, William Frank and Edward Palmer, had become Communists by the early 1940s, and Frank died a hero's death in June 1944, fighting side by side with Bulgarian partisans. Nehru wrote a moving letter of condolence from jail,[152] and sent to his daughter Indira Gandhi a vivid account of Frank's death, facing the firing squad with the clenched-fist salute.[153] An autobiographical fragment left by Frank was edited for publication by his father and came out as *There is a Spirit in Europe* (1947). Frank Thompson remains a Bulgarian national hero.

In 1939 Thompson came to India for the last time, not really 'to dissuade his Indian friends from civil disobedience', as Margoliouth has described it, but, at the request of Lord Lothian, 'to see how the (political) land lay and to bring back a report'.[154] The intention was probably to find out what kind of political concessions could lead to Congress participation in the anti-Nazi war — a bargain that the bulk of the Congress leadership, particularly Nehru, was extremely eager for, right up to the collapse of the Cripps Mission. Certainly the reception and contacts now were very different from 1932: Nehru and Gandhi welcomed him as an old and trusted friend, and Thompson was even invited to attend a meeting of the Congress Working Committee (of which he has left among his papers a vivid and entertaining account).[155] 'The main outcome of his visit was his conviction that Britain had done a most unwise thing in declaring India, willy-nilly, at war, without even asking her consent.'[156] Thompson's

---

Master of Balliol. The Chamberlain admirer, interestingly enough, was Quintin Hogg, later Lord Hailsham — who become Lord Chancellor in Margaret Thatcher's government (I owe this information to E.P. Thompson).

152 'You write with a father's pride and a father's sorrow, and you have reason for both, but many others will share that pride and sorrow. I have thought that if I had a son I would like him to die in some such way before life had stained him and added burdens which are sometimes heavier than death itself': Nehru to Edward Thompson, 9 March 1945. Edward replied: 'there is not much of value in these earth-days. But more and more I am sure that memory, and especially friendship are of worth. I feel that you and I are in close sympathy over all things.' *Selected Works of Jawaharlal Nehru*, vol. 13 (New Delhi, 1980), pp. 572-3.

153 Nehru to Indira Gandhi, 10 March 1945, ibid., pp. 576-8.

154 Theodosia Thompson to H.M. Margoliouth, 11 March 1952.

155 Now partly published in E.P. Thompson's 'The Nehru Tradition', pp. 139-40.

156 Theodosia Thompson.

efforts at mediation came to nothing, for his report was quickly shelved. He never had in any case the kind of high-level personal contacts with officialdom that the far better-remembered Indophile ex-missionary C.F. Andrews had sometimes enjoyed.[157]

Thompson's *Enlist India for Freedom!* brought out by the Left-leaning publishing firm of Victor Gollancz in August 1940 marked a departure in many ways from his earlier writings about India. Rejection of negotiation with the Congress was unequivocally condemned, since it had created a situation in which 'India can speak to us only through British or British-supported officials and a few yes-men.'[158] Jallianwallabagh and the Mutiny were mentioned together, as so often before,[159] communal troubles traced back to British divide-and-rule and 'economic' tensions (clear influence of Nehru here), and princely states condemned as 'the last strongholds in the world anywhere of feudalism'.[160]

The real break, however, comes in the chapter entitled 'Is India Fit for Self-Government?',[161] which needs to be compared with the section with a very similar title in his *Reconstruction of India* written ten years earlier.[162] 'I do not understand what constitutes fitness for a natural right,'[163] Thompson now declares: a decade earlier he had talked repeatedly of the dangers of Indian inefficiency and the need for a long 'process of training'. 'In these last years I have often wondered if the British are fit for self-government', he continues in his best polemical vein − 'No, I have never been able since that byelection to feel sure that Oxford is fit for self-government' − for the Chamberlain admirer had won.[164] This is related to a still more fundamental break: 'today I seem to be able to see only India's poverty, ignorance, misery. I simply cannot understand how as a young man I saw romance and beauty there. . . . We give ourselves more bouquets

---

[157] A High Church Anglican background (till 1919) and St Stephen's College, Delhi, were after all very different from Methodist missionary work at Bankura. Andrews at one time had excellent contacts even at the Viceregal level: 'Thanks to the Hardinges, Andrews moved among the mighty.' Hugh Tinker, *The Ordeal of Love: CF Andrews and India* (Oxford, 1979), p. 75.

[158] Edward Thompson, *Enlist India for Freedom!* (London, August 1940), Preface.

[159] Ibid., pp. 18–19.

[160] Ibid., pp. 50, 59, 69.

[161] Ibid., Part II, Chapter V.

[162] 'Are Indians Fit for Self-Government?' in *Reconstruction of India*.

[163] Ibid., p. 91.

[164] Ibid., p. 92.

than we deserve. . . . The problem has got beyond us, and we have got to hand it over to Indians themselves.' The Indians, Thompson felt, were thinking of reconstruction 'from top to bottom, along the line of an essentially peasant civilization. One reason why Russia has been admired is its work for the peasant.'[165] Five years later, in his last public speech, Thompson drew the same contrast again: 'Today it is clearer than ever that, whatever else we had done in India, we have *not* solved the problem of its poverty, and we have no power ever to solve it. . . . Regeneration can come for a people like that of India only from inside . . . no alien administration has the authority to remove them.' In Russia, Thompson continued, as illiterate a country as India in 1918, 'a miraculous release of submerged talent and power' had taken place through national planning.[166] The 1940 conflation of (presumably Gandhian) peasant utopia with Stalinist Russia had its absurdities, but the contrast was clear enough: Rabindranath by an interesting coincidence would make a very similar point in his last address, *Civilization on Trial* (1941).

In failing health, amidst the many strains of war, separation from his sons (both away in the army), and bereavement, Edward Thompson spent much of his time during his last years 'with the chores of solidarity — meetings, letters and articles, more meetings'.[167] Active solidarity with India during these dark years of post-1942 repression drew him close, not to top Labour politicians[168] who generally spurned his messages, but to 'the socialist, liberal and communist fringe': H.N. Brailsford, Kingsley Martin, Fenner Brockway, Harry Pollitt and the India League of Krishna Menon.[169]

Struck down by cancer and on his deathbed, what gave Thompson the greatest peace and sense of fulfilment was the letter that Nehru wrote him for his birthday, full of deep affection and gratitude for the help and advice he had given him. When he read it he put it down and said, with a quick smile as if he were amused at himself for 'quoting'. 'Now, Lord, let Thy servant depart in peace.' The letter and its response became a cherished

---

[165] Ibid., p. 90.

[166] Typescript of Amritsar Day speech, 13 April 1945.

[167] E.P. Thompson, 'The Nehru Tradition', p. 140.

[168] Theodosia recalled in her letter to Margoliouth that Pethick-Lawrence as Labour Secretary of State for India after 1945 ignored two letters Thompson had written to him. The Tories were now positively hostile: Amery in fact gave instructions that Thompson would not be allowed to visit India during the war.

[169] E.P. Thompson, 'The Nehru Tradition', p. 140.

family memory.[170] Edward Thompson died a few days later, on 28 April 1946.

III

Benita Parry has found in Thompson 'the paradox of moral conscience joined with ineradicable paternalist suppositions. . . . The will to reconciliation coexists with strong currents of hostility towards India, the urge to atone with insistent self-justifications. . . . Thompson does not so much explore paradox as embody it.'[171] Perceptive in some ways, such a conclusion does not, I feel, give sufficient weight to the shifts within Thompson's structure of feelings. And paternalism is perhaps too general a category, for it can be used in polemics to entrap virtually all within superordinate groups (whether defined by race, class or gender) in their relations with subordinates. It is not entirely inappropriate for Thompson in some of his moods, but tends to abstract from too many nuances.

My own reading of Thompson, as I have said earlier, remains very incomplete. Much more thorough work has started in recent years,[172] and all that I am trying here is to tentatively suggest certain alternative lines of approach, in as open-ended a manner as I can.

One hypothesis that I have toyed with is a transition within Thompson from the concept of atonement to a belief in the need for and power of personal relations among cultured friends across racial divides, based on an implicit faith in 'the supreme value of the civilized *individual*, whose pluralization, as more and more civilized individuals, was itself the only acceptable social direction'.[173] 'Atonement, leading on to transformed personal relations, and friendship across races among civilized individuals, are clearly not unconnected — the one might be in a sense a secular version of the other — but there is a change in emphasis, a modified cultural and social ambience.

---

170 Theodosia Thompson. The incident was recalled by E.P. Thompson at my first meeting with him in 1976, and has been subsequently included in his 'The Nehru Tradition'.

171 Benita Parry, pp. 167, 202.

172 Harish Trivedi and Mary Lago have been working on the Thompson Papers, and E.P. Thompson published *Alien Homage: Edward Thompson and Rabindranath Tagore* (Delhi, 1993).

173 Raymond Williams, 'The Bloomsbury Faction', in his *Problems in Materialism and Culture* (London, 1980), p. 165.

The atonement theme, and the related self-questioning of received Methodist Christianity, does seem to become less important in Thompson's writings after the late 1920s. They are not as prominent in *Farewell to India* as they had been in *An Indian Day*. Findlay has now broken away from the mission, and references to Christianity are rare, apart from a brief angry description by Alden of an American Pentecostal group as 'fish-faced bigots'.[174] Thompson by the 1930s seems to have grown beyond the debates within himself about Christianity. He felt impelled to invent two socialist-minded pagan friends for John Arnison, wrote a sympathetic novel about Buddhism, and even on his deathbed could quote a standard Christian text only with a self-mocking smile. Atonement, through gesture rather than political change, had been his predominant theme in the 1920s; *Enlist India for Freedom!*, in contrast, accepted the need for institutional reform — though preferably Dominion Status still, rather than independence.[175] It talked repeatedly, however, of the importance of ties of personal friendship across racial barriers, of the possibilities of 'a civilized and friendly relationship' between England and India. Referring to the excellent command over English displayed by Congress leaders, their ability to even joke in it, Thompson emphasized that 'All over India there are such groups of civilized interesting men and women of the world. . . . India is a part of this modern world. . . . Bring her in more fully, as she longs to be brought in, to the full stream of the world's life.' He made a special point about Nehru's English being much better than Linlithgow's, tried to remind Churchill that both he and Nehru had studied at Harrow, and exhibited a rather pathetic belief that judicious grants from British foundations to 'key men and women' in India could help reduce political tensions.[176]

I have quoted just now from Raymond Williams' analysis of the Bloomsbury group, and it is tempting to infer at this point some affinity deeper than the apparently isolated incident of Hogarth Press publishing *The Other Side of the Medal*. Leonard Woolf in particular had an honourable anti-colonial record. Through the Labour Party Advisory Committee on Imperial Affairs (where his fellow-members included Graham Pole, H.S.L. Polak, John Maynard, and, significantly, G.T. Garratt, co-author of *Rise and Fulfilment of British Rule*),

---

[174] *Farewell to India*, p. 265.

[175] *Enlist India for Freedom!* pp. 116-17.

[176] Ibid., pp. 12-14, 94, 106, 115. It is only fair, however, to set beside such rather irritating passages Basatakumar Chatterji's remarks in *Atonement*.

he often urged Labour leaders 'to do everything in their power to meet the demands in India for self-government and Dominion Status' — advice, Woolf recalls, which was invariably ignored.[177] Bloomsbury in the inter-War years, Williams reminds us, was not just a group of 'withdrawn and languid aesthetes'. It was marked by a distinctive brand of 'social conscience' or 'concern for the under-dog', both at home and (often more easily) in the colonial world. But this sócial conscience was essentially 'a sense of individual obligation, ratified among civilized friends' — very different from 'the *social consciousness* of a self-organizing subordinate class' or subject people. Relating 'to a lower class *as a matter of conscience*, not in solidarity, nor in affiliation, but as an extension of what are still felt as personal or small-group obligations' involved

the specific association of what are really quite unchanged class feelings — a persistent sense of a quite clear line between an upper and a lower class — with a very strong and effective feeling of sympathy with the lower class as victims. . . . Close contacts with them, which the social conscience required, produced a quite unselfconscious and in its own way quite pure patronage. For if this were not given, these new forces could not be expected to be . . . rational and civilized. . . .[178]

It is tempting to apply some of this analysis to Thompson, but dangerous to press it too far. The Bloomsbury milieu was utterly different from that of Thompson: heavily highbrow and upper class, aesthetic and intellectual rather than moral in motivation, self-defined by Leonard Woolf as 'primarily and fundamentally a group of friends. Our roots and the roots of our friendship were in the University of Cambridge.'[179] Thompson was not from Oxbridge, and his later job as tutor in a minor subject like Bengali at Oxford probably did not change things much. In addition, he remained acutely conscious of his non-Anglican lower-middle-class background. 'I can remember when you wouldn't have touched me, a Baptist, with a ten-yard pole', Gregory reminds Thorpe in *Atonement:* 'a Baptist couldn't be con-sidered a gentleman.'[180] 'I have always been one of the depressed classes', Thompson wrote in a private letter in 1927.[181] And he figured briefly in E.M. Forster's jottings, published as *Commonplace Book*

---

177 Leonard Woolf, *Downhill all the Way*, pp. 222, 227.
178 Raymond Williams, pp. 155-6.
179 Ibid., p. 149, quoting from Leonard Woolf's *Beginning Again*.
180 *Atonement*, p. 68.
181 I owe this information to E.P. Thompson.

(1985), as the last in a list of 'Public Bores' drawn up in 1927: 'Edward Thompson of Boar's Hill itself, though he cannot be counted among true boars until borne in silence.'[182] The 'candour' of the Bloomsbury group, as Williams has commented, 'could modulate into tones of quite extraordinary rudeness' about outsiders.[183]

An alternative, more generous,. and possibly more appropriate framework might begin through asking ourselves what was Thompson's own central problematic on Indian matters. The issue uppermost in his perceptions was almost certainly not the continuance or the ending of colonial rule, but a search for human understanding across political, racial and cultural divides. Others, including some distinguished Indian contemporaries of Thompson, did have similar concerns. One notable example would be Rabindranath Tagore, who founded his Visvabharati, 'where the whole world finds its home in one nest',[184] in 1921, the year Non-Cooperation reached its climax. Activists in national liberation or Left movements, in Thompson's times as well as today, are bound to have a strong tendency to brush aside such concerns as immaterial, even dangerous, distractions. They might still have a certain limited relevance in a world teetering on the brink of nuclear holocaust and torn apart by conflicts, not all of which follow neat capitalist/socialist or imperialist/Third World divides.

The limits of such a problematic are clear enough. Political interventions by people like Thompson tend to have an occasional, almost gestural, quality. *Atonement* and *The Other Side of the Medal* were followed by some years of retreat. Rabindranath gave up his knighthood at a time when nationalist leaders were fighting shy of public protests about Jallianwallabagh, but sharply demarcated himself from the mass national upsurge which came two years later. Moving verses which hailed Bengali heroism at a time of intense political repression served as a prelude to a poem about a flower: 'Let me be forgiven, if I sing this song of a jasmine flower in the face of the machine-gun.'[185] The transformation of structural tensions into questions of personal attitudes could also produce a curious opacity. Thompson was acutely aware of Indian, particularly peasant, poverty, but he would always attribute it to ecological

---

182 E.M. Forster, *Commonplace Book* (London, 1985), ed. Philip Gardner, p. 27.
183 Raymond Williams, p. 154.
184 The motto of Visvabharati — 'Yatra visva bhabet ekanidam'.
185 A poem included in Rabindranath's *Purabi*.

factors alone.[186] Even in his last writings, he could at most admit British failure to tackle poverty, not colonial responsibility. The entire drain of wealth and economic exploitation discourse, central to Indian nationalism from Naoroji onwards and one to which Indophile Englishmen had also contributed, seems to have passed him by. Thompson showed surprisingly little awareness, also, of the connections between peasant poverty and zamindar (money-lender) exploitation.

Indian experience led Thompson to rethink his received cultural and religious presuppositions, but here too certain blocks remained. Condemnation of Hindu attitudes towards women is balanced by references to the burning in Europe of heretics and witches, but it is clearly implied that the West had now solved problems of gender domination: 'the best of what Hindu civilization teaches in this respect is a poor thing. So was the best that European civilization taught; but it has been frankly handled, and our ideas have changed.'[187] Suffragettes who had won the vote for women against tremendous opposition only a few years before Thompson wrote this would have certainly found his tone intolerably complacent, and so would women's liberation movements today. Walsh realizes in *Atonement* that 'you can't stay a gentleman if you once start standing over other people'; neither he nor his creator ever realized that the obverse is perhaps more fundamental: one cannot in an important sense be a gentleman (or *bhadralok*, or similar groups in other cultures or societies) without 'standing over other people'.

Thompson's problems and limitations as Indophile Englishman were hardly unique. Tensions not dissimilar, leading up occasionally to similar suspicions of paternalism, can be found in C.F. Andrews, for instance. Andrews of course was a much more prominent figure — intimate friend of Tagore and Gandhi, champion of Indians in South Africa and indentured labourers in Fiji, trade union leader — yet he too had his contradictions, and the very closeness of his simultaneous links with Indian leaders and many British officials made him something like a moderating influence on the course of radical anti-imperialist movements.[188] 'Andrews, you want to be the

186 Introduction to *Bengali Religious Lyrics: Sakta*, p. 15; *The Other Side of the Medal*, pp. 24-5; *Enlist India for Freedom!* pp. 89-90.

187 'A Reply to *Mother India*', in *Nation and Athenaeum*, 30 June 1928.

188 Hugh Tinker's biography contains numerous examples of such efforts at mediation and restraint — *Ordeal of Love*, pp. 71, 165-7, 191, 239-40, 269-70, 275.

Hume of the trade union movement', S.A. Dange once told him during a bitter railway strike in 1927.[189] Thompson, at least, was never important enough politically to have any such ambiguous function. Yet Andrews is remembered and honoured in independent India, perhaps more than any other Englishman;[190] few, very few, would know anything today about Edward Thompson.

It needs to be emphasized, in conclusion, that perhaps none of the alternative frameworks I have probed — repentant paternalist, believer in the pluralization of civilized individuals, seeker of cross-cultural understanding — fully fit the last years of Thompson's life. The changes in Thompson's attitudes reveal something important about the power and elasticity of liberal discourse. The quest for personal contacts across the colonial divide might appear politically somewhat trivial, but it did help to make possible the ideological and emotive acceptance of a by-and-large peaceful transfer of power. Acceptance from both sides, it needs to be added — for we have to recall the relations developed by Nehru, the flaming radical of the 1930s, not only with Edward Thompson but with the Mountbattens.

By the late 1930s Thompson's involvement in the cause of Indian self-government had developed from being mainly gestural to something much more continuous and political. Such regular involvement in the inevitable tedium of solidarity meetings and articles, Thompson's wife has emphasized, 'was a sacrifice', first and foremost: 'Fifty years ago . . . he would have been able to devote himself to poetry without conquering his conscience, perhaps. As it was, and as his conscience was, it was impossible . . . it was . . . his political activity which took him away from poetry.' 'It would be nice', she had pleaded with Margoliouth without success — for the *DNB* entry apparently went in without major modification — 'if the fact that so much of his life was spent in this way were mentioned.'[191] The reissue of *The Other Side of the Medal*, in the centenary year of Edward Thompson's birth, helped a little to redress the balance.

189 Interview with Gopen Chakravarti, in Gautam Chattopadhyay, *Communism and Bengal's Freedom Movement* (New Delhi, 1970), p. 137.

190 'Every Indian educated in the English language knows about him', and Andrew's birth centenary in 1971 was widely celebrated in India. Hugh Tinker, p. xi.

191 Theodosia Thompson to H.M. Margoliouth, 11 March 1952 (Thompson Papers).

POSTSCRIPT (1997)

'Edward Thompson and India', first published in 1989, had been substantially completed by 1986, which explains the reference to Thompson's centenary. It had been written to provide an introduction to a new edition of *The Other Side of the Medal*. The generosity of E.P. Thompson, who gave me access to his father's private papers and provided detailed comments and criticisms of my drafts, stimulated me to go some distance beyond an account of the significance of that specific work. My Introduction expanded into a discussion of the ambiguities and tensions of one kind of British liberal perception of India. But the essay remained based on fairly limited material, and certainly had no ambition of providing any comprehensive assessment of Thompson. Precisely for that reason, one may hope that it has not been rendered entirely superfluous by the considerable volume of scholarly work on Thompson in recent years.[192]

More relevant, from the point of view of my decision to include the essay in the present volume with only minor changes, is the fact that in 1986 what might today be termed the 'Saidian' turn in South Asian scholarship was just beginning, and had not really engaged my attention. My differences and reservations about the particular kind of critique of colonial discourse embodied in Said and several contributors to *Subaltern Studies* have figured prominently at many places in this volume, and I see no need to add footnotes or emendations to resume that polemic once more in an essay which pre-dates that argument. The important question remains: would it be necessary to write in a fundamentally different way about Edward Thompson and India today, given that the study of colonial perceptions and attitudes is precisely the area where Said's influence has been the greatest and most direct? More bluntly: is my essay hopelessly dated?

I can recognize today several specific places in my argument where an awareness of emerging trends in the study of colonial representations would have been helpful. Much valuable work now is

---

[192] My statement that 'not much has been written' about Edward Thompson is no longer appropriate. Recent work, published or in progress, includes Mary Lago's biography, Harish Trivedi's book on Thompson's literary output, Uma Dasgupta on the correspondence with Tagore, Shashi Raina's doctoral dissertation about his writings concerning India, as well as of course E.P. Thompson's *Alien Homage* (see footnote 172).

built around a dialectic of the Self and the Other: the construction of white, male, dominant-class self-images in indissoluble relationships with representations of the colonized black or brown, women, subordinate groups in general. My essay referred to a dichotomy between Christian manly heroism and pagan Indian bestiality as central to British stereotypes about 1857. I investigated the nature and limits of Thompson's efforts to go beyond this dichotomy, drew attention to a correlation between the evolution of his views about India and about Christianity, and mentioned, without further probing, a letter by him written in the 1930s which emphasized a contrast between British Indian officials of the Metcalfe generation and 'the Mutiny men, who seem to have read nothing but the Bible, and the Old Testament mostly'. What I failed to do was to problematize the contrast suggested by Thompson, asking to what extent, and why, aggressive Christian rhetoric of a particular kind became dominant among army men engaged in a massive operation of counterinsurgency, and their panegyrists. How common was such rhetoric in earlier British wars against 'natives' in India? If, as seems likely, 1857 was marked by a significant shift in this respect, could it be because harping on pagan Indian bestiality had become urgent precisely because British military operations and attitudes had become quite exceptionally bestial? Other questions could have been raised, too: for instance the coincidence in time between the well-known shift in British Indian policies after 1857 towards greater 'non-interference' in Indian social and religious practices necessitated by considerations of prudence, and occasional violent diatribes about the ineluctable superstition and brutality of natives for which the Mutiny provided the most convenient locus. One could have ranged further, perhaps. Darwin's *Origin of Species* came out in 1859, posing a formidable challenge to conventional Christianity, and particularly to the Creation myth, for long precisely dated as going no further back than 4004 BC. Did tales of Christian heroism against heathen rebels, retold endlessly for a generation or more after the Mutiny and enjoying great popularity in Britain, provide a mode of recuperation of muscular, Old Testament Christianity in a moment of peril?

Let me come to a second example. I had mentioned, implicitly as one more of Thompson's many inconsistencies, that he was irritated by Indian students who assimilated too well the lessons in European culture taught by him at Bankura. He had become very angry once, for instance, when a pupil quoted Latin back at him. A very common British Indian attitude, of course, though it remains depressing to see Thompson occasionally slipping into Kiplingesque descriptions of the *banderlog*. It is also an attitude that has been described but seldom analytically explored. Homi Bhabha's interesting analysis of mimicry as a key to some of the ambivalences of colonial discourse appears quite helpful here — upto a point. Imitative acculturation is both desirable and threatening for the colonizer, for 'mimicry is at once resemblance and menace', sliding as it can often do towards mockery.[193] The stress upon the ambiguities of mimicry has enabled Bhabha to complicate and introduce an element of play into blunt, over-rigid notions of all-pervasive Western power-knowledge that permit the colonized touched by it no more than derivative discourses. It is more helpful, however, for understanding the anger evoked by too-successful imitation among colonial overlords, than in exploration of the psychology of the colonized — for in effective anti-colonial resistance the slippages of mimicry into mockery could have figured only as a minor trope.

I think a broadly similar comment can be made about Bhabha's other, very influential category of hybridity. It destabilizes myths of 'pure', 'authentic', self-enclosed cultures and identities, common today among both dominant and dominated in situations of growing ethnic or religious conflict. The notion may have become particularly relevant in Western contexts where the need to evolve multi-cultural norms has acquired extreme urgency in recent times. The problem, however, is that hybridity rejects arguments of authenticity only through a trajectory that retains, like the concept of mimicry, what may be an excessive focus on the question of origin. The language used makes it difficult to take adequate cognizance of possibilities of multiple, quite often mutually opposed, appropriations, of developments going so far beyond origins that the point and quality of the initial impetus might become rather unimportant.[194] It is not

[193] Homi Bhabha, 'Of Mimicry and Man: The Ambivalence of Colonial Discourse', *October*, Spring 1984; reprinted in Philip Rice and Patricia Waugh, ed., *Modern Literary Theory: A Reader*, London, etc., 1989, 1992, p. 236, and *passim*. In a perceptive but much lesser-known essay, the anthropologist Gerald Sider has developed a somewhat similar analysis of the contradictions of colonial domination: ' . . . *it cannot both create and incorporate the other*, thus opening a space for continuing resistance and distancing.' 'When Parrots Learn to Talk, and Why They Can't: Domination, Deception, and Self-Deception in Indian-White Relations', *Comparative Studies of Society and History*, 1987.

[194] Partha Chatterjee at first sight may appear to be making a similar point when he argues in a recent article that Bhabha provides no way for distinguishing 'between hybrid and hybrid'. The very next paragraph, as well as most of

just that a multiplicity of different kinds of hybrids should be expected: more significantly, some of them can evolve in ways so autonomous, and/or become so rooted in their country of 'transplantation' as to really become as 'indigenous' as anything that could be meaningfully termed so. Many practices and concepts of indisputably Western origin — parliamentary democracy, socialistic aspirations, social justice through affirmative action ('reservations') — have by now become integral, though of course contested, elements of contemporary 'Indian' life. Calling them hybrids might actually encourage imputations of relative inauthenticity, quite contrary I am sure to Bhabha's intentions. Present-day implications are usually more important than distant origins. In a conflict today between the claims of Hindu Rashtra and secularism, for instance, it would not be all that helpful to point out, correctly, that both formations are hybrids that could not have originated without crucial inputs from Western colonial modernity. What would matter much more are the vastly different consequences in terms of values, power-relations, or sometimes even sheer human survival.[195]

Specific additions or modifications apart, I do not think I would have felt the need to change the basic thrust or tonalities of my essay even if I had had the time or inclination to embark upon thorough rewriting through incorporation of more material. The impact of Saidian moods has varied widely according to the specific areas of cultural studies these moods have influenced. I have argued at many places in this volume that the consequences have quite often been retrogressive in studies of the colonial Indian intelligentsia. Conversely, where the importance and wider implications of colonial representations had been largely ignored earlier — as in apparently disinterested, high-quality Orientalist scholarship, or the canonical texts of traditional English literary studies — the impact of Saidian (and other) critiques has been much more innovative.[196]

---

the essays in the collection that he introduces, makes it clear that the old homogenizing thrust has not been basically modified: what interests Chatterjee is the variety of sites of definition of 'disciplinary practices' that all flow, more or less uniformly, from 'the new discourse of modernity' (in the singular, it will be observed). Partha Chatterjee, ed., *Texts of Power: Emerging Disciplines in Colonial Bengal* (Calcutta: Samya, 1996), pp. 20–1.

195 The above discussion of mimicry and hybridity owes much to Tanika Sarkar.

196 *Orientalism*, of course, and Said's critiques of Conrad, Jane Austen and other canonical figures (*Culture and Imperialism*, London: Vintage, 1993, 1994) — but also much other work, some of it preceding Said, others apparently

Edward Thompson, Indophile Englishman torn by multiple and obvious contradictions, critical of colonial power–knowledge yet complicit with it, is located in another kind of field where applications of Said are so easy as to be largely redundant. Critique here can quickly become synonymous with exposure and debunking, in a mode which to someone of my generation often becomes unpleasantly reminiscent of the cruder kinds of orthodox Marxism of my youth, endlessly engaged in the 'unmasking' of 'liberal illusions' and discovering the 'class essence' of any intellectual position. One tends to slip all too readily into a comfortable reiteration of the already said, surrendering to the ineffable pleasure of discovering 'once more', in the memorable line of Bertold Brecht, 'that right is right'. My essay had sought to push beyond the easy, catch-all formula of paternalism, distinguishing between its various forms: duty and efficiency, atonement, some moves partly transcending both, perhaps, in Thompson's last years. In the words of his historian son, the limits (of missionary and imperial background) were real and obvious enough, 'but what may merit our attention more may be what lies outside those limits or confounds our expectations'.[197]

---

independent of his influence. The examples could include Anouer Abdel-Malik, 'Orientalism in Crisis', *Diogenes*, 44, 1963, Stephen Greenblatt's recent study of late-medieval and Renaissance tales of travel and conquest (*Marvellous Possessions: The Wonder of the New World*, Oxford: Clarendon Press, 1991), as well as the chapters on Marlowe and Shakespeare in the same author's *Renaissance Self-Fashioning* (Chicago, 1980). Neither of these works by the founder of New Historicism, interestingly, make any reference to Said.

[197] *Alien Homage*, p. 3.

5

The City Imagined: Calcutta of the Nineteenth and Early Twentieth Centuries

'Life in Calcutta is no longer what it was in the "good old days" . . . [when] sahibs were sahibs, veritable lords of creation . . . nowadays . . . the baboo has been to England, and back again. . . . There is everything to remind her citizens . . . that she is the capital of the British Raj: Wellesley's stately Government House, the statues of past Governor-Generals . . . the massive blocks of Government houses, the long array of palaces upon Chowringhee, the rows of warehouses and jetties and docks . . . the large European colony . . . the signs upon every hand of opulence and prosperity. . . . a new Calcutta is rising in our midst. The talk is all of an Anglo-Indian Haussman who is to transform the teeming Indian quarter. . . . The electric car and the electric fan tell of the advent of a new era . . . to those who know her, what can there be more fascinating than the City of Palaces?'
> — H.E.A. Cotton, *Calcutta Old and New: Historical and Descriptive Handbook to the City*, Calcutta, 1907.

'The clerks are dozing on their way back from office, their faces worn out by hard work throughout the day . . . many of them will find that there is no oil, salt or coal at home to cook with . . . and yet their wives nag them for ornaments . . . '
> — Durgacharan Roy, *Debganer Marte Agaman / A Visit of Gods to Earth*, Calcutta, 1889.

'Are you strong enough to sunder what fate has bound together / Do you think our lives are yours to make or break?'
— Patriotic song composed by Rabindranath Tagore in
October 1905, and sung in many street processions
during the struggle against the Partition of Bengal.

'O what will happen now if the gentleman's boots get torn /
We won't respond any more to the "Hey, cobbler" call / No.
longer shall we mend boots coming from abroad'.
— Cobbler's song in Amritalal Bose, *Sabash Bangali /
Bravo Bengalees*, first performed at the Star Theatre,
Calcutta, 25 December 1905.

I

For the average educated Bengali today, nineteenth-century Calcutta lives on mainly as a galaxy of great names. Religious and
social reformers, scholars, literary giants, journalists and patriotic
orators, maybe a couple of scientists, all merge to form an image of
'renaissance', *nabajagaran* (awakening), or *nabayuga* (new age), assumed to mark the transition from medieval to modern. Calcutta
enters centrally into this image even though many of the most
distinguished figures — Bankimchandra Chattopadhyay or Rabindranath Tagore, for instance — spent much of their working lives outside
it. And, twentieth-century nationalism, Left politics, and Satyajit Ray
apart, the 'renaissance' today provides the major justification for
recalling the history of the city — as was done with much pride a
few years back, on the occasion of its tercentenary in 1990 — for
Calcutta has been otherwise a quintessentially colonial foundation.
   This standard middle-class view of the city's cultural history has
received some hard knocks in recent years, and most intellectuals
who would like to consider themselves radical and sophisticated no
longer share it. I had done a bit of debunking of our renaissance
myth, myself, some twenty years back, but have increasingly come
to feel the need to get beyond what has become now a rather stale
controversy.[1] We have debated for long whether a renaissance analogy
is appropriate or helpful for understanding nineteenth-century Bengal (or sometimes Indian) middle-class cultural achievements. Perhaps

---

[1] For a brief glance at this debate, and particularly its recent revival, in
somewhat modified forms through critiques of colonial discourse, see Chapter 6, footnotes 2-3 and corresponding text. And fns 2-4.

a more fruitful query could explore when and why such a problematic came to be constituted. It would reveal fairly soon that the Bengal Renaissance has been very much a mid- or late-twentieth-century retrospect. Bankimchandra in 1880 did suggest a renaissance analogue, not, however, with his own times (of the bhadralok culture about which he tended to be deeply ironic and critical), but with religious and cultural developments in sixteenth-century Bengal.[2]

Renaissances are quite often retrospects, not excepting the Italian prototype, which was in large part a nineteenth-century construct. A more serious problem with the Bengal variant has been the tendency to concentrate on outstanding figures and texts alone, whether in eulogy or critique. One result of this persistent elitism has been an implicit dichotomy in history-writing about Calcutta, between intellectual or cultural studies, and social or urban history. The renaissance, or its current inversion through critiques of colonial discourse, floating more or less in a social vacuum, constitutes the central assumption or debating point in the first. High culture in sharp contrast is marginalized or all but omitted in the second, where the thrust is towards aggregates — 'hard' census or other statistics, 'objective' tendencies.

A study of representations that seeks to locate them in specific social contexts — the city imagined in changing ways, by different social groups at different times — may be of some help for an urban history that seeks to get beyond this dichotomy of cultural and social. Representations of Calcutta, by British as well as Bengali residents, seem to have become particularly abundant around the turn of the century. The years around 1900, then, can provide a convenient entry-point for this essay.

II

Around the start of the twentieth century, British residents of Calcutta were writing more about the city than ever before. There already existed, it is true, a not inconsiderable literature of reminiscences, biographies and handbooks acclaiming British achievements and presenting European life in Calcutta in minute and loving detail. But the accounts of early days that have become standard references,

---

2 Bankimchandra Chattopadhyay, *Banglar Itihas Sambandhay Kayekti Katha / A Few words about the History of Bengal*, Bangadarshan, Agrahayan 1287/1880, reprinted in J.C. Bagal (ed.), *Bankim Rachanabali* (Calcutta, 1954, 1969), vol. II p. 339.

like H.E. Busteed's *Echoes from Old Calcutta* (1899) or S.C. Hill's massive collection of documents, *Bengal in 1756-7* (1905), tend to come from these years. Among them, Cotton's *Handbook*, with which I began, stands out in sheer size (over a thousand pages) and mass of historical and descriptive detail.

Detail, it has to be added immediately, with a predictably limited range. A ninety-page chapter entitled 'Historic Houses and Famous Localities' can spare only fifteen of them for Indians, the overwhelming majority of the city's residents, and even this sub-section is introduced through a patronizing comment about the need not to forget the 'Indian helper whose aid has been substantial . . . to the men who have built up the fabric of English rule' (p. 353).[3] Like most other British observers, Cotton was aware that a 'squalor that beggars description' accompanied the 'royal grandeur' of the 'City of Palaces': like them, again, he was quick to naturalize the contrast by attributing it to the innate conservatism of the unchanging East, embodied in the 'prejudices and customs of a religion which is half as old as time.'[4]

The focus, then, of this entire British corpus of writing about Calcutta was on the 'White Town' or *saheb para*, the domain of the Europeans: less than ten thousand in number, according to the 1901 census, in a total city population of 577,066. Its heart was the European business-cum-administrative centre of Dalhousie Square, the headquarters of highly capital-intensive, globally-connected commercial firms, as well as of the governments of Bengal Presidency and (till 1911) British India, an area populous by day but deserted by night. From here it extended southwards through the impressive façade, glittering shops, and massive public buildings (mostly Neo-Classical, with a dash of Victorian Gothic in the High Court and New Market built in the 1870s) of Esplanade and Chowringhee that faced the open green expanse of the Maidan, down to Park Street and the comfortable bungalows, parks and pools that marked the main European residential area to its south. Further to the south-west and south lay the still more fashionable outlying areas of Alipur and what in the twentieth-century would come to be called Old Ballygunge, to distinguish it from the adjoining new Bengali middle-class suburb of the same name.

---

3 Part II, Chapter 2, which has this title, extends from pp. 279-366; of these, only pp. 352-66 are about 'the purely Indian quarter of the north'.

4 Ibid., p. 242. As so often, poverty is quickly exoticized: 'we may be appalled by the squalor of her crowded slums, but we cannot deny the vague and tantalizing charm with which she carries off all her imperfections' (p. 241).

Civic funding and improvements tended to be concentrated on this saheb para, though it did spill over to some extent into the 'native' quarters, particularly during the years (1876-99) when elected Indian councillors had won a toehold in the Calcutta Corporation affairs in the teeth of much resentment and hostility from British business interests. The last three decades of the nineteenth century saw some significant improvements: underground waterpipes and drains in some areas from the 1870s; a pontoon bridge across the Hooghly river in 1874; horse-drawn trams from 1880; gas lights on streets, and then from 1891 a slow replacement of them by electricity; the first telephones in 1882 and a few motor-cars from 1896; and, as mentioned by Cotton, electric lights and fans in a few homes and electric trams from around 1900.[5]

Such mundane things, however, did not interest Cotton very much. About three-fourths of his book consists, rather, of detailed descriptions of the Cantonment area (Fort William, lying on the south-western side of the Maidan, that open space itself being created to strengthen artillery defence after 1757, at the expense of the old Indian settlement of Gobindapur), public buildings, churches, and British statues and monuments. Even as he was writing, the most massive British monument of all had just started coming up at the southern tip of the Maidan: the Victoria Memorial, planned by Curzon but completed only in 1921, a bizarre but not unattractive combination in marble of Renaissance and Mughal architecture, superficially reminiscent of the Taj. Curzon's aims had been political, it needs to be added, and not just aesthetic. He had, in his own words, wanted to shift the Indian quest for national glory from a 'remote and largely unhistorical past' or 'a still more visionary future' to 'the history of India itself in the past two centuries.'[6] Indians, in other words, were somehow to be taught to take pride in the British conquest and exploitation of their country.

Volubility, in literary and monumental representation alike, clearly is a pointer here to inner uncertainties, and this is indicated also

---

[5] A succinct account of the improvements in the last quarter of the nineteenth century was given in A.K. Roy, *A Short History of Calcutta: Town and Suburbs*, Chapter X, included in *Census of Bengal, 1901*, Part I, vol. VII (Calcutta, 1902; reprinted 1982). See also P.T. Nair, 'Civic and Public Services', in Sukanta Chaudhuri (ed.), *Calcutta: The Living City* (Calcutta: Oxford University Press, 1990), vol. I, pp. 224-37.

[6] Hiren Chakrabarty, 'The Victoria Memorial', in Sukanta Chaudhuri (ed.), *Calcutta: The Living City* (Calcutta, 1990), vol. I, p. 256.

by the persistent intertwining of pride with nostalgia in British writings about Calcutta around the 1900s. Two major developments in the early years of the new century would confirm and deepen these uncertainties: the aftermath of the Partition of Bengal of 1905, and the transfer of the Imperial capital to Delhi in 1911.

The grandeur of the 'City of Palaces', at times even described as the second city of the British empire, was based in part on its role as headquarters of British Indian administration. Operationally, though, in many vital respects this was only for some months in the year, ever since Simla had been developed as the summer capital, with Darjeeling as its counterpart for the Bengal government. More fundamental was the twofold economic predominance of Calcutta as the pre-eminent focus of British commerce, shipping, finance, and investments in the East, and as the city where British capital was in command more overwhelmingly than anywhere else in India. On the eve of the First World War, about three-fifths of the total British capital invested in India was based in Calcutta, while according to one estimate 81 per cent of investments in Calcutta were of European origin as compared to only around 3 per cent purely Indian (the comparative figures for Bombay were 41 per cent and 49 per cent).[7] Calcutta was the hub of the vital, British-dominated import–export trade, through which Lancashire textiles poured into the country and foodgrains and raw materials pumped out, with a favourable balance of trade that paid for Britain's trade deficits with the rest of the world. The interlocking structures of the managing agency system kept commerce, finance, railways, tea plantations, coal mines, and jute mills welded together in what amounted to a collective European monopoly of the commanding heights of Bengal's economy. The system was buttressed in decisive ways by racist privilege and exclusive access to the corridors of political authority.[8] And Calcutta lay at the heart of it all, with British-owned jute mills strung along the banks of the Hooghly north and south of the city, and a concentration of business houses, banks, and government buildings in and around Dalhousie Square that served as an effective symbol of the proximity and interdependence of imperial grandeur, power and profit.

[7] Rajat Kanta Ray, *Social Conflict and Political Unrest in Bengal 1875-1927* (Delhi, 1984), pp. 14–16.

[8] The standard analysis is Amiya Kumar Bagchi, *Private Investment in India 1900-39* (Cambridge, 1972).

Proximity, however — not necessarily or always identity or entirely conflict-free symbiosis. The aristocracy from which still came viceroys, governors and the top-most rungs of the British Indian bureaucracy liked to consider themselves a bit above mere trade or money-grubbing (even though their own family origins often would not bear much scrutiny), and capable of taking a 'broader' view of long-term imperial interests. It is interesting, for instance, that Cotton, a High Court advocate with an Oxford degree, says very little about European business activity in his massive account of Calcutta. The 1911 decision to transfer the capital to the much more strategically-located Delhi (near the geographical centre of the empire, and closer to the north-west frontier across which invaders might come) aroused much resentment in British business circles located in Calcutta. *Capital*, principal organ of such interests, interpreted it as a bid to remove the 'Simla clique . . . from the influence of public opinion': the latter being implicitly equated, following the normal practice of *Capital*, with British business opinion. Indian nationalists in fact were not particularly disturbed by the transfer, and some of them welcomed it as clearing the way for some amount of provincial autonomy for Bengal.[9]

The pre-eminence of Calcutta within the colonial economy did gradually decline, in ways related to the decline of that structure as a whole. Indian cotton textiles, spearheaded by Bombay and· Ahmedabad, were able to capture the home market from Lancashire piecegoods during the inter-war years. The world demand for jute declined, while within the Calcutta jute business itself Marwari firms began easing out Europeans. Such developments, however, still lay in the future, in the first decade of the twentieth-century: of more immediate relevance was a suddenly enhanced threat from emergent Indian, and more specifically Bengali educated middle-class *(bhadralok)* nationalism, of which 1905 has remained the abiding symbol.

With Marwari traders and the Bengali, predominantly Hindu, bhadralok, we have moved beyond the saheb para to other Calcuttas. The city in many important respects was, and remains, not one but many: distinct in residential areas, languages and cultures, self-images, but interacting in everyday life in relationships of inequality — and occasional conflict.

---

[9] Pradip Sinha, 'Calcutta and Currents of History', in Sukanta Chaudhuri, vol. I.

III

Around the edges of saheb para, and meeting its indispensable service requirements, had developed what urban historians of Calcutta today describe as a heterogeneous intermediate zone, inhabited by poor whites, Eurasians (products of marriages or liaisons of white and non-white), large numbers of Muslim service groups (preferred by Europeans as servants and cooks as presumably having less stringent pollution taboos), and small communities of Jews, Armenians and Chinese.[10] There were more prosperous Muslims, too, both here and in pockets like Cossipur in the north, Tollygunj in the south, and Garden Reach in the south-west, some of them with considerable urban property. A substantial number particularly of the more 'respectable' Muslim residents were immigrants from outside Bengal, speaking not Bengali but Urdu: some had come in the entourage of defeated courts exiled to Calcutta by the British (the family of Tipu Sultan in Tollygunj, Nawab Wajid Ali Shah of Avadh in Garden Reach). As migration into Calcutta swelled with the opening of railways, the bulk of immigrants came in fact not from Bengal villages but from poorer areas like north Bihar, the eastern United Provinces, and Orissa. They came to constitute the major part of the workforce of the jute mills in the environs of Calcutta, as well as the mass of casual and menial labour. By 1901, 36.3 per cent of the population of Calcutta spoke one or other variety of Hindustani: the speakers of Bengali had no more than a bare majority, constituting 51.3 per cent of the inhabitants.[11]

At the north-western edge of the intermediate zone, adjacent to the European business centre but utterly different visually from it, lay Barabazar, the Great Market. While Dalhousie Square and Clive Street were the abode of sophisticated British firms that concentrated on wholesale business and left retail operations to lesser people located elsewhere, Barabazar remained a traditional 'Oriental' urban market: a maze of bustling shops and narrow lanes crowded at night as much as in daytime. Commerce was fragmented here into a multitude of person-to-person transactions involving a very large number of participants, and enabling what scholars like Van Leur and later Clifford Geertz have described as the long-term coexistence of a mass of peddlers and a few merchant-princes. Barabazar was

[10] See, particularly, Pradip Sinha, *Calcutta in Urban History* (Calcutta, 1978), Chapter II.

[11] *Census of India 1901*, vol. VII, 4, p. 72.

the lynchpin of Calcutta's commerce with other parts of the subcontinent and beyond by river, land and then railways. Here Colesworthy Grant in 1850 found 'Persians, Arabs, Jews, Marwaris, Armenians, Madrasees, Sikhs, Turks, Parsees, Chinese, Burmese and Bengalees.'[12] Bengali merchant-princes, quite prominent in the late-eighteenth and early-nineteenth-centuries as 'banians' or compradores of private British traders, were gradually eased out from the kind of business life that Barabazar symbolized. Their upcountry linkages were weak, and many turned to investment in land in the form of zamindaris, intermediate tenures, or urban real estate. By the late nineteenth century Barabazar's image was coming to be associated above all with the Marwaris, extremely enterprising immigrants from Rajasthan who rose by acting as subordinate agents of British firms in distributing British imports inside the country and collecting raw materials for export or processing into manufactures. After the 1920s, they would gradually displace their erstwhile masters in a drive associated above all with the Calcutta-based Birla family, which also developed some connections with Gandhian all-India nationalism.

Despite their evident and many-sided economic importance, the people of this intermediate zone, and even the enormously successful Marwari businessmen who in more recent years have made some contributions to civic amenities (the Birlas, once again, notably, with their museums, art gallery, a planetarium, as well as a still incomplete giant temple) have remained on the edge of the dominant image of the city. They tend still to be perceived as immigrant birds of passage, without the memories and monumental aura that linger around the British even five decades after independence. That image in the twentieth century has been of a city predominantly Bengali (and, implicitly, high-caste Hindu) in culture, if not in statistics of population or economic success — a city about which all Bengalis can and should take pride. The first decade of the twentieth century was crucial to the making of this imagined Calcutta, for in significant ways, at least as a positive stereotype, it had not existed earlier.

The Calcutta of the Bengalis — predominantly Hindu, with the proportion of upper castes (Brahmans, Kayasthas, Vaidyas) higher

---

[12] Colesworthy Grant, *Anglo-Indian Sketches* (1850), quoted in Sabyasachi Bhattacharya, *Traders and Trades in Old Calcutta*, in Sukanta Chaudhuri, vol. I, p. 204.

than in most other parts of Bengal[13] — lay in the nineteenth century to the north and north-east of the intermediate zone. There was also Bhowanipur, to the south of the European town, where lawyers, doctors and other professional Bengalis were moving in towards the end of the century; Kalighat, adjoining Bhowanipur in the south-west, an older settlement around the Kali temple there; and, from the early twentieth century, the beginnings of a more 'modern' Bengali suburb in Ballygunge.

The families at the apex of old Calcutta's Bengali society have been described as 'compradore-rajas'.[14] They were men who had made their fortunes as agents (banians) to European private traders or intermediaries (dewans) indispensable for East India administration in the early days. Many of them had briefly ventured into independent business in the late-eighteenth and early-nineteenth century, but then moved into landed property or Calcutta real estate as the British collective monopoly consolidated itself with Marwaris as preferred underlings. Their way of life was usually marked by extravagance and conspicuous consumption, and most of the opulent houses of the compradore-rajas were already in various stages of decay by the early-twentieth century. Even in their great days, such palaces had lacked the spaciousness and external grace of the white residential areas, for compradore-rajas turned into urban rentiers had to encourage the peopling of space: opulent houses thus came to be surrounded by slums and brothels.

Early colonial compradore-rajas were fairly often of intermediate-caste origin, indicating a certain social fluidity that was perhaps restricted as what one historian has called the most 'Brahman' of centuries unfolded in subordinate symbiosis with colonial consolidation.[15] The noveaux-riche of old Calcutta patronized the traditional Brahman literati, but also a motley crew of multi-caste *kabiwalas*, with such disconcertingly diverse names as Antony Phiringhee, Nimai Shunri (tapster), Haru Thakur, or Keshto Muchi (cobbler). Somewhat

---

13 The proportion of the three high-castes to the total Hindu population was 28.4 per cent in Calcutta, and 19.2 per cent in its suburbs, in 1881. The figures were high also in a number of East Bengal districts, but there Hindus as a whole comprised only a small part of the population. See the useful table in Anil Seal, *The Emergence of Indian Nationalism: Competition and Collaboration in the Later Nineteenth Century* (Cambridge, 1968), p. 43.

14 Pradip Sinha's term, *Calcutta in Urban History*, pp. 16–17.

15 David Washbrook, 'Law, State and Agrarian Society in Colonial India', in Baker, Johnson and Seal (eds), *Power, Profit and Politics* (Cambridge, 1981).

paradoxically, the creators of the 'new', 'modern', eventually 'renaissance', culture would be overwhelmingly upper caste, even if on occasion reformist or iconoclastic. This, in its own perception, was a middle-class *(madhyasreni, madhyabitta)*, bhadralok world which situated itself below the aristocracy of dewans and banians but above the lesser folk who had to soil their hands with manual labour in countryside or town, and who tended to be lower caste or Muslim. It largely snapped its links with the older culture of compradore-rajas and kabiwalas after the poet Ishwarchandra Gupta (1812–59), developing more refined and somewhat puritanical norms and distinguishing itself from both the luxury and corruption of old-style Babus, and the 'superstitious' ways of the 'uneducated masses'.

Already, by the second quarter of the nineteenth century, some of the more sophisticated of the madhyabitta had started drawing analogies with European middle-class development. The *Bangadoot* of 13 June 1829 described the benefits that could follow from a 'rise of the middle class' as 'too numerous to be mentioned', but not excluding 'freedom . . . in the not too distant future'. It drew a pointed contrast between the experience of England on the one hand, and countries bereft of such a middle class, like Poland and Spain, on the other.[16] Optimism clearly far outran social realities in such analogies. The colonial middle class, particularly in Bengal, would be characterized not really by any association with capitalistic enterprise (signs of which actually diminished with time), but by education (of the new kind introduced by the British, with English as medium at higher levels), predominantly high-caste Hindu status, and a virtually ubiquitous link with land in the form of petty zamindari, or, more often, intermediate tenure holding. The fixing of land revenue in perpetuity in 1793 by Cornwallis' Permanent Zamindari Settlement, without any corresponding ceiling on rent, created over time a vast hierarchy of intermediaries who could batten on a revenue/rent gap that grew without any significant entrepreneurial initiative by zamindars or tenure holders. Constant fragmentation and sale, however, often kept the size of the individual rentier income quite small, and increasingly inadequate for the demands of gentility. Much more than big zamindars, therefore, it was this middle class that went in for Western education in a big way, for such education had become indispensable for the respectable professions of lawyer, doctor, teacher, journalist, writer, government official, or clerk.

16 Cited in Pradip Sinha, p. 95.

Twentieth-century educated common sense has tended to identify the culture of this middle class a bit too closely with Calcutta. 'Which Calcutta?' would be an useful question here, not to elicit banal statements about the renaissance being a minority or elite affair (high culture tending to be that in all class-divided societies), but to emphasize the exclusions even at privileged levels. Nineteenth-century middle-class culture was confined to only one of the three city zones we have distinguished, and left virtually untouched the most influential and prosperous among Calcutta elite groups: the British, of course (barring individual Indophile well-wishers or patrons), but also Marwari business magnates, most Muslim aristocrats, and even the bulk of the opulent compradore-rajas. (We tend to forget how exceptional the Jorasanko Tagores were.) Conversely, the educated middle class or bhadralok was far from being a purely metropolitan phenomenon cut off from the countryside. Many of its members were first-generation immigrants to Calcutta, and there were real, if often diminishing, links with villages through rentier incomes that necessitated at least vacation or Puja visits to rural homes where their womenfolk quite often still resided. A significant proportion spent the bulk of their working lives as professionals, government officials, or clerks outside the city, and suburban towns along the Hooghly and some parts of East Bengal were almost as important for bhadralok culture in the nineteenth century as Calcutta. The Brahmo reform movement, for instance, had some of its principal bases in East Bengal towns, and the Bikrampur region around Dacca reputedly supplied one-third of Bengal Government clerks.[17] The subsequent decline of many mufassil centres probably helped to constitute the twentieth-century identification of the renaissance image with Calcutta alone.

Yet Calcutta was central to the colonial middle class of Bengal, for it constituted the heart of three kinds of institutional networks crucial for the emergence of the nineteenth- and twentieth-century bhadralok as a distinctive formation: the new kinds of schools and colleges which came to be considered the indispensable entry points into the modern liberal professions, the printing press, and clerical jobs in government or mercantile offices. The first has always enjoyed the bulk of scholarly attention, in earlier renaissance discussions and today's cultural studies alike. Relatively little notice, in contrast, has been given to print and office work.

[17] Note by H.H. Risley, 7 February 1904, Government of India Home Public Proceedings A, February 1905, n. 155.

The focus upon what, quite often somewhat vaguely, is commonly termed 'English' education[18] — in praise or blame, as principal agency of 'awakening' or instrument of colonial hegemony producing 'derivative' (maybe at best 'hybrid') discourses[19] — has become unhelpful in several interrelated ways. The ferment brought about by sudden contact with a culture both rich and apparently irresistible in technology and power must not of course be underestimated. But eulogists and critics alike have often somewhat simplified and exaggerated its significance and reach. The tone of much Christian missionary propaganda should be a sufficient reminder that the influence of the nineteenth-century West cannot be equated with 'rationalism' or 'post-Enlightenment modernity' in any total sense. Neither is rationalism unique to the modern West: the most uncompromisingly rationalistic of Rammohan's religious tracts, the *Tuhfat-ul-Muwahiddin* (c. 1804), was written before he had learnt much English and may have had connections with the heritage of Islamic freethinking. And while colonialism no doubt wanted English education to produce clerks to run the administration cheaply and to create an alienated loyalist group, the actual consequences revealed sufficient Indian initiative and appropriation to quickly make the 'educated babu' the principal butt of racist ridicule. Surrender to colonial discourse was seldom total or unambiguous among the new literati — as distinct from many not particularly well-educated zamindars and babus, who mindlessly aped scraps of Western fashion and became the target of merciless satire precisely from men truly steeped in European culture like Michael Madhusudan Dutt or Bankim. The indigenous cultural resources of the English-educated elite also should not be forgotten: 'mimicry', I feel, improves, through complicating, the earlier 'derivative' thesis, but is not in the end a fully satisfactory category for understanding the colonial middle class.

The terms of debate as set by the concentration on English

---

[18] It is not always clear whether one is referring to the use of English as medium of instruction in higher education, the role within it of English Literature studies, or colonial education in general after Macaulay. Such ambiguities persist even in the best writings in the Saidian mode, e.g. Gauri Viswanathan's *Masks of Conquest: Literary Study and British Rule in India* (New York: Columbia University Press, 1989).

[19] Partha Chatterjee, *Nationalist Thought and the Colonial World: A Derivative Discourse?* (Delhi, 1986); Homi Bhabha, 'Of Mimicry and Man: The Ambivalence of Colonial Discourse', reprinted in Philip Rice and Patricia Waugh (eds), *Modern Literary Theory: A Reader* (London, 1989, 1992).

education have also tended to confine attention to a rather small elite among the products of the new schools and colleges. Religious and social reformers/revivalists, literary giants, lawyers, doctors, teachers, journalists and politicians have been the subject of an enormous literature, whether in eulogy or critique. But an intellectual history that tries to become social cannot afford to ignore the numerically much larger stratum of the less successful, if still over-whelmingly high-caste, within the colonial middle class: declining traditional literati, school or college drop-outs, obscure hack-writers, humble school-teachers, and, above all, clerks *(kerani)* in government and mercantile offices. Till the mid nineteenth century, such offices had been largely staffed by Eurasians. This changed with the spread of Western education, for babus with a smattering of English could be increasingly recruited at considerably lower salaries. By 1873 a satirical article in a contemporary journal, entitled 'Reminiscences of a Kerani's Life', was contrasting the 'melodious warblings of DLR' (D.L. Richardson, Professor of English and Principal of Hindu College in the 1840s) with the fate of becoming a lowly clerk in 'Smasher, Mutton, and Co.'[20] It seems helpful, therefore, at least for some purposes, to draw a distinction between two levels in what has generally been considered a more-or-less homogeneous educated middle class. Both the upwardly mobile and the genteel poor were of course most visible in Calcutta, but the distinction was evident also in small towns and villages. In 1925, O'Malley's *Faridpur District Gazeteer* distinguished between a few big zamindars, 'many . . . petty landowners with narrow means', and, 'at the other end', 'ill-paid and penurious priests and struggling clerks, especially those working for private employers, such as landlords and traders.'[21]

High-caste Hindu men constituted the overwhelming majority of the recipients of English education in the nineteenth century, to the exclusion of all but a handful of women and a fairly small, if growing number of lower-caste (and Muslim) males. Debates focussed primarily on the ambiguous legacy of Macaulay tend therefore to relegate women and lower castes to the status of objects of reform/revivalist discourses (which women notably became, of course, from Rammohan onwards), rather than active agents in any sense. A glance at the largely neglected domain of print can help, perhaps, to alter and broaden perspectives.

[20] *Mukherjee's Magazine* (1873), cited in Pradip Sinha, *Calcutta in Urban History*, p. 122.
[21] L.S.S. O'Malley, *Faridpur District Gazetteer* (Calcutta, 1925), p. 55.

Mainstream Indian historiography has paid surprisingly little attention to the colonial introduction of print, yet it is arguable that the consequences here involved more radical departures than those associated with English education. As the Indian experience quickly reconfirmed, mechanical print tends to be associated with simultaneous shifts towards vernaculars, prose, and a wider range of discursivities. The mnemonic aspect becomes less important than in cultures based on a combination of oral tradition and a limited number of manuscripts, and printers and publishers, to make their trade viable, have to reach customers who are literate but without classical education. Vernacular print forges communicational links at a level below the classical language of high culture but above spoken dialects, in ways conducive towards the development of nationalistic identities. The democratizing aspects of printing, further, are normally most prominent in its early days, when it is relatively cheap and not yet controlled by big publishing firms. At the same time, certain more ambiguous, if not retrogressive, dimensions of print culture have also attracted growing scholarly attention at a time when modernity in all its forms is increasingly under attack. Printing diminishes the fluidity of oral traditions through fixing and valorizing written texts and, quite often, alleged 'classical' religious-cultural forms. And it tends to deepen the gulf between literate and illiterate and enhance literate arrogance and elitism, for so much more of the knowledge relevant for efficient everyday living now becomes available only through the written form.

The more negative implications of print are evident enough for colonial India, where an enhanced thrust towards 'classical' standards within both Hindu and Muslim worlds helped to set the two much more definitively apart by condemning as superstitious accretions much popular syncretistic comminglings. Despite print, mass literacy made very slow progress under colonial rule (and its successors), while, particularly in Bengal, formal education quickly became virtually the sole avenue for upward mobility as indigenous enterprise dried up in an area marked by overwhelming British economic preponderance.

Yet it will not do, I think, to consider colonial print culture in primarily negative terms, as no more than yet another disciplinary device restricting a supposedly freer world of pre-colonial popular culture. Printing in Indian languages, like Western education, was introduced as a colonial instrument, an adjunct to administration and Christian proselytization. But, much more evidently than in education, it was quickly appropriated and extended in ways for which mimicry would be a very poor analogy. Missionaries were prominent among the early creators of Bengali prose: but 'missionary Bengali' soon became a term of ridicule. Vernacular prose everywhere accompanied the spread of printing, permitting the systematic discussion of a far wider range of themes than had been normal for verse, and new literary forms and genres developed in considerable abundance. It needs to be emphasized, perhaps, that the Indian colonial intelligentsia of the nineteenth century chose Indian languages, and not English, as their primary, indeed overwhelmingly predominant, media for imaginative expression. 'Indo-Anglian' writing had to wait for postcolonial times to become a significant literary genre, under conditions of intensified globalization.

Vernacular literacy outstripped knowledge of English by a very considerable margin, and here the gender and caste differentials also mattered somewhat less. It is difficult to deny, therefore, that print did have a real, if limited, democratizing impact even in colonial conditions. The novel-reading modern Bengali wife quickly became a major target for conservative satire, while printing seems to have been cheap and accessible enough to have widened opportunities for authors of relatively plebeian origin, and for some women as well as men. Biographical literature, for instance, had dealt mainly with rulers or saints in pre-colonial times. In a recent compilation of sixteen autobiographies, written between 1833 and 1916, in significant contrast, about half are by little-known men. Four are by women: two of them distinguished because of their husbands and sons, the other two entirely obscure.[22] The printing presses of Bat-tala (North Calcutta) quickly started producing large numbers of minor plays and farces, tracts and household manuals and other ephemera, constituting a 'low-life of literature'[23] that historians have only recently begun to explore.

Printing, and the periodical-cum-newspaper writing it made possible, helped to create new forms of sociability, somewhat different

---

[22] Naresh Jana (ed.), *Atmakatha* (Calcutta, 1981). The first printed full-length autobiography is actually by a woman, Rashsundari Devi's *Amar Katha* (Calcutta, 1868). This text has been analysed in detail in Tanika Sarkar, 'A Book of Her Own, A Life of Her Own: Autobiography of a Nineteenth-Century Woman', *History Workshop Journal*, 36, 1993.

[23] To borrow Robert Darnton's phrase: 'The High Enlightenment and the Low-Life of Literature in Pre-Revolutionary France', *Past and Present*, 51, May 1971.

in style and composition from the traditional durbar of princes or zamindars. The best known among these is the middle-class *adda* (prolonged conversational sessions), today considered so typical of Bengali life. It has often centred around a periodical: a long and rich heritage, from *Bangadarshan* through *Bangabasi, Sabujpatra* and *Kallol* to *Parichay* and beyond, to mention only some of the most prominent. There were important audio-visual developments, too. Plays, earlier staged at the houses of zamindar patrons, moved from the 1870s to the newly-founded public theatres of North Calcutta, maintained through sale of fairly cheap tickets and not private patronage. They consequently won audiences that spanned a wide range of social groups and included women as well as men. At a still lower social level, there was, in the early twentieth century, a flood of pamphlet literature from an emerging lower-caste and Muslim literati, the authors of which described themselves as living in obscure villages, often known only by reference to the nearest post office or railway station. The pamphlets quite often bear testimony to yet another kind of sociability associated with print, for their authors acknowledge indebtedness to a large number of subscribers of similarly humble, village or small-town origin to meet their publication expenses.

The forms and channels of sociability which developed around the new educational-professional and print-cultural networks could provide a fruitful theme of research. They contributed to the emergence — under specific conditions of a colonial society not as yet characterized by much in the way of autonomous bourgeois growth — of something akin to a public sphere where standards would be defined and reasoned critiques of authority considered legitimate and proper. Certainly terms like 'public' or 'public opinion' had come to be commonly used by the late nineteenth century, no doubt partly in simple mimesis of the language of British political life, but also reflecting institutional changes in Indian society. To take a stray instance, the author of *An Open Letter to Curzon* (April 1904), protesting against the viceroy's plans of partitioning Bengal, repeatedly used public opinion as his ultimate court of appeal, while remaining careful to define it, through a quotation from Edmund Burke, as the views of men 'above menial dependence'.[24] Conversely, an official justification for the Partition found it advisable to use the argument that it

---

[24] The text of this pamphlet is included in Government of India Home Public Deposit Proceedings, April 1904, n. 39.

had 'emanated from public discussion and public opinion rather than from the government itself.'[25]

Studies of the French Enlightenment, fruitfully influenced by Habermas, have acquired an unprecedented depth and richness in recent years. The significant innovations include an expansion of research interests much beyond the iconic figures, the exploration of patterns of sociability, a sophisticated attention to shifting language-use as a constitutive element in the formation of social categories, and a decisive gendering of perspectives.[26] The potential for a somewhat similar transformation of intellectual into social history does not seem entirely absent for colonial Bengal.

Contemporary responses to office work, the third constitutive element in urban bhadralok experience, were unequivocally negative. The government or British mercantile office was a space where the kerani was subject to foreign authority in a direct, everyday sense, in encounters characterized by racist insult and efforts to impose a novel discipline of clock time. The implications went much beyond the confines of the specific clerical world, for *chakri* by the late nineteenth century had come to signify all that was demeaning and oppressive in colonial bhadralok life. Several essays in this volume explore the many ramifications of this image of clerical work, and in particular its connections with a specifically nineteenth-century image of Kaliyuga.[27] My specific concern here is the way in which representations of clerical life moulded the image of Calcutta itself, giving it a negative tone that in the light of later developments appears somewhat unexpected today.

Nineteenth-century Calcutta had become a real metropolis for the bhadralok, providing education, opportunities for jobs, printed books, a taste for new cultural values. It was also, by and large, a city where the bhadralok did not yet feel at home, an experience embodied in the practice of the Bengali gentleman, till well into the twentieth century, calling his city residence *basha*, reserving the more

25 *Administration of Bengal under Sir Andrew Fraser, 1903-8* (Calcutta, 1908).

26 See, for instance, Roger Chartier, *Cultural Origins of the French Revolution* (Durham: Duke University Press, 1991); Dena Goodman, *The Republic of Letters: A Cultural History of the French Enlightenment* (Cornell, 1994); and Sara Maza, *Private Lives and Public Affairs: The Causes-Celebres of Pre-Revolutionary France* (California, 1993). The contributions of feminist scholarship have been particularly outstanding here. It is a pity that work of such quality still continues to be ignored while repeating stereotypical formulas about a homogenized 'Enlightenment rationality'.

27 See Chapters 6 and 8.

intimate term *bari* for the ancestral village home. Even for the upwardly mobile, the higher rungs of the administration remained a largely European preserve, the most successful of the professionals could never feel secure from occasional racist insult or discrimination, and Bengali presence in the economic life of the city was visibly diminishing. And just below was the world of genteel clerical poverty, inhabited quite often by less fortunate kinsmen.

The striking fact, therefore, was that the nineteenth-century Bengali bhadralok seldom wrote about Calcutta, and tended to emphasize the negative features of its life even when they did: in total contrast to many of their descendants today. Despite the novelty of the metropolitan experience, cityscapes entered rarely into imaginative literature, unlike, say, in Dickens or Baudelaire. It is difficult to think of any extended description of Calcutta written by a Bengali that is not satirical, prior to the accounts of A.K. Roy, a census official, in 1902, and a scion of an old compradore-raja family, Raja Benoy Krishna Deb, in 1905. Calcutta, rather, was often portrayed as the heart of Kaliyuga, the last and most degenerate of eras in the traditional upper-caste Hindu notion of cyclical time, in which aliens rule and hierarchies of caste, gender, and age are inverted. An elementary pun on the city's name permitted its description as the capital of the evil king Kali who in some versions of the myth presides over this dark age.

Durgacharan Roy's farcical account of a visit of ancient Hindu gods to British-ruled India, from which I have quoted, is symptomatic of a very wide range of late-nineteenth-century writings that extend from cheap tracts, prints, plays and farces to the conversations of Ramakrishna Paramhansa, whose early devotees often had a clerical ambience. The format of gods travelling by train from Delhi to Calcutta permitted Durgacharan to compose a kind of travelogue-cum-account of famous persons and places. Yet in his description of Calcutta what dominates are not palaces, distinguished men, novel city amenities, nor even the squalor of the very poor, but clerks streaming to work across the Hooghly, and returning home with worn-out faces in the evening after a day of unremitting humiliation.

The reference to the 'nagging of wives' is also typical. The office, far more completely than the worlds of education and print-culture, was a men-only domain. Unable as yet to do anything effective about British office bosses or colonial domination, the clerk — or rather the writers, readers, or theatre audiences empathizing with him — tended to shift the guilt to women: the 'modern' educated wife.

allegedly unmindful of her domestic duties, ill-treating her mother-in-law, wasting money on imported luxury goods, and forcing her husband to take up demeaning office jobs to obtain the wherewithal for such extravagance. In a further development, the woes of the 'traditional' mother, neglected by her sons who have been entrapped in the snares of the modern wife, could become a symbol of the suffering 'mother'-land. A patriotic message consequently emerged, entangled however within a rejuvenated patriarchy, and without as yet finding any correlative in effective action. Durgacharan's gods observe and mourn, and then listen once again to the tale of the inevitable evils of Kaliyuga before going to sleep.

The bhadralok image of Calcutta, however, started changing fairly rapidly in the 1900s. A.K. Roy and Benoykrishna Deb apart, there was Sibnath Shastri's *Ramtanu Lahiri o Tatkalin Bangasamaj* (Calcutta, 1904). Not formally a cityscape, this presented for the first time a connected history of middle-class educational, social, moral, and religious improvement during the nineteenth century through a chain of biographies of men generally moulded by Calcutta, though not necessarily always residing there. A passage in the early part of *Ramtanu Lahiri* still refers to Calcutta as the source of a 'moral infection'. Significantly, however, this is put in the past tense, and the implication clearly is that the educated bhadralok have been able to remove most of the evils in the nabayuga (new age), brought in through modern education. There is in other words an association of Calcutta with progress, and Sibnath's text would be central to the formation of an influential historiographical model of a nineteenth-century 'Bengal Renaissance' in the next generation.

What really changed perceptions, however, was the Partition of Bengal ordered by Curzon in 1905, and its aftermath. For a few dizzy, inspiring years, Bengali middle-class patriotic dreams appeared capable of realization. The bhadralok seemed on the point of gaining command over the alien city, through struggle.

IV

Lord Curzon, Viceroy from 1899 to 1905, had tried to systematically weaken emergent middle-class Indian nationalism, which had one of its principal centres in Bengal, and in this context he found particularly irritating the close interconnections between Calcutta bhadralok politicians and the East Bengal districts where many of them had their small-town or village homes. Having eliminated in

1899 the elected majority in the Calcutta Corporation (a bugbear for Calcutta-based British business interests, which now obtained a freer hand in matters like licenses and fees), and reduced the autonomy of Calcutta University (felt to be another bhadralok power-base) in 1904, he persuaded the Secretary of State to announce the decision to partition Bengal in July 1905. The public justification given was administrative convenience, but in their confidential minutes officials were perfectly frank about the underlying political motivations: '. . . one of our main objects is to split up and thereby weaken a solid body of opponents to our rule', says H.H. Risley's Note of 6 December 1904.[28] As the new province of Eastern Bengal and Assam had a Muslim majority, while Bengali middle-class nationalism was predominantly though not entirely Hindu, a second, more familiar, kind of divide-and-rule soon took over from the first, with considerably greater ultimate success.

The Partition of Bengal boomeranged very badly, however, so far as Bengali bhadralok nationalism was concerned, and already by October 1905 Curzon was writing angry notes about ineffective police officials composing long minutes while the streets of Calcutta passed under the control of agitators. With remarkable speed, the struggle against the Partition went far beyond the beaten track of 'Moderate' agitation, which had so far consisted of occasional meetings and respectful petitioning. Historians of what is usually termed the Swadeshi movement have analysed in detail the new forms of struggle — boycott of British imported goods and promotion of indigenous swadeshi enterprise, student withdrawal from government-controlled educational institutions and efforts to start 'national' schools and colleges, schemes for arbitration courts in villages in place of official lawcourts, the organization of groups of full-time volunteers, and eventually, in the face of intensified repression and flagging mass support, a shift to methods of individual terrorism. The aims of the struggle similarly broadened out from cancellation of the Partition, through other specific constitutional reforms, to dreams of swaraj: self-rule, independence. Calcutta played a notable, though not necessarily predominant, part in all these developments.[29] What is more relevant in an essay about the city, however, is an effort to trace how

[28] Government of India Home Public Proceedings A February 1905.

[29] Haridas and Uma Mukherji, *India's Fight for Freedom, or the Swadeshi Movement* (Calcutta, 1958); Amales Tripathi, *The Extremist Challenge: India between 1905 and 1910* (Calcutta, 1967); Sumit Sarkar, *The Swadeshi Movement in Bengal, 1903-8* (Delhi, 1973).

the Calcutta scene changed visually, in everyday life, during these years, as well as the more permanent shift in the dominant image of the city: in the tracks, perhaps, of Curzon's bitter remarks about the streets passing under agitator control.

With one major exception — i.e. the brief and socially very retrogressive but extremely powerful agitation against the Age of Consent Bill of 1891, denounced by orthodox Hindus as a gross interference in religious customs by a foreign government — meetings in Calcutta so far had been held inside halls. The Town Hall protest against the Partition announcement on 7 August 1905 began in a similar way, with the scion of a loyalist compradore-raja family in the chair: but the immense crowds that had turned up compelled a spill-over into the fields around the hall, with three separate sets of orators. Soon open-air meetings were being held in parks all over the Bengali areas of the city, though in the absence of loudspeakers Maidan rallies at the foot of the Ochterlony Monument became common only a generation later. The streets regularly filled up with processions, singing patriotic songs which were being composed in unprecedented number, and which breathed a new note of self-confidence and pride. The extract I have cited from one such song, by Rabindranath, might perhaps convey a little of the flavour of those times. Patriotic appropriation of Hindu religious rituals, with consequences that ultimately proved highly ambiguous, was another marked feature of the Swadeshi days. Thus, on 16 October 1905, the day Bengal was partitioned, processions wound their way through north Calcutta lanes to take a ceremonial dip in the river, and wristlets *(rakhis)* were exchanged as symbol of the eternal brotherhood of Bengalis.

The cadres of the Swadeshi movement were mostly students, and more generally bhadralok youth, who systematically picketed shops selling foreign goods (and particularly Lancashire cloth), went around peddling indigenous products, and tried to organize an educational boycott. Their activities led to the first street clashes with the police. Associations or *samitis* of young men proliferated, rooted in many cases in already existing ties of collective life in college hostels and messes (rooms rented by groups of students, often coming from the same district, with a common kitchen), along with the camaraderie evolved through student life and endless tea-shop conversations. Within a few years, some of these connections would develop into revolutionary terrorist groups. This, it needs to be noted, was still a male sociability: one or two exceptional figures apart, women, while regularly hailed now as true repositories of authentic values provided they gave up foreign luxuries, were expected to applaud from the sidelines, persuade husbands to abandon denationalized ways, but not otherwise directly participate in political activities. A leading nationalist weekly even took care to specify on the eve of 16 October that gender segregation had to be maintained while exchanging rakhis[30] — even though the traditional ritual of sisters tying wristlets onto the hands of brothers could in sheer logic have been extended in an entirely opposite direction. Swadeshi cultural nationalism exalted woman as abstract mother-figure, Bangalakshmi, bountiful bestower of good fortune to the land of Bengal. This often went along with fairly aggressive reassertions of patriarchal values and hostility towards what an earlier generation of middle-class reformers had liked to call *stri-swadhinata*, the freeing of women. Absence of women apart, however, the lineaments were emerging already of a radical Calcutta, the 'city of processions', in which students in particular would remain in the forefront of successive waves of militant nationalist, and then Left-wing, politics right down to the 1970s.

Swadeshi Calcutta, predictably, had its principal spatial location in the middle class and Hindu quarters to the north of the intermediate zone, along with Bhowanipur and Kalighat — but there were some penetrations into other areas and social levels. Muslim participation was not negligible, particularly in the early days. Hindu and Muslim students marched hand in hand, for instance, to a massive rally in a North Calcutta square (Rajabazar) on 23 September 1905. There were also a number of extremely active Swadeshi Muslim leaders and orators, invariably described as paid agents in the British records, and special targets of official anger and repression. Effective boycott, again, demanded penetration into Barabazar, and specifically an understanding with the Marwari indentors of Lancashire textiles. For a brief moment, in the autumn of 1905, things looked very promising for the nationalists as many Marwari merchants rejected contracts with British firms. Subsequent developments revealed that the motivation here had been a dispute about trade terms rather than patriotic sentiments, and imports from Lancashire through Marwari intermediaries were soon resumed.

More significant ultimately, though only of limited scale and duration for the moment, was the entry of some bhadralok activists into the field of labour organization. The strike of the clerks of Burn Company, Howrah, in September 1905, protesting, significantly,

[30] *Sanjibani*, 12 October 1905.

against a new mechanical system of recording attendance times that
was considered humiliating, had an electrifying effect: not surprisingly
so, in view of what has been said already about the centrality of the
negative image of clerical chakri dominated by clock-time in much
late-nineteenth-century middle-class discourse. Clerks and white-collar
employees in general, who were usually Bengalis with some degree of
literacy, unlike the bulk of the industrial proletariat, remained the
main focus of Swadeshi labour activity and organization. Thus a
fairly stable Printers Union was set up, and in the summer of 1906
a long strike by stationmasters and clerks of the East Indian Railway
evoked a lot of nationalist support. But there were sporadic efforts
to set up unions in some jute mills, too, and solidarity actions for
tram and dock workers on strike, while labour sympathy for the
Swadeshi cause was widespread enough to impart to 16 October 1905
a bit of the atmosphere of the *bandhs* of more recent times. Most
offices and Indian shops were closed, trams halted by student pick-
eters, carters went off the roads, and even some factories had to close
down. And a fund-raising procession of printers on strike towards
the end of the same year, led by A.C. Banerji, the best-known of the
Swadeshi trade union organizers, demonstrated, however fleetingly,
an impressive unity of the Indian residents of Calcutta across class
lines. 'Even constables and women of the town came forward with
their contributions', Banerji recalls in an unpublished autobiographical fragment, as the procession wound its way through the heart of
middle-class North Calcutta from Cornwallis street to the palace of
the Paikpara zamindar.[31]

The Swadeshi days provide us, in other words, with occasional
brief anticipations of a future in which others beside the bhadralok,
more precisely a significant section of the toilers, would also be able
through struggle to make the city founded by Job Charnock their
own. The clerks of what is called Calcutta's office *para* remain even
today electoral bastions of the Left, at a time when the city's radical
reputation has become in large part no more than a nostalgic memory.

Few, however, of the hopes stimulated by Swadeshi were realized.
Boycott came and went, leaving hardly a dent in the curve of foreign
imports that went on rising till the First World War. A handful of
reasonably successful Swadeshi enterprises were set up, as for instance
Bengal Chemicals and Calcutta Potteries in the eastern suburbs of
the city. Many others quickly withered away, like the bulk of the

---

[31] Sumit Sarkar, *Swadeshi Movement in Bengal*, Chapter v.

national schools, and British control over the decisive levers of economic power was never seriously challenged. In business and education alike, material considerations like relative profitability, access to bank loans, and transport and trade linkages, and the non-existent job prospects of a swadeshi degree proved more powerful than generous patriotic dreams. The trade unions were extremely short-lived, and most of the samitis were quickly snuffed out by police repression. The efforts to reach out beyond bhadralok confines had not really succeeded, and the bulk of the peasants and urban toilers remained indifferent, and at times positively hostile so far as substantial sections of Muslims were concerned. In some East Bengal districts, for instance, where a predominantly Hindu gentry faced an overwhelmingly Muslim tenantry, efforts to enforce the boycott through a combination of Hindu religious appeals and some zamindari pressure contributed to communal riots in 1906-7. By 1908, sections of the patriotic bhadralok in isolation had gone in for methods of individual terror, while others went back to prayers and petitions or became indifferent to politics.

The cobblers' song in Amritalal Bose's play, from which I have given an extract, thus embodied middle-class hopes, not plebeian reality. *Sabash Bangali* in fact at times quite unwittingly revealed some of the social limits of the Swadeshi movement even in 1905, when it was still riding high. The agitation in Pashdanga village remains clearly a matter of schoolboys led by a patriotic headmaster, and no peasant appears on stage. A Muslim swadeshi figure fails to convince when he declares that there could be no communal conflict in Bengal, as Hindus are 'elder brothers' to the Muslims. A clerk's wife is furious that a police constable — belonging by birth to the servant class, she says — has dared lay his hands on her Swadeshi-activist student son. In October 1907, following a clash between the police and a Swadeshi crowd at Beadon Square in North Calcutta, the Bengali bhadralok found themselves being beaten up, and their property looted, by what a non-official enquiry commission described as 'large numbers of low-class people, such as . . . sweepers, etc.'[32]

What remained as the abiding legacy of the Swadeshi years to Bengal, and particularly Calcutta, was a very rich cultural outcrop, richer indeed than that produced by any later phase of nationalism in this part of the country. The patriotic songs composed then, for

[32] Report of the Unofficial Commission of Enquiry into the Riots in Calcutta on 2, 3 and 4 October 1907 in Government of India Home Political, A Proceedings, January 1908, n. 75-80.

instance, have remained an inspiring resource, and not for nationalists alone. There were numerous essays on swadeshi themes, many of them of high intellectual and literary quality, a large number of patriotic plays, two outstanding novels by Rabindranath directly connected with contemporary debates, a new interest in literary and local history and folk culture, and a self-consciously patriotic 'Calcutta School of Art' around Abanindranath Tagore. One needs to add, also, the entry during these years of Bengali youth into what had been so far in large part a preserve of the Europeans, the playing fields of the Maidan: an entry symbolized by the victory of Mohan Bagan football club over its white rivals in the IFA Shield Final of 1911.

Swadeshi lived on, and increasingly so, above all in bhadralok memory and nostalgia about hopes aroused but not fulfilled, or appropriated by others. In 1905, the Bengali middle class had directly challenged the collective economic near-monopoly of British capital, and evolved a range of new techniques of struggle which in many ways anticipated the methods of Gandhian nationalism. Succeeding decades saw the erosion of the British stranglehold over Calcutta's business life, but the principal beneficiaries were Marwaris, not Bengali traders or entrepreneurs. The takeover of boycott, and 'passive resistance' as its extended form, by all-India nationalism under a leader from Gujarat was likewise often read as a decline or marginalization of Bengal and Calcutta in the country's political life. 1921–2 had been another time of high expectations: high-watermark of Hindu–Muslim unity, large numbers of jute mill workers and, for the first time, women of diverse social strata marching in processions and going to jail side by side with middle-class men, at the call of Gandhi, Chittaranjan Das and Khilafat leaders. Anticlimax came swiftly, once again, as Calcutta erupted into unprecedented communal violence in 1926, and the Swarajist Calcutta Corporation which had also briefly aroused great hopes sank into factional squabbles, inefficiency and corruption. The pattern, in fact, has continued beyond the colonial era, in the current ebbing of the dream of social revolution which had been such a vital dimension of Calcutta life from the 1940s to the early 1970s. The Left still rules West Bengal, a remarkable achievement amidst worldwide collapse, but no longer seems capable of arousing much in the way of radical expectations or enthusiasm, at least in Calcutta.

There have been ample reasons, then, for a persistent harking back to an apparently more impressive past, in which a nineteenth-century renaissance is seen to culminate in Swadeshi, with Calcutta lying at the heart of both. It was not accidental that the classic 'renaissance model' was formulated in the 1940s, in a Bengal shattered by the cumulative impact of War, Famine, and Partition. *Notes on the Bengal Renaissance* (1946), by the Marxist Susobhan Sarkar, was explicitly written at a time when 'disintegration threaten[ed] every aspect of our life',[33] while between 1939 and 1952 Brajendranath Banerji and Sajanikanta Das, scholars with a totally different, indeed socially conservative perspective, produced a multi-volume collection of lives of nineteenth-century worthies, the *Sahitya-Sadhak-Charitmala*.

Retrospects tend to eulogize, but can turn at times acutely critical, for the widespread assumption that nineteenth-century bhadralok culture laid the foundations for the Bengal of today could provide occasion to the intelligentsia for self-flagellation as much as pride or nostalgia. Denunciations of the renaissance model have often come at moments when hopes of radical change have flowered and then withered away, notably in the wake of the 1948-9 'Ranadive' years,[34] and then, at a more academic level, following the collapse of the Naxalbari dream.

The consolation-cum-burden of memory, nostalgia, occasional breast-beating, it may seem to cynical observers, has passed from the British chroniclers of European Calcutta of the 1900s to the Bengali intelligentsia of the late twentieth century, that displays a similar antiquarianism about the notable figures, street names and houses of what was once termed the native town. Yet it would be churlish to end on that note alone. There remains something deeply moving about this interest and pride, in the accumulation of quite non-utilitarian knowledge about the city's past by people living, quite often, in atrocious conditions, or, at another level, in the way Calcutta's one new recent amenity, its Metro, is being kept spotlessly clean by its users in a city otherwise notorious for its filth and lack of civic spirit. Other Indian cities — Delhi, Varanasi, Ahmedabad, Madurai, even Bombay — have much more obvious ties linking some or many of its present inhabitants with the visual or cultural reminders of the past. Calcutta, that indisputably colonial creation, has been made its citizens' own through the everyday struggle for survival and the so often frustrated, yet perennial, dreams and endeavours for a better life.

[33] Susobhan Sarkar, *Notes on the Bengal Renaissance* (Calcutta, 1946), p. 1.
[34] The attempt at immediate revolution, after the Calcutta Congress of the Communist Party of India in February 1948, had adopted a new strategy and elected B.T. Ranadive as General Secretary.

6

Renaissance and Kaliyuga: Time, Myth and History in Colonial Bengal

' . . . the youthful band of reformers who had been educated at the Hindoo College, [who] like the tops of the Kanchenjungha were the first to catch and reflect the dawn.'
— Kishorichand Mitra, 1861, quoted in S.C. Sarkar, *Bengal Renaissance and Other Essays* (New Delhi, 1970), pp. 121-2.

'A lot has been said about the benefits of English education, but no one has written about the evils it has brought . . . blind imitation of the English has derailed social reform . . . It would be no exaggeration to say that selfishness is synonymous with today's civilization . . . educated wives no longer perform their domestic duties diligently . . . Europe has so much of commerce and industry: can *chakri* [clerical jobs] alone support so many *bhadralok* [respectable people]?'
— Rajnarayan Basu, *Sekal ar Ekal* (Calcutta, 1874; rpt. 1951), pp. 1, 66, 81, 86.

'See the course of *Kaliyuga*, *dharma*[1] has declined/Vedic ritual and customs have vanished, men and women become the same . . . the Shudra will place his foot on the Brahman's head . . . the son will disobey the father/the mother will be

[1] Kali is the last and the most degenerate of four *yugas* (eras — the preceding ones being Satya, Treta and Dwapar) in the traditional high-Hindu conception of cyclical time. In Kaliyuga, dharma (right ritual and conduct; from the nineteenth century, often taken to be the equivalent of the Western notion of 'religion') is at its lowest ebb. As the rest of the passage indicates, in it low castes (Shudras) dominate over Brahmans and other high castes, and hierarchies of gender and age are also reversed.

the servant of her daughter-in-law . . . so many factories, impossible to list/King Kali is so powerful . . . his commands so rigorous/no one can escape . . . '
— Aghorechandra Kavyatirtha, *Kalir Abasan ba Kalki-avatar Geetabhinoy* (Calcutta, 1902), pp. 3, 7, 80.

'*Kali* comes after *Satya, Treta, Dwapar*/Blessed is *Kaliyuga*, say all Vaishnavas . . . '
— Tarakchandra Sarkar, *Sri Sri Harileelamrita* (Faridpur, 1916), a metrical biography of Harichand Thakur, founder of a low-caste (Namashudra) religious sect.

'Blessed, blessed, be this *Kali* age.'
— Rashsundari Devi, *Amar Jivan* (first published Calcutta, 1868), the first autobiography by a Bengali woman; reprinted in Naresh Jana, *Atmakatha* (Calcutta, 1981), p. 77.

In the extracts above, taken from texts written and printed in colonial Bengal between 1861 and 1916, two well-known intellectuals of high-caste origin, an obscure Brahman schoolteacher-cum-playwright, a member of a low-caste religious sect, and a recently widowed housewife who is known only through the autobiography she composed, are all thinking about their times. They evaluate in distinct ways the changes they have lived through, and sometimes the language they use to conceptualize time itself differs: a new dawn, a Kaliyuga about which it does not seem to matter whether one uses the past, present continuous, or future tense. Kishorichand Mitra and Rajnarayan Basu were both distinguished alumni of Hindu College, Calcutta, founded in 1817 as the first major institution for higher education in the English language on the Western model in Bengal. They differ, clearly, in their estimates of what Western education and colonial rule have brought, but share a commonsensically modern conception of time as the abstract, linear framework in which events happen. The playwright who elsewhere describes himself as a 'poor Brahman', the upper-caste housewife, and the Namashudra author of a metrical biography, refer, in contrast, to a conceptual world familiar to Indologists and scholars of ancient India, but largely assumed to be irrelevant for understanding colonial or modern India. This is the classical Hindu conception of cyclical time, in which Kaliyuga endlessly recurs as the last epoch in an eternally repeated four-*yuga* cycle, the epochs distinguished from each other by their moral qualities. For high-Hindu religion and philosophy, Kaliyuga normally is the most degenerate of times, when Shudras (low-castes) dominate over high-castes and hierarchies of gender and age are reversed: the woman and the Namashudra here have found it to be 'blessed'.

Texts like these were evidently made possible by two major innovations brought in by colonial rule: clock time and print culture, stimulating diverse ways of thinking about time, and enabling even an otherwise obscure housewife to publish an autobiography. The facts here are familiar enough, but a general persistence of simplistic 'impact-response' frameworks in studies of indigenous culture under colonialism have often hindered historians from problematizing or exploring their implications. The unstated assumption has been of a quick, painless, and total transition from cyclical Kaliyuga to linear time, from 'myth' to modern 'history' on the Western model. The specific consequences of the equally belated, and sudden, entry of print-culture have also remained unexplored.

Impact-response frameworks have been of two kinds: eulogistic and denunciatory. As my first extract indicates, Kishorichand's metaphor was being used a hundred years later to substantiate the model of a 'Bengal Renaissance', in which the rediscovery of ancient Hindu cultural achievements by European Orientalists and the inflow of modern Western ideas through English education were supposed to have sparked off a whole series of progressive changes amounting to an 'awakening' to modernity.[2] Rajnarayan's statement, in contrast, points towards alternative viewpoints that displaced acceptance of the 'civilizing' mission of the West by critiques of colonial domination from perspectives that could be traditionalistic, extreme nationalist, or radical Left.[3] A variety of this second approach has recently acquired an international and interdisciplinary audience

[2] S.C. Sarkar's *Bengal Renaissance and Other Essays*, from which I have taken the statement of Kishorichand Mitra, probably represents this approach at its best. See also A.C. Gupta (ed.), *Studies in the Bengal Renaissance* (Calcutta, 1958) and D. Kopf., *British Orientalism and the Bengal Renaissance* (California, 1969).

[3] One could recall Gandhi's controversial statement about Rammohan Roy being a 'pigmy' compared to what he might have been but for Western education. For Left critiques of the 'renaissance' model written some twenty years back, see the articles of Asok Sen, Barun De and Sumit Sarkar in V.C. Joshi (ed.), *Rammohan Roy and the Process of Modernisation in India* (New Delhi, 1975); Asok Sen, *Iswarchandra Vidyasagar and His Elusive Milestones* (Calcutta, 1977); and Sumit Sarkar, *A Critique of Colonial India* (Calcutta, 1985).

through the widespread influence of Edward Said's *Orientalism* and the consequent rise to prominence of colonial discourse analysis in metropolitan academic centres. There are ample signs that this has become a counterorthodoxy, in metropolitan cultural studies as well as in certain sectors of Indian history writing, literary theory, and feminist scholarship.[4]

Eulogy and denunciation can become mirror images, inversions of each other. What they have had in common here at times is an assumption of effective and total acculturation that tends to eliminate the autonomy and agency of the colonial subject. This is at its most blatant in some applications of the Saidian framework where the critique of colonial power–knowledge gets extended into an assumption of complete control or seamless cultural hegemony. The colonial middle class, it appears, is capable of only 'derivative' discourses.[5]

A series of self-validating homogenizations can follow from this basic assumption of total domination by post-Enlightenment rationalist power-knowledge, which is itself a very simplified and over-generalized construct. Domains less affected by it — the uncontaminated pre-colonial or 'popular' — cannot, perhaps, be really explored, as our sources would be overwhelmingly of colonialist or indigenous Western-educated origin, and the tools and categories of today's historians likewise tainted by Enlightenment rationality. Circularity proves convenient, however, for a vague 'community consciousness' can now be postulated as relatively free of internal tensions or structures of oppression: an indigenism that can become extremely retrogressive in its political implications in today's India. More directly relevant for my argument here is the way such a framework, quite as much as in the 'Bengal Renaissance' historiography it repudiates, remains focussed on the high literati, as English education has been merely inverted from being an instrument of awakening to being a principal sign of subordination. Such a concentration on successful and prominent intellectuals of course tends to confirm the basic premise of acculturation/surrender.

[4] For a more detailed account of this Saidian impact, see my 'Orientalism Revisited: Saidian Frameworks in the Writing of Modern Indian History', *Oxford Literary Review*, 16, i–ii, 1994.

[5] There is a possible analogy here with the acculturation thesis of some French historians of early modern European popular culture, formulated around the time *Orientalism* was published: see Chapter II, p. 91, above, and my essay in *Oxford Literary Review*, p. 207.

My intention here is to emphasize difference and variation, open up some of these homogenized blocks; and here divergent perceptions of time, myth and history can provide vital clues. The colonial introduction of clock time in Bengal, for a start, had certain very specific, yet seldom noted, features. Belated entry produced a remarkable telescoping of phases. Clocks and disciplinary time came more or less together here, whereas in Western Europe the transition from medieval clocks showing hours alone, through watches ticking off minutes and seconds, to bureaucratic–industrial structures of time, took some five hundred years – a history, moreover, marked by a great deal of pain, resentment, and resistance.[6] Colonial India had to undergo a similar process, and that under conditions of alien rule, within a couple of generations. The tensions and contradictions bred by such an abrupt and forced transition surely need to be explored.

For the educated middle-class bhadralok of nineteenth-century Bengal, disciplinary time manifested itself primarily in the form of clerical jobs in British-controlled government or mercantile offices – the chakri about which Rajnarayan complained – along with, perhaps, the new educational institutions.[7] Studies of the colonial middle class have generally concentrated on its higher echelons, about whom information is so much more readily available: the reasonably successful English-educated religious and social reformers, writers, journalists, lawyers, doctors, teachers, or politicians. Among such people a sense of moving forward in harmony with time was sometimes noticeable, constituting elements that would later be put together into a 'Renaissance' format, and Kaliyuga disappeared without much fuss or became a not very serious turn of phrase. Foreign rule had bestowed some benefits in the shape of modern culture, and there were hopes that it could be gradually reformed

[6] E.P. Thompson, 'Time, Work-Discipline and Industrial Capitalism', *Past and Present*, 38, December 1967.

[7] Industrial growth was slow in colonial Bengal, and controlled overwhelmingly by British capital (and later, immigrant Marwaris). The emergent working class, too, was largely recruited from non-Bengali upcountry labourers. There were no signs of capitalistic methods in agriculture, and few bhadraloks served in the army. But the Permanent Settlement of land revenue by Cornwallis in 1793 had led to a vast proliferation of rentier interests, many of them quite tiny, and this was the material base for the overwhelmingly upper-caste respectable educated bhadralok. Rentier incomes had to be increasingly supplemented by professional or clerical jobs, for which a smattering of Western education had become essential.

or even eliminated through the efforts of the patriotic bhadralok. A high premium was consequently placed on a variety of forms of predominantly male bhadralok activism: education, religious reform or revival, many-sided efforts to improve the conditions of women, philanthropy, nationalist politics. Yet even the narrative of high-bhadralok activism would be repeatedly punctuated by gaps, relapses into passivity and inward-turning moods, doubts, mordant auto-critiques. Such dimensions become more prominent once we try to enter the world of the less successful bhadralok: declining traditional literati who had failed to adapt to English education, graduates without jobs, college or high-school drop-outs, hack writers, humble schoolteachers, clerks. Here the myth of Kaliyuga remained meaningful, indeed it proliferated through print culture and took on significantly new dimensions.

The evils of Kaliyuga had been associated always with the reversal of proper caste and gender hierarchy, with insubordinate women and Shudras lording it over upper-caste men. But now, as we shall see, the woman on top came to be associated with the lure of money and commodification, while there emerged a totally new and obsessive focus on the harshness and humiliation of office work, or chakri. Kaliyuga thus became a language for expressing the anguish, frustration and resentments of less successful educated men of the higher castes. It offers an entry point into a partially distinct 'lower middle class' world, ideal-typically embodied in the declining traditional rural literati and the city clerk *(kerani)*: a milieu that has been neglected by historians virtually everywhere.[8] The tonalities of Kaliyuga, however, could appeal at times also to the high bhadralok in their darker moods, for colonial domination kept the self-image of the successful enterprising male always fragile, unstable, open to racist humiliation. And so Rajnarayan Basu, too, complains about chakri, and the evils of modern times he talks about have clear affinities with Aghorechandra's depiction of Kaliyuga.

I intend to use two entry points in this exploration of variation and difference. Print culture, as elsewhere, lessened the mnemonic advantages of verse, stimulated a flowering of vernacular prose, and enabled the incorporation into writing of a much larger range of everyday experience. Ample documentation consequently

---

[8] For some discussion of this neglect and efforts to remedy it, see Arno Mayer, 'The Lower Middle Class as a Historical Problem', *Journal of Modern History*, 47, iv, December 1975, and G. Crossick (ed.), *The Lower Middle Class in Britain* (London, 1977).

exists concerning the high-bhadralok oscillation between outward-looking activism and introspective moods. This is central to my argument which questions the unduly seamless representations of the colonial middle class that underly both canonization and debunking. Illustrative samples here will include some biographical material, ways of looking at history, and trends in bhadralok religious life — in particular the strange and significant appeal of Ramakrishna Paramhansa.

The principal evidence for the persistence-cum-modulation of Kaliyuga in nineteenth-century Bengal comes from a somewhat different, less well known corpus: a multitude of cheap tracts, stories, plays and farces, to which a visual component was added by the prevalence of similar themes in the bazaar paintings hawked outside temples like Kalighat in Calcutta. As with the *bibliotheque bleu* of seventeenth- and eighteenth-century France, it is necessary here to avoid the identification of this 'low-life of literature'[9] with a culture that can be termed 'popular' in any unqualified sense. The consumers of the tracts, farces, and prints churned out from the Bat-tala quarter of north Calcutta did not necessarily exclude the most exalted among the bhadralok, while the surnames of their authors indicate most to have been upper caste, indeed very often Brahman. Literacy, even in Bengali, was both low and broadly homologous with caste hierarchy: only 39.9 per cent even among Brahmans in 1911, going down to 4.9 per cent among Nama-shudras.[10] Cheap booklets and prints, peddled by hawkers apart from being sold in bookshops, could however also be read out to people other than the literate. Plays and farces had the potential for reaching even wider audiences in so far as they were actually staged. The Bengali theatre had at first been a matter of private patronage, with performances in rich men's houses alone. But from the 1870s public theatres emerged in Calcutta, creating a ticket-paying audience that could span a wide range of social groups, and which include women as well as men. A fair number of the

---

[9] I am borrowing this term from Robert Darnton, 'The High Enlightenment and the Low-Life of Literature in Pre-Revolutionary France', *Past and Present*, 51, May 1971. For important clarifications of the term 'popular' which I have found very helpful, see Roger Chartier, *Cultural Uses of Print in Early Modern France* (Princeton, 1987).

[10] Census figures, as cited in Sekhar Bandopadhyay, 'Social Mobility in Bengal in the late-19th and early-20th Centuries' (unpublished thesis, Calcutta University, 1985), pp. 183–5.

performances seem to have been scripts for *jatras*, a folk form of entertainment which did not use the Western-style proscenium stage. They were done by wandering groups of players in villages and small towns, as well as cities. Unlike the *bibliotheque bleu*, produced by big Troyes firms and consisting in large part of abbreviated or simplified versions of established high-culture texts, nineteenth-century Bengali cheap printed literature came out from a multitude of small publishers and seems to have been somewhat more distinctive in its subject matter.

Tarakchandra Sarkar and Rashsundari Devi, authors of the last two extracts from which we started, are reminders that the upper-caste male myth of Kaliyuga could on occasion develop interesting low-caste and feminine variants, but data here remain extremely scanty. The other very major problem with the material I am using is that audience reception is difficult to gauge, for data about print-runs and the specific social composition of readership is absent. We know next to nothing about the possibly differentiated ways in which these texts were received, what meanings may have been read into them by varied audiences, and how — if at all — they were related to everyday life. It is in this context that I have found useful a pamphlet describing a most unusual incident in an East Bengal village in December 1904, for here elements of the Kaliyuga myth suddenly seemed to come alive, with consequences both unexpected and ultimately disastrous.[11]

An upper-caste householder, Lalmohan Majumdar of Doyhata village (Munshiganj subdivision, Dacca district, East Bengal), had invited into his home a wandering poor Brahman *sadhu* (ascetic, religious mendicant, holy man), Kalikumar Chakrabarti, who called himself Kalachand. The sadhu claimed powers of miraculous healing, and occasionally that he was Kalki-avatar, the tenth and last incarnation of Vishnu who was supposed to appear at the end of Kaliyuga to set the degenerate world in order again, restoring ideal caste and gender hierarchy. Kalachand was followed into the Majumdar household by two Untouchable disciples, Prasanna, a Namashudra, and

---

11 Madhusudan Chaudhuri, *Kalki-avatarer Mokaddama/Bikrampure bhishan Byabhichar* [Trial of the Kalki-avatar/Terrible Immoralities in Bikrampur] (Dacca, 1905. Henceforward *KM*). This gives copious extracts from the Doyhata court proceedings, and constitutes my principal source for this strange affair. For a more detailed analysis of Doyhata in terms of its varied representations, see my 'Kalki-avatar of Bikrampur: A Village Scandal in Early Twentieth Century Bengal', in Ranajit Guha (ed.), *Subaltern Studies VI* (Delhi, 1989).

Ananda, a Bhuinmali. On the afternoon and night of 8 December 1904, Prasanna suddenly started enacting his own, extremely peculiar version of the end of Kaliyuga. He killed Ananda, apparently with the latter's consent, and the complicity of Kalachand and Lalmohan. This was interpreted by Lalmohan as the killing of Yama, the god of death, which would end all death on earth. Prasanna, however, seems to have thought, and persuaded Ananda to believe, that the latter would be resurrected with a new 'divine body' by Kalachand, whose powers consequently would be recognized by all, even by the British. Prasanna then set fire to neighbouring houses (he was burning 'Lanka', he claimed) and insulted, stripped, and tore the sacred thread of several upper-caste gentlemen. The women of the Majumdar household had to take off their clothes, touch a (presumably sacred) fire, and do homage to Kalachand. Some had their pubic hair burnt, while Lalmohan's wife was ordered to kick her husband's forehead in an exact inversion of *pranam*, the Hindu ritual gesture of deference towards elders, social and gender superiors, and divinities alike. The general atmosphere was one of *yugapralay*, the cataclysmic end of an epoch.

Everyone was remarkably compliant for hours, even though a police station lay only a quarter mile away. Somehow, in the imagination of an enraged Namashudra, what had been associated in high-caste texts with the restoration of Brahman and male authority had suddenly come to mean the insulting of high-castes by an Untouchable and of a husband by his wife. 'All the soldiers of Bharat (India) together will not be able to do anything to me', Prasanna was defiantly shouting when he was at last overpowered and arrested early next morning. He remained defiant and unrepentant in court, while Lalmohan abjectly begged for mercy and Kalachand sought to evade responsibility through an enigmatic silence. Prasanna, one Calcutta paper noted with surprise, seemed 'quite unconcerned with what is going on, commenting freely and gaily on the depositions of several witnesses.'[12] The Dacca sessions court jury, consisting of local bhadralok, recommended surprisingly mild sentences, probably out of a desire to save the two upper-caste accused. The British judge disagreed, and the Calcutta High Court eventually awarded stiffer sentences for all three accused. A local newspaper quickly made a pamphlet out of the Dacca court proceedings, thus constituting our principal source. But Doyhata soon became one of those scandals

12 *Bengalee*, 17 March 1905.

that the bhadralok knew but were embarrassed to write about, and a local history of the Dacca region published in 1909 passed over the affair with a single, cryptic sentence.[13]

Doyhata embodied a brief, explosive encounter between different yet overlapping worlds: respectable high-caste householder belonging to a community exceptionally proud of its learning and culture; wandering poor Brahman mendicant of uncertain reputation who might turn out to be either charlatan or divine incarnation; despised illiterate outcaste normally never allowed inside a bhadralok home who now virtually takes it over for one night. Here we touch the limits of Kaliyuga discourse, the point where it is appropriated by an Untouchable and briefly turned on its head, making the incident itself unmentionable. Doyhata, then, is important, despite or indeed precisely because of its evident a-typicality. Lalmohan, Kalachand and Prasanna may help us to go some distance beyond the sterile polarities that currently dominate the historiography of colonial middle-class Bengal.

II

Lalmohan Majumdar would have remained unknown to the historical record but for the Doyhata case, and not very much emerges even from the court depositions. With *prajas* (tenants), but not the guards or armed retainers that a big landlord (*zamindar*) would have had, he presumably belonged to a small zamindar or tenure-holding high-caste family of the Bikrampur region of East Bengal.[14] The family home seems to have been full of women relatives or dependants: most of the men possibly had jobs in Calcutta or elsewhere. Lalmohan, who had some English education and a smattering of knowledge of Western medicine, had however stayed on in Doyhata village. He was reputed to have been a good family man who made some extra money by dispensing medicine, and did not charge the poor a fee. He appears to have been a fairly typical do-gooding bhadralok — till the coming of Kalachand. The wandering poor Brahman sadhu initially attracted him, not through teachings or miracle-working claims, but by 'his face, it seemed like that of a boy, and *vatsalyabhava* (paternal feelings) were evoked in me.' Soon

[13] Jogendranath Gupta, *Bikrampurer Itihas* (Calcutta, 1909).
[14] Bikrampur was the traditional indigenous name for a region in East Bengal that in British administrative terms comprised Dacca district and the Madaripur subdivision of Faridpur district.

Lalmohan sank into a kind of passivity, lost interest in his medical practice and 'spent much time in idleness . . . saying, if asked about anything, "The sadhu will provide everything, there is nothing to worry about".'[15] This again was succeeded by a brief moment of ecstasy. Lalmohan danced and sang after the killing of Ananda, proclaiming that the yugapralay was at hand.

The data is sparse, but interesting links and affiliations can be teased out from it. However obscure in himself, Lalmohan belonged to an extremely prominent social group, the Bikrampur bhadralok. As in much of East Bengal, the bulk of the population in the Bikrampur region consisted of Muslims or low-caste Hindu (quite often, Namashudra) peasants, but above them towered a thick cluster of predominantly high-caste Hindu rent-receivers. Bikrampur was a land of small, fragmented zamindaris and intermediate tenures, rents from which needed to be supplemented by income from professional or clerical jobs in Calcutta or other towns. Western education, which had become the essential prerequisite for such jobs, came to be exceptionally well developed here, often through the private initiative of the bhadralok themselves. In 1909 the regional historian Jogendranath Gupta mentioned with pride the existence in Bikrampur of 24 High English schools at a time when the whole of the United Provinces outside the district headquarters had only 14. He provided a long list of bhadralok worthies born in that region, renowned for the kinds of reformist, philanthrophic, literary, scientific, or political activities which in twentieth-century retrospect would come together to constitute the renaissance myth.

And yet it was precisely such an activist mileu which in colonial Bengal persistently bred a recurrent undertow of introspection, nostalgia, passivity. Forward-looking male activism was frequently accompanied by a series of intermingled, if logically distinct, Others: past as contrasted to present, country versus city, a deliberate feminization as opposed to active masculinity, the attractive playfulness and irresponsibility of the child or the *pagal* (roughly, madman) as against the goal-oriented instrumental rationality of the adult male.[16]

---

15 Depositions of Lalmohan and his wife Rajlakshmi in the Doyhata case, *KM*, pp. 10, 46.

16 Pagal comes closer, really, to terms like 'holy folly', or to European conceptions of madness postulated by Foucault to have flourished before the 'great confinement' of the seventeenth–eighteenth centuries. For its many nuances in Bengali culture, see June McDaniel, *The Madness of the Saints: Ecstatic Religion in Bengal* (Chicago, 1989).

Such rationality, embodied in the multifarious projects and endeavours of the bhadralok, in any case seemed to end all too often
in whimpers: as when the Brahmo religious reform movement
petered away amidst internal squabbles, or Vidyasagar's bid to improve the lot of Hindu widows failed to change dominant social
attitudes. The failures would have seemed particularly apparent
during what I have elsewhere described as a late-nineteenth-century
hiatus in bhadralok history — the years, roughly 1870–1905, during
which the dream of improvement and reform under British tutelage
turned sour, without as yet being replaced by an alternative viable
patriotic myth of ending the country's ills through drastically modifying or ending foreign rule.[17]

It was during these years, more precisely from around the 1880s,
that nostalgia about the countryside found enduring literary expression through the romantic poetry of nature of Biharilal Chakrabarti
and the early writings of Rabindranath Tagore. A significant shift
had taken place here from the 'epic' style of Michael Madhusudan
Dutta in the 1850s and 1860s, where nature had remained subsidiary
to heroic action in defiance of overwhelming odds, and in which
traditional divinities and incarnations had been treated at times in
a remarkably subversive manner.[18] Calcutta, more generally, which
in twentieth-century retrospect would become the heart of a 'Bengal
Renaissance', figured little in nineteenth-century literary representation, except in negative terms: it was certainly not conceived of,
say, as a new Florence.[19] The colonial metropolis provided the
bhadralok with education, culture, new luxuries and tastes, jobs. As
the political and economic heart of Britain's Indian empire, with
mills, firms and offices controlled by Europeans or enterprising
immigrants like the Marwaris, it was at the same time a city which
often appeared peculiarly beyond the control of the Bengali bhadralok. Here the less fortunate of the bhadralok eked out a living as

17 For a more detailed analysis of this 'hiatus', see Chapter 7.

18 Madhusudan openly declared that he 'despised Ram and his rabble', and
his greatest work, an epic in pioneering blank verse entitled *Meghnadbadh Kavya*,
radically inverted the ancient Ramayana myth about Ram's war against Ravana,
the demon-king of Lanka, which had become central in medieval centuries for
some kinds of Hindu bhakti (devotion: the cultivation of an internal emotional
relationship towards the divinity, rather than the alternative religious ways of
asceticism, knowledge or ritual).

19 For an explication of this point, see Tanika Sarkar, 'The Hindu Wife and
the Hindu Nation: Domesticity and Nationalism in Nineteenth-century Bengal',
Studies in History, VIII, 2, July–December 1992.

kerani, and even the prosperous Bengali gentleman till well into the next century would normally refer to his Calcutta residence as *basa* (lodging), reserving the more privileged term *bari* (home) for the ancestral village or small-town house.

What happened, usually, in personal life as well as in literary representation, was not a rupture or neat separation into activist and inward-turning groups, but a commingling of moods within the same text, movement, or personality. The oscillations of Lalmohan, apparently eccentric and insignificant, thus have wider affinities.

Better-known middle-class personal trajectories constitute one kind of evidence about such tensions and transitions. The Young Bengal (or 'Derozian') group, for instance, Hindu College students of the 1830s inspired by the brilliant young history teacher Henry Louis Vivian Derozio — who had introduced them to the ideas of eighteenth-century rationalism and the French Revolution — have been repeatedly hailed, or denounced, for their youthful iconoclastic rejection of Hindu traditions. Actually most of them made their peace with orthodox society fairly soon, and came to hold respectable administrative or professional positions. Already by the 1840s some of them, in a significant turn towards 'history', had started celebrating the cultural glory and military prowess of Hindus in the past. They failed to develop any effective reform programme: what remained, perhaps, was an inner agony of spirit, finding expression through an epidemic of drinking that blighted many of their lives, as well as through occasional self-critical satire. Thus, in a play by Dinabandhu Mitra, Nimchand Dutta — a brilliant, cynical and dissipated character thought by some to have been modelled on Michael Madhusudan — greets in a drunken stupor a policeman's lantern as Milton's 'Hail, Holy Light!'[20] The surrender to colonial discourse even on the part of those often denounced then and later as denationalized Anglicists was perhaps less total and unambiguous than is often imagined today.[21]

A generation later, to take a second, very different example, a young man of intermediate-caste (Tili) origin started a school in his

[20] For more details, see my 'Complexities of Young Bengal', in *A Critique of Colonial India* (Calcutta, 1985).

[21] For an alternative view, see for instance the recent argument of Ranajit Guha: 'most of the nineteenth-century beneficiaries of [English] education imbibed from it . . . unquestioning servility to the ruling power' through a 'superficial Anglicism.' Ranajit Guha, *An Indian Historiography of India: A Nineteenth-Century Agenda and Its Implications* (Calcutta, 1988), pp. 17–18.

Central Bengal village (Kumarkhali, Nadia district), and then a vernacular journal explicitly designed to voice the sufferings of villagers at the hands of zamindars, British indigo planters, and local officials. Harinath Majumdar (1833-96), nicknamed 'Kangal' (destitute) Harinath, had to struggle against poverty all his life, and incurred through his journalistic exposures the wrath of the local zamindars (the powerful, and exceptionally cultured, Tagores). The journal *Grambartaprakashika*, started in 1863, folded up in 1884 due to lack of funds. It had published in 1872 the first bhadralok account of Lalan Fakir, a major exponent of the Baul tradition of syncretistic folk religious song and ritual. After his journal had collapsed, Harinath, who had had Brahmo (reformist Hindu) connections in his youth, turned towards more emotional and esoteric kinds of religion, and even started writing Baul songs himself under the name of Fikirchand. The story has some interesting sequels. Rabindranath Tagore, son of the zamindar whose officials seem to have tormented Harinath, later contributed greatly towards making Baul poetry, and Lalan Fakir in particular, respectable, even prestigious, among the bhadralok. And Akshoy Maitra, a younger colleague of Harinath who had helped to run *Grambartaprakashika* in its last days, became in course of time a distinguished historian, dedicated to rediscovering the lost splendours of Bengal.[22]

Patriotic history-writing, efforts to tap folk cultural resources, satirical theatre, introspective and emotional forms of religious devotion: such seem to have been some of the ways through which the inner tensions of the bhadralok found expression. In remarkable contrast to what later would become standard form in the renaissance myth, nineteenth-century middle-class cultural achievements were seldom eulogized by their own makers. Bankimchandra Chattopadhyay (1833-94), Bengal's first major novelist, for instance, explicitly used the European Renaissance analogy in 1880 to describe, not contemporary bhadralok activities (target, often, of his merciless satire), but the religious, philosophical, and literary developments of fifteenth- and sixteenth-century Bengal.[23]

Sekal-ar-Ekal, the second extract with which I began, provides striking evidence about this tendency among English-educated

[22] Sudhir Chakrabarti, *Bratya Lokayat Lalan* (Calcutta, 1992); Brojendranath Bandopadhyay and Sajanikanta Das, biography of Kangal Harinath in *Sahitya-Sadhak-Charitmala*, vol. III (Calcutta, 1943).

[23] Bankimchandra Chattopadhyay, *Banglar Itihas Sambandhay Kaekti Katha* (1880), in J.C. Bagal (ed.), *Bankim Rachanabali*, vol. II (Calcutta, 1954, 1969).

worthies to be self-critical about contemporary life. This was a lecture delivered by Rajnarayan Basu (1826–99), distinguished Hindu College alumnus, friend of Michael Madhusudan, and moderate Brahmo reformer. The past *(sekal)* to Rajnarayan was not anything very distant, but childhood memories about elders, the dividing line being the introduction of higher education in English through Hindu College in 1817. The evils of the present for Rajnarayan begin with an alleged decline in male physical strength due to endless book-learning in enclosed classrooms, followed by excessive, time-bound labour in clerical or professional jobs. The Bengali male who matters, then, is the educated bhadralok tied to chakri. Meanwhile the traditional Brahman literati has fallen on evil days, as Sanskrit learning is no longer honoured. The new educated bhadralok has become ensnared by European luxuries, and selfishness is corroding old norms of kinship behaviour and hospitality — except, Rajnarayan adds in a characterisitic conflation of spatial and temporal retrospect, in 'far-off villages' where 'mutual sympathy' still reigns. And women who have received a smattering of education are the worst: they prefer immoral novels to housework and are no longer properly obedient to their husbands. The themes, we shall see, are strikingly similar to the ones often listed under the rubric of Kaliyuga in a large number of near-contemporary plays, farces and religious discourses, even though the term itself never occurs in Rajnarayan's text.

Shifts in religious forms, moods and language constitute probably the most fruitful, if still somewhat underexplored, entry point into the tension-ridden, internally differentiated unhappy consciousness of the nineteenth-century bhadralok. Taken as a whole, nineteenth-century bhadralok piety does give an impression of a thrust towards a novel, socially oriented, ameliorative activism. As elsewhere, however, the self-image of predominantly masculine rationalistic activity and self-confidence was often clouded over by introspective moods, self-conscious 'feminizations', and retreats from adult responsibility.

Such transitions are noticeable within both the major Hindu traditions in Bengal, the Vaishnava devotion to the incarnations of Vishnu (particularly Krishna), and the Shakta worship of the mother-goddess Kali — as well as in the new reformist Brahmo sect founded by Rammohan Roy in the 1820s. The early Brahmos, for instance, like the Protestants on whom they had partially modelled themselves, usually stressed the fatherhood of their theoretically impersonal, formless godhead. In the 1860s, their most active leader was Keshabchandra Sen, engrossed in an enormous variety of social reform activities. By the next decade, however, partly through the influence of Ramakrishna, he had largely withdrawn from reformist activity and simultaneously begun to conceptualize divinity in maternal terms. Rural retrospect, feminization, a turning away from social activism towards the attractive irresponsibility of the child and the pagal — all came together, in fact, in the extraordinary appeal of Ramakrishna (c. 1836–86). A near-illiterate temple priest given to spells of mystic ecstasy, he had lived for some thirty years in a suburb of Calcutta before suddenly becoming a major cult figure among the educated bhadralok in the late 1870s and early 1880s — the 'hiatus' years, again. Ramakrishna's early disciples, in addition, often had a clerical ambience: few among the wealthy or successful professional men initially came to him. The central message was one of quietistic, inward-turning bhakti, and Ramakrishna was often openly scornful of socially activist, ameliorative projects, even of philanthropy. He conveyed his ideas purely through conversation, in a rustic language full of earthy parables that seemed to bring back a rural world from which the city bhadralok now sometimes felt they had unwisely uprooted themselves. Devotees chronicled with respect and admiration Ramakrishna lifelong fondness for women's roles, and they seemed to have found even more attractive his childlike surrender to the Shakta divine mother: 'Attaining *Ishwara* [the divine] makes you into a five-year-old boy.'[24] Hagiographers loved to describe the *balak-bhava* of Ramakrishna, his behaving like a child, one of the acceptable ways of relating to divinity in Shakta traditions: this included lack of inhibitions about nudity and soiling himself in public. Upper-caste Hindu constructions of childhood, it has been pointed out, differ significantly from both Puritanical discipline and romantic glorifications of pure, aesthetically pleasing natural growth. The child may have 'no personal time-table . . . no rules of hygiene or cleanliness imposed from outside. . . . He seems to live by pure whim.'[25] The child model, in other words, could slide into that of the pagal, and, partly through Ramakrishna's influence, the runaway, irresponsible, yet attractive male and the wandering pagal, often of

[24] Here, and later, quotations from Ramakrishna are taken from 'M' (Mahendranath Gupta), *Ramakrishna-Kathamrita*, vol. 5 (Calcutta, 1902–32). A more detailed study of Ramakrishna follows in Chapter 8 below.

[25] Madeleine Biardeau, *Hinduism: The Anthropology of a Civilisation* (Delhi, 1989), pp. 33–4.

poor Brahman origin, as embodiments of holy folly became long-lasting stereotypes in Bengali literature.

Attitudes like these have deep cultural roots, and yet we cannot afford to ignore contextual specificities which may help to explain why it was precisely the Western-educated who felt drawn to Rama-krishna, and that from a particular time. Colonialism had counter-posed to European active virile masculinity the stereotype of the conquered 'native' as effeminate, irritatingly childish, or at best pleasantly childlike. Direct references to colonial domination are extremely rare in Ramakrishna's conversation, but he was subverting, in effect, the distinctions between male and female, adult and child, work and play, that the 'civilizing mission' of the West was making more rigid in nineteenth-century Bengal.[26] The bhadralok, excluded anyway from the privileged male occupations of military and polit-ical command and successful independent entrepreneurship, and relegated to dull and lowly clerical jobs, were perhaps expressing a 'muffled defiance' through a preference for feminization,[27] childlike behaviour, and the irresponsiblility of the pagal. Ramakrishna's message of bhakti could help to create an inner living space detached from the imposed world of formal routinized education and chakri.

Many dimensions of our strange Doyhata tale now begin to fall into broader patterns, though without losing idiosyncrasies of their own: Lalmohan's paternal feelings aroused by the boyish countenance of the sadhu, as a phenomenon rooted deep in the culture of bhakti, and described by him through the appropriate religious term *(vatsalya-bhava)*;[28] his sudden withdrawal from responsible worldly activity; Kalachand, poor Brahman village schoolteacher who had become a kind of religious dropout, a wandering pagal claiming miraculous powers of healing, and, eventually, of world-deliverance as Kalki-avatar. Kalki is an element of the Kaliyuga mythic corpus,[29] and it was through modulations of that age-old structure that a variety of

[26] Ashis Nandy, *The Intimate Enemy: Loss and Recovery of Self under Colonialism* (Delhi, 1983).

[27] I am borrowing this term from Mikhail Bakhtin's analysis of the St Petersburg clerk in 'Poor Folk', *Problems of Dostoevski's Poetics* (Leningrad, 1929; trans., Manchester, 1984), pp. 205, 210.

[28] This is a standard technical term in Vaishnava devotional theory, describ-ing a way of relating to divinity as parent to child.

[29] In some accounts of Kaliyuga, notably the late-medieval text *Kalki-Purana*, the dark age would end with the coming of Kalki, the tenth and last incarnation (avatar) of Vishnu, who as a kind of messiah would destroy all evil kings and restore Satyayuga.

nineteenth-century resentments and hopes found expression. Kaliyuga was a term often on Ramakrishna's lips, and the motif emerged in some profusion in cheap paintings, tracts, plays and farces, the floodgates for which had been opened by the coming of print. It is time to take a closer look at what the late nineteenth century tried to make of Kaliyuga.

III

The many evils of Kaliyuga, a recurrent and powerful format for voicing a variety of high-caste male anxieties for some two thousand years, include disorders in nature, oppressive *mleccha* (impure, alien) kings, Brahmans corrupted by too much rationalistic argument, overmighty Shudras expounding the scriptures and no longer serving the Brahmans, and women choosing their own partners, disobeying and deceiving their husbands, and having intercourse with menials, slaves, and even animals. Kaliyuga was invariably located in the present and would end in a very distant future amidst universal fire and flood, or alternatively through the wars of Kalki, the last incarnation of Vishnu. Born in a 'Sambhalgram' Brahman family, he would in a conflation of Brahman and Kshatriya (royal or warrior) virtue destroy all mleccha kings and restore a Satyayuga in which purified Brahmans would be on top and Shudras and women once again duly subordinated. And then an identical four-yuga cycle would begin again, and so through eternity.[30]

Despite occasional apocalyptic language, Satyayuga was clearly very different from the millennarian dreams of equality and freedom that inspired so many heresies and plebeian rebellions in medieval and early modern Europe. The apocalypse in any case lay far in the future, for Kaliyuga was to last 432,000 years. The message was one of resignation, for the evils were inevitable: they could, however, be made more endurable through modifications in ritual practices. These were the Kali-varjya, things allowed earlier but now discovered to be no longer permissible by Brahman ritual experts — an interesting method of introducing a conservative kind of flexibility

---

[30] *Mahabharata, Vanaparva*, sections 187-90 of the *Markandeya-Samasya* is a principal *locus classicus* of the Kaliyuga myth. I am using an English prose translation by Pratapchandra Roy (Calcutta, n.d.), as well as the authoritative nineteenth-century Bengali translation by Kaliprasanna Sinha (in the Gopal Haldar edition, Calcutta, 1974). See also R.C. Hazra, *Studies in the Upapuranas*, vol. I (Calcutta, 1963), pp. 140, 324-5, for later versions of the myth.

through which caste and gender discipline was tightened up from the twelfth–thirteenth centuries onwards. The high-Hindu ideal was not really the restoration of Satyayuga, which would degenerate again anyway, but a purely individual escape, moksha, from the chain of rebirth (karma) across endless cyclical time. Alternative ways *(marg)* were prescribed for this individual escape: asceticism, intellectual contemplation, ritual, and devotion (bhakti).[31]

Shudras and women, the two social categories sought to be kept subordinate and excluded from the sacred Vedas by Brahmanical power-knowledge, normally constituted the major sources of degeneration in Kaliyuga texts. Bhakti, however, which in the medieval centuries at times inspired powerful movements with much participation, even leadership, of lower castes and women, produced important modifications — indeed, near-inversions — in the dominant image of Kaliyuga. The worst of ages, it also paradoxically became the best of times, for in it, much bhakti literature insisted, deliverance comes easily, and even mere recitation of the divine name may suffice. The paradox extended further, for women and Shudras, the two major sources of Kaliyuga corruption, could attain good simply through performing their duties to husbands and high-caste men. The humble constitute the ideal bhakta (devotee), and subalternity is privileged — provided, of course, it remains properly subaltern. Bhakti and Tantra are repeatedly declared to be the two forms of religious practice peculiarly appropriate for Kaliyuga — and both are explicitly open to women and Shudras, unlike Brahmanical learning and ritual.[32] Bhakti modulations of Kaliyuga thus created a richly ambiguous space for subordinate groups, offering opportunities that were profoundly attractive, at times almost rebellious — and yet always open to ultimate recuperation by dominant hierarchies of caste and gender.[33]

31 Mircea Eliade, *Myth of the Eternal Return* (Paris, 1949; trans., London, 1955), Chapters I, II, IV; P.V. Kane, *History of the Dharmashastras*, vol. III (2nd ed., Pune 1973), Chapter XXXIV.

32 Tantric traditions systematically inverted many orthodox rituals and purity-pollution rules, and some have found in them traces of plebeian materialism, though much appropriated by high castes. Debiprasad Chattopadhyay, Chapter V; N.N. Bhattacharji, *History of the Tantric Religion* (Delhi, 1982), Chapter V.

33 For analysis of the paradoxes of bhakti, both in general and in its conceptions of Kaliyuga, see Kumkum Sangari, 'Mirabai and the Spiritual Economy of Bhakti', *Economic and Political Weekly*, XXV, 27–8, 7, 14 July 1990; W.C. Beane, *Myth, Cult and Symbols in Shakta Hinduism* (London, 1977), pp. 237–9; Madeleine Biardieu, p. 105.

Print culture broadens the potential audience for 'traditional' texts even while stimulating new genres and themes, and Kaliyuga, arguably, became better known than ever before precisely in the century that witnessed the entry of clock time and Enlightenment rationality.[34] Successful zamindars or professional men no longer bothered much about the myth. The reformers among them found its message of stricter caste hierarchy and subordination of women distasteful, while conservatives could content themselves with complacently reiterating the old theme of tighter regulations through Kali-varjya as sufficient for the new challenges. Very different, however, was the deployment of Kaliyuga in a mass of minor plays and farces, as well as in many Kalighat bazaar paintings. Here moods of pessimism, self-doubt and resentment were expressed through black humour and satire. Among 505 plays published between 1858 and 1899 catalogued in a recent massive survey, 31 have 'Kali' in their titles, and a content analysis brings out many more references.[35] Though mostly published from Calcutta, many were performed also by travelling theatre-groups (jatra parties) in small towns and villages. The bazaar paintings, sold 'at a price ranging from a pice to an anna' near Kalighat temple, other pilgrimage centres, and village fairs, were produced by struggling artisans for whom, it has been said, 'the world was passing through a dark age, a Kaliyuga.'[36]

Nineteenth-century Kaliyuga literature and painting made few references to insubordinate Shudras: unlike Maharashtra, lower-caste protest movements were not of much account in Bengal prior to around the turn of the century. Women, as always, remained key targets, but no longer primarily for the sexual immorality they supposedly embodied or provoked. The focus now is on the 'modern' wife, allegedly ill-treating her mother-in-law, enslaving the husband, neglecting household duties to read novels, and wasting money on luxuries for herself. Pictorial and verbal representation at times coincide here: a wife in a farce dresses up her husband in sheep's

---

[34] Thus Bengali translations of the *Kalki-Purana* came out in 1886, 1899, and 1908, and the 1899 version I am using had gone into its tenth edition by 1962. Throughout the nineteenth century, Orientalist scholars, reformers and conservatives showed equal enthusiasm for printing and translating ancient texts.

[35] Jayanta Goswami, *Samajchitre Unabingsha Shatabdir Bangla Prahashan* (Calcutta, 1974).

[36] W.G. Archer, *Bazar Paintings of Calcutta* (London, 1953); Mildred Archer, *Indian Popular Paintings in the India Office Library* (London, 1977); Ashit Paul (ed.), *Woodcut Prints of 19th century Calcutta* (Calcutta, 1983).

clothes, while in a couple of Kalighat paintings a woman leads a sheep with a human head and another boldly strides on top of a prostrate man.[37] The 'modern' wife, in fact, has become emblematic of a perceived threat to kinship obligations and ties through the spread of market values. The crucial innovation in a multitude of late-nineteenth-century farces and tracts is a totally new, obsessive focus upon the miseries of chakri, and the close interrelationship that is assumed to exist between the disorderly wife, the 'modern' craze for money and luxuries, and the clerical job the husband is forced to take up to get the one and please the other. Ramakrishna's conversation repeatedly associated the evils of *kamini* (lust, invariably given a feminine form) and *kanchan* (gold, wealth) with the *dasatya* of chakri (bondage of office job), and the triad recurs endlessly in late-nineteenth-century plays and farces as the hallmark of Kaliyuga.

What made chakri appear intolerable at this specific conjuncture was its connotation of impersonal cash-nexus and authority, embodied in a new work discipline regulated by abruptly introduced clock time, and enforced by foreign bosses through an imperfectly understood alien language of command. The luxuries were foreign importations, modern wives could be plausibly represented as particularly tempted by them, chakri was usually in British-controlled offices — and so a patriotic subtext could emerge fairly easily at this point. In Harishchandra Bandopadhyay's *Kaler Bau* (Calcutta, 1880), for instance, subordination to wives gets·conflated with political subjection to the 'sons of the London queen', and thus the figure of the suffering mother, neglected by her sons who have been entrapped by the wiles of the modern wife, becomes a metaphor for the enslaved 'mother'-land. Unable as yet to resist foreign bosses — or alien rule — effectively, the clerks, or rather the middle or lower-middle-class writers and audiences empathizing with them, displaced part of their resentment on 'their' womenfolk. Emergent nationalist consciousness thus became intertwined with a strengthening of patriarchal assumptions.

Interesting modulations can be noticed also in the alternative, bhakti-inspired, more positive version of Kaliyuga. In many plays from the mid 1880s onwards, the pure women (usually wives) start going beyond the model of exemplary suffering typified by Sita in the Ramayana and traditionally idealized as a subalternity that is peculiarly privileged. They now intervene in ways that are assertive

[37] Bholanath Mukhopadhyay, *Bhyalare mor bap* (Calcutta, 1876); W. Archer, plate 42, p. 70.

and effective, while remaining deferential. Within a continued traditional idiom, a new content is emerging, where the ideal woman's role goes beyond noble endurance of suffering to visualize the prospect of a change of heart brought about by such endurance and fortitude. The women are helped at times by old-world servants, representing the good Shudra, and so a sub-theme extolling simple peasant virtues starts entering this literature.[38] Women and Shudras are thus given a positive role in defending and re-establishing a structure within which they would once again be deferential, but to husbands and social superiors who have been reformed and purified by the efforts of subordinate groups. Such paradoxical ascription of agency is often associated also with inspiration and guidance from wandering poor Brahmans. 'Mad' (pagal) to the conventional world, they are holy madmen who have opted out of the rat race for money and worldly success, emancipated themselves from the world of clock time and office space, and so can purvey divine truth in simple, earthy language. The plays of Girishchandra Ghosh that dominated Calcutta theatre for a generation from the 1880s have a whole gallery of such figures — some of them clearly modelled on Ramakrishna, whose devotee he had become.

The transitions within the Kaliyuga format are epitomized most clearly in Aghorechandra Kabyatirtha's *Kalir Abasan, ba Kalki-avatar Geetabhinoy* (The End of Kali, or The Coming of Kalki-avatar, 1902). The playwright describes himself as a poor Brahman from Central Bengal, now teaching in a Calcutta school, and claims that his play has served as a script for jatra performances in many district towns and villages. This is a fact of some importance for us, for it then becomes not beyond the realm of historical possibility that some of our Doyhata protagonists had seen *Kalir Abasan* — at the Nangalbandh bathing festival, perhaps, where Prasanna first met Kalachand. Developed print culture had by now introduced a premium on textual fidelity, and Aghorechandra tries to be faithful to Kalki-purana — thereby highlighting the occasional self-conscious departures. The evils of Kaliyuga are squarely located in an association of the 'new' insubordinate educated woman with money, and, as we have seen in the extract quoted at the beginning of this essay, there is a reference also to *karkhanas* (factories) with a peculiarly oppressive discipline. The most striking innovation, however, is the situating of Kalki

---

[38] See, for instance, Girishchandra Ghosh's extremely popular play *Prafulla* (Calcutta, 1889), and Satischandra Chattopadhyay' *Chandiram* (Calcutta, 1901) and *Annapurna* (Calcutta, 1889).

himself, both in a recognizably contemporary Bengal setting (and not aeons away in the future), and in a poor Brahman context. Kalki's elder brother almost dies of hunger but is saved by 'Govin-Pagla', a figure of divine folly who goes around preaching the simple bhakti of Hari-nama (reciting the name of the god). The traditional long account of Kalki's many wars is dramatically compressed into a few lines. From embodiment of Kshatriya virtue, Kalki in other words has been relocated in a totally new context of poor Brahmans, wandering folly, and bhakti — which is brought into association immediately with the figure of a deferentially assertive woman, Kalki's mother Sumati. A stronger personality than her husband, she is able to dissuade the latter from killing himself when poverty appears unbearable. But Sumati still reiterates that she is 'only a servant . . . the chief *dharma* of womenkind is to serve their husbands.'[39]

From a dystopia of privileged Brahmans expounded in Sanskrit (the sacred language that women and Shudras were generally forbidden to know), Kaliyuga in colonial Bengal had thus moved to a milieu subordinated to foreign rule and often downwardly mobile, being now written about entirely in the vernacular, by and for fairly humble, if still predominantly high-caste, bhadralok. Print culture facilitated its occasional appropriation also by more subordinate groups. The obscure housewife Rashsundari Devi and the Namashudra hagiographer Tarakchandra Sarkar who hailed Kaliyuga as 'blessed' were not just uttering a platitude common to many bhakti modulations of Kaliyuga. Rashsundari's autobiography chronicles her painful efforts to learn to read and write in secret — an endeavour that went against the grain of the entire Kaliyuga depiction of the educated woman as depraved.[40] Tarakchandra composed the biography of Harichand Biswas (c. 1812–78), founder of the plebeian Vaishnava Matua sect among the Namashudras (once known by the contemptuous label of Chandal) of south-central Bengal: Untouchable poor peasants, agricultural labourers, fishermen, and boatmen, from whose ranks came Prasanna, central figure of our Doyhata tale. The Matua sect in course of time became the core of a powerful Namashudra caste movement. For Tarakchandra, Kaliyuga is glorious not just because salvation becomes easy and open for subalterns who behave properly: in it even divine incarnations seek affiliation with, or come from, downtrodden

[39] *Kalir Abasan* (Calcutta, 1902), Scene VI, p. 78.
[40] For an analysis of Rashsundari, see Tanika Sarkar, 'A Book of Her Own, A Life of Her Own: Autobiography of a Nineteenth Century Woman', *History Workshop Journal*, 36, 1993.

groups. The text lays unusual emphasis on Krishna's cowherd (Gop) origins, makes a passing reference to the 'Muslim weaver Kuber' (Kabir, presumably, the radically iconoclastic medieval bhakti saint of Benaras), and hails the Buddha — standard figure of abuse in much Kaliyuga literature.

In the Balarami sect of the Meherpur region of Nadia, confined entirely to lower castes, we come across a more radical, though much more marginal world, where the yuga-cycle framework itself is deliberately subverted. Balarami oral traditions invariably express hostility towards high-caste landlords. A member of the sect was beaten up, we are told, for refusing to perform the ritual gesture of obeisance *(pranam)* while passing a zamindar. Interestingly, such defiance was taken to be an indication of *ghor Kali* (the depths of Kaliyuga) by the zamindar's companions. Balaram Hadi *(c.* 1780–1850), the founder of the sect, imagined a *divya-yuga* (divine age) superior to the four yugas of Brahmanical orthodoxy, over which presided the supreme and sole deity Hadiram. A note of plebeian materialism is struck here through the caste name of Balaram's Untouchable group. *Hadi* resembles *had* — which means the bones of the human body — and escape from the yuga-cycle meant for the Balaramis not spiritual moksha but an explicitly *physical* immortality.[41] We shall encounter startling traces of not dissimilar conceptions soon, at Doyhata.

I have been dealing, in the main, with literary representations, and what meanings readers or audiences drew out of these texts remain a difficult, possibly intractable, problem. Doyhata, I have suggested, may be of some help here, through its striking pattern of affinities and distinctions. Kalachand was a figure reminiscent in many ways of the numerous poor Brahman wandering pagals who are so ubiquitous in contemporary plays. A schoolteacher in a Faridpur village, not too far from Doyhata, he had become a *ganja* (hemp) addict, and slipped away from his family as a religious mendicant, with disciples at first only from low castes. Lalmohan, hearing about him from a low-caste tenant of his, invited Kalachand into his household, for 'a Brahman's son should not stay with a Chandal.' The precise teachings of Kalachand remain utterly obscure, for British justice, unfortunately for us, was quite uninterested in finding out more about them. The one undisputed aspect seems to be the openness of Kalachand's message to multiple meanings, even wholesale inversion by a Namashudra and his Bhuinmali adjutant-

41 Sudhir Chakrabarti, *Balarami Sampraday Tader Gan* (Calcutta, 1988).

cum-victim. Prasanna, then, becomes the central figure in the concluding part of our story.

IV

With his uninhibited behaviour at Doyhata and in the courtroom,
Prasanna offers us a glimpse into lower depths that remains brief,
tantalizing, and full of mystery. Locating Lalmohan and Kalachand
meaningfully within bhadralok society has not proved too difficult,
even though they had been far more reticent in court. The problem
with Prasanna lies precisely in such contextualization, for his was
an eruption from a largely unrecorded oral culture about which
official and literary Indian testimony alike are silent, confined to
bare statistics, or immersed in stereotypes. Scantiness of background
material makes an exploration through the actions and words of an
evidently unrepresentative figure extremely hazardous: paradoxically,
it also adds to the interest and importance of Prasanna through
sheer lack of alternative material about lower-caste perceptions.

At the most obvious level, Prasanna embodied the fury of a
Chandal unleashed. A newcomer to the village, he could have had
no personal grudge against the Doyhata gentlefolk: his, presumably,
was an elementary caste-cum-class anger, the settling of scores for
a lifetime of humiliation. It needs to be noted, however, that his
entry into the Doyhata scene had been made possible by the
bhadralok themselves, and that the anger was largely articulated
through a rearrangement, *bricoleur*-fashion, of fragments of high
culture. Assumptions of complete subaltern autonomy, of over-sharp
distinctions of cultural 'levels' or 'domains' do not seem very helpful
here. A man like Prasanna would normally never have been allowed
into a bhadralok's home, far less permitted to share a pipe *(kalke)*
with its master — for the touch of a Chandal is supposed to pollute
a high caste. Prasanna could enter because he had become a 'Chandal
sadhu', disciple of a Brahman guru. At first he merely performed
the properly subaltern duty of preparing the ganja for Kalachand
and Lalmohan. He attracted notice, however, because he 'talked so
fast that it was difficult to follow him'[42] — not a trivial detail, for
a man like him would be expected to remain deferentially silent
in high-caste company. Incessant talk then became abuse of superiors, and finally erupted into explosive violence.

[42] *KM*, p. 2; *Bengalee*, 17 March 1905.

And yet even at the most violent moments a sense of limits was retained. There is not the faintest hint of rape, robbery, or attempts to kill anyone apart from the ritual murder of Ananda. More significantly, there were traces of an underlying structure, derived in large part from selective appropriations of bits and pieces of high-caste culture. Prasanna called Lalmohan 'Dronacharya', described the fire he started as an 'yajna', brandished a bow (like Ekalavya, perhaps, the tribal youth who had made Drona his guru in the Mahabharata), called himself Hanuman, and termed the Doyhata he was burning 'Lanka': mixing together with a fine lack of discrimination elements also from that other great epic, the Ramayana. What remained consistently absent was the motif of deference, repeatedly emphasized in the standard version of stories about Ekalavya or Hanuman. Other conflations are also noticeable: thus the cult founded by Kalachand presumably had Vaishnava affiliations, and Prasanna always called his guru 'gossain', preceptor in a tradition which abhors blood sacrifices — and yet the sacrifice of Ananda seems to point towards elements associated more with the alternative, Shakta mode of Hindu devotion.[43]

Doyhata, however, was more than a *bricollage* of well-known fragments of high culture, more, even, than a pattern of ritual inversions of the kind many anthropologists have loved to analyse. Prasanna's actions did involve a whole series of inversions: most fundamentally, a Shudra had taken over bits and pieces from mythic traditions that had exalted proper caste and gender hierarchies and used it to humiliate upper castes and make a woman kick her husband. What he had achieved for one night was indeed a kind of double inversion. The Kaliyuga dystopia had been of an inverted world with Shudras and women on top, which the Kalki-avatar would set right side up again. Prasanna had burst into a re-enactment of this myth by a Brahman sadhu and his bhadralok disciple, and appropriated it to

[43] For the Doyhata details the central reference remains the *KM* pamphlet. *Yajna* is the sacrificial fire, central to ancient Vedic ritual and still retained in modern Hindu ceremonies like marriage. In the Mahabharata, Ekalavya was a tribal youth who had become a master of archery superior even to the epic hero Arjuna, by practising before an image of Dronacharya, military teacher to the Kaurava and Pandava princes. Dronacharya eventually gave Eklavya his blessing — in return for the sacrifice of his forefinger, thus ending the threat to the Kshatriyas. In the Ramayana, Ram recovered his abducted wife Sita by destroying Lanka, the capital of the demon-king Ravana, helped greatly by Hanuman the monkey. Both Ekalavya and Hanuman are usually taken to exemplify subaltern devotion and loyalty.

terrorize the Doyhata gentry. Unlike ritual inversions with ultimate 'safety-valve' functions, again, Prasanna was not acting out any established ritual, but maybe groping towards something new.

The open-ended nature of that Doyhata night was further enhanced by the inclusion of a real and startling innovation: the association of yuga-pralay with *physical* immortality. For Kalachand and Lalmohan, it seems, Ananda was Yama the god of death, brought deliberately into the house by the sadhu as Kalki-avatar — and after his killing 'there would be no more death in this world.' The two low-caste disciples, we have seen, had a slightly different perception, and Prasanna had promised Ananda a *divya-deha* (divine body): both versions, however, share an emphasis upon bodily immortality or resurrection totally absent in the Kaliyuga–Kalki mythic corpus. The roots of this peculiar stress are impossible to determine with any certainty. But the divya-deha promised by Prasanna is a synonym of *divya-tanu* (both refer to a divine and immortal body), and the latter is a technical term in use among Tantrics. Divya-tanu in Tantricism is associated with *jivan-mukti*, which could imply physical immortality as distinct from the moksha of the soul *(atman)*. The underlying theme of *dehavad*, the human body as principal seat of religious practice, is in fact near-ubiquitous in many medieval and later obscure religious cults, largely plebeian in membership, in Bengal and elsewhere. We have already encountered one such group, active in the nineteenth century in a district not very far from Dacca: the Balaramis of Nadia. More directly relevant could be the Nathpanthis, influential for centuries among plebeian groups in East Bengal, including Muslims — whose beliefs and legends combined attainment of bodily immortality with a special hostility towards Yama.[44] But all such beliefs had been 'esoteric', with rituals conducted in secret away from everyday household life, and therefore not too difficult to reconcile with an outward maintenance of due forms. Doyhata was shocking and transgressive through the public importation of these into a bhadralok home.

The embarrassments did not end here. Trial proceedings revealed the bhadralok menfolk in an uniformly unflattering light, as complicit or complaisant in the humiliation of the women of the household.

[44] Louis Dumont, 'World Renunciation in Indian Religions', in his *Religion/ Politics and History* (Paris/Hague, 1970); Debiprasad Chattopadyay, *Lokayata* (Bombay, 1950), Chapter v; Surendranath Dasgupta, *History of Indian Philosophy*, x vol. III (Cambridge, 1981); N.N. Bhattacharji, op. cit.; Sashibhusan Dasgupta, *Obscure Religious Cults* (Calcutta, 1948).

And the women, too, refused to fit into any of the pigeon-holes constructed for them by conventional dominant male discourses. Lalmohan's wife, kicking her husband on the head at the orders of Prasanna, was hardly the disorderly woman-on-top, but neither was she the self-sacrificing, deferentially assertive wife. The proceedings also indicated that the women on the whole had been far more sceptical about Kalachand's claims than their menfolk, thus undermining yet another stereotype, that of them being congenitally more 'superstitious' or 'pious'. The general bhadralok silence about Doyhata, despite its potential as salacious scandal, is thus quite understandable.

A pattern of purification-through-degradation seems to have characterized the actions of Prasanna that night. Upper-caste men and women were forcibly dragged downwards in both social and physical terms though abuse, nudity, having their sacred thread torn, being urinated upon, etc. — and by a Chandal or under his orders. Analogies with Bakhtin's well-known analysis of carnivalesque degradation/ renewal in medieval and Renaissance popular culture through movement downwards into the 'grotesque realism' of the 'material bodily lower stratum' are tempting, but not, perhaps, entirely helpful.[45] Cross-cultural comparisons are tricky things: official Christian and high-Hindu attitudes towards the body are far from identical, for instance, and the implications of their inverted forms are also likely to be different. Inversions reminiscent of the carnivalesque do surface occasionally at nodal points of seasonal cycles: Holi, most notably, as well as in the Charak festival before the Bengali New Year.[46] Where Doyhata differed, quite fundamentally, was in the absence of any community dimension: it had nothing to do with any open community action by Chandals or Bhuinmalis as a whole, and almost certainly the 'Sanskritizing' upwardly-mobile offshoots of the Matua sect would have been as embarrassed by it as the bhadralok themselves. Prasanna remained an individual with a self-assigned special function, performing in public actions that retained a mysterious, esoteric character reminiscent of Tantric rituals. The joyous abandon of community festivals like Holi was conspicuously absent at Doyhata.

[45] Mikhail Bakhtin, *Rabelais and His World* (Moscow, 1966; trans., Bloomington, 1968, 1984), Chapters V, VI.

[46] Holi replaces 'separation by communion and interdiction by license'. (Dumont, p. 51). For accounts of Charak, see Gauranga Chattopadhyay, *Carak Festival in a West Bengal Village*, in L.P. Vidyarthi (ed.), *Aspects of Religion in Indian Society* (Meerut, 1961) and Ralph Nicholas, 'Ritual Hierarchy and Social Relations in Rural Bengal', *Contributions in Indian Sociology*, December 1967.

The affinity/distinction pattern can be extended further: in formal terms, though obviously not in content or consequences, Doyhata fleetingly brings to mind the movements premised upon rumours of sudden, total, miraculous change that were not uncommon in late-colonial India. Birsa Munda's tribal rebellion in South Bihar (1899–1900), for instance, was accompanied by 'rumours of miraculous cures and the resuscitation of dead men', and much was made of a Satyayuga–Kaliyuga contrast in which Satyayuga was obviously very different from the orthodox conception of restored ideal caste hier-archy.[47] Such movements were particularly common in the early years of the Gandhian era, and in them cyclical concepts of time, myths about past golden ages under just kings or benevolent zamindars, mingled with future-oriented impulses. Millennarian hopes like these invariably coalesced around leaders with a reputation for sanctity: Gandhi himself, or wandering religious mendicants. Degradation through reduction to the 'material bodily lower stratum' can also be occasionally glimpsed in such collective, plebeian manifestations: as when rumours circulated in the Gorakhpur region in 1921 that respectable upper-caste people disobeying Gandhi's commands ran the risk of finding themselves covered with excreta. Rough, bawdy jokes often enhanced morale at moments of acute confrontation with authority. It is in such collective protests, and not at Doyhata, that we can expect to find elements of Bakhtinian carnivalesque.[48]

Yet newspapers noticed the strange gaiety of Prasanna in court, 'commenting freely and gaily on the depositions of several witnesses,' making sarcastic remarks about the other accused, judges, and the jury.[49] This could not be the rollicking, triumphant, Rabelaisian laughter celebrated by Bakhtin as allegedly characteristic of the culture of the marketplace in late-medieval and Renaissance towns, nor could Prasanna's sarcasm and gaiety compare with the well-known genre of gallows speeches in eighteenth-century England or France, with its 'aspect of the Carnival, in which rules were inverted, authority mocked, and criminals transformed into heroes.'[50] The essential component of a plebeian audience was missing in the

[47] Ranajit Guha, *Elementary Aspects of Peasant Insurgency in Colonial India* (Delhi, 1983), pp. 267, 294–7.

[48] Shahid Amin, 'Gandhi as Mahatma: Gorakhpur District, Eastern U.P., 1921–2', in Guha (ed.), *Subaltern Studies III* (Delhi, 1984); Tanika Sarkar, *Bengal 1928–34: The Politics of Protest* (Delhi, 1987), Chapter I.

[49] *Bengalee*, 17 March 1905.

[50] Michel Foucault, *Discipline and Punish* (Paris, 1975; Peregrine, 1979), pp. 57–69.

bhadralok-dominated courtroom. Prasanna's could only be the wry, resigned, yet defiant smile of the isolated plebeian, caught in the machinery of bhadralok-administered colonial power–knowledge, aware that no one in court was really interested in finding out what he had meant by his actions, what inspiration and meanings he had derived from the teachings of his gossain.

The most populist of historians is unlikely to make a hero out of Prasanna, whose actions merely brought death to a man of even humbler caste, a night of agony for some innocent women, and purely temporary humiliation for a few bhadralok. Doyhata might be a reminder for us of lower-caste fires underground, but it is also a warning against tendencies towards valorizing all more-or-less autonomous plebeian or subaltern action. The carnivalesque is not necessarily a realm of pure freedom emancipated from cruelty and oppression. In twentieth-century India, and most recently at Babri Masjid and in the countrywide riots that followed in the winter of 1992–3, elements reminiscent of the Bakhtinian carnivalesque have manifested themselves also in fratricidal conflicts between Hindus, Muslims and Sikhs.

And yet, precisely through his 'laughter', Prasanna did attain a certain dignity in court, even, if we like to read it that way, a fleeting acuteness of perception. When Lalmohan was abjectly trying to wriggle out of all responsibility, the Chandal interjected: 'No, he did nothing, he just had three or four *kalkes* [pipe for smoking hemp] of ganja with us.' Asked then by the judge to sign a statement taking full responsibility for what had happened, Prasanna replied, 'If I had known how to write, why, then, I would have become a judge and earned five to seven hundred rupees.'[51] Superb sarcasm, that allows us to rejoin the problematic with which we had begun. Education had been at the heart of the entire 'renaissance' enterprise of the bhadralok, and its meagre fruits in the shape of subordinate chakri had fuelled resentments expressed through a renewed Kaliyuga mood. Beyond this dichotomy lie caste and class dimensions, deeply affected by colonialism but extending before and after it: dimensions often elided in models of 'renaissance' awakening and critiques of colonial acculturation. Prasanna's last comment, with which he departs from the historical record forever, points towards that little-explored and ambiguous world.

[51] *KM*, p. 74.

7

Vidyasagar and
Brahmanical Society

Ramakrishna: "The work *(karma)* that you are doing is very good. . . . But as your devotion *(bhakti)* and love for Him grows, your work will lessen. . . . Man cannot improve the world, only He is doing it: He has made the sun and the moon, given affection to mothers and fathers, benevolence *(daya)* to the great, *bhakti* to the *sadhu bhakt.* . . . Look, how wonderful the universe is. How many things: sun, moon, the stars; how many different kinds of living beings. Big and small, good and bad, some with more powers *(shakti)*, some with less."

Vidyasagar: "Has He given more *shakti* to some, less to others?"

— 'M' (Mahendranath Gupta), *Ramakrishna-Kathamrita,*
Volume III (Calcutta, 1908; 15th edition, 1982),
pp. 15, 10. 5 August 1882.

I

The *Ramakrishna-Kathamrita* will appear an odd, perhaps positively eccentric, starting point for an essay on Vidyasagar. Ramakrishna's visit to Vidyasagar's house was never reciprocated, and in many ways the two clearly represented opposite poles. Mahendranath Gupta, the compiler of *Kathamrita,* who had arranged the visit at Ramakrishna's request, was in 1882 headmaster of a North Calcutta school started by Vidyasagar. He resigned his job soon afterwards, upon hearing that the latter had made an adverse comment about his neglect of his duties because of over-frequent visits to Dakshineswar.[1]

Mahendranāth's account of Ramakrishna's conversations with

[1] Biographical note on 'M' (Mahendranath Gupta), appended to *Ramakrishna-Kathamrita,* Volume I (Calcutta, 1901, 1980).

Vidyasagar, based on his diary notings but published a quarter of a century later, seems to have been structured with exceptional care. It begins with praise of Vidyasagar by the diarist-compiler for great learning and unequalled compassion ('dayar sagar'): there is not a word about Vidyasagar the social reformer, no reference at all to widow remarriage. Then, step by step, Ramakrishna is presented as establishing the inferiority of 'mere' learning and philanthropy to devotion. There is a brief moment of agreement, when Vidyasagar admires Ramakrishna's statement that no one can know or describe what divinity is. But from there the paths diverge radically once more. For Vidyasagar, as described by Mahendranath, the unknowability of the supramundane makes it our supreme duty to try to do everything possible to improve this-worldly life.[2] For Ramakrishna, in total contrast, ignorance becomes the premise for faith and devotion, and it is folly and arrogance for men to think of improving the world. The universe inevitably consists of big and small, some with more power and others with less: it is beautiful because it is divinely structured in terms of hierarchical inequality. This reiteration of the principle of *adhikari-bheda*, much used in nineteenth-century Brahmanical discourses,[3] provoked Vidyasagar to make a retort implicitly asserting that inequality is not natural but social, and hence open to human remedial action. The retort clearly rankled with Ramakrishna, for the *Kathamrita* describes him recalling it on two later occasions as proof of the folly of Vidyasagar.[4]

Opposed mentalities, indeed world outlooks: but I think it is helpful to remember that Vidyasagar and Ramakrishna came from rather similar social worlds. Not primarily because Birsingha and Kamarpukur are villages close to each other, both then part of Jehanabad (Arambagh) subdivision of Hooghly district, but in terms of origins in rural, poor Brahman families in an area centred around Khanakul-Krishnanagar, noted for centuries for its Brahmanical learning. Families, moreover, which were or had become extremely

---

[2] Vidyasagar once teased a Brahmo preacher who had lost his way while coming to his house: 'Why do you think you know the road to heaven any better? You'd better give up this business fast.' Chandicharan Bandopadhyay, *Vidyasagar* (Calcutta, 1895, 1969), p. 54.

[3] For a discussion of the centrality of this notion, see Chapters 8 and 9, *passim*.

[4] 'Vidyasagar is so learned, has such a reputation, yet he said such a silly thing, asking whether He could have given more powers to some, less to others —'. *Kathamrita*, II, p. 64 (15 June 1883). See also ibid., III, p. 205 (28 July 1885).

poor: few among the other famous men of nineteenth-century Bengal rose from such conditions of extreme genteel poverty.[5] For both Vidyasagar and Ramakrishna, the move to Calcutta was crucial, but then their paths to influence and fame became utterly different. The social ascent of Vidyasagar, enjoying excellent relations with high British officials and leading zamindars particularly in the 1850s and 1860s, and with a monthly income at times of three to four thousand rupees from his textbook publishing business, was in external terms much more spectacular than that of the humble pujari-cum-mystic at Rani Rashmoni's Dakshineswar temple. Before coming to visit Vidyasagar, Ramakrishna took unusual care to see that his buttons were in place, and in course of their conversation said that Vidyasagar was like a big ship, while people like him were no more than fishing-boats.[6] Yet by the early 1880s there was also a strong element of paradox in their respective positions. The 'ocean of learning' was feeling more and more isolated among the Calcutta bhadralok, and had come to prefer the company of unlearned Santals at Karmatar, while it was precisely the English-educated who were flocking to Dakshineswar. When Ramakrishna died in August 1886, the liberal English newspaper *Statesman* was impressed by the manner in which his ashes had been 'reverentially carried' by his 'followers — all graduates and undergraduates of the university.'[7]

A juxtaposition of Vidyasagar with Ramakrishna can raise some interesting questions about different trajectories emerging from a little-explored world of poor high-caste literati: the underside, so to say, of the colonial 'educated middle class' about which so much has been written in praise or condemnation. Nineteenth-century studies have oscillated between eulogies of 'renaissance awakening' inspired by Western or English education, and critiques of colonial

---

[5] Vidyasagar's father Thakurdas was earning Rs 10 a month when he brought his son to Calcutta in 1828, and though prices of most things then were extremely low, the Hindu College fee was Rs 5 per month. Rani Rashmoni's deed of endowment of February 1861 provided Rs 5 for Ramakrishna as pujari of her temple, plus stipulated amounts of cloth and food. *Vidyasagar Charit* (autobiographical fragment, published posthumously in 1891, reprinted in Tirthapati Datta, ed., *Vidyasagar Rachanabali*, Volume I, Calcutta, 1994, p. 411); Sambhuchandra Vidyaratna, *Vidyasagar-Jivancarit* (Calcutta, 1891; reprinted, ed. Kumudkumar Bhattacharya, Calcutta, 1992), p. 13; *Ramakrishna-Kathamrita*, Volume II (Calcutta, 1904, 1982, p. iii).

[6] *Ramakrishna-Kathamrita*, Volume III, pp. 3, 16.

[7] *Statesman*, 25 August 1886, reprinted in Ranabir Raychaudhuri, ed., *Calcutta A Hundred Years Ago* (Calcutta, Nachiketa Publications, 1988), p. 126.

cultural subjugation brought about by the same institutions and ideas. The influence, or imposition, of the culture of the post-Enlightenment West figures as absolutely central in both interpretive models, while the 'middle class', in a second assumption common to otherwise opposed poles, tends to get portrayed in excessively homogenized terms.[8]

It has never been easy to slot Vidyasagar into either of these alternative frames, for he combined indisputably 'modernistic' ideas and reform initiatives with a rejection of all the external signs of 'Westernism' and evident rootedness, by education and way of life, in 'traditional' Brahman literati culture. At times such problems have heightened the quality of research. Benoy Ghosh's study, for instance, remains impressive through its grasp over detail and valuable insights, even though its 'awakening' or 'renaissance' mould would not be acceptable to many today.[9] And the early-1970s critique of the renaissance in terms of colonial constraints undoubtedly attained its point of maximum subtlety and depth in Asok Sen's *Iswarchandra Vidyasagar and His Elusive Milestones.*[10]

Sen's study had been a wide-ranging analysis of the constraints upon Vidyasagar, exploring the interrelations between education, social-reform endeavours, and the changing contours of colonial political economy. With the displacement of Marx by Saidian critiques of colonial discourse, emphasis has shifted from such specific explorations of the ways in which modernizing initiatives had been frustrated in colonial conditions to supposedly more radical repudiations of post-Enlightenment modernity and radicalism. 'Modernity', rather than the structures of capitalist colonialism, has become the principal polemical target, and the social is collapsed into the narrowly intellectual and discursive. The nineteenth-century literati now appear as more homogenized than ever, with their trajectories set by ideas inevitably tainted by their origin in the modern West. What, often with considerable vagueness, is called nationalism gets deconstructed into a series of disciplinary projects that are either derived from, or at best run parallel to, the patterns of colonial power-knowledge.[11]

[8] For a fuller elaboration of my problems with both these frameworks, see Chapter 6 in this book.

[9] Benoy Ghosh, *Vidyasagar o Bangali Samaj*, Volumes I, II, III (Calcutta, 1957, 1958, 1959; combined volume, Calcutta, Orient Longman, 1973).

[10] Published Calcutta, Riddhi-India, 1977.

[11] The most authoritative and influential expositions of this current orthodoxy have come of course from Partha Chatterjee, *Nationalist Thought and the*

Significantly, perhaps, few attempts have been made so far to incorporate Vidyasagar into this anti-modernist interpretive frame.[12] Some recent writings point, rather, in a different and to my mind more fruitful direction. Brian Hatcher and Sekhar Bandopadhyay have highlighted in distinct ways the relevance of Brahmanical ideas and contexts for understanding Vidyasagar. Hatcher's is an unusual, if narrow, focus upon Vidyasagar's educational plans and school textbooks: he finds in them not a simple acculturation by Victorian notions of improvement and discipline, but a coming together of 'bourgeois and Brahmanical educational ideologies within a Bengali idiom of moral pedagogy.'[13] In a brief but very original and important essay, Sekhar Bandopadhyay has argued that the relative failure of widow remarriage and other nineteenth-century social-reform initiatives cannot be explained solely by the 'structural weaknesses of the reformist effort'. One needs to take into account also 'the power of tradition that refused to be reformed', as embodied in hierarchies of caste and gender that were necessarily interlocked, since caste purity depended in large part on strict regulation of marriage and female sexuality.[14] These were consolidated in some ways under British rule, but certainly did not originate from colonialism. Bandopadhyay rejects the tendency common nowadays to romanticize the precolonial 'popular' as a realm of freedom. He argues that the Brahmanical 'ideology of discipline' and 'public control over private life' had penetrated deep into so-called 'popular' Hinduism in Bengal well before the colonial presence. The taboo

---

Colonial World: A Derivative Discourse? (Delhi, Oxford University Press, 1986), and *The Nation and Its Fragments* (Delhi, Oxford University Press, 1994). For the (slightly) revised version emphasizing parallel disciplinary projects, see Partha Chatterjee, ed., *Texts of Power: Emerging Disciplines in Colonial Bengal* (Calcutta, Samya, 1996).

12 With the partial exception, perhaps, of Shivaji Bandopadhyay, *Gopal-Rakhal Dvandva Samas: Upanibeshbad O Bangla Shishusahitya* (Calcutta, 1991), pp. 134–42, and *passim*.

13 Brian A. Hatcher, *Idioms of Improvement: Vidyasagar and Cultural Encounter in Bengal* (Calcutta, Oxford University Press, 1996), p. 117, and *passim*.

14 H.H. Risley had declared in 1891 that 'caste is mainly a matter of marriage'. Five years later, Jogendranath Bhattacharya, leading Nadia pandit and expert in Hindu law, quoted Risley with appproval and reiterated: 'The most important regulations by which the castes have been made exclusive are those which relate to marriage.' H.H. Risley, *Tribes and Castes of Bengal*, Volume I, *Introductory Essay: Caste in Relation to Marriage* (Calcutta, 1891, 1981), pp. xlii; Jogendranath Bhattacharya, *Hindu Castes and Sects* (Calcutta, 1896, 1968), p. 9.

on widow remarriage, for instance, was far from being restricted to high castes alone, as has often been assumed. Turn-of-the-century census reports found it normative among the bulk of intermediate and even lower castes, with only very lowly-placed groups still remarrying widows without inhibition.[15] Both resistance to, and (I shall argue) occasional support for, Vidyasagar's campaign was therefore not necessarily always confined to the upper-caste elite.

Hatcher's careful analysis remains in the end more textual than social, slipping at times into a bland language of disembodied 'cultural encounter'. The Brahmanical focus in both Hatcher and Bandopadhyay, I feel, needs to be sharpened through a more layered, non-homogenized view of the high-caste literati world that would also give due regard to the many changes within it in the course of the nineteenth century. Vidyasagar's rise from poor-Brahman origins should be seen not just in terms of the heroic endeavour of an individual, but within a wider context of multiple pressures and opportunities playing upon the world of traditional pandits and ritual experts.

The unusually abundant biographical literature on Vidyasagar[16] (itself a feature that needs to be problematized, I shall argue) permits many glimpses of a pandit world in movement. Most of Vidyasagar's teachers in Sanskrit College, for instance, seem to have been first-generation migrants into Calcutta: Gangadhar Tarkabagish, grammarian, from Kumarhatta-Halisahar; Joygopal Tarkalankar, famous scholar of Sanskrit literature who had assisted Colebrooke and Carey and helped to edit the early Bengali newspaper *Samachar Darpan*, from Bajrapur village in Nadia; Premchandra Tarkabagish, master of Alankar (aesthetics), from Rayna (Burdwan district); Sambhuchandra Vacaspati, Vedanta expert, from Ujirpur village in Barisal; and Joynarayan Tarkapanchanan, who trained Vidyasagar in Nyaya, from the south-western environs of the city (Behala-Barisha, followed by Salkia).[17] Vacaspati apart, they had all come from villages or small

---

[15] Sekhar Bandopadhyay, 'Caste, Widow-remarriage and the Reform of Popular Culture in Colonial Bengal', in Bharati Ray, ed., *From the Seams of History: Essays on Indian Women* (Delhi, Oxford University Press, 1995), pp. 9, 11, 14, and *passim*.

[16] No less than four full-length biographies of Vidyasagar were published within a decade of his death in 1891: by Sambhuchandra Vidyaratna (1891), Chandicharan Bandopadhyay (1895), Biharilal Sarkar (1895), and (in English) Subolchandra Mitra (1902). There has also been an abundance of anecdotes.

[17] Benoy Ghosh, pp. 74–95, has carefully collated the information about Vidyasagar's teachers from biographical literature and the research of Brojendranath Banerji. Of the early biographies of Vidyasagar, Sambhuchandra is

towns within a fifty-mile or so radius of the new metropolis, for
this also had been the heartland, from the fifteenth-sixteenth century
onwards, of Vaidik and Rarhiya Brahman scholarship and training
in Smriti and Nyaya. Most famous of all had been the Nadia belt
from Nabadwip to Bhatpara, which had produced Raghunandan
and Raghunath Shiromani, masters of Nabya-Smriti and Nabya-
Nyaya, and had enjoyed another late efflorecence in the eighteenth
century through the patronage of Maharaj Krishnachandra of Nadia.
The belt of old Brahman settlements and *tols-chatuspathis* extended
southwards along the Bhagirathi from here through Halisahar, down
to what are today the south-eastern outskirts of Calcutta — the
Harinabhi-Rajpur-Changripota-Majilpur area, while across the river
there was a parallel stretch from Ambica-Kalna and Guptipara
through Tribeni down to Serampur and Uttarpara. And finally there
was the region from which came Vidyasagar, Ramakrishna — and
Rammohan: the Khanakul-Krishnanagar pandit samaj, with influence extending to Brahman settlements in the subdivisions of adjoining Arambagh and Ghatal. With a touch of local pride, Vidyasagar
in an official report once described the village of Krishnanagar as
'the chief centre of Hindu learning next to Nuddea.'[18]

The pandits who had moved to Calcutta quite often lived in
conditions of marked poverty[19] — but presumably prospects had
become worse still in their original villages by the early nineteenth
century, making city life preferable. Brahman scholars and ritual
experts had been accustomed to live 'not off the land but off
patronage':[20] as *sabha-pandits* of maharajas and rajas, on bits of
revenue or rent-free *brahmottar* or *devottar* lands donated by zamindars, and from gifts and fees from local notables and from householders with whom they had hereditary *jajmani* connections. They
were therefore among the rural groups most vulnerable in times of

particularly informative about his Sanskrit College teachers: see pp. 16–32 of
his book.

18 Vidyasagar's Report on Progress of Normal and Village Schools, January
1857, included in General Report on Public Instruction, Lower Provinces, Bengal
Presidency, 1856–7, Appendix A, and reprinted in Arabinda Guha, ed., *Unpublished Letters of Vidyasagar* (Calcutta, Ananda Publishers, 1971), p. 29.

19 Benoy Ghosh has used the biography of a near-contemporary of Vidyasagar,
Girishchandra Vidyaratna, to illustrate this poverty. Girishchandra's father had
run tols in Rajpur and then North Calcutta, living virtually in a hovel. Harishchandra Bhattacharya, *Girishchandra Vidyaratner Jivani* (Calcutta, 1909), cited in
Benoy Ghosh, p. 78.

20 Hatcher, p. 36.

trouble, and such times came in quick succession to South-Western and Central Bengal from the mid eighteenth century.

There had been the Maratha raids, affecting parts of the south-west and the west, followed twenty years later by the much more devastating famine of 1770, when Midnapur, Hooghly, Burdwan and Nadia had figured among the worst-affected districts.[21] Vidyasagar's corner of Bengal was among the regions where the famine had been followed by decades of near-anarchy. His grandfather developed the habit of always travelling with an iron staff, with which he once beat off and killed a bear just a few miles from Midnapur town.[22] Patronage flows must have been further restricted by the quick changes in superior land rights through Company revenue experiments culminating in the Permanent Settlement. The new rigorous regime of Sunset Laws would have made grants to Brahmans often appear an ill-affordable luxury. The British in the 1830s attempted large-scale resumption of revenue-free grants, while an enterprising zamindar like Joykrishna Mukherjee of Uttarpara, who had been part of the zamindari united front critical of this move, later became unpopular among many Hooghly Brahmans by resuming rent-free tenures on his own estates.[23] The decline of traditional crafts under the new regime of one-way free trade could also have deepened indirectly the crisis of rural literati families. It must have affected the old textile centre of Khirpai, for instance, close to Birsingha and the place where Vidyasagar's grandmother had probably sold the yarn she used to spin on her *charkha* as her only resource, in the years when Thakurdas had been too young to earn, and her husband had become a wanderer.[24] And finally, over the *longue durée*, there were the consequences of the shift in river-flows eastwards, making the old heartland of Brahmanical culture irreversibly part of a moribund delta — a process quickened after the mid nineteenth century by railway embankments blocking old drainage patterns and

---

[21] N.K. Sinha, *Economic History of Bengal*, Volume II (Calcutta, Firma K.L. Mukhopadhyay, 1962), pp. 50–3.

[22] *Vidyasagar-Charit*, p. 409.

[23] The Calcutta *dals* headed by Radhakanta Deb and the Tagores came together on this issue to float the Bengal Landholders' Society in 1838. Nilmoni Mukherjee, *A Bengal Zamindar: Joykrishna Mukherjee of Uttarpara and His Times, 1808–1888* (Calcutta, Firma K.L. Mukhopadhyay, 1975), pp. 56–8. The later resumption of Brahman grants by Joykrishna led Vidyasagar to briefly oppose the zamindar whose name had figured at the head of the petition seeking legalization of widow remarriage, in 1855. Mukherjee, p. 274.

[24] *Vidyasagar Charit*, p. 399.

probably contributing to the devastating entry of malaria. An early
biography of Vidyasagar bears witness to the panic inspired by
malaria through an unexpected precision about places and dates:
malaria first appeared, Chandicharan Bandopadhyay tells us, in
Muhammadpur village in Jessore in 1825, spread over Nadia, Barasat
and 24 Parganas, and then struck Burdwan and Hooghly in 1867-9.[25]

For a generation or two, in contrast, the expanding colonial
metropolis of Calcutta appeared as a zone of new opportunities for
a significant part of the traditional literati. 'Native' life in Calcutta
was initially dominated by noveau riche families, members of which
amassed fabulous fortunes as banians and dewans through profitable
collaboration with early British traders and administrators, experi-
mented in independent entrepreneurship, and then settled down as
urban real-estate owners and zamindars. Most of them came from
non-Brahman, and indeed at times low-caste, groups. Such 'compradore-rajas'[26] were eager to patronize Brahman scholars and ritual
experts in their *sabhas* ('courts') as part of their quest for respectability,
and it is significant that the citadel of nineteenth-century Calcutta
orthodoxy was constituted by a Kayastha family, the Debs of Sobhabazar. Nabakrishna Deb, grandfather of Radhakanta, had built
the family's fortunes through highly profitable collaboration with
Clive and Warren Hastings. He is also reputed to have brought many
learned Brahmans to Calcutta to adorn his court, among them
scholars like Jagannath Tarkapanchanan and Baneswar Vidyalankar.[27]
The various *dals* or factions of early-nineteenth-century Calcutta
around rival notable families all had need of the services of Brahman
pandits: even Young Bengal seems to have had one in tow, in
Gourishankar Bhattacharyay, who helped Derozians bring out the
Jnananeswan and later edited the reformist *Sambad Bhashkar*.

The continued prestige of pandits and ulema in colonial Calcutta
till the 1830s was related even more, perhaps, to certain distinctive
features of Company judicial administration. Hastings had laid down
in 1780 that matters of 'inheritance, marriage, caste and other
religious usages or institutions were to be administered to Hindus

25 Chandicharan Bandopadhayay, *Vidyasagar* (Calcutta, 1895, 1969), p. 497.

26 Pradip Sinha's term: see his *Calcutta in Urban History* (Calcutta, 1978),
pp. 16-17.

27 Loknath Ghosh, *The Native Aristocracy and Gentry of India* (Calcutta, 1881;
I am using its Bengali translation, *Kalkatar Babu-Vrittanta*, Calcutta, 1983,
pp. 74-5). Raja Binaya Krishna Deb, *The Early History and Growth of Calcutta*
(Calcutta, 1905), pp. 60-1.

according to the laws of the Shaster', and to Muslims by those of the Shariat.[28] 'Judge-pandits' and experts in Islamic law therefore had to be appointed to assist Englishmen in the civil courts of the Company, and in the 1820s and 1830s they were appointed from Sanskrit College students who had mastered their Smriti texts and passed a subsequent Law Committee examination. In 1829, Vidyasagar's educational plans were decided after much family confabulation by the argument that joining Sanskrit College would open up for him considerable prospects of profitable employment.[29]

Till around the 1830s, then, Company administration needed the reproduction on a fairly extended scale of the Sanskrit (as well as Persian-knowing) literati, and the channelling of official patronage to the Calcutta Madrasa and the Sanskrit College made good administrative sense even apart from the classical tastes of emerging Orientalist scholarship. Sanskrit College (and even more Fort William College, where Company officials learned Indian classical and vernacular languages) offered Indian scholars and experts salaries that were fairly high for the times. For the less fortunate or able, there was the possibility, given the continued high demand for Sanskrit, of starting 'tols' in Calcutta. William Ward counted twenty-eight of them in 1820, possibly an underestimate. Vidyasagar's father Thakurdas had put up initially with a distant relative who was running such a chatuspathi, when a move to Calcutta had been forced on him by financial need. Some thirty years later, in the 1840s, Ramakrishna likewise came to Calcutta in the wake of his elder brother Ramkumar, who thought running a tol in the city offered better prospects than eking out a livelihood as Smriti expert cum astrologer in the obscure village of Kamarpukur.[30]

By the mid 1840s, however, Sanskrit College graduates were finding it increasingly difficult to get jobs, a problem that Vidyasagar tried to tackle by advising Hardinge in 1846 that teachers of the

[28] J.D.M. Derrett, 'The British as Patrons of the Sastra', in his *Religion, Law and the State in India* (London, 1968), p. 233.

[29] Thakurdas, Vidyasagar's father, however, who had had to give up hopes himself of following the family profession of teaching Sanskrit due to sheer financial need, and had become a bill-collector for a shopkeeper instead, wanted his son to ultimately set up a *chatuspathi* in Birsingha. He made Vidyasagar turn down the offer of a Judge-Pandit's job in Tripura, after he had performed brilliantly in the Smriti and Law Committee examinations when only seventeen. *Vidyasagar Charit*, p. 414; Chandicharan Bandopadhyay, p. 53.

[30] Swami Saradananda, *Sri Sri Ramakrishna-Leelaprasanga, Volume I, Purvakatha O Balakbhabh* (Calcutta, 1911, 1982), pp. 122-3.

101 vernacular schools the Governor-General had just decided to start should be recruited entirely from them. Vidyasagar's appointment as Principal of Sanskrit College in January 1851 was directly connected with the crisis the College had come to face due to the employment crunch.[31] At a much less exalted level within the world of the traditional literati, Ramkumar by the early 1850s was finding survival as pandit of a Calcutta tol extremely difficult. He, along with his brother Gadadhar (Ramakrishna), had to become pujari in 1855 at the new temple of Dakshineswar just built by Rani Rashmoni — initially with considerable heartburning, for temple priests were considered rather low in the pecking order of Brahmans, and the brothers, even worse, were accepting the patronage of a Kaibarta.[32]

Incidents like these were indicators of bigger changes. The window of opportunity that Calcutta had opened for the traditional literati was clearly closing, as a result of the triumph of Macaulay and the 'Anglicists'. The 1840s also marked the end of large-scale Bengali entrepreneurship, with the collapse of the Union Bank in 1847 being often taken as the benchmark. This further reduced potential patronage — even though the sabhas and pandits around leading families did not wither away immediately, and we shall see Vidyasagar trying to utilize them at times for his reformist projects. There was now less need of judge-pandits, too, for a formidable body of 'Anglo-Hindu' jurisprudence had emerged which by 1864 could 'assume' that sufficient expertise had accumulated to obviate the need for such appointments. The practice of having such judge-pandits for each district court started withering away from the 1840s.[33] Above all, English education was becoming virtually the sole channel for retaining or winning respectability and employment for a *madhyabitta* or middle class that could not live on zamindari or tenure-holding alone, and yet (unlike peasants, labourers, the bulk of lower-castes

[31] Chandicharan Bandopadhyay, pp. 82–3; Subolchandra Mitra, *Life of Pandit Isvar Chandra Vidyasagar* (Calcutta, 1902; reprinted, New Delhi, Ashish Publishing House, 1975), p. 113.

[32] Swami Saradananda, *Volume II, Sadhakbhava* (Calcutta, 1982, pp. 70–5. Kaibartas in the mid nineteenth century were mostly fishermen and agriculturists of intermediate-caste status in south-western Bengal, with a major concentration in Midnapur. Over the succeeding decades the cultivators among them (the Hele, as distinct from the Jele, Kaivartas) were able to win for themselves the more prestigious name of Mahishya through a major caste movement.

[33] Sambhuchandra Vidyaratna, p. 40.

and Muslims) could afford, though often with great difficulty, to go to college. But college fees were pretty high for the times (Presidency charged twelve rupees a month in the 1870s, and Vidyasagar started his Metropolitan Institution mainly to provide a cheaper education for the more indigent among the bhadralok),[34] and so only a limited number among the madhyabitta really had the chance of successful professional or service careers as lawyers, prominent writers, journalists, doctors, officials, or politicians. Below them a substratum proliferated that, over time, came to be associated — ideal-typically and for generations in Bengali literature whenever it sought to depict poverty — with the figures of the indigent traditional literati and the clerk in government and mercantile offices caught in the toils of *chakri*.[35] Already in 1823, Bhabanicharan Bandopadhyay in his *Kalikata Kamalalay* had distinguished between *madhyabita lok* and *daridra athaccha bhadra lok* (poor but respectable folk). He described the latter, however, as surviving through doing odd jobs for the big 'dewanjis'.[36] Patronage of the rich Indian was clearly more visible then than regular office work, entered into through some amount of formal education. Clerical jobs down to around the mid century seem to have been more the domain of the Eurasians. A smattering of English, picked up through personal contacts, had been sufficient for Thakurdas to get a bill-collector's job with a businessman, and Vidyasagar in the 1840s and 1850s was able to get fairly important official posts for some friends and clients through contacts with prominent Englishmen.

With time, however, both education and employment became more bureaucratized, and the drudgery and humiliation of chakri, under foreign bosses and subordinated to a new discipline of clock time, became the crucial element in a late-nineteenth-century revival of the ancient trope of Kaliyuga.[37] By the 1880s, Ramakrishna would be describing in a vivid passage the plight of a college graduate, running from office to office, desperately begging for a job: for the

[34] Chandicharan Bandopadhyay, p. 369.

[35] Two obvious examples would be Haripada kerani in Rabindranath's poem *Kinu Goalar Goli*, and Harihar in Bibhutibhushan Bandopadhyay's *Pather Panchali*, now internationally known through Satyajit Ray's trilogy.

[36] Bhabanicharan Bandopadhyay, *Kalikata Kamalalay* (Calcutta, 1823; reprinted in Bandopadhyay, *Rasarachanasamagra*, Calcutta, Nabapatra Prakashana, 1987), p. 7.

[37] I have tried to explore this theme in a number of essays: see Chapters 5, 6 and 8, and 'Colonial Times: Clocks and Kaliyuga in Nineteenth-Century Bengal' (paper presented at Paris, Maison des Sciences de l'Hommes, June 1996).

professions and the services open to Indians were getting over-crowded, and newspapers were already full of complaints about educated unemployment. Changes in agrarian relations probably also contributed to the sense of a madhyabitta crisis. Thanks to the proliferation of intermediate tenures under the Permanent Settlement, a significant part of professional and even clerical groups also had some connections with land.[38] Fragmentation, however, tended to make such incomes from petty zamindari or tenure-holding insuffient, particularly after many easy ways of rent-enhancement had been restricted by the tenancy laws of 1859 and 1885. The pattern of some years of hope and social ascent, followed by frustration, that we have traced through the traditional literati was reproducing itself after a gap of a few decades in the life of the 'new', English-knowing intelligentsia.

Vidyasagar, I feel, needs to be placed within this broad context of a changing, multi-layered madhyabitta society. Multi-layered, though, not in the sense of rigid or insuperable partitions — both Vidyasagar and Ramakrishna in very different ways illustrate in fact just the opposite. The importance of keeping in mind the internal differentiation of the bhadralok world is precisely because the dividing lines were permeable. The most eminent of the bhadralok could have kinsmen eking out a living from clerical chakri, or among the ranks of the educated unemployed. He could recall, or imagine, lower-middle-class life as his past, or perhaps his future, and the racist humiliations which even the most successful of Indian officials or professional men would occasionally encounter could make vivid for them the indignity and degradation which was the constant lot of the clerk. The image of the *kerani* conse-quently had a power and reach much in excess of the actual, physical number of clerks, and a focus upon the 'daridra athaccha bhadra' is analytically helpful for highlighting pressures and tensions in some ways common to the entire madhyabitta.

The manifestations of these pressures in everyday family life, marriage relationships, and widowhood are vital for my enquiry, for this obviously was the domain central to all Vidyasagar's reformist concerns. In a brief essay, written many years ago, I had argued that

[38] A rough estimate made by the 1891 Bengal Census found half the merchants, one-third of the shopkeepers, a tenth of schoolteachers, pleaders and lawyers, one-fourth of the doctors, and one-sixth of the 'clerical class' to have 'some interest in land, generally as intermediate tenants.' *Census 1891, Volume III (Bengal)*, ed. C.J. O'Donnell (Calcutta, 1893), p. 291.

the fairly unusual concentration on the 'women's question' in middle-class male circles through much of the nineteenth century needs to be problematized, for it cannot be explained entirely in terms of mimesis of the West. Young men, moving to the city in quest of education and jobs, married off in their teens by parents to brides much younger and generally illiterate, could have faced acute problems of conjugal adjustment — particularly if they happened to be first-generation reformers, Derozian or Brahmo, with nuclearity imposed on them through ostracism by their relatives. Issues like widow-burning, women's education, gender seclusion, arranged marriage, child marriage, polygamy, and the prohibition of widow marriage would be 'under their eyes every day and hour of their existence within the precincts of their own respective domiciles.'[39] These in addition were problems which the nineteenth-century intelligentsia would have thought to be within their reach, remediable — unlike, say, foreign rule, prior to the rise of effective, middle-class-led nationalism. Programmes emerged consequently of *stri-swadhinata*: in effect, a fairly limited and controlled emancipation of wives within a framework of more companionate conjugality, undertaken entirely at male initiative, and sometimes accompanied by a refurbished patriarchy as reformist husbands within nuclear units sought to impose new norms of religious and social conduct on not-too-enthusiastic wives.[40]

This, however, could only have been one kind of scenario among many. Our hypothetical young men doing reasonably well in Calcutta might soon have large numbers of relatives (or village-cum-jati affines) staying with and/or dependent on them. Out of a salary of fifty rupees a month as chief pandit of Fort William College in the mid 1840s, Vidyasagar was sending twenty home to his father in Birsingha as virtually sole support for the big joint family there, while maintaining in Calcutta with the remainder three brothers, five nephews, an old servant and a number of indigent boys whose education he was paying for.[41] The successful few might try to break

[39] The quotation is from Maheshchandra Deb, *A Sketch of the Condition of Hindoo Women*, presented to the Derozian Society for Acquisition of General Knowledge in January 1839, and reprinted in Gautam Chattopadhyay, ed., *Awakening in Bengal in the Early Nineteenth Century* (Calcutta, 1965), p. 90.

[40] Sumit Sarkar, 'The Women's Question in Nineteenth Century Bengal, in Sarkar, *A Critique of Colonial India* (Calcutta, Papyrus, 1985), pp. 71–6.

[41] Sambhuchandra Vidyaratna, p. 40; Chandicharan Bandopadhyay, p. 78; Benoy Ghosh, p. 159, and *passim*.

away, fuelling charges of selfish, iconoclastic modernity: for the less fortunate or able, insistence on customary obligations could become an important strategy for survival. One response, therefore, to the pressures of changing colonial life, that probably deepened over time as they impinged upon one sector after another of the madhyabitta, was a renewed insistence upon the virtues of the 'traditional' upper-caste Hindu undivided family. This was counterposed against the encroachment of market values and selfish, insubordinate individualism, and portrayed in ideological terms as a world characterized by mutuality of deference and benevolent paternalism, where kinship obligations had been sacred, and an endless hospitality had kept doors always open for everyone of equivalent status. That the burdens of such hospitality and openness would rest inevitably on the unpaid labour of wives and the toil of servants would of course be either elided, or prettified into a model of Annapurna, the mother or wife as bounteous provider of food, from whom services somehow flowed with tireless grace and beauty. Such norms constituted the implicit ideal Other of the many representations of Kaliyuga in a mass of mid- and late-nineteenth-century tracts, plays and farces, produced by obscure authors among whom one notes a high proportion of Brahman surnames. In them the evils of contemporary life were regularly attributed to insubordinate, expensive, educated wives, neglecting domestic duties, making husbands disregard kinship obligations, nagging them for money and jewellery, and pushing menfolk into the humiliating dependence of clerical chakri.

Let us take one example, typical in everything except its surprising location: 'The one priceless resource this enslaved and lifeless society of Bengal can have is the ideal Hindu household . . . [where] relatives are looked after, responsibility is taken for one's community and caste (jatigoshthi), poor and helpless sons and daughters of departed relations are brought up with care. . . . ' All these, however, are becoming things of the past: 'Today people are entirely dominated by calculations of selfish gain. . . . Peace and happiness had reigned over Bengal's homes once, because women had been satisfied with little, and poor relations in trouble had been given shelter in well-off households.'

The passage comes from Chandicharan Bandopadhyay's very sympathetic biography of Vidyasagar, which unlike several others supported women's education and widow remarriage.[42] But Chandicharan, we shall see, clearly did not agree with Vidyasagar's views

[42] Chandicharan Bandopadhyay, *Vidyasagar* (Calcutta, 1895, 1896, 1909, 1969), pp. 17–18.

about the undivided family, and a clue regarding his reasons is provided by repeated references to poor relations. He was a Brahmo from a Jessore-Khulna poor Brahman background, and owed his education and career to a relative who had been better off.

I have argued elsewhere that Ramakrishna, whose conversation was full of allusions to the evils of *kamini*, *kanchan*, and the *dasatya* of *chakri* (lust, money, the bondage of office-work), needs to be placed in the setting of this late-nineteenth-century revival of Kaliyuga themes — but with a difference. We are told that many parents in the early 1880s disliked his influence over boys and young men, for they were afraid he was encouraging them to neglect studies and careers. For the bulk of his listeners, his was a message of *grihastha bhakti*, a move into a self-created inner, devotional space from where one could go on discharging one's domestic duties, but in a detached, non-worldly manner: neither any leech-like clinging to joint-family connections for material survival, therefore, nor activist efforts to transform domestic relations and reduce human suffering through human endeavour. For an intimate circle, he may have advised the path of sanyas or renunciation — which Vivekananda would later drastically modify in an activist direction, reviving Vidyasagar's philanthropy, but not much of his transformative social programme.[43]

Chandicharan Bandopadhyay will be of help again, as we try now to move closer to Vidyasagar, approaching him through cross-sections of his writings and activities concerning Sanskrit College, primary and women's education, gender — but first of all through a glance at representations of him in biography and anecdote. The passage I have quoted is a comment inserted into an account of Vidyasagar's ancestry, largely based, as all such accounts have been, on a posthumous autobiographical fragment. Its context is Vidyasagar's description of the household of Radhamohan Vidyabhushan, maternal uncle of his mother. This had been a joint family run in an ideal manner, without quarrels, and with a great reputation for generous hospitality. Bandopadhyay expressed surprise that despite seeing at first hand such an ideal Hindu household, Vidyasagar was 'bitterly opposed to the undivided family. He used to say: "Where husbands are run by their wives [a brief Kaliyuga motif even here!], where there is no affection between brother and brother, it is futile to try to maintain the joint family. . .".' A quick separation of brothers could reduce

---

[43] For a detailed analysis, see my 'Kaliyuga, Bhakti, and Chakri: Ramakrishna and His Times', in this volume.

conflict. Also, 'If a happy [and, implicitly, nuclear] family becomes prosperous, it is possible to help considerably one's brothers, their sons and daughters, other relations — but within a family torn by quarrels it is impossible to do any good even with a lakh of rupees.'[44]

There was much bitter personal experience behind such a remark, we shall see: but the point can bear a wider generalization. Vidyasagar sought, all his life, to transform his upper-caste surroundings in specific, concrete ways through tremendous, basically individual endeavours. Despite the total absence of inherited wealth or landed property (something quite unusual for such a prominent and materially successful man), he was able to achieve and maintain personal independence through skilful utilization of the three basic determinants of nineteenth-century colonial middle-class life in Bengal: education, chakri, print culture. Vidyasagar learnt English late, from his English contacts and from friends who had studied in Hindu College, but mastered it sufficiently to translate or adapt numerous texts, even Shakespeare's *Comedy of Errors*. He rose high in a still somewhat informal structure of educational administration (Head Pandit of Fort William College, Assistant Secretary and then Principal of Sanskrit College, Assistant Inspector of Schools for Midnapur, Hooghly, Burdwan, and Nadia), but simultaneously was careful to establish financial independence through the Sanskrit Press Depository (1846-7), a printing-press-cum bookshop and publishing concern. That gave him enough private income to sustain an exceptional independence in official employment, and then the ability to quit when he realized by the late 1850s that his advice would no longer be acceptable to a more bureaucratized officialdom eager after 1857 to cut down expenses. His income from textbooks and the bookshop was very high for the times.[45] Nearly all of it he spent, however — at times running deep into debt — on widow remarriage, and philanthropy.

For Vidyasagar's was never an individualism divested of collective concerns, and he refused to abandon his roots in Brahmanical, and specifically poor Brahman, society, even while seeking to change its

44 Chandicharan Bandopadhyay, p. 18.

45 In the year ending 30 June 1870, for instance, the Sanskrit Press Depository published 27 editions, with a total print-run of 253,000 copies. Buckland estimated Vidyasagar's annual income from publishing at around Rs 3500–4000 a month. Swapan Basu, *Samakale Vidyasagar* (Calcutta, 1993), p. 179, citing C.E. Buckland, *Bengal under the Lieutenant-Governors*, Volume II (Calcutta, 1902), p. 1035.

norms in specific ways: he soared, we might say, but refused to roam. Therein, upto a point, perhaps lay his strength, and certainly much of his human greatness — but also, I intend to argue, some of the roots of compromise, failure and tragedy.

II

We look back on past happenings and figures as through a glass, darkly, through representations, never face to face. Discrepancies and fissures within and among representations, however, may help us at times to avoid getting entirely trapped in a hall of mirrors. 'Sources' and their conditions of production, as well as our own perspectives, need to be constantly problematized, made part of the narratives we are trying to build about the past.

Later scholars have tended to take for granted the existence of an unusually large number of near-contemporary biographies of Vidyasagar, and the equally exceptional abundance of anecdotes, and then happily gone ahead to use them as quarries of valuable information. But why four biographies within eleven years of his death, when Rammohan, for instance (who, unlike Vidyasagar, left some kind of movement after him) had to wait nearly fifty years for the first?[46] And why so many anecdotes, unequalled numerically by those about any other nineteenth-century luminary? The puzzle deepens when we recall that the biographies were written in a decade dominated by social reaction and revivalism, not reform. For Vidyasagar's death in 1891 had coincided with a massive upsurge in Bengali middle- and lower-middle-class society against the official proposal to raise the age of consent from ten to twelve.[47]

Several of the biographers themselves present an even greater surprise. No doubt it was natural enough for Sambhuchandra Vidyaratna to write an appreciative life of his distinguished elder brother, even though he had once made Vidyasagar very angry by initially opposing the widow remarriage of the reformer's son, Narayanchandra.[48] And Chandicharan, as we have seen, was a Brahmo who

[46] The first full-length biography of Rammohan, by Nagendranath Chattopadhyay, came out only in 1881.

[47] For a detailed analysis, see Tanika Sarkar, 'Rhetoric against Age of Consent: Resisting Colonial Reason and the Death of a Child-Wife', *Economic and Political Weekly*, XXVIII, 36, 4 September 1993.

[48] This marriage, arranged by Narayanchandra on his own initiative, much to his father's delight and pride, occasioned the famous letter of Vidyasagar to

supported women's education and widow remarriage, though he had reservations about Vidyasagar's dislike of the joint family. But Subol Mitra was unenthusiastic about widow remarriage, and the section about it in his English biography, though detailed and valuable, clearly is tilted on the side of Vidyasagar's critics.[49] The really interesting, indeed, paradoxical, case is Biharilal Sarkar, connected from 1883 till his death in 1921 with the *Bangabasi* newspaper group that spearheaded the virulent anti-reformist crusade against the Age of Consent bill, and who remained consistently conservative on every social issue. The edition I am using contains an autobiographical sketch that begins with an evocation of the principle of adhikari-bheda, and refers to the way he had peddled from door to door Bengali translations of shastric texts brought out in cheap editions by the *Bangabasi* press.[50] We learn from the ensuing biography that one such text had been Panchanan Tarkaratna's edition of *Parasar-Samhita*, which had sought to explicitly refute Vidyasagar's interpretation, upon which the reformer had grounded his scriptural justification for widow remarriage. The failure of widow remarriage, Biharilal states without equivocation, had been a 'great good fortune for Hindu society'. Another blessing was that no law had been passed banning polygamy despite Vidyasagar's efforts, and Biharilal has doubts even about the usually more acceptable issue of women's education. Education for Hindu women, he argues, has produced 'poison'. It should have been geared towards fostering 'Annapurnas. . . . Not writing and reading [*lekhapara*], but learning the duties proper to Hindu wives — that is what education for them should mean.'[51] And yet such a man had felt impelled in 1895 to write a long biography of Vidyasagar, which was in fact the most carefully

---

Sambhuchandra (27 Sravana 1277/1870) rebuking him for the request he had evidently made to hold back, as Sambhuchandra's in-laws were threatening to sever social connections. The letter went on to declare: 'The introduction of widow remarriage is the greatest deed of my life. I have spent my all in this cause, and if need be, remain prepared to give my life for it. . . . I am not a mere slave to custom (*deshachar*) . . . what I think to be justified or necessary for the good of myself or my society, I will do: I will never be held back by fear of other people or relatives . . . It is my conviction that in such matters everyone must be free to decide on his own . . . ', Benoy Ghosh, p. 450.

[49] Subolchandra Mitra, *Life of Pandit Isvarchandra Vidyasagar* (Calcutta, 1902, 1975), Chapter XVI, pp. 260–324.

[50] Biharilal Sarkar, *Vidyasagar* (Calcutta, 1895, 1900, 1910, 1922; ed., Asit Bandopadhyay, 1986), pp. 25, 30, 31.

[51] Ibid., pp. 181, 171, 310, 151.

compiled of all the early accounts, and provided the basic matter for Subol Mitra's English *Life*.

No biography of Vidyasagar can avoid giving considerable space to his reform endeavours. A strategy of displacement is often at work, however, shifting emphasis and, particularly, praise to his *panditya* and *daya* (learning and compassionate philanthropy). Mahendranath Gupta's presentation is thus entirely typical. For Biharilal, to take the most obvious example, Vidyasagar's drive for widow remarriage flowed out of an unacceptable excess of compassion. His book ends with an appeal to 'Hindus' to 'energetically perform their proper, strictly *shastra*-determined duties with Vidyasagar's sincerity and determination.'[52]

In biography and anecdote alike, Vidyasagar's learning and philanthropy invariably gained a special lustre from his poor Brahman origins and conquest of adverse circumstances through sheer personal grit, determination, and self-discipline.[53] Instances of self-respect and independence of spirit while in government service are also lovingly narrated in virtually all writings and tales about him. Anecdotes, which need to be recognized as 'among the principal products of a culture's representational technology',[54] are particularly revealing of the patterns of selectivity and emphasis at work in constituting memories about Vidyasagar. Written accounts and verbal narration of stories, of course, should not be segregated from each other in a case like Vidyasagar's, for the spate of early biographies clearly contributed to the preservation of tales by recording many of them in print. But stories spread very much further, in repeated cycles of orality and reading as they were reproduced in a variety of printed forms (school texts about the great man, for instance) and passed down in conversation. Unlike biographies, anecdotes have a built-in license to be selective, for they are free of the need to appear

---

[52] Biharilal Sarkar, p. 369. Subolchandra Mitra also feels that Vidyasagar 'materially injured the Hindu religion' through an excess of 'kindness and self-reliance', which led him to try to remedy the 'apparent distress of Hindu widows' and the 'ostensible miseries of Kulin women' (p. 673–4).

[53] For Subolchandra Mitra, to take a characteristic example, Vidyasagar provided an object lesson that 'poverty is no bar to the attainment of success.' (p. 85). He also emphasized that Vidyasagar, 'nothing but a common man of the middle station of life', 'in liberality . . . surpassed the richest millionaires' (p. 415). Hatcher has aptly commented that Vidyasagar's life became an exemplar of the moral pedagogy he had tried to inculcate through his textbooks: p. 185.

[54] Stephen Greenblatt, *Marvellous Possessions: The Wonder of the New World* (Oxford, Clarendon Press, 1991), p. 3.

comprehensive. It is significant, therefore, that there seem to be few specific stories about what Vidyasagar himself had declared to be the greatest deed of his life — widow remarriage — at least as compared to the flood of tales illustrating Vidyasagar's compassion, conquest of adverse circumstances, and independence of spirit. The early biographies would be known today only by specialists, the more recent accounts only by a fairly limited number. But the average educated Bengali is quite likely to be familiar with tales of Vidyasagar as a student from a wretchedly poor family, reading under street lamps to save money on fuel, and cooking for his father in a tiny, filthy kitchen full of cockroaches.[55] Equally famous is his declared intention to live by selling potatoes, if need be, while chucking up his first Sanskrit College job. Anecdotes about dignity and independence in relation to white bosses are perhaps the most loved of all: Vidyasagar calmly putting up his feet on the desk to avenge a like insult from the English principal of Hindu College, and allegedly throwing a slipper at the actor playing the part of an indigo planter in a performance of Dinabandhu Mitra's *Nil-Darpan*. The protonationalistic ring in some of these tales is significant, though more perhaps as imagined retrospect than reality: the one about *Nil-Darpan* is probably a later emendation, for it was absent in the biographies of the 1890s.

That dominant representations of Vidyasagar have been selective appropriations is thus fairly obvious, and perhaps only to be expected. What still remains mysterious is why this sanitization had to take the form of volubility and not silence: why conventional and even conservative men found it imperative to write and talk incessantly about a reformer whose efforts had largely failed. The emphasis in biographies and anecdotes upon poor Brahman origins, ascent through self-help, and maintenance of dignity and independence before foreign employers might provide an important clue, for these were precisely the values that the madhyabitta, and particularly its poorer and less successful substratum, were likely to have admired, aspired towards, but generally failed or lacked the courage to sustain in their own lives. And while the compassion of Vidyasagar is known to have extended to Santals and famine-stricken peasant

[55] Asked by Hatcher to paint a portrait of Vidyasagar, a scroll-painter in Midnapur came up with a picture of a youthful Iswarchandra reading under a street lamp. The same story figures in many modern texts for children. Hatcher cites as one example Rabidas Saharay's *Amader Vidyasagar* (Calcutta, 1985). Hatcher, pp. 76–7.

women, it lay in the nature of things that its most regular recipients would be poor bhadralok. These were the people with whom he would have had everyday social contact, who could benefit from the low fees charged by the Metropolitan Institution, and for whom his excellent official contacts could sometimes provide jobs.

The available data about the three early biographers (other than his brother) appear quite relevant here, for all came from this mileu of poor bhadralok. Chandicharan Bandopadhyay (1858–1916) never had the resources to complete his education and depended on the patronage of a manager of the Narail zamindari estate. Biharilal Sarkar (1855–1921), too, did not get beyond the First Arts class, for the business ventures of his father, a former clerk at the Surveyor-General's office, had ended in financial ruin, and Biharilal had had to take up a job at a printing press. Subolchandra Mitra (1872–1913) likewise started as a humble press employee, though he later became the best known of the three through a fine dictionary-cum-encyclopaedia. None of the three could have had personal memories of the 1850s, when Vidyasagar's educational and reform campaigns had been at their height, but they could well have known many who had been recipients of his *daya* in the decades when philanthropy had perforce become his principal activity. 'Who will be able to count', the otherwise often critical Biharilal asked rhetorically, 'the number whose chakri had been arranged by Vidyasagar?' And Chandicharan lavished particular praise on the Hindu Family Annuity Fund Vidyasagar had initiated in 1872 to provide, on an insurance principle, an allowance of five rupees a month for widows and dependants of 'Bengal's *madhyabitta daridra bhadra paribar* [poor, respectable middle class families].'[56]

In a more speculative vein: the temporal location of all the early biographies of Vidyasagar in the decade immediately following the Age of Consent agitation may not have been entirely coincidental. Triumphant revivalism was clearly not averse to an appropriation of a suitably sanitized Vidyasagar, in the hegemonizing spirit of wasting no icon. (The ascendant Hindutva of recent years has similarly made many efforts to absorb even Ambedkar.) But maybe there was also a more complex and ambiguous connection. Hindu-revivalist nationalism had with apparent success inverted Vidyasagar's premises for reform in the most extreme conceivable manner. No compassion was wasted on Phulmonee, a child of ten or eleven raped

---

[56] Biharilal Sarkar, p. 216; Chandicharan Bandopadhyay, p. 503.

to death by her husband in 1890. Rather, as the agitation attained its height in the early months of 1891, newspapers like *Bangabasi* and *Dainik-o-Samachar-Chandrika* defiantly admitted that Hindu shastras did impose a harsh discipline on women (in particular, child-wives and widows), did cause much suffering, even at times death: yet such suffering was necessary for the honour and glory of the Hindu community/nation, and alien interference could never be tolerated.[57] But such arguments, it should be noted, implicitly accepted what had been the starting point of Vidyasagar's reform drive: that some Hindu texts and customs imposed gross suffering on women.[58] The intense, taut, almost hysterical rhetoric could have sometimes concealed an inner tension, a half-formed self-doubt, maybe even an occasional pang of guilt that needed to be suppressed through excessive vehemence. By the mid 1890s the movement had subsided, and Vidyasagar himself was safely dead.[59] Incessant talk and writing about a suitably sanitized Vidyasagar could have provided a certain necessary release of tension, precisely in circles that had been, and remained, fundamentally conservative.

The sanitizing process did have one outstanding contemporary critic, however — Rabindranath Tagore. In a speech at the annual Vidyasagar Memorial meeting in July 1895, Tagore declared that Vidyasagar's true greatness lay 'not in compassion [*daya*], not in learning [*vidya*]', but in a determined, uncompromising humanism which had made him look at the life of women in a fundamentally distinctive way. Furthermore, 'Vidyasagar had been alone in Bengal. It is as if he had no kith or kin in this land. . . . He was not happy here. . . . He had a deep contempt for this weak, petty, heartless, lazy, arrogant, argumentative people, for in every way he was their opposite . . . '[60] Strange words, in a way, spoken amidst apparently

---

[57] Tanika Sarkar, 'Rhetoric against the Age of Consent'. Of particular relevance for my argument is the quotation given in this essay from *Dainik-o-Samachar-Chandrika*, 11 January 1891: 'Fasting [by widows] on ekadashi is a cruel custom and many weak-bodied widows very nearly die of observing it . . . '.

[58] Such an admission was present also in the criticisms of widow remarriage made by Biharilal and Subolchandra: Vidyasagar had been motivated by an excess of compassion that subverted a necessary, though admittedly painful, discipline.

[59] He had also 'redeemed' himself slightly in the eyes of conservatives just before his death, by giving a somewhat ambiguous opinion about the Age of Consent bill when officially asked for his views. See footnote 149 and corresponding text, below.

[60] Rabindranath Tagore, *Vidyasagarcharit*, 13 Sravana 1302/1895; reprinted,

universal praise for the departed reformer which had been joined in with enthusiasm even by conservatives. But they fit rather well with certain anomalies that occasionally burst through the placid surfaces of conventional narratives about Vidyasagar, and find further confirmation in the pattern of stresses and silences that characterize the autobiographical fragment published after his death.

The biographies repeatedly present Vidyasagar as an ever-dutiful and considerate son, elder brother, and father who maintained from Calcutta a big joint family in Birsingha. Vidyasagar's devotion to his mother in particular has become legendary. Yet despite the mass of personal detail, whether authentic or apocryphal, some things remain mysterious, and there are sudden explosions, never fully-explained ruptures, in the accounts of his family relationships. Around 1867, to end 'intermittent quarrels among the members of the large family', Vidyasagar arranged 'separate boarding' for his brothers and only son, giving each of them a monthly allowance.[61] One brother brought a case against him a couple of years later about the ownership of the Sanskrit Press Depository.[62] And then there was that series of mysterious letters, all dated 12 Agrahayan 1276/1869, through which Vidyasagar bade 'lifelong farewell' to mother, wife, brothers, and Birsingha village (through the village pradhan). The letters at the same time stipulated in minute detail monthly allowances for each relative and money for the philanthropic institutions he had started in his village. He never visited Birsingha again.[63] And finally came the disinheritance of his son Narayanchandra, around 1872. Once again, the biographies reveal nothing of the reasons for this.

Charitrapuja (1907); *Rabindra-rachanabali*, Volume IV (Calcutta, Viswabharati, 1940, 1975), pp. 502, and *passim*.

[61] Subolchandra Mitra, pp. 482–3.

[62] Chandicharan Bandopadhyay, p. 405; Subolchandra Mitra, p. 500. Mitra states that Vidyasagar had arranged a deputy-magistrateship for this brother, Dinabandhu, earlier, by speaking about him after much hesitation with the Lieutenant-Governor: indication, simultaneously, of the still rather informal official appointments system, and the burden of ingratitude that seems to have been often Vidyasagar's lot.

[63] The ostensible reason for the break was a rather strange incident, in which Vidyasagar, for once, had promised not to encourage a particular widow remarriage, but his brother Sambhuchandra had gone ahead and arranged it. It can hardly explain such a dramatic rupture, affecting also his wife and mother who could not have anything to do with the affair. Chandicharan Bandopadhyay, pp. 414–17. For the full text of these letters, see Benoy Ghosh, pp. 454–7. The most complete account of the whole murky affair is in Asok Sen, pp. 161–2.

The autobiographical fragment is at first sight disappointing, for it is mostly about Vidyasagar's ancestry and ends with him at age nine, just joining Sanskrit College. It has been used in virtually all accounts of Vidyasagar, but so far as no more than a repository of information about his genealogy. Brian Hatcher is a partial exception, since he goes some distance towards treating it as a constructed text through which Vidyasagar tried to communicate 'his own self-understanding'.[64] But his analysis stops with the suggestion that the choice of stresses in the fragment indicates Vidyasagar's continued reverence for the Brahman as man of learning, while also conveying a sense of crisis affecting rural Brahmans due to disorderly times and economic distress.[65] What I find much more revealing is an implicit, recurrent note critical of the high-caste joint family. Radhamohan Vidyabhushan of Patul village, along with his entire extended family, had given succour to his sister, Vidyasagar's maternal grandmother Ganga, after her husband had gone mad through Tantric excesses. For Chandicharan, this was convincing proof of the enduring value of the joint family. Vidyasagar did describe the Patul household in loving detail, but immediately added that such an ideal family was utterly atypical: 'Affection among brothers usually does not last long in an undivided family.'[66] The ancestor about whom Vidyasagar left by far the longest account, and whom he clearly admired most, was not a pandit running a tol, but his exceptionally independent-minded grandfather Ramjoy Tarkabhushan, who had broken with his joint family after quarrelling with elder brothers, left the original homestead of Banamalipur, and become a wanderer for many years. He retained a tremendous sense of dignity and self-respect even in his old age, rejected an offer of land from the local zamindar, and was openly contemptuous of the prominent men in Birsingha village.[67]

The second, recurrent stress in the fragment is about how,

64 Hatcher, p. 23, and Chapter I.

65 The fragment emphasizes the expertise of several ancestors in Sanskrit grammar, Smriti, and Nyaya, and mentions Thakurdas' lifelong regret that poverty had forced him to give up plans for a pandit's life and take up the job of bill-collector for a Barabazar shop selling imported ironware. Hatcher, Chapter I; *Vidyasagar-Charit (Swarachita)*, in Tirthapati Datta, ed., *Vidyasagar Rachanabali*, Volume I (Calcutta, 1994), pp. 400, 414.

66 *Vidyasagar-Charit*, pp. 405–6.

67 Vidyasagar recounts, with evident approval and delight, that Ramjoy called the village big-wigs cows, not men. Warned once about some human excreta on the path, he had replied: 'I can see only cowdung.' Ibid., p. 408.

repeatedly, it is the women who have to bear the burden of family quarrels among men. What is more, Vidyasagar seems to be indicating, they often bear this undeserved suffering with a fortitude, dignity and loving kindness rare among men. There is, in other words, not just compassion for women but respect, admiration, and a strong sense of male guilt — and the respect, it can be argued, was related to individual qualities and actions, not primarily to status as elders or even to motherhood as such.

Admiration for Ramjoy does not blind Vidyasagar to a realization that much of the price of his independence had to be borne by grandmother Durgadevi. She had had to bring up six sons and daughters by spinning yarn and selling it at Khirpai. Ill-treatment by in-laws had forced her out of Banamalipur: she returned to her home village of Birsingha, but there too faced much unkindness from her brother's family. (This, then, was the counter-example to Patul, and for Vidyasagar evidently far more characteristic of the extended family at work.) And then there is the story of an unnamed middle-aged widow running a roadside foodshop, who fed Thakurdas gratis regularly at a time when he was virtually starving on the streets of Calcutta — a generosity, Vidyasagar emphasizes, 'that would have been unthinkable if the shopkeeper had been a man.' The other woman who figures prominently in Vidyasagar's narrative is Raimoni, another widow, sister of Jagatdurlabh Sinha, in whose house he initially put up in Calcutta. Her kindness and deep affection had given him solace when, as a boy who had left home for the first time, he was missing his grandmother. 'I have never seen a woman to equal Raimoni', he declares, and mentions her as justification for what many have called his 'partiality' towards women.[68] Surprisingly, if we recall the biographies and the many anecdotes, the autobiography says virtually nothing about Vidyasagar's mother. We should not build too much on an absence in what is an unfinished fragment, but here perhaps is another hint that the Vidyasagar of the biographies and anecdotes has been excessively sentimentalized.

The concluding chapters of Vidyasagar's biographies tend to become long catalogues of his philanthropic deeds. Interrupting this flow, however, particularly in Chandicharan, are occasional references to Vidyasagar's caustic remarks about his own social group, the high-caste bhadralok men: remarks so sharp that they make this

---

[68] Ibid., pp. 401, 411. Both Biharilal and Subolchandra dilate on Raimoni's kindness, but avoid mentioning that she was a widow.

'ocean of compassion' seem almost a misanthrope. 'Why does he
abuse me — I don't remember having ever tried to help him in any
way?' Chandicharan reports Vidyasagar saying, in his last days, that
the country could improve only if the present breed of men were
totally uprooted, and human beings of a new kind planted on
freshly-tilled soil. 'I much prefer my uncivilised Santals to your sort
of respectably-dressed men of Aryan descent.'[69]

Biting, cynical, sarcasm, amidst a continued stream of philanthropic acts: the contradictions here are at the heart of Vidyasagar's
lifelong endeavours and tragedy, as a man who valued his links with
high-Hindu society, and yet had developed a very different set of
values and sought to reform his milieu in specific but quite fundamental ways. The remaining sections of this essay will explore the
unfolding of this dialectic of affinity and difference, first through
Vidyasagar's educational initiatives, and then in terms of attempted
reform of gender relations.

III

Vidyasagar never wrote a systematic treatise on education. The precise
significance of his extremely innovative ideas and projects have to
be reconstructed from scattered texts — official letters and notes,[70]
school primers and textbooks written by him, and documents relating
to Vidyasagar in the files of the government education department
and archives of Sanskrit College.[71]

The changes Vidyasagar sought to make in Sanskrit College, as
Assistant Secretary (1846–7) and later as Principal (1850–8), were not
just about reforms in a particular institution, for they can be seen
to imply ultimately a distinctive educational-cum-social philosophy.
Even the innovations that might appear trivial today, such as
Vidyasagar's insistence on punctuality and regular attendance by
students and teachers,[72] acquire greater meaning when one remembers

[69] Chandicharan Bandopadhyay, pp. 518–20.

[70] The most important of these are Vidyasagar's proposals for reorganizing
Sanskrit College (16 December 1850), his Notes on the Sanskrit College, drawn
up at the request of Lieutenant-Governor Halliday (12 April 1852), and the
controversy with J.R. Ballantyne, Principal, Benaras Sanskrit College, in 1853.

[71] These have been usefully collated and published in Arabinda Guha, ed.,
Unpublished Letters of Vidyasagar.

[72] Vidyasagar introduced a pass system for students wanting to go out during
college hours, and tried to shame latecomers among teachers by standing at
the gate every morning at 10:30. Chandicharan Bandopadhyay, pp. 92, 104–5.

that clock time was no more than a generation or two old in India in the 1840s, having been a belated, colonial import. Its history has been surprisingly neglected in studies of colonial India. Bound up, as elsewhere, with new pressures for regularity and tighter work schedules, clocks and watches acquired somewhat distinct and varied implications through their links with structures of colonial power. The three principal early sites for time-discipline in colonial Bengal were educational institutions, government and mercantile offices, and the railways.[73] Indigenous responses to it clearly had a differential character. Vidyasagar is a reminder that systematized, rule-bound education governed by clock time was widely perceived as indispensable for middle-class self-improvement under colonial conditions. Punctuality no doubt often remained a burden, but its normative role in schools and colleges was not questioned. Things were quite different in the alienated world of chakri or office work under foreign bosses, where disciplinary time entered into a distinctively late-nineteenth-century vision of Kaliyuga.[74]

Vidyasagar's plan of 16 December 1850 suggested a series of changes in the syllabus of Sanskrit College, all in a recognizably modern, rationalistic direction. It simultaneously sought to bring Sanskrit teaching into close contact with the development of both Bengali and English education. Thus, for Sanskrit grammar, which students so long had been forced to memorize through the very difficult *Mugdhabodha*, Vidyasagar suggested the learning of the basic rules 'dressed in the easiest Bengali', followed by graduated Sanskrit readings. (He would himself soon supply the appropriate Sanskrit grammar in Bengali, the *Vyakarana-Kaumudi*.) Training in English, too, was necessary, but only in the higher classes, to avoid the danger of getting swamped by it at the expense of the vernacular. Sanskrit College students, the plan emphasized, must 'acquire great proficiency in Bengali' and 'derive useful information' through it (for which he was already providing the wherewithal, through textbooks like *Jibancharit* and *Bodhodaya*), 'and thereby have their views expanded before they commence their English studies'. They could also learn Jyotish (mathematics and astronomy) much more profitably through Bengali translations of contemporary English texts,

---

[73] Modern factories start getting important only in the later decades of the nineteenth century, and much of the workforce even then consisted of immigrants. Relatively few Bengali-speaking people were recruited into that other site of time-discipline — the modern colonial army.

[74] For a fuller discussion, see Chapters 6 and 8.

instead of Lilavati and Bhaskaracharya, which Vidyasagar thought 'very meagre' by modern standards. Even more striking is the evident attempt to reduce the importance in the syllabus of the Smriti teachings of Raghunandan (whose texts constituted the principal barrier to reforms like widow remarriage or a higher age of consent throughout the nineteenth century) and the Navya-Nyaya of Raghu-nath Shiromani (whose logic Vidyasagar thought had been 'similar to that of schoolmen'). Along with Navya-Nyaya, the philosophical portions of the pre-Vidyasagar syllabus had a strong tilt towards Vedanta, characteristic of high-Hindu metaphysics since medieval times. It included texts specifically refuting 'the Bouddha or atheis-tical doctrine' and all other non-Vedantist schools. In their place, Vidyasagar wanted to introduce the *Sarvadarshanasangraha*, through which, he argued, the student would be able to see how 'the different systems have attacked each other, and have pointed out each other's errors and fallacies. Thus he would be able to judge for himself' — particularly since some courses in European philosophy would also be introduced.[75] In 1858 Vidyasagar brought out a critical edition of this fourteenth-century text of Madhavacharya, which he said had become a very rare manuscript.[76] It may not be irrelevant to note that the *Sarvadarshanasangraha* remains the primary source for the little information we have about the suppressed ancient Indian materialist tradition of Lokayata, associated with Carvaka.[77]

That the implications of Vidyasagar's reform plan went very much beyond mere syllabus revision becomes clear from his *Notes on the Sanskrit College* (12 April 1852), which summed up with admirable precision and logic the core of his educational perspectives. 'The creation of an enlightened Bengali Literature', Vidyasagar now de-clared, 'should be the first object of those who are entrusted with the superintendence of Education in Bengal.' This required the 'exertions of those . . . competent to collect the materials from European sources and . . . dress them in elegant, expressive and

---

[75] The full text of Vidyasagar's plan for the reorganization of Sanskrit College, submitted to F.J. Mouat, Secretary, Council of Education, on 16 December 1850, is included in Debkumar Basu, ed., *Vidyasagar Rachanabali*, Volume I (Calcutta, 1974), pp. 376–92. The quotations in this paragraph are taken from this report.

[76] Ibid., pp. 364–5.

[77] S.N. Dasgupta, *A History of Indian Philosophy*, Volume I (Cambridge, 1922); Debiprasad Chattopadhyay, *Lokayata: A Study in Ancient Indian Materialism* (New Delhi, People's Publishing House, 1959, 1978), Chapter I.

idiomatic Bengali.' But for this, Vidyasagar felt, mastery of Sanskrit was also essential, as 'mere English scholars are altogether incapable of expressing their ideas in elegant and idiomatic Bengali. They are so much anglicized that it seems at present almost impossible for them to do so even if they later learn Sanskrit.' It is very clear then that 'if students of the Sanskrit College be made familiar with English Literature, they will prove the best and ablest contributors to an enlightened Bengali Literature.'[78]

In September 1853 Vidyasagar had to defend his syllabus against criticisms made of it by J.R. Ballantyne, Principal of Benares Government Sanskrit College. In course of that exercise he had to formulate its underlying assumptions with greater clarity and polemical sharpness. Ballantyne had suggested a greater emphasis on the 'correspondences' between select aspects of European and Indian philosophical traditions as a way of reconciling the Brahmanical literati to the coming of Western ideas. This involved a very different pattern of choice between philosophical schools, than Vidyasagar's. The Benares principal wanted less of Mill's *Logic*, the inclusion of Bishop Berkeley's *Inquiry*, and the introduction of a commentary written by Ballantyne himself which had emphasized the alleged similarities between that classic text of European philosophical Idealism, and Vedanta and Sankhya. This was the specific context for Vidyasagar's blunt and aggressive statement about Vedanta and Sankhya being 'false systems of philosophy': a remark that has been often torn out of context to indicate either Vidyasagar's laudable Westernized modernity, or (with some justice) his philosophical naivete and dogmatism. But Vidyasagar's position, it must be emphasized, was not an uncritical preference of Western to Indian thought, for Vidyasagar was equally dismissive of Berkeley. The really interesting thing about the reply to Ballantyne is the way it anticipated, and sought to refute, what by the late nineteenth century would become a central strategy of much Hindu revivalism, as well as of a brand of Orientalism from which it was often highly derivative.[79] 'Lately a feeling is

78 The text of the *Notes* has been reprinted in many places: I am using Indramitra, *Karunasagar Vidyasagar* (Calcutta, 1969, 1992), pp. 652-4.

79 Ballantyne as Principal of Benares Sanskrit College, interestingly, contributed quite directly to the later development of Hindu revivalism by insisting on the need to evolve a Sanskritized Hindi, distinct from Urdu. As early as 1847, he was advising his pupils that they should try to make the Hindi used by the pandits of the 'holy city' of Benares 'the standard of all India'. 'It was the duty of himself and his brother Pundits not to leave the task of formulating

manifesting itself among the learned of this part of India, specially
in Calcutta and its neighbourhood, that when they hear of a
Scientific truth, the germs of which may be traced out in their
Shastras, instead of shewing any regard for that truth, they triumph
and the superstitious regard for their own Shastras is redoubled.'
Vidyasagar went on to make a most uncomplimentary characterization of the 'learned of India' as a 'body of men whose longstanding
prejudices are unshakeable' — referring presumably to the traditional
Brahman literati, not the Sanskrit College students he was trying to
train in a new way. He went on to reiterate and expand the alternative
cultural perspective he had outlined in April 1852. Instead of trying
'to reconcile the learned of the Country',

what we require is to extend the benefit of education to the mass of
the people. Let us establish a number of Vernacular schools, let us
prepare a series of Vernacular class-books on useful and instructive
subjects, let us raise up a band of men [who] should be perfect masters
of their own language, possess a considerable amount of useful information and be free from the prejudices of their country. To raise up
such a useful class of men is the object I have proposed to myself and
to the accomplishment of which the whole energy of *our* Sanskrit College
should be directed.[80]

Beginning, then, in 1844 with the suggestion for tackling the
employment problem facing Sanskrit College graduates through
giving them jobs in Hardinge's experimental village schools, Vidyasagar in course of a decade had progressed to an integrated plan
for cultural renovation of the literati of Bengal. Considered in the
perspective of conventional histories of education, Vidyasagar's
scheme may be seen as a bringing together of Orientalist, Anglicist,
and Vernacularist positions, achieved through significant changes
within each of them. Translated more meaningfully into social

---

the national language in the hands of the villagers, but to endeavour to get rid
the unprofitable diversity of provincial dialects —.' This was in reply to a rather
puzzled interjection of a student of his that it was difficult to understand 'what
you Europeans mean by the term Hindi, for there are hundreds of dialects
. . . and what you call the Hindi will eventually merge in some future modification of the Oordoo, nor do we see any great cause of regret in this prospect.'
Christopher R. King, 'Forging a New Linguistic Identity: The Hindi Movement
in Banaras, 1868-1914', in Sandria B. Freitag, *Culture and Power in Banaras*,
(Delhi, Oxford University Press, 1990), pp. 184-5.

[80] Vidyasagar to F.I. Mouat, replying to Ballantyne's obsevations; 7 September
1853. Text in Benoy Ghosh, pp. 525-30.

terms, it needs to be understood as an attempt to bridge the growing gap between the traditional pandits and the Westernized, English-educated intelligentsia: not through some kind of eclectic compromise, however, which roughly had been Ballantyne's advice, but by a determined effort to transform and get beyond both poles. Vidyasagar hoped to impart a fundamentally new vernacular-cum-rural turn to pandits and English-educated alike, and considerably broaden the social basis of the intelligentsia as a whole. That such a trend could unfold in mid-nineteenth-century Bengal, it needs to be added, should considerably complicate the Westernist/traditionalist dichotomy in terms of which so much colonial middle-class history has been conceptualized.

Vidyasagar had had ample opportunities of watching this rupture grow at first hand, for classes in Sanskrit College in his time took place in the same building as Hindu College, with the two institutions, however, carefully segregated from each other by walls. His class-friends would all be Brahmans (plus a few Vaidyas), mostly poor. Hindu College was catering to a more multi-caste clientele, including many sons of the relatively low-born Calcutta nouveaux riches, but it was at the same time considerably more exclusive in economic terms. Vidyasagar himself had managed to straddle both worlds, through mastering English and developing personal ties with a host of Hindu College products (including many of the Young Bengal variety), but he would have realized how insuperable the barriers might soon appear to many. And indeed the long-term consequences of the failure of Vidyasagar's dream have been very far-reaching. The logical implication of his educational strategy was a reunification of the literati on a basis oriented towards modernistic change, which would be at the same time geared towards mass vernacular education, and therefore at least potentially more democratic than pre-colonial Brahmanical culture. Instead, as the rift widened, the world of the old-fashioned pandits became increasingly narrow, immersed in futile grumbling about the many evils of Kaliyuga, often blindly conservative — while the 'Anglicized' have often swung between complete alienation and recurrent searches for 'roots' in (largely invented or spurious) 'traditions'. In total contrast to Vidyasagar's vision, the occasional unificatory moments have tended to develop around revivalist-nationalistic programmes — right down to our own times, one is tempted to add, in Hindutva's twin base among Vishwa Hindu Parishad sadhus and a Non-Resident Indian oriented elite that is highly Westernized in a consumerist sense.

Two things were indispensable if Vidyasagar's plans were to succeed. There was the need for an 'enlightened Bengali Literature', in particular a vernacular discursive prose capable of tackling in a creative and attractive manner a much wider range of themes than had been possible or necessary in pre-colonial times. The other, interrelated, prerequisite was the rapid spread of vernacular education. The two together could help to constitute a public space open to argumentation, and based on expanding literacy and print culture.

The first condition was largely met, for this was an autonomous area where the intelligentsia could operate on its own, and where the coming of print culture enabled wide dissemination and created some possibilities for financial independence. Western education on the whole was a stimulus rather than hindrance to the development of indigenous languages, in significant contrast to what happened in some other parts of the colonized world. Vidyasagar's own seminal and multiple contributions to the development of modern Bengali prose have of course been very widely recognized. They ranged from mundane but necessary things like the introduction of standardized punctuation[81] and syntax, the careful compilation of glossaries of new terms for modern concepts,[82] to the creation of a style that was chaste, dignified, yet free from the inaccessible and excessively Sanskritized ornateness of the Bengali which many pandits still liked to use.[83] Rabindranath even felt this to have been Vidyasagar's greatest single achievement, and described it as an emancipation of the language simultaneously from 'rustic

[81] Vidyasagar's introduction of commas and semi-colons made Bengali prose both more rigorous and more accessible, as a comparison, say, with Rammohan immediately reveals. On the importance of punctuation, see the perceptive comments of Carolyn Steedman, who reminds us that even for written English, rules for punctuation were still 'in the process of being established' in the second half of the nineteenth century. *The Radical Soldier's Tale* (London, Routledge, 1988), p. 73, and *passim*.

[82] Vidyasagar's *Jivancharit* (1849) included a list of the Bengali terms he was coining for words like 'colonial', 'prejudice', 'museum', 'natural law', 'theatre', 'revolution', and 'university'. Debkumar Basu, Volume I (Calcutta, 1966, 1969, 1974), p. 234-6.

[83] Many among the old-fashioned literati disliked Vidyasagar's Bengali. Chandicharan Bandopadhyay, p. 178, relates a story of Sanskrit scholars at a shastric debate in the palace of the zamindar of Krishnanagar ridiculing a pandit who had given a vyavastha (opinion on a point of religious law) in Bengali that seemed too close to Vidyasagar's: 'What have you done? This can be too easily understood!'

barbarism' and 'parochial scholasticism'.[84] And for a man capable of the considerable literary qualities of a text like *Sitar Banobas*, it must have been a major sacrifice to devote one's writing talents almost entirely to composing, as part of a deeply felt social commitment, school textbooks, adaptations, and reform tracts.[85]

The expansion-cum-improvement of vernacular schools in villages required, however, considerable financial inputs from the state and/or the rural gentry, as well as active support from the literati, old and new. For a brief period in the mid 1850s the conjuncture appeared favourable for Vidyasagar's dream. Colonial educational policy was not quite the monolith, determined solely by Macaulay's notorious Minute of 1835, that is sometimes assumed nowadays. Bengal officials in the early 1850s had been impressed by the apparent success of the 'circle' experiment started in the North-Western Provinces under Thomason that had tried to set up a model school in each revenue district as a way of improving vernacular education. Wood's Education Despatch of 1854, though in the end contained within the 'filtration' framework, had also visualized some expansion in vernacular education through the grants-in-aid system by which costs would be shared between the government and local patrons.

Around 1855–6 — the peak years also of his social reform drive — Vidyasagar was enjoying excellent relations with many high British officials in Bengal, from Lieutanant-Governor Halliday downwards. This had helped him to develop links with a number of prominent zamindars, in particular some 'improving' landlords like Joykrishna Mukhopadhyay of Uttarpara, who had recently acquired large estates in Hooghly district, and who around 1855 was combining efforts to promote new crops like potatoes and sugarcane with the establishment of both English and vernacular schools in the areas under his control.[86] Vidyasagar, finally, had become a major figure by the mid 1850s among the literati, both traditional and new: active in the Brahmo-led Tattwabodhini Sabha and Patrika, friend of many

[84] Rabindranath Tagore, *Vidyasagar-carit*, p. 478.

[85] Bankimchandra's remark in 1871 that 'beyond translating or primer-making Vidyasagar has done nothing' therefore appears peculiarly uncharitable. *Calcutta Review*, April 1871, quoted in Swapan Basu, *Samakale Vidyasagar* (Calcutta, 1993), p. 157.

[86] In June 1855, for instance, Joykrishna and his brother proposed the starting of fourteen village vernacular schools, and were able to obtain from the Lieutenant-Governor a grant-in-aid of Rs 189 a month for each. Nilmoni Mukherjee, *A Bengal Zamindar*, pp. 102, 160.

with Young Bengal antecedents, and yet numbering among his closest associates pandits like Madanmohan Tarkalankar, who helped him start the Sanskrit Press Depository, and Taranath Tarkavacaspati, who combined running a tol at Ambica-Kalna with far-flung business interests. The peak of Vidyasagar's educational and reform campaign seems to have coincided in fact with a last flurry of enterprising landlordism and middle-class entrepreneurship in Bengal.[87] Vidyasagar's, in other words, was not quite a lone venture in the Bengal society of the 1850s. A British Inspector of Schools would note in April 1859 that 'the learned Pundits of Sanskrit College have, as a body, been seized with a love of publishing books.' They had become interested 'in European Science and Literature' and 'were writing in a language that ordinary people may read.' Through their efforts, and particularly 'under the able superintendence of Ishur Chunder Vidyasagar', the Bengali language was becoming 'capable of being the elegant vehicle of scientific and other information.'[88]

In May 1855, Halliday appointed Vidyasagar Assistant Inspector of Schools for the four districts of Hooghly, Burdwan, Midnapur and Nadia, conjointly with his principalship of Sanskrit College, with a combined salary of Rs 500 a month. By the end of that year he had already established some twenty model schools, applying to Bengal Thomason's circle system, and also started a normal school to train village headmasters at Sanskrit College under the superintendence of his close friend, the rationalist Akshoykumar Dutta. In a parallel move Vidyasagar, who had already displayed his commitment to women's education by enthusiastically backing Bethune's school for daughters of respectable families in Calcutta in 1849, utilized his new official position to start forty girls' schools in villages between November 1857 and June 1858.

Precision is needed about what exactly was new in these two initiatives of Vidyasagar, for it is possible both to exaggerate or unduly downplay their significance. The surveys made in 1835–8 by

[87] Thus the prominent Derozian Ramgopal Ghosh had prospered through rice trade with Burma, while Taranath Tarkavacaspati around 1850 was supplying imported yarn to 1200 weavers in Ambica-Kalna and Radhanagar, and exporting cloth to many places in north India. He was connected also with trade in timber and ghee. Such literati connections with successful business enterprise would become very rare after the 1850s. Benoy Ghosh, pp. 161–2.

[88] H. Woodrow, Inspector of Schools, East Bengal, in General Report of Public Instruction, 1858–9, Appendix A, p. 30, cited in Arabinda Guha, ed., *Unpublished Letters of Vidyasagar*, p. 19.

William Adam, Rammohan's Unitarian friend, had found a fairly widespread system of indigenous vernacular education in the villages, with some 100,000 *pathshalas* for the 'indigent classes' in Bengal and Bihar, mostly under non-Brahman (often Kayastha) *gurumohasayas*. Adam discovered 'the desire to give education to their male children' to be 'deeply seated in the minds of parents even of the humblest classes', and thought that the pathshalas, of course quite radically modified and improved, could be 'the institutions — through which primarily, although not exclusively, we may hope to improve the morals and the intellect of the Native population.'[89] Vidyasagar's plan of normal and model schools can be seen, therefore, as in a way a belated effort to implement Adam's suggestions.

The impressive number and apparent absence of direct Brahman control has led to an occasional romanticization of these pre-colonial schools, which in some ways fitted in better with rural conditions than the new system which colonial rule, actively helped by reformers like Vidyasagar, eventually established.[90] Poromesh Acharya has recently provided an important corrective here, emphasizing both the extremely limited nature .of the education supplied by these schools even at their best, as well as the split-up and hierarchized nature of the entire indigenous educational system which allowed little scope for social mobility. Pathshala education, of course entirely in Bengali, was basically confined to writing, arithmetic, and a bit of revenue and commercial accounting. (Reading was less important, since there were no printed textbooks and a necessarily very limited number of manuscripts — which put a premium on memorizing.[91]) The pathshalas, in

[89] William Adam, *First Report on the State of Education in Bengal, 1835*, ed. Anathnath Basu (Calcutta, Calcutta University, 1941), p. 7.

[90] Thus the pathshalas used to have classes from early morning to ten, and again from three to sundown, and were often closed during the harvesting season: certainly arrangements far better suited to rural conditions and a hot climate than the 'modern' system. The changeover to a ten-to-four schedule was in the 1860s, after Vidyasagar had resigned his official positions, but it came about through the influence of the Normal School for gurus which he had started. Kazi Shahidullah, 'The Purpose and Impact of Government Policy on Pathshala Gurumohashoys in Nineteenth-Century Bengal', in Nigel Crook, ed., *The Transmission of Knowledge in South Asia*, (Delhi, Oxford University Press, 1995), pp. 120, 122, 125.

[91] One might recall in this context the terms which Vidyasagar's village teacher is said to have used when advising Thakurdas that his son should be taken to Calcutta and taught English: 'His handwriting is very beautiful.' Chandicharan Bandopadhyay, p. 23.

other words, were geared to the everyday needs of would-be petty za-mindari officials, traders, and better-off peasants: a source of strength, but also a limit. Adam's Reports were actually quite critical of the very limited content of indigenous elementary education.[92] The village school structure had little or nothing to do with the tols, chatuspathis, and madrasas — centres of Sanskrit and Arabic or Persian learning which were the preserve of Brahman males and other learned groups. The educational apparatus consisted of 'separate classes of institutions without any link or relation of any kind, each catering to a distinct class or community.'[93] The relative absence of high castes from village schools was thus a mark of inferiorization and hierarchy (a crucial instance of adhikari-bheda, in fact, the principle which Ramakrishna had extolled and Vidyasagar questioned in their only conversation), not autonomy. The *Chanakya-slokas*, for instance, which pupils were often made to memorize in the pathshalas, combined maxims of worldly wisdom with frequent reaffirmations of Brahmanical suprem-acy: the Brahman was the guru of all other castes, it declared, just as the husband was guru to his wife.[94]

The changes Vidyasagar and other mid-nineteenth-century colonial officials sought to introduce in the pathshala involved expansion of its curriculum to include history, geography, ethics, and natural philosophy (i.e. elementary science), much greater use of textbooks, promotion through examinations, and in general an integration within the theoretically 'complete and continuous' system that was being worked out for colonial education.[95] Hierarchies did not end, of course, particularly those based on economic or class differentials, and may even have been sharpened at times, both through the dichotomy in medium of instruction (English at higher levels) and by some of the changes brought about in the pathshalas.[96] At the

[92] 'there is no text or schoolbook used containing any moral truths or liberal knowledge. . . . ' Adam, p. 9.

[93] Poromesh Acharya, 'Indigenous Education and Brahmannical Hegemony in Bengal', in Crook, p. 98.

[94] Poromesh Acharya, pp. 105–11.

[95] Hatcher, p. 106; Poromesh Acharya, p. 98.

[96] In 1863, a British official noticed a 'marked difference' in the appearance of pupils of 'improved', as compared to unreformed pathshalas. In the latter, cultivators' children were prominent, those of 'the better class of villagers' relatively rare. Normal school pupils in contrast were largely 'the Brahmin and writer-caste boys.' Report of Inspector Medlicott, Government of Bengal Educa-tional Proceedings, No. 51, January 1863, cited in Kazi Shahidullah, p. 125. School fees in the new system were rigorously collected, and payable in cash only;

same time, there was a new theoretical equality of opportunity independent of caste status, a chance for talented boys of families with some but not much resources to climb up an uniform educational ladder through personal grit, determination, and self-discipline.

There was much more gradual and limited, but still strikingly new, opening for some girls, too, against formidable opposition. The widespread belief was that educated wives became widows, and while daughters in high-caste families could be occasionally taught a little within their parents' homes, the idea of sending them out to school was deeply shocking, and a very early marriage anyway obligatory. Conditions were no different in the villages: Adam's First Report made the categorical statement that 'there are no indigenous girls' schools.'[97] It is true that Radhakanta Deb, the great champion of sati against Rammohan and Bentinck and of ascetic widowhood against Vidyasagar, had been at the same time a promoter, of a kind, of the education of girls and is even said to have published a tract about it. This had specified, however, that only girls of poor parents could be sent out to school, while respectable families should have their daughters taught within the home — in both cases only till they were married off. A number of girls' schools were set up in Calcutta in the early 1820s, mostly at missionary initiative, but they were, significantly, located in the poorer parts of the city. The initiative then seems to have died out for a generation, and we may speculate whether the conservative consolidation against the ban on sati and Derozian iconoclasm may not have had something to do with this hiatus. What was striking about Bethune's endeavour in 1849 was that daughters of respectable families were now being encouraged to go out to a school, being transported there in a carriage that displayed a Sanskrit quotation said to have been hunted up by Vidyasagar.[98] In course of his drive for girls' schools in villages, too, Vidyasagar took special pride in those being attended by daughters of respectable, high-caste families, thus once again challenging directly conservative bhadralok prejudices.[99]

---

school timings no longer made adjustments for agrarian rhythms; and the curriculum had become more abstract, detached from labour processes (e.g. the shift from zamindari and mahajani accounting to formal Western mathematics).

[97] Adam, p. 7.

[98] The above paragraph is based on Chandicharan Bandopadhyay, Chapter VII, and Benoy Ghosh, Chapter IV.

[99] Vidyasagar's report to H. Woodrowe, officiating Director of Public Instruction, 10 December 1857, emphasized the importance of the girls' school he had managed to start at Koolingram, Burdwan district, as those sending

The characteristic features — and limits — of Vidyasagar's pedagogy are revealed most clearly through a glance at his primers and text-books.[100] Three themes stand out. There is the motif of the poor boy making good through diligence, devoted effort, and single-minded pursuit of learning. *Jivancharit* and *Charitabali* use material from William and Robert Chambers' *Exemplary and Instructive Biography* (Edinburgh, 1846) to present brief life-histories of leading Western scientists, along with those of Grotius, Valentine Duval (a shepherd boy who rose to become a historian), and Jenkins (son of an African prince who managed to get a British education). The concentration on scientists (Copernicus, Galileo, Newton, Herschell, Linnaeus) indicates Vidyasagar's rationalist preferences, and so perhaps is the insertion here of Grotius — founder of an international law which theoretically puts the same limits on the powers of all states, big or small, and prominent advocate of toleration in an age of religious bigotry. The life-histories are adaptations from English, yet a revealing displacement seems to be at work in many of the comments: diligence, which in the Western exemplars is by no means constricted to formal book-learning alone, tends inevitably, in the conditions of colonial, middle-class Bengal, to get focussed solely on a single-minded pursuit of education. The biography of Duval ends with Vidyasagar remarking that *yatna* and *parisrama* (devoted effort and exertion) would have led the shepherd-boy nowhere had he not harnessed that devotion to learning.[101] The *Varnaparichay* and, even more, *Bodhoday* made the point sharper: 'Those who are diligent about becoming educated will live happy lives because they will be able to earn money.'[102]

their daughters there 'are, for the most part, respectable men.' A later report of his claimed that with consistent Government support he could have started girls' schools 'in almost every village in the districts under me, except perhaps the District of Nuddea.' The qualification is revealing, for Nadia was the citadel of Brahmanical learning and orthodoxy. Arabinda Guha, pp. 35, 36.

[100] The key texts here include *Jivancharit* (1849), *Bodhoday* (1851), *Nitibodh* (1851: published in the name of Vidyasagar's close friend Rajkrishna Bandopadhyay, but with the first seven sections written by himself), *Charitabali* (1856), and, of course, *Varnaparichay* in two parts (April, June, 1855). *Varnaparichay* went through 152 editions totalling 3,500,000 copies in Vidyasagar's lifetime, and remained the standard Bengali primer right down to contemporary times. Sibaji Bandopadhyay, *Gopal-Rakhal Dvandvasamas: Upanibeshbad o Bangla Shishusahitya* (Calcutta, Papyrus, 1991), p. 135.

[101] I owe this point to Hatcher, p. 181, who does not, however, make this distinction between Western exemplar and Indian adaptation explicit.

[102] *Bodhoday*, in Gopal Haldar, ed, *Vidyasagar Rachanasangraha* (Calcutta, 1972), Volume I, p. 182. The theme, of course, has become a Bengali proverb:

The theme of improvement through education is inextricably bound up with a tremendous insistence on discipline, connoting both rigorous self-control and strict obedience to the commands of parents and teachers. The *Varnaparichay*, as Sibaji Bandopadhyay has emphasized in an important study, is structured throughout by a binary contrast between disciplined diligence and errant disobedience, culminating at the end of Part I in the opposition of Gopal who will succeed in life, and Rakhal who will never learn to read.[103] This is a discipline, it should be added, that is presented in terms utterly stark and bleak, abstracted from human affect and paternalistic glosses. Children are actually told in one lesson that they should always try to please their parents, for if the latter had not been kind enough to feed and clothe them, their sufferings would have known no limit.[104] The Utilitarian, materialistic tone of Vidyasagar's textbooks in fact provoked some contemporary criticism from both orthodox Hindus and some Christian missionaries.[105] These are understandable enough, but the peculiar bleakness of the world of *Varnaparichay* remains a bit puzzling: it is almost as if Vidyasagar sometimes is fighting a part of himself, suppressing an inner Rakhal, projecting the path of discipline and obedience as something made necessary by a heartless world.[106] *Varnaparichay* ends with a really strange and cruel tale, quite out of place one would think in a children's primer. Bhuban, an orphan boy spoilt by his loving aunt, becomes a thief, is condemned to be hanged, and as a parting 'gift' bites off his aunt's ear while saying goodbye.

Improvement, or social ascent, through stern discipline: but only upto a point, within limits set by existing property relations. *Bodhoday* affirms a highly status quoist version of a kind of labour theory of property: 'The things we see around us must belong to

---

'Lekhapara kore je garighora chare se.'

[103] Sibaji Bandopadhyay, pp. 134–42, and *passim*.

[104] *Varnaparichay*, Part II, in T. Datta, ed., *Vidyasagar Rachanbali*, Volume I (Calcutta,1994), p. 1264.

[105] Biharilal Sarkar, p. 153, was critical of the *Bodhoday*, which had declared that sense impressions constitute the only source of knowledge, and defined matter as objects that can be perceived. The missionary leader John Murdoch objected to the use of the 'secularist' *Varnaparichay* in Christian schools. Swapan Basu, p. 130.

[106] Vidyasagar's autobiographical fragment begins by recalling how disobedient he had been in his childhood and how often his father had had to scold or beat him: a relevant personal detail, but which does not, I feel, fully explain this tone.

one or other person. An object belongs to whoever has worked to produce it, or has inherited it from his forefathers. No one else has any right to it. Whoever owns an object should continue to own it.' No respectable *(bhadra)* person should be a beggar, while having property is conducive to continuous effort. Vidyasagar's school texts are full of warnings about the immorality of theft: 'One shouldn't lay one's hand on something belonging to another person, even if one's life is at stake.'[107] There was, then, a clear class limit — and sometimes a caste frontier, too, though here it was more a question of expediency than believed-in principle. Vidyasagar had insisted in 1851 on opening Sanskrit College to Kayasthas, and in 1854 to other 'respectable castes'. But in 1855 he rejected as inexpedient a suggestion that a Subarnabanik student should also be admitted.[108] Though often very prosperous, he argued, 'in the scale of castes the class stands very low', and he did not want to further 'shock the prejudice of the orthodox Pundits of the Institution.'[109] Despite a concern for primary education in the countryside very rare among members of his class, Vidyasagar, it needs to be added, was probably not the unqualified advocate for mass enlightenment that later admirers have at times made him out to be. Hatcher has cited a letter of his written in September 1859, which argues that educating 'one boy in a proper style' was preferable to providing a smattering of learning to large numbers, for poor children would be taken out of school and put to work by their parents in any case.[110] Vidyasagar did set up a night school for 'sons of the cultivating class' in Birsingha in 1853, but this seems to have been a special gesture made for his home village, and not part of his overall schemes.[111]

Still it is possible to be over-harsh about Vidyasagar. Ranajit Guha has described his schoolbook morality as nothing but 'hard-

---

[107] *Bodhoday* (1851, 1886), in Debkumar Basu, ed., *Vidyasagar Rachanabali*, Volume I (Calcutta, 1966, 1974), pp. 282–3.

[108] Subarnabaniks were a prosperous trading community in Bengal who had a surprisingly low-caste status: supposedly because they had offended Ballal Sen, eponymous founder of the specific caste structure of Bengal.

[109] Letters dated 28 March 1851 and 21 November 1855, in Benoy Ghosh, pp. 542–5.

[110] Letter to Rivers Thompson, 29 September 1859, cited in Hatcher, p. 111.

[111] Vidyasagar also ran a free day-school and a girls' school at Birsingha, along with a charitable dispensary. His total expenses for these came to as much as Rs 500–600 a month. Subolchandra Mitra, pp. 240–1.

baked, bourgeois individualism',[112] and certainly there are not only similarities but obvious connections (through Chambers, for instance) with nineteenth-century middle-class British ideologies of improvement as moulded by amalgams of Evangelicalism and Utilitarianism.[113] Texts like *Varnaparichay* comprise the part of Vidyasagar's work that might appear readily assimilable to today's very influential emphasis on 'disciplinary' projects, either derived from colonial discourses or running parallel with them.[114] Hatcher's book has effectively drawn attention, in significant contrast, to the possibility of the more indigenous roots of Vidyasagar's pedagogical values, in particular the traditions of *nitishastra*, embodied in texts like *Chanakya-slokas* and *Hitopadesha*, which also contained elements of an ethic of this-wordly improvement through strenuous learning.[115] But Hatcher, like the analysts of colonial discourse, remains within the parameters of a search for 'influence' or origins. What tends to remain unasked is the question of the precise social contexts which made the emphasis on discipline appear unavoidable. (Not necessarily pleasant or attractive: the bleak world of *Varnaparichay*, its almost Machiavellian realism and ruthlessness, perhaps signifies a recognition of necessity rather than blithe imitation or enthusiastic acceptance.) With the closing of opportunities for military careers and the decline of indigenous business enterprise, education in Bengal, by the mid nineteenth century, was becoming virtually the sole channel for respectable upward mobility: education, further, of a far more formal, examination-centred kind, for which the old kind of pathshala, however much in tune with earlier conditions, was quite unsuited. Recruitment into services and professions was becoming increasingly dependent on examinations and educational degrees. The informal patronage that Vidyasagar could still distribute through his personal relations with top British officials would soon

[112] Ranajit Guha, *An Indian Historiography of India* (Calcutta, K.P. Bagchi, 1988), p. 61.

[113] For later generations, Samuel Smiles' *Self-Help* has come to epitomize this ideology: here, however, there can have been no direct influence, since that text was published only in 1859.

[114] See, for instance, Partha Chatterjee, ed., *Texts of Power: Emerging Disciplines in Colonial Bengal* (Calcutta, Samya, 1996). For a more nuanced version of a similar argument, see Sibaji Bandopadhyay.

[115] A prize-winning Sanskrit poem by Vidyasagar in his student days, composed at a time (1838) when he had not mastered English, had already announced that 'though a man be weak, poor, or of low birth, through learning he earns the respect worthy of a king.' Hatcher, pp. 165-7.

become a thing of the past. And, once again, instead of a homogenized 'middle class', a focus on its poorer elements seems helpful
for situating Vidyasagar's initiatives. The strenuous moods of his
school texts were not primarily meant for the gilded youth of
Calcutta. They become meaningful only when placed in a context
of genteel poverty, and here Vidyasagar's projects implied a striving
for a real though limited expansion, an attempt, in the words of
Asok Sen, to extend 'opportunities of education for the poorer
gentry in small towns and villages of Bengal.'[116]

The attempt went some distance beyond them, perhaps, in terms
of long-term appropriations by groups about whom Vidyasagar
himself had shown little or no concern. Recent research has unear-
thed a mass of early-twentieth-century vernacular tracts composed
by an emerging literati of Muslims and lower-caste authors located
in obscure villages or small towns of rural Bengal.[117] They are imbued
with an improvement ethic reminiscent often of Vidyasagar's combination of education with puritanical virtues and discipline, though
there is also a greater focus on life outside the classroom, in particular
on agricultural development. Given the continued, massive circula-
tion of texts like *Varnaparichay*, one might even suspect a certain
amount of direct, if unintended, influence.

Such developments lay much in the future in the 1850s. For
Vidyasagar, the tragedy was that the favourable conjuncture that
he had sought to utilize for major educational and other initiatives
proved extremely shortlived. Educational administration was getting
more bureaucratized under a brash young ICS Director of Public
Instruction, Gordon Young, who did not get on with Vidyasagar.
Much more important was a new mood of financial stringency,
fairly obviously connected with counterinsurgency expenses in the
wake of 1857. Vidyasagar had gone ahead in the early summer of
1857 in starting girls' schools in his four districts, on the strength
of a verbal assurance from Halliday that if 'the inhabitants would
provide suitable school houses, the expenses for maintaining the
schools would be met by the Government.' In the next year 'the
Supreme Government . . . refused their sanction to their establishment except under the Grants-in-aid Rules. My labours have
thus become fruitless and the interesting little schools will have to

---

[116] Asok Sen, p. 42.

[117] I am indebted for this point to the very original research of Pradip Kumar
Dutta: 'Hindu–Muslim Relations in the Bengal of the 1920s' (unpublished
thesis, Delhi University, 1996), Chapter II, and *passim*.

be closed immediately.'[118] Towards the end of 1858 Vidyasagar resigned in disgust from all his official posts. ·

Barriers of another kind, relating to the development of vernacular education for boys, become evident from an earlier report of Vidyasagar in January 1857. He had pointed out then that 'the success of Vernacular Education will depend materially upon the encouragement given in the way of providing the Alumni of these institutions with offices under Government.' Vidyasagar suggested that vernacular students should therefore be nominated 'to lower posts in the Judicial or Revenue Departments' — a proposal, needless to state, that was entirely ignored.

Colonial constraints — in the form of very material considerations and structures, not abstract ideas — are therefore entirely clear in the case of Vidyasagar's educational ventures. They had coalesced with the elite Brahmanical traditions of high castes, sometimes strengthening, but hardly creating them: for there is no evidence whatsoever of any major attempt at mass education (or organized efforts to improve the conditions of women, for that matter) by bhadralok men in pre-colonial times. The philanthropy of the more enterprising zamindars, on which too Vidyasagar had thought he could depend in the 1850s, was often a bit double-edged at its best,[119] and died away as enhancement of rent became more difficult with the tenancy acts of 1859 and 1885. And deepening employment problems clearly constricted middle-class attitudes over time. Bhadralok protests poured in when Lieutenant-Governor Campbell suggested some diversion of funds from higher towards primary education in 1870.[120] Even anti- colonial nationalism did not change attitudes fundamentally. The 'national education' of the Swadeshi era concentrated on trying to float an alternative university, and certain interesting experiments in districts like Barisal and Faridpur to start autonomous nationalist-oriented village schools among Namashudras and Muslims, which had worried the government considerably, soon died away.[121]

[118] Extract from General Report of Public Instruction, 1858–59, Appendix A, in Arabinda Guha, p. 36.

[119] There had been complaints in 1847 that Joykrishna Mukherjee was funding his Uttarpara English school by enhancing the rents of his tenants at Boinchee. Nilmoni Mukherjee, p. 108.

[120] Asok Sen, pp. 38–9.

[121] Sumit Sarkar, *Swadeshi Movement in Bengal, 1903–1908* (New Delhi, 1973), Chapter IV.

A report of an inspector of schools just a few months after Vidya-sagar's resignation can serve as an appropriate, if depressing, epitaph for this section. At Jowgong village near Boinchee, Burdwan district, where a girls' school founded by Vidyasagar was still getting an official grant of Rs 32 per month, 'not a girl, boy or pundit was in attendance' when it was visited on 25 January 1859. The inspector went from there to the neighbouring village of Koolingram, which, as we have seen, Vidyasagar had singled out for special mention in December 1857 as an instance of successful overcoming of the initial hostility of 'respectable men'.[122] A few girls could be seen there in January 1859, but ' the poor Pundit of the Girls' School had . . . no friends'. The headmaster of the boys' school was leading the opposition, and the girls' school had had to shift to another village a mile away.[123]

IV

Many stories have been current about the origins of Vidyasagar's passionate concern for the plight of women, in a society where child marriage was normative, widow remarriage prohibited, austere widowhood stringently enforced among high and most intermediate castes, and polygamy considered prestigious among Kulin Brahmans, Kayasthas, and Vaidyas. His mother first advised him to take up the cause of widows — according to one account. Others refer to first-hand experiences during visits to Birsingha in his college days: seeing a child-widow of his own age having to fast on *ekadosi*, and hearing about another forced into infanticide by parental command. He was particularly shocked when a favourite teacher of his at Sanskrit College, the elderly Vedanta scholar Sambhu-chandra Vacaspati, married a child to run his household for him a few months before his death. (Vidyasagar is said to have wept on meeting the child-bride, doomed to early and lifelong widow-hood, and walked out of his teacher's house, refusing to touch water there henceforth.[124]) Two widows are prominent, as we have seen, in his own autobiographical fragment, but as exemplars of warmth and compassion rather than suffering.

122 See fn. 90 above.
123 Report of E. Lodge, Inspector of Schools, South Bengal, 10 March 1859, cited in Arabinda Guha, pp. 50-1.
124 Chandicharan Bandopadhyay, pp. 59-61, rejects as inauthentic the story about his mother, and relates the tales about infanticide and Vacaspati. Subol-chandra Mitra, p. 262, gives the story about ekadosi.

What is common to all these anecdotes is an emphasis on personal experience that can be read as a confirmation of the inference I had drawn from Maheshchandra Deb's essay.[125] There are no references at all to any stimulus provided by Western models of marital relations. And, contrary to an interpretive model which today is very influential, all biographies about Vidyasagar agree that the counter-posing of shastra against *deshachar*, texts versus customs, eventually the core of his widow remarriage and anti-polygamy tracts, came as deliberate strategy, formulated after he had become convinced that certain practices were harmful and evil.[126] Vidyasagar's reform tracts hardly bear out the assumption so often made nowadays that 'the discursive struggle in which the social reformers were engaged was over tradition and culture; women were simply the site of this contestation.'[127]

Vidyasagar's first essay on social reform, *Balyabibaher Dosh* (Evils of Child-Marriage, 1850), was marked in fact by a total absence of textual exegesis. Partly for that reason, it was also his most radical statement on gender relations, and it was able within the space of a few, brilliantly written pages to unfold an integrated, comprehensive critique of child marriage, arranged marriages, marital oppression, taboos against educating women, and the horrors and evils of austere widowhood.[128]

---

[125] See above, footnote 39 and corresponding text.

[126] Chandicharan Bandopadhyay, pp. 237–8, vividly describes sleepless nights spent by Vidyasagar hunting for shastric arguments to prove the case for widow-remarriage, before he came across the Parasar passage he would make famous. The story may be overdramatized, as it seems unlikely that Vidyasagar would not have known about the passage earlier (see fn. 142 below), but the essential point regarding the primacy of personal experience over text is reiterated by Subolchandra Mitra, p. 262, who adds that he 'rightly' took no public step before discovering the shastric justification.

[127] Ratna Kapur and Brenda Cossman, *Subversive Sites: Feminist Engagements with Law in India* (New Delhi, Sage, 1996), p. 47, a pioneering feminist study of Indian legal discourse which unfortunately accepts at this point a little uncritically Lata Mani's thesis about the debate around sati. I have stated elsewhere my difficulties with Mani's argument, namely that nineteenth-century debates about the conditions of women were primarily a means to the end of establishing textualized versions of tradition, even when applied to Rammohan: see my 'Orientalism Revisited: Saidian Frameworks in the Writing of Indian History', *Oxford Literary Review*, 16, 1994.

[128] *Sarvasubhakari*, 1850; Gopal Haldar, ed., *Vidyasagar Rachanabali*, Volume II (Calcutta, 1972), pp. 3–9. This was an article in a shortlived monthly brought out by some Hindu College friends of Vidyasagar; it was published anonymously,

The essay began with a trenchant denunciation of *both* text and custom, shastra and *laukik vyavahara*. The two in combination have produced, and sustain, all that Vidyasagar found objectionable in existing marital practices. Throughout the essay, he judged the existing institutions and practices against an ideal norm of companionate conjugality based on adult mutual love *(pronoy)* — and that, Vidyasagar says, can flow only from an 'unity of minds'.[129] This is impossible if girls are married off at eight, nine, or ten — which happens because *smriti-shastras* have promised some imagined otherworldly boons from such action, and people are also afraid of flouting long-continuing custom. All marriages, further, are arranged by parents as advised by often corrupt *ghataks* (professional go-betweens), and the couple do not even see each other before the ceremony — and so 'in our country sincere marital love is rare: the husband is merely the breadwinner, the wife a domestic servant *(grihaparicharika)*.' Child marriage, again, is directly connected with women being kept without education, for, even if they had been taught a little at their parental homes, after marriage will begin life in an 'alien house *(paragriha)*', totally subjected to the authority of fathers and mothers-in-law, and filled with an endless round of 'cleaning the house, preparing beds, cooking, serving food, and other duties which would have to be learned with perfection.' The early marriage of girls also increases the number of widows, 'and who has not witnessed first-hand the unbearable sufferings of widows? . . . All chance of pleasure must end as soon as their husbands die . . . they will not be allowed a drop of water, even if critically ill, on days of ritual fasting. . . . ' Never again would Vidyasagar condemn so uncompromisingly the rules of austere widowhood, identify patrilocal marriage for women as life in an 'alien' home, or indeed critique child marriage directly. These did not become part of his action programmes, nor did he return to the interconnections he had worked out here between the need to raise the age of marriage, promotion of women's education, and improving the lot of widows.

The major plank of Vidyasagar's argument in this pamphlet is thus individual and conjugal happiness — but there is also a second register, of morality and social welfare that on the whole has figured

---

but there is complete unanimity among biographers and critics that the author was Ishwarchandra.

129 I intend to argue below that this implicit recognition of ideal conjugality as necessarily based on the union of adult minds and bodies is quite central to a proper assessment of Vidyasagar.

more in social reform literature but remains somewhat low-key here. The rigours of lifelong widowhood, imposed often on young girls, cause much immorality and lead to abortions and infanticide. Children born of too early marriage tend to be weak and unhealthy, nor can they get proper training from mothers who have been kept uneducated. Young men married off in their teens neglect their studies and are overburdened by the financial responsibilities of maintaining wife and children: earning money has to become the sole aim of life, leading, once again, to immoral ways. Vidyasagar, interestingly, comes close for a moment here to what became a standard late-nineteenth-century Kaliyuga theme, and figured often in Ramakrishna's conversation as the link between kamini, kanchan and chakri — but then his argument moved in a very different direction, prioritizing this-worldly happiness and welfare, not devotion or asceticism. Ramakrishna would certainly not have shared his enthusiasm for conjugal love.

Did the later, and very much better known, tracts advocating widow remarriage and criticizing Kulin polygamy on largely textual grounds then mark a retreat for Vidyasagar, with gender injustice becoming no more than a site for arguments about valid and invalid tradition? Such a critique would be less than fair, for it fails to analyse the options that were open (or not open) to Vidyasagar when formulating a specific programme of reform and trying to organize a movement on its basis. The tract against child marriage could be daringly radical and reject shastric exegesis, precisely because it was more of a consciousness-raising exercise than a specific proposal for an immediate, concrete reform. It raised no demand for a new law: did not need to, in strict logic, for of course there was no law prohibiting adult marriage — as widow remarriage was prohibited and its issue illegitimate till 1856. The basic point that has to be made is that under British Indian law personal and family matters were supposed to be regulated in accordance with the shastras for Hindus, and the shariat for Muslims.[130] Reform through external

---

[130] Warren Hastings' Regulations had laid down, in 1772 and again in 1780, that 'inheritance, marriage, caste and other religious usages or institutions were to be administered to Hindus according to the laws of "Shaster".' Numerous changes were made, of course, but in consultation with indigenous experts (hence the need for 'judge-pandits' in courts) — till the 'assumption', made in 1864, that judicial knowledge of Hindu law was complete. In practice, occasional consultations continued even afterwards. J.D. Derrett, *Religion, Law and the State in India*, p. 233, and *passim*.

state legislation, and reform-from-within through scriptural exegesis and community debate, which today often get counterposed against each other (as in current controversies about Muslim Personal Law, for instance), were actually interdependent in Vidyasagar's time. He had to find shastric justifications for widow remarriage, if it was to become legal under 'Anglo-Hindu' law: reason and humanity alone would not be sufficient. The intertwining of Brahmanical tradition and colonial law becomes clear when seen from the opposite side, too. The petition organized by Raja Radhakanta Deb against the Widow Marriage bill in March 1856 combined alternative interpretations of the shastras and appeals to age-old custom with the argument that 'the proposed law is also at variance with the several Statutes of the British Parliament and the Regulations of the East India Company.'[131]

The author of *Balyabibaher Dosh* was not yet particularly important in official or elite Indian circles. The widow-remarriage tracts, in contrast, were published in 1855-6, at the peak of Vidyasagar's influence, and the plunge into shastric exegesis was obviously in significant part an attempt to convince leading pandits who, through their importance in the *sabhas* of big zamindars and at high-caste ritual occasions, could in turn help him get the support of the big men of Hindu society. Vidyasagar in other words was trying to utilize and manipulate, for reformist purposes, the traditions of the medieval raja–pandit nexus that had spilled over in modified forms into the Calcutta-based *dals* of the nineteenth century.[132] Soon after publishing his first tract justifying widow remarriage, Vidyasagar even tried to win over the Sobhabazar Raj, approaching Radhakanta Deb through a nephew who had become an ally of his. That attempt failed,[133] but he was able to get a substantial section of leading

---

[131] The petition, which obtained 36,764 signatures, went on to cite regulations enacted in 1772, 1793, and 1831, and the unanimous opinion of the judges of the Sadr courts given to the Law Commission of 1837 that legalization of widow remarriage would 'at once dislocate the whole framework of Hindu jurisprudence.' A similar combination is visible in the petition made by the 'Professors of the Hindu law' of 'Nuddea, Tribeni, Bhatpara, Bansberia, Calcutta, and other places' denouncing the efforts of a *'Modern* pandit, Vidyasagar', 'in conjunction with a few young men of the rising class'. For the texts of both these documents, see Subolchandra Mitra, pp. 302-17.

[132] See the excellent discussion in Sekhar Bandopadhyay, pp. 22-3.

[133] Radhakanta organized two shastric debates, but at the end of the second awarded the shawl that traditionally signified victory at such occasions to Brajanath Vidyaratna, leading Smriti expert of Nabadwip. Subolchandra Mitra,

zamindars, along with a number of pandits like Taranath Tarkavacaspati and some Sanskrit College teachers, to line up with Brahmos and Young Bengal intellectuals in the petitions that were organized from October 1855 onwards asking for the legalization of widow remarriage.[134] Vidyasagar's subsequent campaign against Kulin polygamy in 1856-7 also got the support of many prominent zamindars: probably more easily, for in its extreme forms (Kulins with a hundred wives or more, many of whom never saw their husbands after marriage) this was an undeniable scandal, confined moreover to a limited circle of high-caste families claiming a peculiarly high status.[135] A law on the subject may well have been enacted but for the 1857 rebellion. In the late 1860s, when Vidyasagar revived the demand and published his two tracts against polygamy, support was forthcoming for a time even from the Sanatan Dharmarakshini Sabha that had lately been organized to defend Hindu orthodoxy.[136]

As Sekhar Bandopadhyay has emphasized, Vidyasagar's reform campaigns thus included an element of continuity with earlier ways of seeking change through *vyavasthas* (authoritative rulings on social matters) from prominent pandits.[137] There had been several attempts earlier to get individual widow marriages sanctioned in this way, notably one by Raja Rajballabh of Dacca in the mid eighteenth century, which had been blocked by the pandits of Maharaja Krishnachandra of Nadia. Shortly before Vidyasagar published his first tract on widow remarriage, Shyamacharan Das, a man of intermediate-caste (Nabasakh) status living in North Calcutta, had managed to

---

pp. 268-9. Brajanath remained one of Vidyasagar's most bitter and formidable antagonists down to the 1880s.

[134] The signatories included the Maharajas of Burdwan and Nadia, and the heads of both branches of the Tagore family (Debendranath and Prasannakumar), and the first petition was headed by the unimpeachably respectable and orthodox Joykrishna Mukherjee of Uttarpara. Altogether some 25,000 signatures could be collected for reform: less than the number collected by its opponents, but still fairly impressive. Chandicharan Bandopadhyay, pp. 255-6; Nilmoni Mukherjee, pp. 142-3.

[135] Polygamy had become rampant because it often became the principal source of livelihood for Kulin young men, who would be paid handsome sums by the parents of daughters eager to move their families up in the hypergamous scale.

[136] A support that Vidyasagar cited as a particularly telling argument in his favour in the introduction to his first *Bahubibaha* tract (1870). This also gives a brief history of the earlier campaigns against polygamy. Haldar, ed., *Vidyasagar Rachanabali*, Volume II, pp. 167-9.

[137] Sekhar Bandopadhyay, p. 28.

get a favourable vyavastha for the remarriage of his widowed child from a number of leading pandits. (The ruling used a passage from Manu but was careful to limit permission for remarriage to Shudra widows who had remained virgins.[138])

Vidyasagar's tracts, then, were in a sense sophisticated vyavasthas, geared to an audience of fellow pandits and their patrons. But this was only one register among several on which he was playing. Right at the beginning of the first *Bidhaba-bibaha* pamphlet, there is a memorable appeal to a conception of public, vernacular space that is fundamentally new. This was the space that he was simultaneously trying to create, through vernacular prose and reformed elementary education, in endeavours that, like widow remarriage, attained their climax precisely around 1855-6. Tired of the endless controversy on the matter that had been so long confined to pandits animated by mutual jealousy, Vidyasagar declares he has decided to present his views 'in the language spoken by the people, to bring it to the notice of the general public [*sarbasadharan*]. Now let everyone read and discuss, in an impartial manner, whether widow marriage should be introduced or not.'[139] The shastric passages are therefore always translated, and the discussion, though inevitably complicated, is conveyed through a prose far simpler than what had been current in scholarly discussion in Bengali before Vidyasagar. And textual exegesis, ever so often, is interrupted by passages marked by deep compassion for suffering womankind, anger, and a profound sense of male guilt. The best known of these is of course the eloquent condemnation of deshachar at the close of the second *Bidhaba-bibaha* tract, highlighting (in that order) the sufferings of widows and the flood of immorality and abortion which is caused by male cruelty sanctioned by that custom. As in the *Balya-bibaha* pamphlet, an implicitly positive recognition of the naturalness of physical, sexual needs underpins Vidyasagar's polemic: 'You think that with the death of the husband, the woman's body becomes like a stone. . .' . The tract ends with the famous lines:

---

[138] Vidyasagar reprinted this vyavastha in the second edition of his initial widow-remarriage tract (1857), at the same time pointing to its subsequent repudiation by most of the signatories as a crass instance of opportunism. Haldar, *Vidyasagar Rachanabali*, Volume II, pp.15-19. Chandicharan Bandopadhyay, pp. 224-5, lists a number of earlier attempts to get widow marriage accepted.

[139] Ibid., p. 21.

Let not the unfortunate weaker sex [*abala*] be born in a country where the men have no pity, no dharma, no sense of right and wrong, no ability to discriminate between beneficial and harmful, where preservation of what has been customary is considered the only duty, the only dharma . . . By what sin do women come to be born in Bharatvarsha at all?[140]

There are other, less-known passages, too, that outstrip the limits of shastric interpretation. Space permits only one more reference. The first *Bahubibaha* pamphlet begins with the general proposition that women everywhere are subordinated to men, because 'they are physically weaker, and because social rules are so bad': 'But in no country are the conditions of women so bad as in our unfortunate land, due to the excessive barbarism, selfishness, and thoughtlessness of men.' And the long lists of Kūlin men with many wives that Vidyasagar goes on to offer, giving precise names and locations, are interspersed with an angry sarcasm: 'The younger [of two Kulin sisters] has a husband aged 25-26. He has not so far managed to marry more than 32 times.'[141]

The more purely textual sections of the widow-marriage and anti-polygamy tracts are unlikely to attract many readers today: a pity, for they have a brilliance of their own. Vidyasagar displayed here a mastery over text and interpretative logic that was able to subvert, or appropriate for his own purposes, a number of standard orthodox arguments. The example of 'Kali-varjya' is particularly relevant for us, for once again we see Vidyasagar come close to the trope of Kaliyuga, and then move off in a completely different direction. Kali-varjya had been the method by which ancient texts had been modified or pruned, almost always in socially restrictive ways, and often with reference to controls over women, by medieval Smriti experts like Raghunandan.[142] Vidyasagar appropriated the same scholastic tool to prise open a textual space for widow marriage. The lynchpin of Vidyasagar's argument, as is well known, is a passage in *Parasara-samhita*, permitting the remarriage of women in five specific

---

[140] Haldar, ed., pp. 164-5.

[141] Ibid., pp. 171, 218-19.

[142] Raghunandan had listed, among practices allowed by some *Dharmasastras* but no longer permissible in the Kaliyuga, sea-voyages, twice-born jatis marrying women of lower castes, going on too-distant pilgrimages, Brahmans using Shudra cooks — as well as a practice which had often been interpreted as widow marriage. The relevant passage was quoted, and glossed differently, by Vidyasagar in his first widow-marriage tract: Haldar, ed., p. 28.

cases, one of which is the death of the husband.[143] But there were many contrary texts which had to be got out of the way. Vidyasagar eliminated the *puranas* among these through the argument that Parasara as a dharmashastra had to be given precedence over them, and then made maximum use of the claim, made in the *Parasara-samhita* itself, that this was the text specifically applicable to Kaliyuga: the other texts, where they contradict it, are Kali-varjya. Vidyasagar's use of Parasara, and not, say, Manu, which had been cited by pandits to allow the remarriage of Shyamacharan Das' daughter, indicates his desire to open the space for widow remarriage to the maximum degree possible within the shastric mode of argument. (Manu, it will be recalled, had been read by the pandits to permit only the remarriage of Shudra widows who were also *akshata-yoni*, i.e. *virgo intacta*.) Vidyasagar's second tract specifically controverted the argument that remarriage is only permitted for low-caste widows, and he also quietly dropped all reference to virginity as a prerequisite.

The shastric rejection of polygamy seems to have been a more difficult task. With all his obvious enthusiasm for monogamous conjugality, Vidyasagar could not prove a complete case for strict monogamy from the Hindu scriptures. All that he could establish, mainly on the basis of Manu, was that the texts had laid down a number of specific conditions under which a man could take more than one wife — there was no unlimited and arbitrary right to multiple wives, as had become the practice among Kulins in Bengal.[144] The

143 'A woman is permitted by the shastras to remarry if her husband has disappeared, has died, been found impotent, has abandoned the world, or has been outcasted.' Haldar, ed., p. 26. Biographers like Chandicharan Bandpadhyay (p. 237) present Vidyasagar's discovery of this text in dramatic terms, as coming in a revelation after many nights of sleepless study of the shastras. This seems a bit unlikely, as the Derozian journal *Bengal Spectator* had already referred to the passage in July 1842 while advocating widow remarriage. Indramitra, *Karunasagar Vidyasagar* (Calcutta, 1969, 1992), pp. 242–3. A Sanskrit scholar like Vidyasagar would surely have known his Parasara anyway: the real problem was how the texts contradicting this passage could be shown to be irrelevant.

144 The permitted grounds In Manu are nearly all highly gender-unequal: the husband could marry again, not only if his wife dies, but also if she is barren, bears daughters only, drinks, is unfaithful, extravagant, always ill, and even if she talks back at him. Contrary to today's widespread communal stereotype which somehow associates Islam uniquely with many wives, the scriptural-cum-customary grounds for monogamy in Hindu traditions have been quite remarkably weak, and only postcolonial legislation has made a (partial) change. See the passages cited in Vidyasagar's two *Bahubibaha* tracts (1870, 1873), reprinted in Haldar, ed. pp. 173–5, 413–15.

argument in the first tra¢t against polygamy then shifts rather quickly to non-shastric grounds: a highly derogatory sketch of the history of Kulinism in Bengal, followed by statistics giving the names, ages, number of marriages, and locations of prominent polygamous men in Hooghly district.[145]

Vidyasagar's shastric arguments justifying widow remarriage and restricting polygamy provoked a flood of attempted refutations from pandits, mostly it seems from the Nadia-Jessore and 24 Parganas belt of solid Brahmanical orthodox scholarship, but joined in later by some erstwhile allies, notably Taranath Tarkavacaspati. Vidyasagar plunged with zest into the scholastic debate, making his sequels far longer than the initial tracts, and carrying on the battle right into his last days. Leafing through his voluminous replies to critics (the second tract against polygamy runs to nearly 200 closely printed pages in the edition I am using), one does at times get the impression of the reformer trapped in a scholastic morass, lost in an endless polemic of interest to fellow pandits alone, moving away in fact from that vision of widening, lay, public space that had animated him in 1850 and 1855. There is a sense of helpless anger, too, finding vent perhaps in bouts of violent, even vulgar, abuse that Vidyasagar sometimes published under pen-names, replying in kind to no doubt equal or greater scurrility on the other side.[146]

A more crucial problem lay in the built-in limits of a strategy of reform 'from within', by shastric exegesis. A number of areas dear to Vidyasagar's heart, as revealed by the 1850 pamphlet (notably, child- and arranged marriages) had to be left out as clearly validated by the scriptures, and the scholastic method also had a tendency to create problems for other, subsequent, reform agendas. Rammohan may have unwittingly added to Vidyasagar's difficulties by hunting up and publicizing the texts praising austere widowhood in order to controvert those that insisted on sati. Vidyasagar sought to eliminate one kind of polygamy which Manu had permitted

---

[145] One hundred and thirty-three are listed for Hooghly district, with the number of marriages ranging from 80 to 5. A list follows for the single village of Janai, near Calcutta, with 64 names of men having from two to ten wives. Ibid., pp. 201-12.

[146] See for instance the passage in *Ratnapariksha* (1886) where Vidyasagar, writing under the alias of 'Worthy Nephew', expresses regret that his earlier polemic has led to the death of 'Uncle Vidyaratna' (Brojobilas Vidyaratna, the Nadia Smriti scholar who had been opposing him from 1855), and now he doesn't know whether this should be classed as Brahman-slaughter or cow-slaughter. Haldar, ed., p. 512.

(marrying a woman of lower caste) by emphasizing that in Kaliyuga intercaste marriage was strictly prohibited.[147] His polemic against Kulinism also used the argument that it often led to delayed marriages for girls in the absence of suitably high-status bridegrooms — and this, Vidyasagar emphasized, clearly contradicted the shastric command that marriage had to be consummated before the first menses.[148] Perhaps it was this passage in his own earlier writing that contributed to Vidyasagar's surprising ambiguity on the Age of Consent issue, when his opinion was officially asked for shortly before his death.[149] And finally, as Bankimchandra acutely pointed out in 1873 in a critique of Vidyasagar's demand for a law against polygamy, scriptural arguments were in a sense redundant, as Hindus guided themselves far more by customs, and texts at times prescribed rules which it would be quite impossible to implement strictly.[150]

We have been looking at Vidyasagar's reform initiatives so far in terms of texts and polemics. But this can be no more than a partial view, for with all its obvious limitations the issue of widow marriage did become for a time something like a movement, not confined to pandits or even always only to highly literate people. Vidyasagar, as is well known, did not stop with getting widow marriage legalized. From November 1856 onwards he went to enormous trouble, expenditure, and sometimes real physical danger to organize widow marriages,

[147] Ibid., p. 176.

[148] Ibid., p. 188.

[149] Vidyasagar found it impossible to support the bill in its existing form, as he thought fixing the minimum age of consent at twelve could go against the *garbhadan* rite immediately after menses. His alternative suggestion was to make consummation before first menses a penal offence, irrespective of age. As girls can menstruate very early, this would not have given protection against physical and emotional injury in many cases. Subolchandra Mitra, who enthusiastically gives long extracts from this note of 16 February 1891, rejects however a widespread opinion that it represented a kind of recantation of earlier attitudes: for two months before his death Vidyasagar warmly welcomed the marriage of the Brahmo activist Durgamohan Das (who had earlier tried to get his own widowed stepmother remarried) with a widow with several children. Mitra, p. 652–5.

[150] Bankim, however, used this potentially radical argument to reject Vidyasagar's demand for an anti-polygamy law, which he thought to be unnecessary. A passage in his article was quite prophetic in the way it anticipated what later became, and remains, a recurrent argument: it was unfair to pass a law curtailing Hindu (male) rights unless a similar restriction was imposed on Muslims too. *Bahubibaha* (*Bangadarshan*, 1280/1873), reprinted in Jogeshchandra Bagal, ed., *Bankim Rachanabali*, Volume II (Calcutta, 1954, 1969), pp. 314–19.

and by 1867 had personally arranged about sixty of them.[151] Most of the big names, the rajas and zamindars who had joined him in petitioning the government for the law, quickly backed out, often defaulting on earlier commitments of financial help. He did continue to get enthusiastic and active support from a number of young men, most of them Brahmos, through the late 1850s and 1860s and beyond, and much of the information we do have about specific widow marriage cases in fact comes from Brahmo biographies and histories.[152] During and just after the campaign for legalization of widow remarriage, interest and excitement was high enough to generate a large number of poems and songs, some ridiculing the move, others hailing it, and even 'cultivators, street-porters, cab-men and other lower-class people indulged in' them.[153] The best known of the verses is of course the one wishing long life to Vidyasagar, which appeared on the borders of some saris woven at Santipur. (As weavers have been a low-status group in caste society, this in itself is an indication of a reach beyond the bhadralok.) But more significant perhaps than such momentary excitement, yet peculiarly difficult to recuperate, are the long-term personal experiences into which a movement like widow marriage necessarily translated itself. For widow marriage meant, above all, young men, and girls growing up into young women, entering into a domesticity that flouted traditions, in the face of an enormous amount of everyday petty slander, persecution, ostracism.

Here our sources tend to fail us, for nearly all accounts stop with the first few highly-publicized marriages in Calcutta, followed by some discussion of Vidyasagar as lonely, tragic hero. The flood of anecdotes, so voluminous on philanthropy, also narrows down quite suddenly. Indramitra's *Karunasagar Vidyasagar*, which brings together the largest number of anecdotes, is a collection of 737 pages: only 62 of them deal with widow marriage.

[151] Vidyasagar mentioned this figure in a letter published in *Hindoo Patriot*, 1 July 1867, in connection with a proposal that had been made to raise a public fund to help him repay the debts he had incurred while organizing these marriages. He rejected the offer, but evidently felt it necessary to explain how so much had been spent.

[152] In his preface to the third edition (1863) of his first widow-marriage tract, Vidyasagar referred to the excitement and agitation generated in the Dacca region by his pamphlet, necessitating the reprint. Vidyasagar is not known to have many contacts in East Bengal, but the Brahmo movement acquired some of its principal bases in the areas of bhadralok concentration there, like Bikrampur, Barisal, and parts of Mymensingh and Sylhet.

[153] Subolchandra Mitra, p. 279.

We can get a few stray and momentary glimpses, however, of developments that should have called into question a number of very well-established assumptions but have been almost entirely ignored. Vidyasagar has usually been seen as a reformer of urban, educated bhadralok society, whose work had Calcutta as its focus. Yet the *Tattvabodhini Patrika* of Bhadra (August–September) 1858 contrasted the five widow marriages that had been achieved in Calcutta over the twenty months since the wedding of Srishchandra Vidyaratna in November 1856 with the seven in just two months in Hooghly villages (or very small towns) around Birsingha, beginning in June 1858. It mentioned Ramjibanpur, Khirpai, Chandrakona, Basuli; there were two more at Chandrakona next month, and the first widow marriage in Vidyasagar's home village in July 1862. By August 1862 *Somprakash* could report some twenty to twenty-two marriages in three years in this fairly small corner of Hooghly district, where Vidyasagar clearly had established some kind of a rural base.[154] Widow marriage, further, was not an entirely high-caste matter: thus Sambhuchandra Vidyaratna describes the '20-25' marriages that took place during 1864-5 as involving 'Brahmans, Kayasthas, Tantubay (weavers), Vaidyas, Telis, etc.'[155]

Vidyasagar's letter in *Hindoo Patriot* of July 1867 gives some hints about how the movement had been organized in the villages — as well as the kind of problems it was facing. Explaining why widow marriage had proved so expensive, Vidyasagar stated that apart from the heavy sums he had spent on the first wedding to establish its respectability, '*dals* or parties' were being 'maintained in several villages in the Mufassil', and anyone 'acquainted with the constitution of Hindoo society' would know that this was an expensive proposition 'even ordinarily'. But this was not an ordinary situation: many cases had been brought against 'the promoters of the movement in the Mufassil', and sometimes physical force was also being deployed. All this was demanding heavy litigation expenses.

Most remarkable of all, illuminating in concrete detail one instance of what Vidyasagar described in general terms in his letter, are the notes he had kept (in English) among his papers about a

---

154 Indramitra, p. 292. Sambhuchandra Vidyaratna mentions 'nearly fifteen' widow remarriages organized in Jehanabad villages like Ramjibanpur, Chandrakona, Sola, Srinagar, Kalikapur and Khirpai in Asar-Sravana 1265 (June-July 1858). Numerous such marriages, he states, took place in this area down to 1865. Sambhuchandra Vidyaratna, p. 104.

155 Sambhuchandra Vidyaratna, p. 116.

series of incidents in Kumarganj village, adjoining Birsingha. Long extracts from these are tucked away in a corner of Subolchandra's biography, but seem to have somehow gone unnoticed by later scholars.[156] The party at Kumargunj supporting widow marriage had been excluded from the ceremonies in the village Shiva-temple at the time of 'Churrukpooja', at the end of the Bengali year. When they tried to enter the temple to offer puja separately, they 'were beaten back with great violence', and local police officials at first refused to record their complaints. Worse was to come, for then the 'Zamindar of the village Baboo Shib Narain Roy' of Jurul began 'oppressing with impunity those of the Royots of his Talook Comergunj who belong to the widow marriage party.' Shib Narayan sent durwans to forcibly round up the pro-reformers, who were dragged to his presence and 'dismissed with 10 strokes of shoes and a fine of Rs 10 each. . . . Several of them have left the village with their respective families.' The terror had a wider impact: 'The news having reached the inhabitants of pergonnas Burda and Chandrakona, those who are willing to marry their sons and daughters have fallen back, through fear of consequences.' Further, the zamindar was clearly being backed by not only subordinate police officials but the Deputy Magistrate of Jehanabad: the local state apparatus, in other words. Numerous complaints to the latter, including several lodged by Vidyasagar himself, had had no result. The Deputy Magistrate passed orders against continuation of the acts of oppression, but Vidyasagar had learnt from a friendly police amla that 'the Khan Bahadur' had told his subordinates to ignore these, render no help to the widow marriage party, but 'endeavour to give them trouble if possible. . . . It is notorious that Baboo Shib Narain Roy often calls on the Deputy Magistrate at an advanced hour of the night.' The net result was that 'the party at Coomergunge' which had 'consisted of about 60 families' was reduced to four or five. Vidyasagar concluded his notes in a mood of complete despair. As 'those, who joined the cause at

---

[156] Subolchandra Mitra, pp. 511-16. There is a passing reference to the Kumarganj developments also in Biharilal Sarkar, p.282. From Vidyasagar's autobiographical fragment, we learn that Kumarganj was the weekly market-place (*hat*) for Birsingha, located in Chandrakona police-station, Jehanabad (Arambag) sub-division. There is no indication of date, but it must have been before 1869, when Vidyasagar left Birsingha permanently. Subolchandra places the extracts just after his account of Vidyasagar's relief work during the 1866 famine, and a date, *c.* 1867, seems indicated also by the reference in general terms to similar developments in the letter of 1 July 1867.

my solicitation and are suffering from their act' are not being relieved and their oppressors are going unpunished, 'I must leave the world, for what is the good of my remaining in it when there is no chance of success of the cause. I have resolved to devote my existence to it and if it fails, life would have no charm to me and existence would be useless.'

There is a little bit of data also in Vidyasagar's notes about the social composition of the two parties in the Kumargunj region. The Deputy Magistrate would of course be high-caste, and the zamindar probably also so. Some names are given of Vidyasagar's 'Royot' supporters: Damoo, Sriharee, Nilcomal, Gopal, and a 'Sreenibas Doss'. The one surname, as well as its absence in the other cases, suggests a subordinate, probably lower-caste status. But the peasants are clearly divided, for Vidyasagar's supporters at one point get beaten up by the 'Goallas [Sadgops] of the opposite Party'. An anthropological study of Birsingha in the 1950s located the Sadgops as an upwardly mobile jati, dominant in the neighbouring villages and becoming so in Vidyasagar's home village, where the other major groups were Brahmans and Bagdis.[157] One is tempted to speculate about a link between the 'Goalla' hostility to widow marriage and possible Sanskritizing aspirations at work already in the 1860s, but of course this is no more than guesswork.

The Kumargunj affair certainly raises some questions regarding the common stereotype about nineteenth-century social reform being an affair of the English-educated high bhadralok alone, generally backed by the foreign rulers and confined to issues which did not affect the rural masses. Despite Vidyasagar's contacts with leading British officials, an informal alliance between the state machinery at the local level and landlord power evidently frustrated all his initiatives in an area where he would have been most influential.[158] The implicit caste dimensions are equally interesting. In an important article some years ago, Lucy Carroll pointed out that for lower castes

[157] The study, made incidentally by a descendant of Vidyasagar, found the village Siva temple controlled by a Brahman family, surnamed Ray (a relation of Shib Narayan Roy, perhaps), who had land granted by the Maharaja of Burdwan. Village religious festivals were still the foci of social conflict. Gouranga Chattopadhyay, *Ranjana: A Village in West Bengal* (Calcutta, 1964).

[158] There seems to have been a brief spell earlier where the local authority at Jehanabad had been helpful. Interestingly, the deputy magistrate who Sambhuchandra remembers as helping Vidyasagar then was the well-known Muslim intellectual Abdul Latif. Sambhuchandra Vidyaratna, p. 104.

already practising widow marriage Act XV of 1856 could have been unwittingly retrogressive, and indeed in some ways represent a paradoxical extension of Brahmanical norms. It deprived widows who married of all succession rights to the property of the deceased husband, even though lower-caste customs had been more liberal in that respect at times.[159] But, at least in Bengal where Brahmanical norms had penetrated fairly deep into lower-caste society, it is dangerous to associate the 'popular' with any unqualified realm of freedom from upper-caste taboos and restrictions. The Kumargunj data seem rather to indicate that the ambiguities and divisions on reform issues could have their counterparts at other social levels, too, with some of the upwardly mobile seeking to 'Sanskritize' themselves by imposing greater controls on women, while at the same time the problems and misery caused by the widow marriage ban could also stimulate quite contrary tendencies. In 1922, a big Namashudra conference broke up partly through a bitter controversy as to whether widow marriage should be prohibited or encouraged, and during the mid 1920s Digindranarayan Bhattacharya, the rebel Brahman closely identified with lower-caste movements, revived and indeed extended Vidyasagar's programme by campaigning against the practice of widows being made to go without water on ekadosi.[160]

Vidyasagar had sought respectability for widow marriage by making their forms as conventional as possible, and in his letter of July 1867 claimed to have spent no less than Rs 10,000 on the marriage of Srishchandra, giving massive presents to pandits, ghataks and kulins. The reference to go-betweens confirms the obvious: these were presumably all arranged marriages, independent of the bride's consent. Yet despite this strategic emphasis on conventionality, something entirely unconventional was happening, with implications that could at times go a bit beyond the norms set by the founder of the movement. In 'normal' marriages, the child or very young girl was doing what every rule and custom of her society told her to do: in widow marriage she, along with the man she was marrying, was engaged in a violation of norms which no amount of apparent conformity could really disguise. And though

---

[159] Lucy Carroll, 'Law, Custom and Statutory Social Reform: The Hindu Widow Remarriage Act of 1856', in J. Krishnamurty, ed., *Women in Colonial India*.

[160] Sekhar Bandopadhyay, 'Social Mobility in Bengal in the late-19th-early-20th century' (unpublished thesis, Calcutta University, 1985), p. 480; Digindranarayan Bhattacharya, *Bidhabar Nirjala Ekadosi* (Serajgunj, 1923, 1926).

the emphasis was always on getting child widows remarried, neither Vidyasagar's arguments nor the law itself made any mention of age or virginity being a condition. In practice, widows marrying again would have been likely to be of somewhat maturer age than first-time child brides. It is unlikely that a socially dangerous second marriage could have been imposed on them.

Some of the verses composed during the height of the agitation do convey a real sense of rebellion: mostly in ridicule and outrage, but just occasionally in what seems to be celebration. Take some of the lines of the song said to have been inscribed on Santipur saris, of which only the first is commonly remembered. 'O when will that day dawn, when the law will be proclaimed / Orders will be passed in every district and region / Widow marriages will come in a rush / We will live happily, with husbands of our own choice / When will the day come, when the sufferings of widows will end. . . . '[161]

That, of course, was optimistic imagination, not reality: but an autobiography by a little-known Brahmo from Bikrampur, Gurucharan Mahalanobis (1833–1916), does reveal an instance of woman's agency. Gurucharan, unusual among Brahmos in never having formal English education, married a widow in 1862. Remarkably, as described in detail by Gurucharan, he had known her for some time before the marriage, and it was she who had taken the initiative. Indeed, there is a hint of a bit of romantic competition over the young man between her and another young girl who had also lost her husband. Vidyasagar, Gurucharan reports, was quite pleased when told of these unusual happpenings, and commented that an intelligent person should never agree to marry someone s/he had never seen. He did not come to the wedding — for Gurucharan, as a fervent young Brahmo who had discarded his sacred thread, refused to follow the Hindu forms — but remained close to the Mahalanobis family.[162]

The limits of Vidyasagar's ideas and reform activities still remain clear, particularly from today's feminist perspectives. The problems did not consist only in the kind of inconsistencies that we have seen emerging from his reform-through-texts strategy. The fundamental impulse, as in all nineteenth-century male *stri-swadhinata* (women's freedom — 'freeing women' would perhaps convey the implicit meaning better) initiatives, was 'protectionist' rather than

---

161 The full text of this song is given in Subolchandra Mitra, pp. 279–80.

162 Gurucharan Mahalanobis, 'Atmakatha', manuscript, c.1913: pub., ed. Nirmalkumari Mahalanobis (Calcutta, 1974), pp. 46–53.

egalitarian.[163] It sought through legal reform to improve the lot of the abala (weak), a term much in use in reformist discourses. Paternalist concern certainly differed from conventional patriarchal discipline, but it could slide towards ideologies of control. Vidyasagar was not entirely free, perhaps, from a certain fear of the 'over-independent' woman going beyond the bounds of (reformed and humanized) conjugality. All his tracts do have a moralizing strand, though to be sure usually on a minor key, which portrayed theoretically austere widowhood as in practice a realm of sexual license. (A license, it should be added immediately, that basically men enjoyed at the expense of widows, who would be left to bear the costs in terms of illicit abortion, infanticide, and scandal: Vidyasagar's moralism did also have a point.) Such fears probably help to explain the most obvious limit, even contradiction, in Vidyasagar's programme. It made no attempt at all (unlike Digindranarayan later on) to improve the lot of the widow who could not, or maybe did not wish to, marry again. When his own daughter returned home as a widow, Vidyasagar is said to have imposed the same austerities on himself for some time. A moving tale, within limits: there is no report that Vidyasagar ever asked her to defy the traditional rules, the inhumanities of which had been a major impulse behind his entire reform drive. There are also a few indications that by the late 1860s and 1870s an increasingly frustrated and cynical Vidyasagar was falling behind some of the younger Brahmos in the extent to which he was prepared to endorse radical patterns of behaviour. He rejected Miss Carpenter's proposal for starting a normal school to train women teachers on the grounds that 'respectable Hindus' would not allow 'their grown-up female relatives to follow the profession of tuition', while 'unprotected and helpless widows', whose services might be available, might not be 'morally . . . fit agents for educational purposes. . . . '[164] A last, very personal, inconsistency: there are many instances of husbands educating their wives in the nineteenth century, but Dinamoyee Devi, wife of the great educator and champion of companionate conjugality, seems to have remained virtually illiterate, spending much of her time looking after Vidyasagar's parents in Birsingha.

The failure, indeed absence of effort, to modify the conditions

[163] See the useful theoretical distinctions drawn in Ratna Kapur and Brenda Crossman, pp. 22–33.

[164] Vidyasagar to William Grey, 1 October 1867, reprinted in Subolchandra Mitra, p. 466.

of most married women, as well as of widows who did not remarry, may help us to understand the somewhat paradoxical appeal of a figure like Ramakrishna by the closing decades of the century. The saint's conversations were full of references to the dangers flowing from womankind: yet middle-aged and elderly wives and widows flocked to Dakshineswar. Like the men caught in the toils of chakri, they sought solace from the burdens of household routine in the message of *grihastha bhakti*, which promised a certain distancing through the cultivation of an inner devotional space, even while remaining immersed outwardly in the mundane everyday. Similarly, the withering of hopes in the transformative potential of education, as pressures on the middle class increased, may have had something to do with the resonance of Ramakrishna's denigration of formal learning, precisely among the educated.[165]

The biggest limit of all, so far as prospects of change in gender relations were concerned, was of course the absence, as yet, of autonomous, organized women's initiatives. Domestic domination and injustice — located 'within the precincts of their own respective domiciles', to use again Maheshchandra Deb's clumsy but expressive phrase, has always been peculiarly difficult to organize against, which is one reason why selfconscious feminist movements and even perceptions have been fairly rare in history. A few of the preconditions for them did start to emerge in Vidyasagar's times, however, sometimes as distant consequences of his work.

The spread of women's education, combined with the questioning of norms that Vidyasagar had provoked, led on towards the beginnings of a female literary public sphere in the decade that immediately followed the peak of his educational and reform initiatives. Three instances will have to suffice. The *Bamabodhini Patrika* was founded in 1863, run by reformist Brahmo men but greatly stimulating writings by women.[166] The same year saw the publication of Kailasbashini Devi's *Hindu Mahilaganer Heenabastha*. Kailasbashini had initially become literate at the behest of her husband, but her learning process still included an element of subversion, for it had to be kept a secret from her parents-in-law. Its results, as her husband confessed in his preface to the book, had surprised him, for the text by this neo-literate woman had needed no correction from her

---

165 See Chapter 8 of this book.

166 Bharati Ray is editing a valuable collection of extracts from this journal: Ray, ed, *Sekaler Narishiksha: Bamabodhini Patrika, 1270-1329 / 1863-1922* (Calcutta, 1994).

erstwhile teacher. In the sheer range of its survey of women's disabilities *Hindu Mahilaganer Heenabastha* rivals Vidyasagar's polemic against child marriage, for it includes within its sweep unequal treatment from childhood onwards, keeping girls uneducated and immersed in female rituals (*vratas*) which Kailasbashini considered meaningless, marrying them off in childhood into loveless conjugality, and exposing them to the miseries of Kulin polygamy. The accounts of married life and austere widowhood are especially poignant: child-brides torn from parental homes live as if in a prison, she says, caged like birds and animals. The agony of widows observing ekadosi provoked Kailasbashini to remark that only God can understand the wonders of the Hindu religion.[167] And then in 1868 there was Rashsundari Devi's *Amar Jivan*, the product of the lone, heroic efforts of an obscure, otherwise entirely conventional housewife, who had learnt her letters in fear and secrecy and gone on to publish the first autobiography in the Bengali language.[168]

Vidyasagar failed, in so far as the number of widows daring to remarry has remained almost negligible, and much social obloquy persists even today. But the legal reform he was able to push through, and even more the debates he provoked, did unsettle grossly unjust gender norms that had been part of a doxa of commonsense, immune from rational debate and questioning. That, maybe, is where reformist efforts to change laws can help, even when they remain largely unimplemented, or much misapplied.

There is also a paradoxical way in which the extent of resistance to widow remarriage itself bears witness to the significance and radical implications of Vidyasagar's crusade. Whatever the degree of their continued prevalence in practice, child marriage and polygamy are no longer considered normative, but the widow who remarries still generally invites criticism or worse. Widow remarriage was, and remains, disturbing, because it had implications that went some distance beyond what is quite often assumed in feminist circles today to have been the outer limit of nineteenth-century male reformism; a notion of companionate marriage that in essence represented yet another form of control over feminine sexuality. Vidyasagar's campaign, and the law it was able to push through,

---

[167] Kailasbashini Devi, *Hindu Mahilaganer Heenabastha* (Calcutta, Gupta Press, 1863).

[168] For Rashsundari, see Tanika Sarkar, 'A Book of Her Own, A Life of Her Own: Autobiography of a Nineteenth-Century Woman', *History Workshop Journal*, 36, 1993.

implicitly challenged the basic Hindu notion of the pure woman as *ardhangini*, half her husband's body even after the latter's death (and hence entitled to a share in his property as long as she does not remarry), who is permitted to have sex in the entire course of her life with one male partner, her husband, alone. (Here lay also the core of the double standard in Hindu conjugality, for there was no corresponding restraint on men.) The subversion implied in Vidyasagar's work was that he achieved the legalization of the remarriage, not of child-widows or virgins alone, but of adult women who would have had full-fledged sexual relations with their husbands, and may have borne children. The 'Great Unchastity Case' of 1873 drove the point home more sharply. It decided, going against general Hindu public opinion, that a widow who had not remarried but was proved to have committed 'adultery' subsequently (i.e. been 'unfaithful' to her deceased husband after his death) would retain her share of her husband's property. Vidyasagar, somewhat hesitantly, supported the majority judgement: 'I do not want to condone immorality. But how can property, once inherited, be taken away again?'[169] Bourgeois property right clearly triumphed in his mind in this case over customary norms of chastity.[170] It is also noteworthy that Vidyasagar's tracts on marriage sedulously avoided the standard language of describing the husband as the supreme, near-divine, preceptor of the wife. It emphasized repeatedly, rather, the dimension of mutuality, the meeting of adult minds and bodies. Vidyasagar obviously remained far from any questioning of the limits of ideal monogamous marriage, but he was still an uncompromising critic of double standards, and the weight he was prepared to give to theoretical equality of rights remains quite remarkable.[171]

The protectionist compassion of Vidyasagar was recuperable into socially innocuous philanthropy, and that quickly became, and remains, the dominant way of representing him. But his was a compassion associated above all with anger, and a deep sense of

[169] Biharilal Sarkar, p. 332.

[170] My assessment of the significance of widow marriage has been greatly helped by Tanika Sarkar, 'Talking about Scandals: Religion, Law and Love in Late Nineteenth Century Bengal', *Studies in History*, 13i, 1997.

[171] The second widow-remarriage tract, for instance, did some skilful bending of the shastras to reach the conclusion that 'carefully studied, the makers of the shastras may be seen to have wanted the same rules for men as for women.' Haldar, Volume II, p. 156.

male guilt. It is this which distinguishes his widow-marriage campaign from apparently similar later moves, notably under Arya Samaj auspices, where there was a shift in emphasis to the need for breeding faster and better for religious community and/or country. Anger and guilt, too, have been often diffused or displaced on to external targets, in the heyday of anti-colonial nationalism, but also in much more recent times, through writings where Western 'post-Enlightenment modernity' becomes the primary polemical target.

We cannot afford to lose touch with Vidyasagar's anger and guilt, directed primarily towards gender relations in his own society. For we live in times when wives are regularly burnt for dowry, a lower-caste woman activist is raped for campaigning against child marriage, and the murderers of Roop Kanwar, burnt as sati at Deorala in 1987, are acquitted in court.

8

Kaliyuga, Chakri and Bhakti: Ramakrishna and His Times[*]

'[Head]-master: "Tell me, does he read a lot of books?"'
Brinde [servant-girl]: "Why should he need books? Its all in his
words."
The master had just come from his books. He was amazed to
discover that Thakur Sri Ramakrishna never read books.'

> — From description of Mahendranath Gupta's
> first visit to Ramakrishna, February 1882, in
> 'M' *Ramakrishna-Kathamrita*, ı, p. 17.[1]

The sudden entry of print culture and Western education, along
with the creative indigenous response to them through vernacular prose, valorized book-learning to an unprecedented extent
among the colonial middle class of nineteenth-century Bengal. Sacred
Hindu texts became widely available in written form for the first

[*] Reprinted, with minor changes, from *Economic and Political Weekly*, xxvıı
29, 18 July 1992. Another version has been published as 'An Exploration of
the Ramakrishna–Vivekananda Tradition', in the series *Socio-Religious Movements
and Cultural Networks in Indian Civilisation: Occasional Paper I* (Shimla, Indian
Institute of Advanced Study, 1993). Earlier drafts of parts of this essay have
appeared as 'The Kathamrita as Text: Towards an Understanding of Ramakrishna Paramahansa' (Occasional Paper No. 22, Nehru Memorial Museum and
Library, New Delhi, 1985), and 'Ramakrishna and the Calcutta of His Times'
('The Calcutta Psyche'), *India International Centre Quarterly*, Winter, 1990-1. The
present text owes much to the searching criticisms and correction of Tanika
Sarkar and to comments by Hitesranjan Sanyal and Dipesh Chakrabarty.
[1] I am using the 1980-2 reprints of 'M' (Mahendranath Gupta)'s 5-volume
Sri Sri Ramakrishna-Kathamrita (first published, Calcutta, 1902, 1904, 1908, 1910,
1932). Henceforward *KM*. The translations are mine.

time, and printed matter became far more accessible than manuscripts could ever have been. Higher education, now being made indispensable for respectable jobs and professions, was imparted through a foreign language, far removed from everyday speech, which could be learnt only through books. Contact with a culture which claimed superior status by virtue of its rationality and science stimulated efforts to use self-consciously 'rational' arguments to modify or defend institutions and ideas now felt to be 'traditional'. Time acquired new meaning and disciplinary authority through an equally abrupt entry of clocks and watches, and there was among some a sense of moving forward in consonance with its linear progress. Foreign rule, however humiliating, had brought the gift of 'modern' culture for the new English-educated literati, and maybe its evils could be reduced or eliminated through gradual reform. A premium, consequently, was placed on varied forms of social activism: education, religious and social reform, revivalism, philanthropy, patriotic endeavour.

And yet, at the very heart of it all, there was that strange, sudden trek of the Calcutta bhadralok in the late 1870s and early 1880s to a man who seemed to represent the very opposite of all such valorizations and initiatives. Ramakrishna Paramahansa (c. 1836–86), hitherto an obscure Dakshineswar temple priest of humble village Brahman origin, had virtually no English, and not even much formal vernacular (or Sanskrit) schooling. He thought little of rationalistic argument, considered organized efforts to improve social conditions futile, preached an apparently timeless message of *bhakti* in rustic language, and claimed to have seen, many times, the Goddess Kali face to face. The cult that developed around Ramakrishna remained an essentially bhadralok affair in Bengal, with some extensions later, again invariably among educated people, in other provinces and abroad through the efforts of Vivekananda and the Ramakrishna Mission. Some fifty years after Ramakrishna's death, a short story imagined two devout elderly women meeting at Benaras: the city lady was full of Ramakrishna, the village woman had never heard of him.[2] Today, an average middle- or lower-middle-class Hindu household in Bengal can be expected to have a portrait of Ramakrishna somewhere, along with, quite possibly, a well-thumbed copy of the *Kathamrita*.

---

[2] Bibhutibhushan Bandopadhyay, *Drobomoyeer Kashibas*, in Bandopadhyay, *Galpasamagra* (Calcutta, 1975).

It was the *Kathamrita* which first aroused my interest, as a historian, in Ramakrishna, with its claim to be a diary-based record of the conversation of the Dakshineswar saint between February 1882 and August 1886. Not just scattered saintly *obiter dicta*, in other words, but actual conversation: here, it was tempting to assume, we have something close to G.M. Young's definition of the ideal social history document through which we can eavesdrop on the people of the past talking among themselves. More significantly, the *Kathamrita* was a product of something like a liminal moment, a two-way crossing of social frontiers — the rustic Brahman becoming the guru of the city bhadralok, the latter falling under the spell of an idiom, values, and personality very different from their own. Both trajectories needed to be problematized and explored, for perhaps they could add something to our understanding of village culture and religion on the one hand, and the contradictions of bhadralok life on the other.

The passage in the *Kathamrita* which describes Mahendranath Gupta's first visit to Ramakrishna introduces us to this intersection of apparently very distinct worlds. The diarist-author had stood third in the BA examinations in 1874, and in 1882 he was headmaster of a North Calcutta school controlled by Ishwarchandra Vidyasagar[3] — the 'ocean of learning', famous social reformer, and philanthropist. It was natural for a man like Mahendranath to assume that wisdom and reading books were all but synonymous: the five-volume compendium he prepared from his diary, however, would eventually celebrate the surrender of men like him to a near-illiterate villager who never read books. Brinde, the servant-girl, almost certainly illiterate, had no problem in accepting that true wisdom and holiness had nothing to do with written culture. But Ramakrishna was not interested in having devotees like her, and he is said to have disliked the crowds of villagers that came to see him when he occasionally visited Kamarpukur, where he had been born.[4] The *Kathamrita*, as well as biographical accounts of Ramakrishna, in contrast, repeatedly describe how the saint often went out of his way to win over bhadralok devotees.[5] This might appear to be a 'natural' process of

[3] Biographical sketch of Mahendranath Gupta, appended to *KM* I.

[4] *Life of Sri Ramakrishna Compiled from Various Authentic Sources* (Mayavati 1924, Calcutta, 1964), pp. 290–1. Henceforward *Life*.

[5] The major canonical biography is Swami Saradananda, *Sri Sri Ramakrishna-Lilaprasanga* (Calcutta, 1911–19, 1979). Henceforward *L*. All intimate disciples of Ramakrishna were of educated bhadralok origin, with the solitary exception of Latu, the Bihari servant of Ramchandra Datta.

upward mobility. It was conditioned, however, by a colonial situation which had obliged many members of the traditional village or small-town-based upper-caste literati to move to the metropolis, try to take to English education, or − like Ramakrishna − become a rather new kind of guru for middle-class bhadralok. The ascent into urban bhadralok society also left traces in Ramakrishna's discourse in a changing pattern of stresses and silences which can tell us something about varied appropriations of apparently common religious traditions at different social levels.

For men like Mahendranath there was clearly an initial hesitation, but also a passionate eagerness to cross this threshold. The attraction for opposites here reveals a deep disquiet among sections of the bhadralok, at least in some moods, about assumptions and styles of activity which on the surface ruled their lives. There were reasons, we shall see, why such a sense of aridity and dissatisfaction manifested itself precisely in the 1870s and 1880s. A certain differentiation within bhadralok social space also needs to be taken into account. English education brought reasonable success in professions and services for some, though even there the highest rungs would be occupied by Englishmen. For many more, it came to connote only humble clerical jobs *(chakri)* in government or mercantile offices, once again usually British-controlled. Ramakrishna's message developed a particular resonance in this second, often half-forgotten, world of the unsuccessful bhadralok. Chakri, I intend to argue, is crucial for understanding Ramakrishna and situating him within the overall context of colonial domination. It helps also to highlight a sense of internal difference, inadequate awareness of which, I feel, has made the recent studies of the *Kathamrita* by Partha Chatterjee somewhat monochromatic.[6] The Ramakrishna tradition, at least arguably, may have become in our own times an undifferentiated 'religion of urban domesticity'. Reading that back into the beginnings of that cult, in terms of a homogenized colonial middle class confronting Western cultural domination, appears to me to be more than a little teleological.

If Ramakrishna attracted bhadralok through his 'Otherness', this was to a considerable extent an Other constructed by the bhadralok themselves. There is no direct written testimony left by the saint: we know about him only from bhadralok disciples and admirers,

6 Partha Chatterjee, 'A Religion of Urban Domesticity: Sri Ramakrishna and the Calcutta Middle Class', in Partha Chatterjee and Gyanendra Pandey (eds), *Subaltern Studies VII* (Delhi, 1992); see also Chatterjee, *The Nation and Its Fragments* (Delhi, 1994), Chapter III.

and the texts they composed simultaneously illuminate — and transform. This is not necessarily a disadvantage, for the logic of bhadralok appropriations constitutes our major field of interest. The *Kathamrita* occasionally beckons beyond it towards a less assimilated Ramakrishna, by virtue of its effort to preserve direct conversation and its relatively non-canonized character.[7] But on the whole it is not a perhaps unapproachable 'original' Ramakrishna-by-himself, but Ramakrishna as constituted in the gaze of the late-nineteenth-century bhadralok, who is of central importance in any exploration of the Ramakrishna–Vivekananda tradition.[**]

The *Kathamrita* was published from fifteen to fifty years after the sessions with Ramakrishna, and covers a total of only 186 days spread over the last four and a half years of the saint's life. The full text of the original diary has never been made publicly available. Considered as a constructed 'text' rather than simply as a more-or-less authentic 'source', the *Kathamrita* reveals the presence of certain fairly selfconscious authorial strategies. There is in particular a deployment of paradox which simultaneously points towards an overarching harmony. The high degree of 'truth-effect' undeniably conveyed by the *Kathamrita* to twentieth-century readers is related to its display of testimonies to authenticity, careful listing of 'types of evidence',[8] and

---

[7] Thus the Ramakrishna described in the *KM* (its author, incidentally, never formally joined the Ramakrishna Mission) did not wear saffron, used polished slippers or shoes, slept on a bed under a mosquito net: visitors were often surprised by his appearance and dress (*KM* III, p. 1). Later iconic representations of Ramakrishna invariably present him in the garb of a conventional sanyasi. The one contemporary photograph that exists is hardly ever used in the canonical literature. I have seen only one reproduction of it, in Brojen Banerji and Sajanikanta Das, *Sri Ramkrishna Samasamayik Drishtite* (Calcutta, 1952). This shows Ramakrishna in a dance of ecstasy with Brahmos at Keshabchandra Sen's house in September 1879: he is not markedly different in dress from the other bhadralok, apart from a rather shabby rusticity.

[**] I feel now that my initial paper on Ramakrishna, entitled 'Kathamrita as Text: Towards an Understanding of Ramakrishna Paramahansa', despite its title, was insufficiently aware of these dimensions. I am grateful for the comments and criticisms of Hitesranjan Sanyal and, particularly, Dipesh Chakrabarty, as well as others attending the seminar at the Calcutta University History Department, where I presented the paper mentioned above in 1985.

[8] Each volume of the *KM* begins with an analysis of 'Three Kinds of Evidence' — 'direct and recorded on the same day', 'direct but unrecorded', and 'hearsay and unrecorded' — and the text claims to be based on the first type. Vivekananda's praise of the author for having kept himself 'entirely hidden', unlike Plato with Socrates, is quoted, along with testimonies from Ramakrishna's wife

meticulous references to exact dates and times. We are reminded that the nineteenth century had brought a new vogue for precise biographies and histories. But the man whose conversation was being presented had been attractive to the bhadralok partly because he had been bored by formal logic,[9] preferred parables and analogies to precise argumentation, and often expressed a deep aversion for the discipline of time.

There is, then, a deliberate foregrounding, throughout, of the learned literate knowledge/unlearned oral wisdom polarity. We never meet Brinde again: her one appearance was clearly to set the scene for this contrast. Quotations from high-Hindu sacred texts *(shastras)* and references to abstract religious and philosophical doctrines embellish the *Kathamrita* as chapter headings and footnotes – in obvious stylistic contrast to Ramakrishna's own colloquial idiom. The point being made, however, is precisely that there is no fundamental conflict. The paradoxes which abound in the *Kathamrita* raise doubts about bhadralok assumptions (like the inherent superiority of textual learning which underlay Mahendranath's initial query to Brinde) but eventually reinforce accepted categories.[10] A wonderful affinity is shown to prevail between Ramakrishna's unlearned wisdom and the shastras, mutually confirming the avatar status of the saint and the eternal validity of the holy's texts. As the *Lilaprasanga*, the canonical biography brought out by the Ramakrishna Mission, stated in 1911: 'The coming of the *thakur* this time as an illiterate was to prove the truth of all the shastras'.[11] We need to ponder over the implications of a textual strategy – and movement – that felt the need to simultaneously display and reconcile learned/ illiterate, city-educated/rustic differences.

Ramakrishna, then, was an appropriated and partially bhadralok-constructed Other with whom an urban group plagued with a sense of alienation from roots could relate without undue discomfort. Late-nineteenth-century Bengal had its rural rebels, its troublesome tribal, low-caste, or Muslim illiterates: the 1870s and 1880s in particular were marked by acute agrarian tension over rents and tenant rights. Bhadralok society, even the clerical underdogs of which

---

and some other prominent disciples.

[9] *KM* I, p. 30 (5 March 1882).

[10] For an argument stressing this dual nature of paradox particularly in religious discourse, see Megan McLaughlin, 'Gender Paradox and the Otherness of God', *Gender and History*, III 2, Summer 1991.

[11] *L* I, pp. 264–5.

could at times have a bit of rental income through petty intermediate tenure-holding in the Permanent Settlement hierarchy,[12] naturally preferred empathy with the countryside through a figure like Ramakrishna. Despite the apparent vehemence of his rejection of book-learning and activism, acceptance of Ramakrishna, we shall see, did not usually involve any sharp or total break with normal forms of bhadralok life and activity. These could still be carried on, but in a new way, enriched by a spirituality and inner life suited to the times, which helped to mitigate a deepening sense of anomie.

There was little obviously new in Ramakrishna's teachings. That may have been one of his strengths, for through Ramakrishna the city bhadralok could imagine themselves to be reaching back to lost traditional moorings in the countryside, in simple faith conveyed through rustic language. The central message was one of bhakti, valorizing, as bhakti has often done, quiet inner devotion over textual exegesis, time-consuming ritual, and external action. The catholicity of 'many views, many paths' (yata mat, tato path) which became one of Ramakrishna's principal titles to fame, also has many earlier — and nineteenth-century — counterparts. What is significant, and valuable for historical analysis, is the way Ramakrishna contextualized such themes through parables and similes drawn from contemporary everyday rural and bhadralok life. Thus the critique of the printed word takes the form of a comment about English-educated people who refuse to believe that a house is collapsing before their eyes till it is confirmed by that characteristic nineteenth-century innovation, the newspaper.[13] And very specific forms of bhadralok social activism are listed in a story Ramakrishna seems to have particularly liked to relate, for it is repeated no less than six times in the *Kathamrita*:

Sambhu Mallik wanted to talk about hospitals, dispensaries, schools, roads, and tanks . . . Giving just alms at Kalighat, not seeing Kali herself! (Laughter) . . . So I told Sambhu, if you meet *Iswara*, will you ask him to build some hospitals and dispensaries? (Laughter). The *bhakta* will never say that. He will rather say, *Thakur*, let me stay near your lotus-feet, keep me always near you, give me pure *bhakti*.[14]

12 See, for instance, Asok Sen, 'Agrarian Structure and Tenancy Laws in Bengal, 1850–1900', in Sen, *et al.*, *Perspectives in Social Sciences 2* (Calcutta, 1982).

13 *KM* I, p. 219 (22 October 1885).

14 *KM* I, p. 51 (27 October 1882). The passage is repeated with minor variations in *KM* I, pp. 127–8 (15 June 1884); *KM* II, p. 166 (11 October 1884); *KM* III, p. 215 (18 October 1885); *KM* IV, p. 50 (5 January 1884); and *KM* V, p. 202 (6 December 1884).

His audience was clearly appreciative, in the early 1880s. We will have to consider why, and for how long — since Vivekananda would subsequently make systematic philanthropy the central thrust of the Mission he founded in Ramakrishna's name.

Images drawn from quotidian life have been common in Indian religious discourses, and particularly in bhakti. But the precise situating of such images, in juxtaposition with other kinds of historical evidence, is much easier with a firmly datable nineteenth-century figure like Ramakrishna than it would be, say, with Kabir or Mirabai. Thus Ramakrishna's conception of evil repeatedly linked together *kamini, kanchan*, and the *dasatya* of chakri: lust, as embodied invariably in women, gold, and the bondage of the office job. Wives with their luxurious ways instil into their husbands a thirst for money, and this in turn forces men into office work. The temptations of kamini and kanchan are age-old themes, but their association with chakri is new. We meet this triad again in a multitude of late-nineteenth-century vernacular plays, farces and tracts as the correlated evils of Kaliyuga, the last and worst of the four-fold succession of eras in the traditional Hindu conception of cyclical time. A 2000-year-old motif took on new specific contours under colonial rule, which had abruptly introduced the discipline of clock time, and imposed it so far mainly in government offices and mercantile firms.

Language is vital here: we can get close to Ramakrishna, who left behind no systematic exposition, only through images. The parables through which Ramakrishna expounded his conception of bhakti held out the image of a traditional, paternalistic, caring overlord, to whom the devotee could come close through faithful service — the polar opposite of the impersonal, alien, sahib of the nineteenth-century office. The alternative, and on the whole preferred, model was an escape from all effort and tension, even those of loving service, through an unquestioning, childlike surrender to the Mother Goddess, Kali. The first kind of devotion represented a well-known Vaishnava *bhava* (mood), the second embodied the alternative Shakta tradition as modified in the eighteenth century by Ramprasad, Ramakrishna's favourite poet. But bhakti in both forms, I intend to argue, had been modulated by felt evils of a specific, historically conditioned kind. It had at first a mainly clerical lower-middle-class ambience, but could attract the more successful bhadralok, too, in their more inward-turning moods.

For Ramakrishna, the woman to whom one could not relate as to a mother invariably represents the threat of kamini, lust incarnate. Not least among the many paradoxes of the Ramakrishna movement is the way a saint with such apparent misogynist traits came to have many enthusiastic women devotees: middle-aged or elderly bhadralok housewives and widows, even actresses of prostitute origin. This was happening after a generation of male bhadralok initiatives concentrated on women's questions and seeking what by the 1860s was being called 'stri swadhinata', the 'freeing' of women through education and reform from the more obvious of patriarchal disabilities and prejudices (sati, the ban on widow remarriage, polygamy). Ramakrishna cared nothing about such efforts, and yet one of the principal leaders of social reform, the Brahmo Keshabchandra Sen — who had persuaded the government to pass a very modern marriage law for his sect in 1872 — became in the late 1870s the first really prominent bhadralok to become an admirer of the Dakshineswar saint. Once again, the interrelations between Ramakrishna and the bhadralok offer an entry point into crucial tensions and contradictions, this time related to gender. There were interesting shifts within the Ramakrishna movement, too. Sarada Debi, Ramakrishna's wife, was kept very much in the background in the saint's lifetime, living in a tiny room, cooking and looking after her husband, and talking to women devotees alone. Ramakrishna rigorously abstained from sexual relations with Sarada, and worshipped her as embodiment of the Divine Mother one night as the culminating point of his years of passionate spiritual quest (sadhana).[15] After Ramakrishna's death Sarada Debi became a major cult figure of the movement in her own right, revered as Sri Ma or Holy Mother. Shifting constructions and images of womanhood in fact will be quite central to our analysis: gender has to be not an afterthought, but at the very core of any understanding of Ramakrishna and Vivekananda.

My principal focus is on the initial interaction between Ramakrishna and the Calcutta bhadralok in the late 1870s and early 1880s as embedded above all in the *Kathamrita*. This provides, I argue, an exceptionally privileged but little-explored ground for understanding some of the ways in which Hindu religious traditions came to be modified to meet the new pressures and demands of colonial middle-class life. What we call Hinduism today is, in its crystallized form, to a considerable extent a relatively new, late-nineteenth-century

---

15 *Life*, p. 250.

construction, and the Ramakrishna movement played a significant role in its emergence.[16] This happened particularly through the varied appropriations of Ramakrishna that continued across time and seemed to abruptly change their nature a decade or so after Ramakrishna's death through the efforts of his best-known disciple. Vivekananda achieved a tour-de-force which apparently inverted much of his master's teaching. He gave crucial importance to organized philanthropy, serving the 'daridranarayan' (God embodied in poor folk): the conversation with Sambhu Mallik consequently had to be excised totally from the canonical biography.[17] Emphasis was shifted from bhakti towards the other two *margas* (ways) of high-Hindu spiritual quest, Vedantic *jnana* (knowledge) and karma (redefined now as social service rather than ritual), and Ramakrishna's catholicity was made into an argument for the essential superiority of an aggressive and muscular Hinduism. Vivekananda's tours abroad and across India raised the social status of the Ramakrishna movement in Bengal, and the humble world of clerical chakri lost some of its centrality.

Vivekananda, however, must not be reduced to a mere series of inversions of Ramakrishna, for the shifts were related to the opening up of dimensions virtually unknown to his master. Schematically, these can be represented as the problematizations of western domination, of 'Bharatvarsha' seen through the prism of an ideally unified Hindu world, and of the village, low castes, and poor people generally as standing in need of wholesale upliftment. Vivekananda, again, like Ramakrishna before him, quickly became open to multiple appropriations, though in his case the existence of authenticated writings and correspondence make the question of a 'real' or 'original' Swamiji less chimerical. There is Vivekananda the 'patriot-prophet', patron-saint for a whole generation of Swadeshi enthusiasts, revolutionary terrorists, and nationalists in general. More relevant today, and ominously so, is the image of the Swami as one of the founders of twentieth-century 'Hindutva', of an unified and chauvinistic Hinduism.

I can only hope to lightly touch on some of these many dimensions here. A comprehensive discussion obviously demands a separate paper, which would also have to explore in detail the

---

[16] I am borrowing the term 'crystallization' from W. Cantwell Smith, 'The Crystallization of Religious Communities in Mughal India' in his *On Understanding Islam: Selected Studies* (Hague, 1981), Chapter 9.

[17] *L* I, pp. 370-3, gives a longish account of Ramakrishna contacts with Sambhu Mallik, but completely omits the conversation quoted six times in *KM*.

new social compulsion and aspirations of the 1890s which must have conditioned Vivekananda's initiatives. But it is equally impossible to leave Vivekananda out of any study of Ramakrishna. His influence has indelibly marked nearly all the texts we have about Ramakrishna — though the *Kathamrita* less so than most[18] — and there was never any conscious or complete rupture. We cannot ignore the question as to how that continuity remained possible. Vivekananda was recognized by most people as Ramakrishna's authentic heir, and his reputation, in fact, helped to establish, extend, and perpetuate Ramakrishna's own image as apostle of an apparently very different kind of devotion. A quietistic, inward-looking bhakti, which in certain circumstances can develop into its apparent opposite: there are implications here of deep contemporary interest and concern.

II

Ramakrishna's interaction with the Calcutta bhadralok has given us an initial impression of a series of opposites which attract each other, a bridging of different 'worlds' or 'levels', of frontiers that were 'difficult' and yet 'had to be crossed'.[19] It is time to attempt greater precision about what worlds we are talking about, and when and why they were sought to be bridged.

Binaries like elite/popular, city/country, or bhadralok/peasant are of limited help in exploring the tensions that structure the *Kathamrita*. Ramakrishna, for a start, was not a peasant, but a poor Brahman from Kamarpukur village in Hooghly district. The family plot was tiny; it was, nevertheless, cultivated by agricultural labourers.[20] Gadadhar Chattopadhyay (born in 1836) as a boy played with children of low-caste artisans. His high-caste status helped him to become a friend, however, of the local zamindar's son, and the scanty formal schooling he received was at a *pathshala* run in that landlord's house. Around 1850 he was brought to Calcutta by his elder brother

---

18 The contrasts between *KM* and *L* are particularly relevant here — see Walter G. Neevel (Jr), 'The Transformation of Ramakrishna' in Bardwell L. Smith, *Hinduism: New Essays on History of Religion* (London, 1976).

19 'A difficult borderland and . . . frontiers that had to be crossed' — terms used by Raymond Williams while discussing writers like George Eliot, Thomas Hardy, and D.H. Lawrence in an analysis of a somewhat similar problematic, in *The Country and the City* (London, 1973), p. 316.

20 *L* I, *Purbakatha o Balyajivan*, p. 41; *Life*, p. 5.

Ramakumar. The paddy grown on the family plot was not sufficient to balance the rising cost of cloth and other necessities, and Ramakumar's own income as *smriti* expert from rulings on ritual disputes was also drying up.[21]

Kamarpukur, once noted for weaving and other crafts, had started to decline. It was afflicted by 'Burdwan fever' (malaria), and hit, like so many parts of the West Bengal moribund delta, by a combination of ecological change, disruption of drainage due to railways, and decline of crafts before imported manufactures. The traditional high-caste literati, experts in Sanskrit learning alone, were facing a crisis as English education increasingly became the prerequisite for entry into the respectable professions.

Ramakrishna's own family, however, was saved from ruin by the patronage of the upstart Kaivarta zamindars of Janbazar in Calcutta. Rani Rashmoni had just completed the Dakshineswar temple but was finding *pujaris* (priests) difficult to get because of her low-caste origin. Ramakrishna and Ramakumar eventually obliged.[22] Ramakrishna's passionate and wayward sadhana soon made him abandon formal priestly duties and many at that time thought he had gone mad. Rashmoni and then her son-in-law Mathur, however, continued looking after his simple needs. A deed of endowment stabilized Ramakrishna's position in 1858, though on a rather minimal basis.[23] Other patrons and devotees started coming in after Mathur's death in 1871: the philanthropist Sambhu Mallik, who had a garden house adjoining Dakshineswar temple; a high official of the Nepal durbar posted in Calcutta named Biswanath Upadhyaya; and, from 1875, after Ramakrishna had sought out and impressed the Keshab Sen circle, a growing number of English-educated professional men, clerks, and students.[24]

Details like these, placed against a background of crisis of the traditional literati, help us to understand some of the complexities in Ramakrishna's attitude towards well-off learned folk, the masters of the written or printed word. They add a deeper social meaning to the orality/literacy contrast with which we began and which in different forms will accompany us throughout our essay. *Baramanush* or *baralok*

---

[21] *L* I, pp. 122-4.

[22] *Life*, pp. 45-57.

[23] The cash payment amounted to Rs 5 per month, together with stipulated quantities of food and cloth, *KM* II, p. ix (for text of deed of endowment); *L* II; *Dibyabhave o Narendra*, p. 350.

[24] *Life*, pp. 250-8, 269-70, 297-303, 307-10, 370-5, 430-50, 470-1.

(rich, literally big people) patrons were essential for survival, even if they occasionally happened to be of low-caste origin or embodied cultural values in many ways alien to Ramakrishna. They had, in fact, to be sought for — and yet were resented at the same time.

Ramakrishna loved to recall that his father, despite poverty, had never accepted gifts from Shudras.[25] That to him was the role-model of the unbending old-world Brahman, asserting ritual purity at all costs over wealth and power: admirable, but unrealistic, for Ramakrishna himself was spending his adult life as a dependant of a Kaivarta zamindar. From this, perhaps, followed a self-mocking description. Ramakrishna once confessed that from boyhood on he had been a 'sukher paira [pigeon that seeks comfort]. I frequented well off households, but ran away from houses where I saw suffering.'[26] Ramakrishna admits to a weakness, mildly ridicules himself, and at the same time confesses that he had been unable to rid himself of an unfortunate trait. Implicit here is the danger of an opposite, degenerate model of the Brahman turned self-seeker, currying favour from rich but low-caste patrons — the very type, one could add, of the decadent Brahman of many texts denouncing Kaliyuga. The 'mad' sadhana through which Ramakrishna eventually gained recognition as holy man and preceptor typified a third, subtler form of negotiation with the baramanush of the world, through which patronage could be won without loss of self-respect. In the days of his 'madness', when recognition was still to come, Ramakrishna had prayed: 'Mother, if the zamindars of my desh [village home] show me respect, I will believe that all this [his visions] is true. Then even they came to talk to me on their own.' Acknowledgement by the baramanush remains indispensable, but the zamindars now come 'on their own' to the hitherto humble, unknown temple pujari. Holy madness also gives a licence to mock authority. Ramakrishna recalled with considerable satisfaction that his 'madness' had permitted him then to say 'things bluntly and straight out to people. I showed no deference for anyone, had no fear of baralok.'[27] He had even slapped Rani Rashmoni once, for being inattentive during a devotional song.[28] The years of tempestuous sadhana were over, and Ramakrishna was now a respectable guru of the bhadralok: he still looked back on those mad years with pride.

[25] Life, p. 7; L I, p. 40.
[26] KM V, p. 45 (10 June 1883).
[27] KM II, p. 49 (4 June 1883).
[28] KM II, pp. 2-3 (16 October 1882).

The ambiguity persisted throughout. Thus Ramakrishna, by then quite a well-established figure, took special care to button himself up while going to visit Vidyasagar. In course of their conversation, however, he informed Vidyasagar that the celebrated reformer was like a ship, he himself a tiny boat. But ships may run aground in small streams, boats sail freely on rivers big or small.[29] Subservience and resentment, we shall see, would jostle at the heart of Ramakrishna's central conception of bhakti, with divinity at times patterned by him on the model of the baramanush patron in a relationship that was acceptable but not tension-free. For a man like Ramakrishna, resentment would always fall far short of overt critique. The occasional mockery of the powerful would be inextricably mingled with deference. Ramakrishna's attitudes recall, perhaps, that 'sideward glance' of 'muffled challenge' with which the St Petersburg clerk looks at his superiors in Dostoyevski's *Poor Folk*.[30] Such ambiguity towards power would be shared by many of Ramakrishna's bhadralok audience, and, more particularly, by its clerical component.

If Ramakrishna was ambivalent towards the superior ones of his world, the baralok, a second kind of ambiguity surfaces in the parables drawn from nature and rural life which are so abundant in his discourse. Virtual absence of formal learning kept Ramakrishna's original world not too distant from the oral culture of peasants, artisans, and village women. But birth in a high-caste family with some reputation for ritual expertise already meant a certain distancing, and Ramakrishna himself moved away from the village towards the new world of city bhadralok. The *Kathamrita* conversations provide rich evidence about the tensions of a never-quite-completed movement: they help us to appreciate, too, the ways through which Ramakrishna's language itself became an additional attraction for his urban devotees. Late-nineteenth-century bhadralok writing had changed recently in the direction of greater chastity and decorum, with the prose of Vidyasagar and Bankimchandra rejecting as vulgar the style associated with earlier literary figures like Iswar Gupta. Such self-imposed restraints perhaps at times became slightly oppressive, as creating an uncomfortable distance from everyday speech. The *Kathamrita* insisted on keeping Ramakrishna's colloquialisms, and presented to its readers a language that seemed attractively earthy and unsophisticated, and yet perfectly understandable.

[29] *KM* III, p. 16 (5 August 1882).
[30] Mikhail Bakhtin, *Problems of Dostoyevski's Poetics* (Leningrad, 1929, Moscow, 1963; trans. Manchester, 1984), pp. 205, 210.

The remarkable thing about Ramakrishna's nature imagery is the unselfconscious ease with which he passes from similes conventionally beautiful, to others that would seldom be mentioned in chaste late-nineteenth-century bhadralok writing. The sea, blue from a distance but colourless close by, indicates the equal validity of *sakar* and *nirakar* types of devotion — conceiving divinity as with or without form.[31] Steadfastness in yogic devotion is conveyed by the image of a bird sitting with total concentration on its egg.[32] But villagers defecating around a Kamarpukur pond can serve Ramakrishna's purpose as well, and as often as sea or birds,[33] and there are also caustic comments about the Brahmo habit of dwelling constantly on the beauty of God's creation. They admire the garden, said Ramakrishna, and forget to look for its owner or *babu*.[34] There is no 'dissociation of sensibility'[35] in Ramakrishna, no marking out of a distinct realm of subject or diction as proper or poetic. Nature in his conversation is different from the way it is represented in the occasional formal set descriptions Mahendranath Gupta gives of the surroundings of Dakshineswar, in imagery derived through Bankimchandra's prose ultimately from canons of Sanskrit aesthetics. It differs also from the style of the 'romantic' poetry of nature being developed, precisely around the 1880s, by Biharilal Chakrabarti and Rabindranath.

Nature to Ramakrishna was not yet a spectacle of sheer beauty, to be admired through a distinct and self-conscious aesthetic sensibility. It was also something impregnated with human labour. It is remarkable how often the everyday toil of peasants, artisans and women is made to convey messages with a positive content — unlike, we shall see, most of Ramakrishna's images drawn from city life. The peasant, sticking to his ancestral land even if crops have failed in a year of drought, working carefully and hard to bring just the right amount of water to his field from a distance, is often made to epitomise the perseverance needed for true bhakti.[36] The housewife

31 *KM* I, p. 59 (28 October 1882).

32 *KM* III, pp. 19–20 (24 August 1882).

33 *KM* I, p. 74 (December 1882).

34 *KM* II, p. 75 (28 November 1883); *KM* V, p. 62 (18 August 1883); *KM* I, p. 150 (19 October 1884).

35 The phrase used by T.S. Eliot to emphasize the contrast between the literature of the times of Shakespeare and Donne, and that of Milton and his successors. See also Raymond Williams, *Country and City*, for a similar disjunction in the evolution of the pastoral.

36 *KM* I, p. 71 (14 December 1882); *KM* II, p. 33 (8 April 1883); *KM* IV, p. 84 (23 March 1884); *KM* V, p. 104 (2 January 1884), 135 (22 February 1885).

who prepares fish in various ways to suit the distinct palates of her many children becomes the symbol of the multiplicity of paths to the divine.[37] The bhakta can remain in the world but not be lost in its temptations, like village women minding their babies, talking to customers while they work at the *dheki* (husking machine), careful that their hands do not get injured.[38] Evident in such parables is a love and delight in the sensuous details of rural workaday life, where individual labour can be seen to produce immediate, palpable results: land yielding crops, women turning fish into many dishes, grain being husked into rice. City life — and more particularly the life of the intellectual and the clerk — must have appeared singularly bereft of this feel of sensuous productivity, to Ramakrishna as well as to his audience.

The valorization of rural labour, again, is often associated with the questioning of the dry abstract arrogance of formal written culture, the *jnana* of pandits or of the English-educated. Seeing is better than hearing, and hearing is better than reading, Ramakrishna liked to say.[39] True religious awareness is like the practical knowledge about varieties of yarn picked up by the apprentice, never from books, but through serving a master-weaver.[40] Such passages indicate not a general 'withdrawal' from jnana and karma, as has been recently argued,[41] but a valorization of village labour and oral practical wisdom over city life and the written culture of the literati, old or new.

Ramakrishna's fables are often imbued with a strong note of peasant wisdom and practicality. The pandit crossing the Ganga boasts of his shastric knowledge. But then a storm begins and he does not know how to swim. His companion says: 'I may not know *Sankhya* and *Patanjali*, but I can swim.'[42] Of the three friends who meet a tiger in the forest, the true bhakta is the one who climbs up a tree, not the man who resigns himself to death, or even the third who calls on Iswara for succour. The bhakta loves God so much that he says: 'Why bother Iswara with this?' His of course is also the most practical choice.[43]

Perhaps a note of 'plebeian' practicality can be inferred also from

[37] *KM* I, p. 21 (February 1882).
[38] *KM* III, p. 59 (27 December 1883); *KM* IV, p. 146 (14 September 1884).
[39] *KM* I, p. 216 (22 October 1885); *KM* III, p. 75 (30 June 1884).
[40] *KM* II, p. 39 (15 April 1883).
[41] Partha Chatterjee, 'A Religion of Urban Domesticity'.
[42] *KM* IV, pp. 74-5 (24 February 1884).
[43] *KM* II, p. 46 (2 June 1883).

Ramakrishna's passionate desire to see Kali face to face during the days of his intense sadhana.[44] Later on, too, he insisted that he was literally seeing and talking with the goddess during his frequent trances — and this was the sole claim to superior religious power Ramakrishna ever made. Once again, *seeing* was held to be superior to hearing, say, a text read out by a pandit. Interesting in this context is Ramakrishna's denigration of reading, though that too uses the eyes: evidently he was not particularly used to silent reading, that central practice of developed literate culture. 'Seeing' would be the only way through which plebeians with little or no education could claim devotional equality with, or primacy over, the baralok masters of textual learning. As with the work of peasants, artisans or women, devotion here yields direct, sensuous results.

Direct perception had been privileged as the only valid form of knowledge in the *pratakshyabad* of the ancient Indian materialist tradition of Lokayata, which has been denigrated down the ages as a philosophy of the vulgar people.[45] Perhaps we have in Ramakrishna traces of a 'religious materialism' not utterly dissimilar to what Carlo Ginzburg has diagnosed for his sixteenth-century North Italian miller — minus, of course, that social radicalism which makes Menocchio so remarkable.[46] But Ramakrishna, as usual, perhaps like Hindu traditions in general, straddles different levels or worlds. The primacy of visual perception is assumed also in a wide variety of Hindu religious and philosophical traditions, though this is *manaspratyaksha*, spiritual or mystic seeing, rather than anything comparable to everyday visual experience. One recalls the justly famous ancient hymn which claims to have seen the Absolute Purusha, resplendent like the sun, dispelling all darkness. Sanyasis claiming yogic powers, along with preachers of bhakti, have often counterposed their superhuman powers of seeing the divine against the Brahman claim to textual knowledge,[47] and Ramakrishna clearly fits in with such traditions.

Such affinities are not surprising, for continued familiarity with the rural world of nature, labour and oral culture is accompanied

---

[44] *L* I, Sadhak-bhava, pp. 111–14; *Life*, p. 68.

[45] Surendranath Dasgupta, *History of Indian Philosophy*, vol. III (Cambridge, 1961); Debiprasad Chattopadhyay, *Lokayata* (New Delhi, 1959, 1975), Chapter I.

[46] Carlo Ginzburg, *The Cheese and the Worms* (Harmondsworth, Penguin Books, 1982).

[47] Madeleine Biardeau, *Hinduism: The Anthropology of a Civilization* (Delhi, 1989), pp. 73–5.

in Ramakrishna by a certain distancing. The labour of artisans, peasants, and women has become a parable of perseverance and devotion: little remains of the sweat and pain of toil. This is a rural Brahman sensibility, perhaps, which does not aestheticize village life — unlike romantic literature — but seeks to reduce it to lessons in religion and morality.

A similar process can be seen at work in the selection Ramakrishna made, in the *Kathamrita* conversations with bhadralok devotees, of some forty-odd songs from his favourite composer, Ramprasad Sen. The songs of this eighteenth-century Kali-bhakta can still be heard in village lanes and on the lips of beggars. They often present a faith heroically preserved in and through enormous suffering, poverty, inequality and exploitation:

> Who calls you, Tara, compassionate to the poor!
> To some you give wealth, elephants, and chariots.
> While others are fated to work for wages, without enough of
>   rice and *sag*. . . .
> You have brought me to this world, and beaten me as iron is
>   beaten.
> I will still call to you, Kali, See how much courage I have.[48]

Little remains of this anguish, suppressed anger, and sublimation, of what is recognized to be injustice, in the songs sung by Ramakrishna to city audiences of middle-aged householders and educated young men. His choice highlighted the more obviously doctrinal pieces, along with the ones where the mood of triumphant union with Kali marginalizes or eliminates suffering. To borrow for a moment from Weber, a movement is taking place from a 'theodicy of suffering' towards a 'theodicy of good fortune'.[49]

Ramakrishna's parables of village life do occasionally mention instances of zamindari oppression — but always as things which have to be accepted, facts of life no different from droughts or other natural calamities.[50] Rural hierarchy is accepted and even idealized at times in the figure of the benevolent baramanush patron. This

---

[48] Sibaprasad Bhattacharji, *Bharatchandra o Ramprasad* (Calcutta, 1967), p. 218; Sasibhushan Dasgupta *Bharater Shakti-Sadhana o shakta-Sahitya* (Calcutta, 1960), p. 230.

[49] Max Weber, 'The Social Psychology of World Religion', from H.H. Garth and C. Wright Mills, *Max Weber, Essays in Sociology* (London, 1948, 1977), pp. 271-5.

[50] See, for example, *KM* II, pp. 271-7 (2 June 1883); *KM* II, p. 61 (15 June 1883).

contrasts significantly, we shall see, with Ramakrishna's views on certain forms of power in city life.

Ramakrishna spent thirty-five years of his life in a suburb of Calcutta, but it was only during the last ten years or so that he suddenly gained acceptance and renown among the Calcutta bhadralok. The timing coincided, significantly, with a kind of hiatus in bhadralok history. By the 1870s and 1880s, the 'renaissance' dream of improvement and reform under British tutelage was turning sour. The Brahmos had split up, Vidyasagar was increasingly frustrated and lonely, and racial tensions were mounting under Lytton and through the Ilbert Bill furore. The alternative, patriotic vision of solving the country's ills by drastically modifying or overthrowing foreign rule did not, however, appear really viable till around 1905. Organizations like the Indian Association or the early Congress still had a very limited appeal, even among the bhadralok.

The hiatus bred, in the first place, a disquiet about the multifarious schemes and endeavours of the bhadralok, so many of which seemed to end in a whimper. Ramakrishna's rejection of social activism, embodied for instance in his scornful comments about Sambhu Mallik's philanthropy, thus won an appreciative audience — even though its own foundations were rather different. Subordination of external action to inner piety came natural for someone affiliated to traditions of bhakti and there was, perhaps, also an element of plebeian cynicism. Philanthropy merely boosted the ego of the do-gooding baramanush: it was sheer arrogance for anyone to think that he had the power to really improve the world.[51]

For the bhadralok, the hiatus between the myths of renaissance improvement and nationalist deliverance encouraged moods of introspection and nostalgia. There was a partial turning away from forward-looking male activism towards a series of logically distinct but often intermingled 'Others': past as contrasted to present, country *vs* city, a deliberate feminization as opposed to active masculinity, the attractive playfulness and irresponsibility of the child and the *pagal*[52] as against the goal-oriented instrumental rationality of the adult male. One can now begin to understand the scope and power of Ramakrishna's appeal, which fitted in with,

[51] See, for instance, *KM* II, p. 157 (11 October 1884), where Ramakrishna recalls a conversation with Kristodas Pal, or his meeting with Vidyasagar, *KM* III, p. 15 (5 August 1882).

[52] See note 63 for reference to the culturally specific meanings of *pagal* (usually translated as 'mad') in Bengal.

and helped to stimulate, such broader trends. His earthy parables seemed to bring back a rural world from which the city bhadralok now sometimes felt they had unwisely uprooted themselves. Ramakrishna's lifelong love for women's roles — acting feminine parts in boyhood, dressing up as a woman for a time in Mathur's house, even allegedly having periods[53] — was chronicled with respect and admiration by Mahendranath Gupta and other biographers. Feminization in any case had a respectable pedigree in certain forms of Vaishnava devotion.[54] Even more attractive was Ramakrishna's childlike surrender to the Shakta divine mother: 'Attaining Iswara makes you into a five-year old boy'[55] — a womb-reversion, almost, allowing uninhibited scope to what in other contexts would be termed irresponsible, unmanly, irrational behaviour.

What was happening, however, was not a rupture or neat separation into activist and inward-turning groups, but a commingling of moods. In Bankimchandra's *Anandamath*, for instance — published incidentally in 1882, the year in which Mahendranath began his trips to Dakshineswar — the sanyasis are engaged in a hard masculine project of overthrowing British-backed Muslim rule, and they explicitly distinguish their Vaishnavism from the non-violent bhakti of Chaitanya. Yet their 'Bande Mataram' hymn is addressed to a nurturing bounteous motherland, and the novel contains a dream sequence where Kalyani sees Vishnu cradled and enveloped by an indistinct all-embracing mother-figure.[56] In Bengali poetry the 'epic' style of Michael Madhusudan Dutta in the 1850s and 1860s had glorified heroic action in defiance of overwhelming odds. Precisely around the 1880s, this began to be partially displaced by the more introspective Romantic lyricism of Biharilal Chakrabarti and Rabindranath, where nature was given a new centrality. A rural retrospect became prominent also in autobiographies, which were now being composed in unprecedented number thanks to the simultaneous entry of print culture and vernacular prose. They were coming to acquire a 'developmental' format, in which a man's life became 'a study of his progress towards and absorption into his historical role'[57] — and yet it was

53 *Life*, p. 176.
54 See for instance, Ramakanta Chakrabarti, *Vaisnavism in Bengal* (Calcutta, 1985), Chapter XI, and *passim*.
55 *KM* I, p. 214 (22 October 1885).
56 Bankimchandra Chattopadhyay, *Anandamath* (1882) — *Bankim Rachanabali*, I (Calcutta, 1360/1953).
57 Benedict Anderson, 'A Time of Darkness and A Time of Light', in A. Reid

reformist authors using this format who seemed to linger most over idealized memories of childhood spent in traditional rural families.[58] Introspection and intimate detail, marginalized in the central narrative of adult public activity, could be given freer rein in memories of childhood, and these consequently became channels for 'expressing difficulty and ambivalence'.[59]

Probably under Ramakrishna's influence, the Brahmos associated with Keshabchandra Sen began conceptualizing and addressing divinity in maternal terms. Ramakrishna's spell helped to turn another once-militant Brahmo, Bejoykrishna Goswami, into a Vaishnava mystic who wanted to 'become like a child, just like what he had been in infancy'.[60] The childlike behaviour valorized by Ramakrishna or Bejoykrishna, it must be added, was modelled on a construction of childhood, possibly specific to upper-caste Hindu society, which was different from both Puritanical discipline and romantic glorification of pure natural growth. The Hindu child 'is closely integrated into family life without having any of its responsibilities. He has no personal timetable . . . no rules of hygiene or cleanliness imposed from outside . . . He seems to live by pure whim . . . '[61] Biographers of Ramakrishna love to describe what they term his balak-bhava (the mood of relating to divinity as a child), including lack of inhibitions about nudity or soiling himself in public.[62] The child model thus slides into that of the pagal, and, partly again under Ramakrishna's influence, the runaway irresponsible male and the pagal as embodiment of holy folly became long-lasting stereotypes in Bengali literature.[63]

Direct references to colonial domination are extremely rare in

---

and O. Mann, *Perceptions of the Past in South East Asia* (Heinemann, 1979, 1982), p. 226.

[58] For a more detailed discussion, see my 'Renaissance, Kaliyuga and Kalki: Constructions of Time and History in Colonial Bengal', paper presented at International Roundtable of Historians and Anthropologists, Bellagio, August 1989, reproduced in revised form as Chapter 6 in the present book.

[59] Carolyn Steedman (ed.), *The Radical Soldier's Tale* (London, etc, 1988) — pt I, p. 103.

[60] Mahatma Bijoykrishna Goswami in *Jivan-Vrittanta* (Calcutta, n.d.), p. 387.

[61] Madeleine Biardeau, *Hinduism*, pp. 33-4.

[62] See, for instance, the section entitled 'Balakbhava' in Satyacharan Mitra, *Sri Sri Ramakrishna Paramahansa: Jibani o Upadesh* (Calcutta, 1897), pp. 150-2.

[63] See pp. 312, 344-5, for the figure of the pagal in late-nineteenth and early-twentieth-century Bengali literature. For a study of the pagal in religious life, see June McDaniel, *The Madness of the Saints: Ecstatic Religion in Bengal* (Chicago, 1989).

Ramakrishna's discourse, but surely it is not far-fetched to see in the series of 'Others' fostered by his example traces of an implicit rejection of values imposed by the nineteenth-century west. Colonialism counterposed to European active virile masculinity the stereotype of the conquered native as effeminate, irritatingly childish, or at best pleasantly childlike.[64] The educated Bengali did not surrender, without qualification, to this 'colonial discourse', as uncritical admiration of Edward Said has led some to assume. Excluded anyway from the privileged male occupations of military and political command and successful independent entrepreneurship, and relegated to dull and lowly clerical jobs, such people were perhaps expressing a muffled defiance through a preference for feminization, childlike behaviour, and the irresponsible unreason of the pagal. These provided a wider scope to certain human possibilities than the rigid code of Victorian responsible male behaviour sought to be imposed as the bhadralok's role model. Ramakrishna and his devotees freely expressed their emotions, plunged into ecstatic dances, wept in public: the *Kathamrita* describes the master uninhibitedly fondling and 'playing' with his teenager disciples.[65] Ramakrishna in effect subverted the distinctions between adult and child, male and female, work and play, which the 'civilizing' mission of the west was making more rigid in colonial Bengal. Such subversion was particularly attractive during the hiatus between the renaissance and the nationalist myths, but its appeal extended beyond the 1870s and 1880s and had a specific social dimension. It stood in marked contrast particularly to the imposed world of formal routinized education and time-bound chakri.

Not all sections of the Calcutta bhadralok were equally open to Ramakrishna's influence in the late 1870s and early 1880s. Rani Rashmoni and Mathur of the Janbazar family apart, the really big zamindars of Calcutta showed little interest in Ramakrishna. A few well-off householders became devotees, he was occasionally invited to the garden-houses of the rich, and there were some sessions with Marwari businessmen of Barabazar.[66] But on the whole the insistence of Ramakrishna's first biographer, Ramachandra Datta, that his master had been the guru not of the rich but of the *madhyabitta*

---

[64] Ashis Nandy, *The Intimate Enemy: Loss and Recovery of Self under Colonialism* (Delhi, 1983), pp. 7–8, 11–16, 52–3.

[65] *Life*, pp. 32, 323–5, 338, 345 and *passim*.

[66] *KM* I, Chapter 21 (20 October 1884, pp. 178–86), is an account of a visit of Ramakrishna to the Marwaris of Barabazar.

(middle class)[67] seems acceptable — with the further, vital, clarification that the higher or more successful stratum of the Calcutta professional middle class also remained more or less immune from the spell of Dakshineswar in the saint's own lifetime. The disciples who became sanyasis under Vivekananda suffered from acute scarcity of funds till the late 1890s. Lawyers, journalists, teachers (except Mahendranath),[68] and writers seldom figure in the *Kathamrita*, and politicians like Surendranath Banerji never bothered to pay Ramakrishna a visit. Among the major figures of what today is often called the Bengal Renaissance, only Keshabchandra Sen became close to him, and it was journals run by the Nababidhan Brahmo group that first made Ramakrishna known among the English-educated.[69] There were brief encounters — usually at Ramakrishna's initiative, and none of them too happy — with leaders of the other two Brahmo factions (Debendranath Tagore and Shibnath Shastri), with the Hindu revivalist orator Sasadhar Tarkachudamoni, as well as with Vidyasagar, the poet Michael Madhusudan, and the novelist Bankimchandra.[70] But the one major literary figure who became a devotee, the actor-playwright Girishchandra Ghosh, had failed in the school-leaving examination and had then spent years as a clerk. It is the world of chakri, of clerical jobs in mercantile and government offices, that really dominates Ramakrishna's Calcutta milieu. His devotees included a sprinkling of deputy-magistrates and subjudges, along with a few who held relatively senior jobs in mercantile offices: the upper rungs in both kinds of service would have been British preserves. More often, the disciples were struggling clerks or young men who might soon have to start looking for clerical posts.[71]

The stresses and silences about Calcutta in Ramakrishna's discourses confirm and supplement the inferences derived from data about

67 Ramachandra Datta, *Sri Sri Ramakrishna Paramahansa Dever Jivan-Vrittanta* (Calcutta, 1890, pp. 86-9.

68 Mahendranath's near-uniqueness is indicated by the nickname of 'master' (teacher), which he came to be known by in Ramakrishna's circle. Evidently there were no other teachers around.

69 For details about Ramakrishna's relations with Brahmos, see Brojen Banerji and Sajanikanta Das, and Sankariprasad Basu, *Vivekananda o Samakalin Bharatvarsha* (Calcutta, 1979), Chapter 13.

70 *KM, passim*. Bankimchandra, for instance, horrified Ramakrishna by declaring with provocative cynicism that food, sleep, and sex were the principal goals of human life. Vidyasagar remained polite, but never followed up Ramakrishna's sole visit to him.

71 For some details, see my 'Kathamrita As Text', pp. 24-6.

his city contacts. Despite long years in Dakshineswar (a northern suburb of the metropolis) and lengthy sojourns at the Janbazar mansion in the heart of central Calcutta, Ramakrishna remained in many ways an outsider to the city. The poignant nostalgia of the *dasi* (servant woman) is a favourite image of his, serving her master's family with devotion, looking after his children, and yet thinking all the time of her distant village home.[72] It conveys, perhaps, something of his own mood. Ramakrishna could display, even in the 1880s, a rustic sense of wonder at times about city marvels.[73] But, in total contrast to rural labour, most urban work processes failed to arouse his interest — even though Dakshineswar was an area where jute mills were springing up. The city rich do not constitute a distinct category in his conversation, being conflated with the rural zamindar in the image of the baramanush, baralok, or babu. The limits of Ramakrishna's city contacts and appeal are indicated also by the silence about the middle-class professions of law, journalism and teaching. The one specifically urban life-situation which becomes really vivid in Ramakrishna's discourse is the life of the clerk (kerani): 'What a mess! A salary of twenty rupees — three children — no money to feed them properly; the roof leaks, no money to repair it; impossible to buy new books for the son, to give him the sacred thread; have to beg eight annas from one, four annas from another!'[74] Other passages graphically describe the unemployed kerani desperately running around for another job, as well as the travails of time-bound office work.[75]

A poor Brahman like Ramakrishna had a natural empathy for clerks — poor, overwhelmingly upper caste, with bhadralok aspirations but without the resources, often, to fulfil them.[76] I have argued elsewhere that the anguish and frustrations of genteel poverty in this world of the unsuccessful bhadralok — pandits losing patronage in the new era, obscure hack-writers, humble schoolteachers, clerks, unemployed educated youth, high-school or college boys with highly uncertain job prospects — produced a late flowering

---

[72] *KM* I, p. 22 (February 1882); p. 131 (15 June 1884); *KMV* p. 7 (2 April 1882).

[73] *KM* I, p. 52 (27 October 1882). This describes his 'childlike' pleasure about the sights and sounds of the white part of the city: gas lights, well-lit houses, girls playing the piano.

[74] *KM* V, p. 109 (9 March 1884).

[75] *KM* V, p. 44 (2 June 1883), p. 4 (2 April 1882).

[76] For Ramakrishna, as we have just seen, the many burdens of the kerani include, notably, trying to educate his son and meeting the costs of the sacred thread investiture ceremony.

of what may be called 'Kaliyuga literature' in mid- and late-nineteenth-century Bengal.[77] Embodied in a mass of cheap vernacular tracts, plays, and farces, and finding a visual counterpart in many Kalighat paintings,[78] these constitute the most relevant context for understanding Ramakrishna and his appeal. This 'low life of literature',[79] together with Ramakrishna's conversation (in which the Kaliyuga motif recurs with some frequency), provide an entry into a grossly neglected world. Historians of the 'Bengal Renaissance' have concentrated on the well-known intellectuals, the older kind of work on nationalism focused on politics inspired or manipulated from the top, while *Subaltern Studies* concerned itself primarily with peasant movements and consciousness.[80] What for convenience may be termed lower-middle-class groups have entered historical narratives, if at all, mainly under economistic rubrics as victims of educated unemployment or price-rise. Yet their importance in a variety of late-nineteenth-century and twentieth-century movements is obvious enough − and so is, in cultural terms, their vital intermediate role. Theirs has been a predominantly high-caste, yet depressed world, − entry into which has been the first step in upward mobility for neo-literates from lower down the social hierarchy. And if the Kaliyuga myth has been relatively open to occasional appropriations from below,[81] it could also extend its appeal to the late-nineteenth-century high bhadralok in their more introspective and pessimistic moods. This was possible, I intend to argue, particularly because of the new and crucial centrality of chakri within the Kaliyuga literature of colonial Bengal.

For some two thousand years, from the Vana Parva of the

[77] See my 'Kalki-avatar of Bikrampur: A Village Scandal in Early Twentieth-century Bengal' in Guha (ed.), *Subaltern Studies VI* (Delhi, 1989), as well as 'Calcutta in the Bengal Renaissance', in Sukanta Chaudhuri (ed.), *Calcutta the Living City*, vol. I (Delhi, 1990), and 'Kali-yuger Kalpana o Aupanibeshik Samaj', in G Chattopadhyay (ed.), *Itihas Anusandhan 4* (Calcutta, 1989). See also Chapters 5 and 6 of this book.

[78] W.G. Archer, *Bazar Paintings of Calcutta* (London, 1953); Mildred Archer, *Indian Popular Paintings in the India Office Library* (London, 1977).

[79] I am borrowing this term from Robert Darnton, 'The High Enlightenment and the Low-Life of Literature in Pre-Revolutionary France', *Past and Present*, no. 51, May 1971.

[80] In its initial phase, that is to say: today some of its practitioners are more interested in the Saidian project of deconstructing a colonial discourse assumed to be all-pervasive.

[81] For an example, see my 'Kalki-avatar of Bikrampur'.

Mahabharata onwards, Kaliyuga has been a recurrent and powerful dystopia, a format for voicing a variety of high-caste male anxieties. Its many evils — located in the present and the future, for Kaliyuga is supposed to have begun soon after the end of the Mahabharata war — traditionally include oppressive *mleccha* (alien and impure) kings, Brahmans corrupted by too much rational argument (the 'science of disputation'), overmighty Shudras expounding the scriptures and ceasing to serve the Brahmans, girls choosing their own partners, and disobedient and deceiving wives having intercourse with menials, slaves, and even animals.[82] The nineteenth century made a selection, with new stresses, from this impressive catalogue. Brahman corruption and rationalistic criticism of traditional verities were obviously relevant themes. Little was made (except in some later, early-twentieth-century texts[83]) of the Shudra threat, which never became much of an issue in nineteenth-century Bengal (as contrasted to Maharashtra). Women remain a key target — but no longer primarily for sexual immorality: pride of place now went to the 'modern' wife, allegedly ill-treating her mother-in-law, enslaving the husband, and wasting money on luxuries for herself.[84] The crucial innovation in a multitude of late-nineteenth-century tracts and farces was the close interrelationship postulated between the disorderly wife, the 'modern' craze for money, and the chakri the husband is forced to take up to get the one and please the other — precisely, in other words, Ramakrishna's triad of kamini–kanchan–chakri.

And so the gods, on a visit to colonial India in *Debganer Marte Agaman* (1889), keep meeting 'clerks . . . dozing as they return home from office. Their faces are worn out after the whole day's work . . . The *sahib*'s kicks and blows the whole day, and when they return . . . the nagging of wives . . . '[85] A play entitled *Kerani-carit* (1885) makes the discipline of time its central focus: 'We lose the day's salaries if we reach office a minute late . . . half the salary goes on

[82] These, along with natural calamities, are the principal features of Kaliyuga in 'Vana Parva' ('Markandaya Samasya', 187-90) of the *Mahabharata*. I am using the English translation of Pratapchandra Roy (Calcutta, n.d.), vol. III, pp. 397-413, along with the standard nineteenth-century Bengali version of Kaliprasanna Sinha — Gopal Haldar (eds), *Mahabharata* (Calcutta, 1974), vol. II, pp. 194-200.

[83] Thus Pasupati Chattopadhyaya's *Kalir Bamun* (Calcutta, 1922) hits out at a lower-caste 'Sanskritizing' movement.

[84] Jayanta Goswami, *Samajchitre Unabinghsha Satabdir Bangla Prahasan* (Calcutta, n.d.), summarizes the plots of a large number of plays and farces around these themes.

[85] Durgacharan Roy, *Debganer-Martea Agaman* (Calcutta, 1889).

fines . . . : there is not a single gap in our day's routine.' The clerk's wife complains that she now sees little of her husband, but is quickly consoled by the thought that the salary will fetch her jewellery.[86] And while little is said directly about colonial domination as mleccha rule, Harischandra Bandopadhyay's *Kaler Bau* (1880) contains a powerful sub-text. 'Slaves to government officials, we have to spend our time in home as slaves to the wives', complains a husband. The figure of the suffering mother, neglected by a son who has been entrapped by the wiles of the modern wife, becomes here a metaphor for the enslaved 'mother'-land, the *Bangamata* who has become the 'slave *(dasi)* of the London queen'.[87]

Placed in this context, Ramakrishna's oft-repeated comments about kamini and kanchan cease to sound like a mere reiteration of age-old verities and acquire a specific late-nineteenth-century resonance. As in many contemporary farces and Kalighat paintings, kamini at times conveys a fear of loss of male authority within the household: 'Men are made fools and worthless, by women . . . If the wife, says, "Get up", he gets up — "Sit down", he sits down.' A caustic remark about an ex-devotee, now busy running errands for his wife, drew appreciative laughter from Ramakrishna's audience. But the central link is between kamini and the *dasatya* of chakri (bondage of the office-job), mediated by kanchan — and direct references to colonial domination, extremely rare otherwise in Ramakrishna's discourse, here put in an appearance. 'Look, how many educated people trained in English, with so many degrees, accept chakri, and receive kicks from their master's boots every day. Kamini is the sole reason for all this.'[88] Ramakrishna once told a favourite disciple that he should jump in the Ganga rather than 'become a slave of someone by taking a job'.[89] He was also quite explicit about what is objectionable about office-work: 'Your face seems to have a dark shadow upon it. That's because you are working in an office. In the office you have to handle money, keep accounts, do so much other work. You have to be alert all the time.'[90]

The precise nature and implications of this aversion to chakri,

---

[86] Prankrishna Gangopadhyay, *Kerani-carit* (Calcutta, 1885). See also Anon., *Kerani-darpan* (Calcutta, 1874), with its vivid account of time discipline and racist humiliation in office work (I owe this reference to Anamitra Das).

[87] Jayanta Goswami, p. 1036.

[88] *KM* III, p. 143 (12 April 1885); *KM* I, p. 73 (14 December 1882).

[89] *KM* II, p. 201 (1 March 1885).

[90] *KM* I, p. 121 (15 June 1884).

running through late-nineteenth-century Kaliyuga literature and Ramakrishna's conversation, need some analysis. Chakri was generally ill-paid and increasingly difficult to obtain: but the 'salary of twenty rupees' mentioned by Ramakrishna was not really negligible by contemporary standards, and educated unemployment was not yet the explosive issue it would become later. What made chakri intolerable at this specific conjuncture was rather its connotation of impersonal cash nexus and authority, embodied above all in the new rigorous discipline of work regulated by clock time. Disciplinary time was a particularly abrupt and imposed innovation in colonial India. Europe had gone through a much slower and phased transition spanning some five hundred years: from the first thirteenth- and fourteenth-century mechanical clocks with hour-hands alone, through the later innovation of watches counting off minutes and seconds, down to the developed eighteenth and nineteenth-century apparatus of disciplinary time in modern armies, bureaucracies, hospitals, schools, prisons, and factories.[91] Colonial rule telescoped the entire process for India within one or two generations.

In Bengal, particularly, government and mercantile offices (along with the new type of schools and colleges) became the principal locus for the imported ideas of bourgeois time and discipline. Factories were still rare (and mainly, so far, involved white employers and migrant non-Bengali labourers), capitalist farming non-existent, and few Bengalis served in the army. Calcutta in the late nineteenth · century, however, was the headquarters of British Indian bureaucracy, mercantile enterprise, and education. Regular hours of work throughout the year in offices must have contrasted sharply with the seasonal variation in labour tempo normal to village life. Mughal bureaucracy had had its clerks, of course, but jobs in British-controlled offices under bosses seeking to impose Victorian standards of punctuality and discipline must have still meant a considerable departure. Timebound office work, again, had to be performed in the unfamiliar enclosed space of the modern city building. In school and office alike, there was the additional problem of an often imperfectly understood foreign language of command.

Chakri thus became a 'chronotope' of alienated time and space,[92]

---

[91] E.P. Thompson, 'Time, Work-Discipline, and Industrial Capitalism', *Past and Present*, no. 38, December 1967; Michel Foucault, *Discipline and Punish* (London, 1979).

[92] Mikhail Bakhtin, *The Dialogic Imagination* (Texas, 1981), *passim*. The dual

late-nineteenth-century Kaliyuga's heart of darkness, the principal format through which awareness of subjection spread among colonial middle-class males. Unable as yet to resist foreign bosses effectively, the clerk — or the writer empathizing with him — often passed on the blame in part to women. Awakening political consciousness thus became intertwined with a strengthening of patriarchal prejudices.

In course of time this predominantly lower-middle-class discourse on chakri merged with broader critiques of colonial domination, formulated by more sophisticated intellectuals. The office was one obvious and highly visible site of racial discrimination, manifested in salary differentials and the everyday behaviour of white bosses. British rule, it came to be argued, was directly responsible for making Indians dependent on servile clerical jobs, for it had destroyed handicrafts, ruined agriculture through excessive taxes, and blocked independent business through 'one-way' free trade. Remedies were now sought through autonomous efforts at technical and 'national' education, swadeshi enterprise — and, increasingly, political struggle. Within offices, too, the first signs of clerical organization and protest would become manifest from around 1905.[93]

All that lay in the future: for the moment, Ramakrishna could evoke a profound response through his promise of escape into an inner world of bhakti, into which one could retreat even while carrying on the duties imposed by a heartless time- and rule-bound society. This was Ramakrishna's specific, original contribution to the general critique of chakri. Over this inner world presides, significantly enough, an Ishwara who, in Ramakrishna's parables, gets repeatedly conflated with the idealized figure of the traditional baramanush or babu — someone utterly different from the impersonal, distant office boss (usually called *manib* in the *Kathamrita*

---

burden of disciplinary time and foreign language is neatly summed up in a 'funny' story that can still be heard in Bengal about the clerk's life, perpetually rushing from home to shopping to office and back: 'Running, running, office come — *tobuo to* Sir late *hoy'* [Sir, still I am late]. I owe this reference to Sukumari Bhattacharji. For some interesting evidence about a hostility to 'naukri' based on aversion towards disciplinary time persisting among artisans till today, see Nita Kumar. *The Artisans of Banaras: Popular Culture and Identity, 1880-1986* (Princeton, 1988), Chapters 2, 4, and *passim*.

[93] For some details, see my *Swadeshi Movement in Bengal 1903-8* (New Delhi, 1973), Chapter v. Interestingly the first strike that attracted widespread attention and sympathy was by the clerks of Burn Iron Works, Howrah, and it was around a question of time-discipline. The clerks were protesting against a new mechanical system of recording attendance, ibid., pp. 200-2.

conversations). The raja, zamindar, or old kind of city patron[94] pleased with the *seba* (devoted voluntary service, as contrasted to bondage or *dasatya*) of his *khansama* (servant), might ask the latter one day to sit next to him.[95] A poor man's son in this paternalistic, personalized mode of authority could become rich overnight if the baramanush wed his daughter to him.[96] It is essential, however, to get to know the babu directly, even if his officials *(amlas)* try to block your way — after which even the amlas will respect you. Maybe there is a hint here of the age-old rural dream in many lands of the distant overlord, just king, 'little father' of the poor. 'Willed submission'[97] was an acceptable way of relating to such figures, at least in retrospect: they can serve, therefore, as prototypes of the divine.

Running through all such parables is an implicit 'Other': the modern British-controlled office governed by impersonal rules and abstract time-schedules where the amlas are as troublesome as ever, but the superior (sahib) is no longer approachable. A story frequently related from the mid-nineteenth-century onwards about Ramprasad seems relevant here. The composer is supposed to have been caught by an official scribbling verses about Kali all over the account book of his employer. The eighteenth-century Calcutta baramanush, far from dismissing him, was moved to tears, and gave Ramprasad a lifelong pension. The written version of this tale seems to have originated with Iswar Gupta in 1853–4, in a pioneering biographical essay which, incidentally, identified that bygone age as a lost golden Satya-yuga, in which patrons like Krishnachandra Roy of Nadia still knew how to treat with honour the traditional literati. The essay simultaneously valorized unlearned wisdom over formal training in poetry and religion alike.[98] The anguish of a declining traditional high-caste literati, and the misery of clerical chakri, thus come together to constitute the core of late-nineteenth-century Kaliyuga sensibility.

Kaliyuga, however, is not necessarily a symbol of pessimism alone. The worst of ages, it paradoxically has also been seen as the best of times. In it, according to much bhakti literature, deliverance comes

[94] *KM* IV, p. 11 (25 February 1883), p. 68 (2 February 1884), *KM* V, p. 104 (26 December 1883).

[95] *KM* II, p. 63 (15 June 1883).

[96] *KM* III, p. 83 (30 June 1884), pp. 160–1 (9 May 1885).

[97] For the centrality of 'willed submission' to bhakti, see Kumkum Sangari, 'Mirabai and the Spiritual Economy of Bhakti', *Economic and Political Weekly*, xxv, 27–8, 7–14 July 1990.

[98] Extracts from Ishwarchandra Gupta's essay are given in Jogendranath Gupta, *Sadhak Kavi Ramprasad* (Calcutta, 1954).

easily, for mere recitation of the name of Hari may suffice. The paradox extends further, for women and Shudras, the two major sources of corruption in all pre-modern Kaliyuga texts, 'can attain good simply through performing their duties' to husbands and twice-born men.[99] Subalternity is privileged — provided, of course, it remains properly subaltern. The humble constitute the ideal bhaktas. Bhakti and tantra, the two forms of religious practice repeatedly declared to be appropriate for Kaliyuga, are both explicitly open to women and Shudras, unlike Brahmanical learning and ritual. Extreme degeneration could also foreshadow a total reversal, with Vishnu coming as Kalki-avatar to restore Satya-yuga. Here, however, the Brahman male takes over again, for the restored norm will be of ideal caste and gender hierarchy.[100]

A 'gender paradox'[101] thus underlay conceptions of Kaliyuga: the insubordinate, unchaste woman was a principal source of evil, but bhakti too had a feminine face, being personified by the pure dutiful wife or mother. This paradox took on new forms in the nineteenth century as certain modulations were made in the remedial dimensions of Kaliyuga. From the 1880s onwards, most notably in the plays of Girischandra Ghosh and those influenced by him, the ideal woman (usually a wife) emerged as *active* helper in the restoration of moral order. Going beyond the model of exemplary patient suffering typified by Sita, she intervenes in a manner which is deferential yet assertive: a mode that anticipates, perhaps, some aspects of Gandhian passive resistance or satyagraha.[102] The woman may be helped by an old-world servant, representing the good Shudra, and gradually a sub-theme extolling simple peasant virtues starts entering the literature.[103] Inspiration for remedial action comes from figures of holy madness, sometimes obviously modelled on Ramakrishna, and, occasionally, the Kalki-avatar himself enters to restore Satya-yuga.[104]

[99] *Vishnupurana*, cited in Kumkum Sangari. I am grateful to Kumkum Sangari for drawing my attention to this important paradox. See also W.C. Beane, *Myth, Cult and Symbols in Shakta Hinduism* (London, 1977), pp. 237–9, and Madeleine Biardieu, p. 105.

[100] Here there is a significant contrast with the egalitarian dimensions of Christian apocalypse.

[101] See Megan McLaughlin, fn 10 above.

[102] For some examples, see my 'Kalki-avatar of Bikrampur', and Chapter 6 of this book.

[103] Ibid.

[104] Aghorchandra Kabyatirtha, *Kalir Abasan, be Kalki-avatar Geetabhinoy* (Calcutta, 1902).

Ramakrishna's own ways of confronting the evils of Kaliyuga had, however, certain significantly distinct nuances. Nineteenth-century Kaliyuga literature could pass over easily from denunciation of the disorderly woman to the exaltation of the pure Hindu wife, for the evils it pilloried amounted to little more than a shrewishness which could be tamed or reformed. The evil woman in Kaliyuga literature was insubordinate, quarrelsome, lazy and luxurious, but seldom really dangerous or sexually frightening. The trope had flourished on the margins of a much broader bhadralok discourse which from the 1820s had insistently and obsessively probed Hindu conjugality as its central concern. By the late nineteenth century, a very wide spectrum of Hindu sensibilities had come to regard the pure Hindu wife as the last unconquered space in a universe increasingly dominated by alien western values.[105]

Ramakrishna was emphatically not interested in probing or celebrating Hindu conjugality, for deep within him lay an acute physical revulsion for heterosexual intercourse. He frequently equated it with defecation, and expressed a fear and abhorrence of the female body which aroused male lust: 'Blood, flesh, fat, entrails, stools, urine — how can one love such a body?' The 'limbs and openings' of women's bodies appeared 'enormous' to him.[106] Sex to him consequently was not any less disgusting when pursued within marriage: rather, it could then become associated with kanchan and the need for salaried jobs, and therefore doubly dangerous.

The redemptive wife was thus no resolution for Kaliyuga anxieties to Ramakrishna. Women became tolerable only if somehow totally desexualized, which for Ramakrishna meant looking on them as mothers — bringing them in other words under the powerful taboo of incest. 'After much effort', Ramakrishna says, he was able to tolerate women devotees, by identifying all women as 'manifestations of Ma Anandamoyee'.[107] A shift in discourse from conjugality to motherhood, we shall see, did become common towards the end of the century,[108] and by 1905 Durga–Kali had

105 Tanika Sarkar, 'The Hindu Wife and the Hindu Nation: Domesticity and Nationalism in Nineteenth-century Bengal', *Studies in History*, July, December 1992.

106 *KM* III, p. 19 (24 August 1882), and many similar passages; *KM* IV, p. 201 (5 October 1884).

107 *KM* IV, p. 201.

108 See Tanika Sarkar, 'Bankimchandra and the Impossibility of a Political Agenda', *Oxford Literary Review*, 16 i, ii, 1994.

emerged as collective redeemer and patriotic icon, a powerful symbol of the 'mother'-land.

Ramakrishna's mother goddess, however, offered only individual solace, not any overall deliverance from the afflictions of Kaliyuga. Nor did the apocalyptic solution of an imminent Kalki-avatar appeal to him much. There does exist one startling passage in the *Kathamrita* where Ramakrishna can be seeing toying with such dreams while recalling insults suffered from Dakshineswar Temple officials: 'The Kalki-avatar will come at the end of Kaliyuga. A Brahman's son — he knows nothing, suddenly a horse and sword will come . . . '[109] Kalki as a Brahman 'who knows nothing', and is, presumably like Ramakrishna himself, poor, seems to be a late-nineteenth-century innovation. It turns up again in *Kalir Abasan* (1902), written by the 'poor Brahman' head pandit of a Calcutta school. And, in December 1904, a wandering poor Brahman sadhu who had once been a village schoolteacher turned up at a rural bhadralok household in Dacca district, actually claiming to be Kalki-avatar.[110] More indications, perhaps, of the social ambience of the Kaliyuga motif in late-nineteenth and early-twentieth-century Bengal.

Ramakrishna's main response to Kaliyuga was, however, along the paths of devotional and not apocalyptic bhakti. This took two basic forms in his discourse: the evocation of the paternalistic baramanush model as counterpoint to the alien world of chakri, and the way, more emotionally satisfactory for him, of total surrender to the Shakta mother goddess, becoming again a five-year-old child. Both ways were structured in terms adapted from patterns of religious discourse available to Ramakrishna. It is time to turn to the more formal, specifically religious, structure of Ramakrishna's teachings.

III

The more technically 'religious' aspects of Ramakrishna's discourse compel the problematization of a whole range of assumptions and themes. Conventional orality/literacy distinctions, for a start, begin to appear rather different as we listen to a holy man, quite often called illiterate by his disciples, using with considerable expertise abstruse doctrinal and philosophical concepts normally assigned to the realms of high or textual culture alone. Following a pattern

---

[109] *KM* IV, p. 101 (20 June 1884).

[110] For details of this Doyhata incident, see my 'Kalki-avatar of Bikrampur', and Chapter 6 in this book.

common in much hagiography, the *Kathamrita* and other accounts by devotees simultaneously stress Ramakrishna's uniqueness, and his manifold connections with a variety of religious practices and doctrines: village cults, obscure sects like the Kartabhaja, the world of Tantrism, mainstream Vaishnava and Shakta traditions, even fleetingly Christianity and Islam. A saint, in hagiography, has to have very distinctive features (in this case, particularly, unlearned wisdom and supreme catholicity) and yet fit into normal religious modes. The problem of recurrence and uniqueness, or linkages and distinctions, concerns historical analysis, too, and goes beyond the (by no means unimportant) issue of Ramakrishna's personal qualities. What it can reveal also are some of the ways through which religious traditions were being reshaped amidst the new pressures of colonial life. Thus, it is insufficient to merely acclaim Ramakrishna's justly famous catholicity as a 'traditional' or 'age-old' feature of 'Hinduism': its precise origins and features, the nature of its appeal, and changing implications require exploration. Again, Ramakrishna evolved into a rather new kind of guru, related to yet distinct from established types of religious preceptors. He was, perhaps, a guru suited particularly well to the demands of colonial urban bhadralok life, and anticipates in some ways (not all) the 'god-men' of today. The two models of bhakti which constituted the core of his teachings, and which we have already seen manifested through parables, also have doctrinal aspects, antecedents, and linkages, among which that between mother-worship and deep aversion for sexuality demands particular attention. Ramakrishna's conversation and attitudes here offer important insights into shifting late-nineteenth-century images of gender, which in their turn were bound up with the development of discourses of nationalism. Finally, the possible audience-specific features of Ramakrishna's discourse need to be kept in mind. His devotees included middle-aged householders, an inner circle consisting mainly of adolescents of college- or even school-going age, respectable housewives and widows, actresses of prostitute origin, and a lone disciple of non-bhadralok status, his Bihari servant Latu. Ramakrishna's message could well have varied slightly with his audience — and here the *Kathamrita* begins to fail us, for it offers direct access only to the first group. Audience-specificity raises the question of varied appropriations, and so we are led into a brief study of what became the dominant reading, that of Vivekananda.

Ramakrishna's conversation often has surprisingly deep 'textual' foundations, even where it seems to be most context-determined, or a product of homespun wisdom alone. Thus bhakti to him, as in much contemporary Kaliyuga literature, was the counterpoint to the new nineteenth-century world of chakri which reduced the quantum of free time and left little room for contemplation or ritual. But the association of Kaliyuga with lack of time is also a very old theme, with bhakti as the corresponding appropriate and 'easy' response for men who have lost in physical stature, span of life, and moral worth alike.[111] A more startling example is Ramakrishna's preference for the bhakti of a kitten, clinging helplessly to its mother in total dependence, over that of the baby monkey, who holds on to its parent with a certain will and effort of its own. The two images actually come unaltered from a philosophical dispute, way back in the thirteenth century in far-off Srirangam (Tamil Nadu), between the 'Tenkalai' and the 'Barkalai' sects of the Sri Vaishnavas, followers of Ramanuja, the founder of Visista-advaitabad.[112]

Ramakrishna was particularly knowledgeable about the doctrinal categories of Gaudiya Vaishnavabad — not surprisingly, as Vaishnava bhakti in Bengal since the days of Chaitanya has combined mass appeal with a uniquely rich theological literature, in the vernacular as well as in Sanskrit. He made, for instance, an analysis of three types of devotees (*sattvik*, *rajasik*, and *tamasik* bhaktas) which goes back to the *Bhagavat Purana*, adding a brilliant gloss that identified these subdivisions with types drawn from contemporary bhadralok life.[113] Ramakrishna was also perfectly capable of making precisely-defined doctrinal choices: of *raganuga* (emotional or ecstatic) bhakti, for instance, over the more ritualised *vaidhi*. A much more unusual — indeed, somewhat puzzling — choice was Ramakrishna's preference for Ramanuja's philosophy of Visista-advaita, as against the orthodox

---

111 *Haribhakti* (Calcutta, 1909-10), a Vaishnava tract in simple language, argued that in Kaliyuga repetition of *Harinama* alone had to be sufficient for salvation, for the path of contemplation ('jnana') was blocked by 'worries about rice, dal, oil and salt . . . others get nervous about being late for office, and can think only of the angry face of the boss . . . ' The theme of a compensatory easy way due to dimunition of time in Kaliyuga is already present in the *Vishnupurana* (*c.* 100-500 AD) — W.C. Beane, p. 238; and Kumkum Sangari.

112 *KM* I, p. 23 (February 1882); *KM* II, p. 69 (26 September 1883); *KM* III, pp. 60-1 (27 December 1883). The third reference draws an analogy between the (inferior) devotion of the baby monkey and the more ritualized *vaidhi* form of bhakti: the kitten, in contrast, embodies *raganuga*. For the thirteenth-century origins, see Jitendranath Bandopadhyay, *Panchopasana* (Calcutta, 1960), p. 103: then, too, Tenkalai was the less ritualized variant.

113 *KM* I, p. 57; Jitendranath Bandopadhyay, pp. 15-17.

Gaudiya Vaishnava version of dualistic bhakti, *achinta-bhedabheda*, about which he remained completely silent.[114] For the rest, a discourse on the five standard *bhavas* (moods) of Gaudiya Vaishnavabad was a regular feature of his conversation: relating to divinity as subject to ruler *(shanta)*, servant to master *(dasya)*, parent to child *(vatsalya)*, friend to friend *(sakhya)*, and lover to beloved *(madhur)*. He had tried out all these during the days of his 'mad' sadhana, he told his disciples, but had now settled down into dasya. The model of acceptable authority, seba willingly offered to the traditional baramanush or baralok — Ramakrishna's counterpoint, as we have already seen, to the dasatya of chakri — thus also had a firm doctrinal foundation.

What can explain such long lineages, the apparently textual bases of the discourse of a man supposedly illiterate? Despite the testimony of the servant-girl Brinde, Ramakrishna perhaps did have a few books, and he is said to have given one of them, a medieval monistic (Advaita Vedantic) text, to his favourite disciple Narendranath (Vivekananda). This *Ashtavakrasamhita* uses the image of an ocean in its account of the highest stage of high-Hindu spiritual realization, and resemblances have been found between such passages and Ramakrishna's descriptions of his frequent experiences of samadhi in terms of immersion into an endless ocean.[115]

But the bulk of Ramakrishna's doctrinal knowledge evidently could not have come from private reading of books. The *Kathamrita* forces upon us a keener awareness of the complex interpenetrations of literacy and orality. Historians in recent years have been moving away from sharp elite/popular, textual/oral disjunctions towards an understanding of ways in which elements of high textual culture could sink into and intermix with predominantly oral practices. Distinctions may persist, not through any rigid separation of traditions, beliefs or artefacts, but in differential appropriation or use of a broadly common heritage.[116] Such interfaces are perhaps particularly

---

[114] I remain grateful to the late Hitesranjan Sanyal for drawing my attention to this problem.

[115] J. Moussatef Masson, *The Oceanic Feeling: The Origins of Religious Sentiment in Ancient India* (Dordrecht, 1980), pp. 37–43. Masson thinks that Freud's use of the term 'oceanic feeling' in his *Civilization and Its Discontents* (1930) was derived from Romain Rolland's study of Ramakrishna.

[116] Roger Chartier, 'Culture as Appropriation: Popular Cultural Uses in Early Modern France' in S. Kaplan (ed.), *Understanding Popular Culture* (Mouton, 1984); Chartier, *Cultural Uses of Print in Early Modern France* (Princeton, 1987), Introduction.

marked in a culture like that of Hinduism, which has had a literate elite for well over two thousand years, but which still tried till the late eighteenth century to keep its most sacred texts in purely oral form. Orality here in fact became an instrument of high-caste domination: Ramakrishna could have relatively easy access to 'high' knowledge, despite poverty and lack of formal education, as he happened to be of Brahman birth.

In contrast to the specialized textual learning of the pandit, the traditional renouncer, holy man or sanyasi normally picked up his skills through apprenticeship to a master and/or contacts with other similar wandering sadhus. Transmission, in other words, was through predominantly non-textual means, from watching, hearing about, or participating in a variety of religious practices. Ramakrishna, for whom, as we have seen, seeing and hearing were always privileged over reading, clearly belonged to a world of this kind, which could be high and non-textual at the same time, and which was furthermore marked by great heterogeneity.

The striking feature of Ramakrishna's original village world, as revealed by his occasional reminiscences and later accounts of Kamarpukur by devotees, was certainly catholicity. Gadadhar encountered in boyhood a multiplicity of cults — Dharma, Gajan, Manasa (or Vishalakshmi), Shitala — with mainly plebeian devotees but occasional high-caste participation. Devotional practices easily crossed sectarian barriers and could vary within the same family. Thus Gadadhar's father Khudiram began as a devotee of Shitala, and later made Raghuvir (Ram) his chosen deity, while the prosperous Pyne family of merchants worshipped both Siva and Vishnu. Ramakrishna's elder brother Ramkumar became a worshipper of Shakti without this troubling his Vaishnava father. The boy Gadadhar could imbibe mainstream Hindu traditions through watching folk theatre performances of epic and puranic tales (there were three such jatra parties in Kamarpukur), and he soon started acting them out himself with friends. In addition, two pilgrim routes intersected at Kamarpukur, from Burdwan to Puri with its Vaishnava associations, and from Calcutta to the Saivite centre of Tarakeswar. Gadadhar developed an early interest in the constant flow of pilgrims and sadhus through his native village.[117]

Numerous 'sadhu-sants, sanyasis and bairagi babajis' used to pass through Dakshineswar, too, Ramakrishna once recalled, taking the

---

[117] *L* I, *Purba-katha o Balya-jivana*, pp. 27-9, 40, 48-9, 51, 116.

river route down to the great pilgrimage centre of Gangasagar. 'They
don't come here any longer, now that the railway has been constructed.'[118] A whole series of mentors thus came Ramakrishna's way, as,
fired by an intense desire to literally see Kali face to face, he pursued
a sadhana initially passionate and wild enough to be thought by many
to indicate possession or madness.[119] They brought with them formal
knowledge of diverse doctrines and rituals, and so helped to structure
Ramakrishna's devotional practices into recognizable and established
forms. The flow of sanyasis through Dakshineswar thus provided a
substitute, in Ramakrishna's case, for the years of wandering which is
a standard constituent in the life-histories of many religious leaders
— in the nineteenth century for men as different as Sahajananda Swami
(the founder of the Swaminarayan sect), Dayananda, and Rammohan.

The mysterious and beautiful Bhairabi Brahmini came first,
around 1861, and instructed Ramakrishna in Tantric practices and
concepts which have provided an 'esoteric', often somewhat disreputable, substratum to much of mainstream Bengal Shakta and
Vaishnava traditions. Bhairabi assured Ramakrishna that his unusual
states indicated not possession or madness but *mahabhava*, akin to
what had been manifested in Chaitanya. She was followed by Vaish-
navacharan, a Vaishnava pandit who was also a member of the largely
low-caste Kartabhaja sect. Initiation into orthodox Vaishnava traditions came from the Ramayat sadhu Jatadhari, while between 1864
and 1866 Totapuri, a sadhu from Punjab, guided him on the very
different path of Vedantic contemplation of the Absolute. Ramakrishna also made brief forays into Islam and Christianity, though
these never became major constituents of his thought.[120]

The striking feature of these years of mad sadhana was thus
religious experimentation. Ramakrishna, flouting all conventional
norms of Brahman *pujari* behaviour,[121] took up, followed, and then
discarded the practices of one tradition after another. The Ramakrishna we meet in the *Kathamrita* was significantly different. He
remained on the whole now on a single preferred path of devotion
(a combination of dasya with santan-bhava, bringing together elements from Vaishnava and Shakta traditions), though still supremely

---

118 *L* II, *Gurubhava-Uttarardha*, p. 44.
119 *L* I, Sadhakbhava, p. 82.
120 *Life*, pp. 139–40, 176, 189–205; *L* I, Sadhakbhava, pp. 206–74.
121 Thus his sacred thread had 'flown off by itself, as if in a summer storm'
— *KM* II, p. 2 (16 October 1882). Discarding the sacred thread is right and proper
for a sanyasi — but then Ramakrishna had never formally taken sanyas, either.

catholic in his acceptance of many paths to the divine. It was this more relaxed, self-confident Ramakrishna, firmly grounded once again in normal caste practices,[122] secure in his guru status, less of a seeker and more the dispenser of holy wisdom, who went on his own initiative to meet Keshabchandra Sen in March 1875 — beginning an interaction with Brahmos, and, more generally, with the English-educated: the people he once described as 'Young Bengal'.[123]

The conversations of this later Ramakrishna in the *Kathamrita*, as well as — to an enhanced extent — hagiographical accounts, bear on them the marks of this trajectory, for they indicate certain patterns of selectiveness in references to the years of religious experimentation. The stresses and silences here are significant in several different ways. Conditioned by the transition from poor Brahman villager to guru of English-educated city bhadralok, they simultaneously point to broader shifts within religious practices themselves and help us to understand the precise (and changing) meanings and implications of Ramakrishna's famous catholicity.

The village cults of Dharma, Gajan, Manasa, or Shitala figure only in reminiscences about boyhood, and the tone remains purely descriptive, without either praise or blame. They never enter Ramakrishna's many listings of alternative valid paths, where only main-stream forms of high-Hinduism are mentioned along with references to (undifferentiated) Islam and Christianity. Such cults, Ramakrishna evidently thought, were irrelevant, perhaps almost unknown or forgotten among his bhadralok devotees, or in metropolitan life in general. Manasa, other local or plebeian forms of the mother-goddess like Chandi, and Dharma had provided the standard themes in much of pre-colonial Bengali literature. Ramakrishna's relative silence is a possible indication, therefore, of a shift in the nineteenth-century bhadralok milieu towards more Sanskritized high-Hindu forms of devotion, grounded in Brahmanical texts made much more widely accessible through printing and translation.

Tantrism, along with the Kartabhajas, figure much more prominently in the *Kathamrita* conversations, and one of Ramakrishna's favourite songs came from another 'obscure' sect, the entirely low-caste Sahebdhani.[124] Reference or exposition, however, is usually combined with warnings, and the ambiguous tone deepened, to verge on virtual

---

[122] *KM* II, p. 113 (21 September 1884).

[123] *L* II, p. 44.

[124] Sudhir Chakrabarti, *Sahebdhani Sampraday Tader Gan* (Calcutta, 1985), pp. 52-3.

silencing, in later hagiographical literature composed under Vivek-ananda's shadow. Tantrism down the centuries has provided a cru-cially important underside to Hindu religious traditions in Bengal. It constituted the doctrinal core of Shakta practices, influenced many types of Vaishnavism, and formed a vital substratum in the rituals and doctrines of predominantly low-caste 'esoteric' Sahajiya cults — among which the Kartabhaja and the Sahebdhani are late examples. Open, unlike much of Brahmanical knowledge and ritual, to low-castes and women, the Tantric perspective of attaining spiritual goals in and through the body involves the ritual transgression of conven-tional norms about meat, fish, wine and sexual intercourse (symboli-cally, or with a wife alone, in dakshinachara, but literally and with any member of the circle, in vamachara). *Coitus reservatus*, the key element in such ritualized sex, could be replaced, however, in more respectable forms of Tantrism by the mystic union of Shakti and Siva within one's own body through rousing the *kundalini*, or by the sublimation of sex into the childlike love for the mother-goddess.[125] Disreputable, yet often deeply attractive, Tantric and Sahajiya tradi-tions have had a powerful appeal for low castes and women — while providing at the same time a kind of secret second life to many high-caste men (as autobiographical literature well into the twentieth century occasionally reveals).[126]

Ramakrishna's conversation reveals considerable knowledge about Kartabhaja and Tantric practices and technical terms.[127] The Karta-bhaja, whose practices included ritual violation of caste — and possibly sexual taboos at an annual festival at Ghoshpara — figure in one catalogue of valid forms of devotion, on par with Vaishnava, Shakta, Vedantic and Brahmo.[128] And another account of their teachings is

---

[125] Sir John Woodruffe, *Sakti and Sakta* (Madras, 1918, 1965), Chapter 27; Heinrich Zimmer, *Philosophies of India* (New York, 1951, 1956), pt. III, Chapter V; Chintaharan Chakrabarti, *Tantras: Studies on their Religion and Literature* (Calcutta, 1963); N.N. Bhattacharji, *History of the Tantric Religion* (Delhi, 1982). Dakshin-chara and Vamachara refer to the 'right-hand' and 'left-hand' varieties of Tantric ritual. Kundalini is the 'serpent power' which supposedly lies coiled on the lowest extremity of the spinal cord, and has to be aroused. See Bhattacharji, Chapter II.

[126] See, for instance, Motilal Roy, *Jivan-Sangini* (Calcutta, 3rd ed., 1968), pp. 39-48, and *passim*.

[127] So much so that the *Kathamrita* was used by Zimmer to illustrate his presentation of Tantrism, while Ramakrishna's 'lucid' exposition of Kartabhaja tenets is taken to be authoritative in Ramakanta Chakrabarti, *Vaisnavism in Bengal* (Calcutta, 1985), Chapter XX.

[128] For the Kartabhaja, apart from Sudhir Chakrabarti and Ramakanta

immediately followed by the assertion that 'only the low can become high . . . cultivation is difficult on uplands'.[129] Yet disciples were repeatedly warned also that the Kartabhaja combined 'big words . . . with licence. Theirs is a very dirty sadhana, like entering the house through a latrine'.[130]

A similar ambivalence characterizes Ramakrishna's many references to Tantrism, which, arguably, was much more fundamental to his entire way of thinking than has been generally acknowledged.[131] Tantrism, as expressed particularly through the songs of Ramprasad, probably helped Ramakrishna to blend together — as Ramprasad had done a century before — the two major traditions of Bengal Hinduism: Shakta and Vaishnava. The much quoted equation of money with soil *(taka mati, mati taka)* has an obvious affinity with the Tantric affirmation of the identity of 'cremation-ground and dwelling-place, gold and grass'.[132] Affinities are noticeable also between Ramakrishna and his near-contemporary Bamakshepa, the pagal Tantric sadhu of Tarapith cremation-ground in Birbhum — another poor brahman without formal learning who likewise combined catholicity with intense devotion to Kali. Bamakshepa, who avoided Calcutta and deliberately flaunted a rough and bawdy style of speech, perhaps indicates what Ramakrishna could have been if he had remained fixated in his pagal phase, and not evolved into a guru preferring a purely urban bhadralok audience.[133]

The *Kathamrita* discourse, however, is replete also with warnings about Tantric sadhana with women — even though that precisely was what Bhairabi Brahmani had taught Ramakrishna, making him

---

Chakrabarti, see Debendranath De, *Kartabhaja Dharmar Itibritta* (Calcutta, 1968, 1990). I owe the last reference to Ratnabali Chatterji.

[129] *KM* IV, p. 169 (19 September 1884); *KM* II, pp. 30-1 (8 April 1883).

[130] *KM* V, p. 181 (23 March 1884).

[131] Walter Neevel has argued that Ramakrishna's ideas can be understood 'more adequately in the categories of Tantric thought and practice than in the concepts of Sankara's advaita which the-biographers primarily employ.' 'The Transformation of Ramakrishna' in Bardwell L. Smith, *Hinduism: New Essays in the History of Religion* (London, 1976), p. 76. Following Zimmer, Neevel emphasizes the allegedly 'world-affirmative' aspects of Tantra, as opposed to Vedantic-ascetic renunciation; this, he argues, links Ramakrishna with Vivekananda's social service. Zimmer, however, had pointed out that Tantric 'dionysian' affirmation was of the world 'just as it is' — this could as well rule out ameliorative action.

[132] Jitendranath Bandopadhyay, *Panchopasana* (Calcutta, 1960), p. 270.

[133] Jogindranath Chattopadhyay, *Bamakshepa* (Calcutta, 1918).

sit on the lap of a beautiful nude young woman as the culminating point of a long process of training.[134] The Tantrism Ramakrishna himself talked about followed the safer forms of arousing the kundalini, and pursuit of santan-bhava. Conversations using or expounding Tantric terms are prefaced with the remark that these were 'secret matters' *(guhya katha)*, and Mahendranath preferred to put the bulk of such passages in the later volumes of the *Kathamrita*, published when Ramakrishna's reputation as pre-eminent saint of the bhadralok had become unassailable. He also took care to include, as an appendix to the last volume of the *Kathamrita*, a violent attack on vamacari Tantrism by Vivekananda.[135]

The vital, yet difficult and embarrassing interface between Tantric-Sahajiya traditions and Ramakrishna is reminiscent of similar problems encountered four centuries back by Chaitanya and his followers.[136] It clearly points also towards a contemporary transition. Tantric traditions were being made more respectable through excisions, and at times sought to be suppressed altogether, in bhadralok circles as stricter ideas about gentility developed in the shadow of 'Victorian' norms in the late nineteenth century.[137]

The multiplicity of religious experiences and experiments, along with the transition we have noticed from the years of mad sadhana to the more domesticated guru of the *Kathamrita*, conditioned the best-known feature of Ramakrishna's teachings — a specific blend of enormous catholicity with clear expression of preference. Catholicity for Ramakrishna was inseparable from bhakti: all forms and paths were valid, provided they were followed with genuine devotion. The mother loves to prepare varied dishes for her children, to suit their different tastes.[138] The sheer breadth of Ramakrishna's tolerance for other faiths evokes wonder and admiration today: 'There is a pond with three or four *ghats* — Hindus call what they drink *jal*, Muslims *pani*, the English water. He is called Allah by one, god by others,

---

[134] *L* I, pp. 204–5, Ramakrishna, we are assured, went immediately into samadhi.

[135] *KM* V, p. 181. I would like to acknowledge my indebtedness on this point to the ongoing work of Jeff Kripal, Chicago University research scholar, and particularly his 'Revealing/Concealing the Social: A Textual History of Mahendranath Gupta's Ramakrishna's Kathamrita', Bengal Studies Conference, 1990.

[136] Hitesranjan Sanyal, *Bangla Kirtaner Itihas* (Calcutta, 1989), *passim*.

[137] One illustration of this would be Woodruffe's *Sakti and Sakta*, with its playing down of Vamachara and argument that Tantra presents Vedic truths in forms appropriate for Kaliyuga.

[138] *KM* I, p. 21 (February 1882).

some say Brahma, others Kali, still others Ram, Hari, Jesus or Durga.'[139]

Ramakrishna's catholicity would soon come to be displayed as a timeless essence of Hinduism: its precise meanings and implications become clearer, however, if contextualized against a background of shifting lines of demarcation between religious traditions. By the 1880s a variety of pressures and influences were helping to generalize certain identities and conflicts, and a transition from 'fuzzy' to 'enumerated' communities was well under way.[140] The early 1890s would see, for the first time, Hindu–Muslim riots spread across a large part of the subcontinent on a single issue (cow protection), while Christian missionary propaganda also provoked acute tensions at times. To Ramakrishna, however, Jesus could still come between Hari and Durga in a listing of varieties of devotion, and there is no developed sense of a sharply distinct 'Hindu' identity — let alone any political use of it.[141] The total lack in him of the modern sense of history that print-culture and colonial textbooks had stimulated kept Ramakrishna immune also from the myth of 'medieval Muslim tyranny' evident in bhadralok discourse from the 1820s onwards. Whether out of innocence or deliberate choice, Ramakrishna represented a kind of protest against the creation of sectarian walls. Yet in his own way he did bear witness to changing times. Ramakrishna's acquaintances with Islam (or Christianity) were fairly minimal,[142] and the religious or philosophical concepts he used came entirely from what today would be considered 'Hindu' traditions — unlike much of pre-colonial bhakti, with its close interrelationships with Sufism, or, at a very different level, Rammohan.

A two-fold transition was under way in the late nineteenth century: the sharpening of distinctions between a 'Hindu' and other religious identities, and the blurring of differences now being perceived as internal to Hindu dharma (in the sense, actually rather new, of Hindu 'religion' or 'Hinduism'). Ramakrishna himself had no conception of hostile 'Others' in Christianity or Islam: his catholicity, nonetheless,

---

[139] *KM* I, p. 42 (27 October 1882).

[140] I am borrowing these terms from Sudipta Kaviraj.

[141] Consider for instance the following passage, 'You can reach *Iswara* through any *dharma*, pursued with sincerity. Vaishnavas, Shaktas, Vedantists, Brahmos will all attain *Iswara*, and so will Muslims and Christians'. *KM* II, p. 19 (11 March 1883). What is missing is the sense of 'Hindu' as a cohesive identity or dharma.

[142] *Life*, pp. 207–8, 253–5.

did not really involve any 'syncretism' between Hindu and other religions. It related principally to divisions within the Hindu world. Doctrinal tensions within nineteenth-century middle-class Hindu society had been sharpened by Christian polemics against idolatry and Brahmo efforts to replace image-worship by adoration of the formless (nirakar) Brahman, who was nirguna — not to be described in terms of humanly conceived qualities. There were debates also about the relative efficacy of contemplation, devotion, and ritual (jnana, bhakti and karma). Ramakrishna provided a healing touch in such conflicts — particularly welcome, perhaps, for Brahmos tired of internecine strife who became the earliest among his bhadralok admirers. Doctrinal subtleties and textual debates were irrelevant, he assured his devotees, as sakara-saguna worship (of divinities with form and qualities, given representation in images) and nirakar sadhana, jnana, bhakti, and karma, were all but alternative paths of attaining the same goal. Ramakrishna's catholicity embraced, we have already seen, Vedic-Pauranic texts and rituals, Tantrism, and obscure sects like the Kartabhaja and the Sahebdhani. Vaishnava and Shakta concepts, images and songs intermingled in his sessions with devotees, and kirtan and Ramprasad alike could send him off into the ecstatic condition that his disciples liked to call samadhi.

For the Ramakrishna of the *Kathamrita* years, however, celebration of difference always went along with clear expression of preferences. An obvious primacy was given to bhakti, and, as ecstatic devotee of Kali, Ramakrishna was bound to prefer sakara worship. One can get to a roof in many ways, Ramakrishna liked to say, by staircase, ladder, or rope — but the ways must not get mixed up: 'You have to stick firmly to one way to get to *Iswara*.'[143] To each his own, so to say — but each should normally also stick to his own. Stable choice, rather than any really open or fluid syncretism or experimentation, despite his own earlier history, was Ramakrishna's advice in the 1880s.

Here we encounter the crucially important concept of *adhikari-bheda*: immense catholicity, going along with firmly conservative maintenance of rules appropriate for each level, jati, or *sampraday* (community), which are all conceived as having a place in a multiplicity of orthopraxies. Adhikari-bheda had emerged as a formal doctrine in the seventeenth–eighteenth century as a high-Brahmanical way of accommodating difference in philosophy, belief and ritual. A particular application of it was the concept of *smarta panchopasana*

---

[143] *KM* IV, p. 135 (7 September 1884); *KM* V, p. 14 (13 August 1882).

— the equal validity and orthodoxy of devotion to Ganapati, Vishnu, Siva, Shakti, and Surya.[144] The roots, perhaps, go much further back, to the notion, basic to Hindu concepts of hierarchy and caste, of each human group having its *svadharma* (one's own religious path).[145]

Adhikari-bheda is open to somewhat different implications, depending on whether looked upon 'from below' or 'from above'. Adhikari-bheda catholicity has allowed the formation and survival of a multitude of practices and beliefs, numerous sampradayas with a fluidity and openness in their initial phases which makes even classification as Hindu or Muslim not always easy.[146] 'Living spaces' have thus opened up for subordinate groups — low castes and women — within the interstices of an order marked by great caste and gender inequality and oppression: moments during which caste could be disregarded, rituals and taboos of superiors mocked or turned on their heads.[147] Such living spaces, however, also help hierarchy and oppression to endure by making them appear less unendurable. A recent fine study of Mira and Kabir has indicated how this dialectic of protest and subordination manifested itself, above all, through bhakti.[148]

Catholicity, grounded in adhikari-bheda, can also have an opposite thrust. In official, high-caste doctrine, adhikari-bheda often becomes synonymous with, not fluidity or openness, but neat compartmentalization, the drawing-up of more definite boundaries, and the arrangement of the various philosophies, rituals, beliefs and sampradayas in a fixed hierarchy culminating in high-Brahman practices and Advaita Vedantist philosophy. Mid-nineteenth-century conservative Bengali Hindu texts like Loknath Basu's *Hindu-dharma-marma* (Calcutta, 1856, 1872) and Nandakumar Kabiratna's *Sandeha-nirasana* (Calcutta, 1863) have a conception of orthopraxy at first sight almost as broad as Ramakrishna's, but this is used essentially as a polemical weapon in defending the *status quo* in orthopraxy against Christians, Brahmos, and 'atheists and rationalists'.[149] Reformers are condemned

---

144 Umeshchandra Bhattacharji, *Bharat-darshan-sara* (Calcutta, 1949), pp. 287–8; Jitendranath Bandopadhyay, *Panchopasana*, Chapter IV.

145 Madeleine Biardieu, p. 45.

146 Two obvious examples would·be the Bauls of Bengal and the legend about Hindus and Muslims quarrelling over Kabir's body.

147 For some examples, see Sashibhushan Dasgupta, *Obscure Religious Cults* (Calcutta, 1946), and Sudhir Chakrabarti.

148 See Kumkum Sangari.

149 Thus, 'varna-bhiveda (caste distinctions) are essential for mukti sadhan (quest for salvation) . . . since the Supreme Lord has given different *shakti* (powers) to different *jatis* . . . What is bad is to lose one's *dharma*. The possibility

as intolerant — banning even voluntary sati, forcibly trying to modify age-old customs of marriage and widowhood, insulting the simple faith of the masses in image-worship. Caste was irrelevant at the highest levels of Vedantic jnana and sanyas: being unimportant, no effort was needed to attack it in everyday practice.

The adhikari-bheda of Ramakrishna has to be situated within this continuum between the two logically opposed poles of extreme fluidity and precise definition of hierarchy. Thus caste, on the whole, was not particularly prominent in his discourse, and he often recalled how, in the days of mad sadhana, his own sacred thread 'had flown off by itself'.[150] But Ramakrishna, too, argued that caste becomes unimportant through a natural process of spiritual realization alone, and once used an abusive epithet about those who tried to end it through conscious effort. A joke he made was resented as an instance of high-caste prejudice by a Teli devotee.[151] In more general terms, we have seen Ramakrishna move in personal life from extreme religious experimentation towards an insistence on each sticking to his own practices and beliefs in a world of fairly rigid divisions. But this was still some distance removed from a single, clear-cut hierarchization exalting the supremacy of Vedantic monism based on the jnana of learned, high-brahmanical culture. Ramakrishna occasionally admitted this superiority in theory, but loved to reiterate his own preference for dualistic bhakti through Ramprasad's words: 'I do not want to become sugar, for I love its taste.' Ambiguity persisted also in the relationship between Vedic-Pauranic and Tantric traditions. In Vivekananda, we shall see, the transition would be completed, with Vedantic jnana firmly placed at the apex of a single, well-defined hierarchy. This was accompanied by a much sharper definition of dividing lines between Hindu and other religious traditions. In Ramakrishna, in contrast, the term 'Hindu' is not particularly common, and the Hindu/Muslim/Christian demarcation often does not seem qualitatively too different from the distinctions between Shakta, Vaishnava and Brahmo. The post-*Kathamrita* canonical literature, however, tended to read back such firm hierarchization and dividing lines into Ramakrishna, emphasizing his affinities

---

of salvation remains so long as any *dharma* is devoutly followed.' Lokenath Basu, *Hindu-dharma-marma* (Calcutta, 1856, 1873), pp. 2, 67.

150 *KM* II, p. 2 (16 October 1882).

151 *KM* II, pp. 27–8 (8 April 1883).

with Vedanta.[152] The sacred thread and conventional sanyasi attire, to take another example, came back in most standard iconographic representation of Ramakrishna, in significant contrast to *Kathamrita* descriptions and the seldom-reproduced 1879 photograph.[153]

Along with Ramakrishna's catholicity, many facets of the bhadra-lok cult that developed around him as guru provide entry points into a religious world in process of being reshaped and crystallized into modern Hinduism. The guru in Indian traditions has taken on multifarious and changing forms. Guru cults have been indispensable for most lower-caste Hindu or *be-shara* Sufi heterodoxies, as necessary concomitant to their rejection of the textual expertise of brahmans and mullahs.[154] *Diksha* (initiation) from a guru is indispensable also for Tantric sadhana and many forms of Vaishnava devotion, and orthodox high-caste families often have kula-gurus, giving initiation through a secret mantra. Fundamental usually to all these forms is an initiation rite, and a conception of *parampara* or lineage. Thus the relationship between kula-guru and the families initiated by him would be inheritable on both sides in a pattern similar to the lineage in matters of puja and life-cycle rituals between the upper-caste *jajman* and the family *purohit*. The guru would normally expect complete deference and obedience, might sometimes acquire a reputation for miraculous powers, and even come to the regarded as true object of worship. The kula-gurus of orthodox families had a guiding role in crucial family decisions, while the gurus of lower-caste sects or Tantric circles presided over distinctive and generally secret rituals, involving ecstatic song and dance and, at times, ritualized sex. The subterranean world of non-brahmanical heterodoxies developed as a corollary an enigmatic *sandhya-bhasha*, or language of twilight, rich in double meanings, full of images drawn from everyday life which seemed simple but had deeper meanings for the initiated.[155]

Ramakrishna's circle was distinctive here in many ways. The need to find and stay near a *sat-guru* (true guru), presumably himself above all, was a constant refrain in Ramakrishna's conversation. But relations

---

152 Walter Neevel; *L* I, II, *passim*.

153 The photograph was published in Gurudas Barman, *Sri Sri Ramakrish-nacarit* (Calcutta, 1910), a never-reprinted biography, which lies today in the Rare Book Section of the National Library (Calcutta). It has been reproduced, to the best of my knowledge, only once — in Brojen Banerji and Sajanikanta Das.

154 Madeleine Biardieu, pp. 73-5.

155 Sashibhushan Dasgupta, *Obscure Religious Cults, passim*. See also Daniel Gold, *The Lord as Guru: Hindi Sants in the Northern Indian Tradition* (Oxford, 1987).

with disciples remained relaxed and informal. Ramakrishna never claimed special miraculous powers, often expressed contempt for such *siddhai*, and disappointed some devotees by consulting a doctor during his last fatal illness. There were usually no initiation rites or mantras,[156] no insistence on total obedience, and not even very much outward deference as the Thakur uninhibitedly 'played' with his boys and went together with them to watch plays. Ramakrishna did not seek to displace the diksha-giving kula-guru in the lives of his upper-caste disciples: his remained a purely emotional influence, more or less independent of specific life-cycle moments or situations, and perhaps all the more powerful because of this relative detachment from everyday life. An open-market fluidity, suited to a metropolitan, mobile society thus distinguished Ramakrishna from more traditional types of gurus, and the printed word played a crucial role in the spread of his reputation.[157] There were some tendencies, however, towards the end of Ramakrishna's life and particularly after his death, towards a reabsorption of Ramakrishna into more familiar patterns of religious leadership. The *Kathamrita* records debates among disciples about Ramakrishna's possible avatar-status,[158] the *Lilaprasanga* mentions some miraculous incidents,[159] many devotees began worshipping him formally after his death, and Sarada and the swamijis of the Ramakrishna Mission started giving diksha to new recruits.[160]

The *Kathamrita* accounts of sessions with Ramakrishna repeatedly highlight the Thakur's frequent trances, and these obviously enhanced his appeal. Ramakrishna, from boyhood on, had periodically lost consciousness, become motionless as a statue, and then seemed to be talking on very familiar terms with figures (usually Kali) visible to him alone. The possible physical or psychotic explanations here are less important than the interpretations given by different cultures to trance states.[161] Considered in early days to be a form of illness

---

156 *KM* IV, p. 191 (20 October 1885), *KM* V, p. 121 (24 May 1884).

157 Particularly, in the late 1870s, the journals brought out by the Keshab Sen group. For details, see Brojen Banerji and Sajanikanta Das, *passim*.

158 Girishchandra Ghosh and Ramchandra Datta in particular upheld the avatar thesis, and the *KM* records sharp debates around this issue with Mahendralal Sircar — in, particularly, *KM* IV, pp. 258, 264, 266-7, 275-6 (23-4 October 1885).

159 These amount to no more than supernatural visions seen by Ramakrishna and not external transformations.

160 See below.

161 I.M. Lewis, *Ecstatic Religion: An Anthropological Study of Spirit Possession and Shamanism* (Harmondsworth, Penguin, 1971, 1975), p. 39.

bordering on lunacy, or instances of spirit possession (and as such apparently responsible for attracting large crowds during Rama-krishna's brief visits of Kamarpukur),[162] the trances came to be invariably interpreted by bhadralok devotees as samadhi: the mystical communion in high-Hindu sadhana in which the individual *jivatma* merges for a while with *paramatma* or Brahman, the ultimate in spiritual realization. A monistic Vedantic stamp was thus put on a man who on the whole seems to have preferred the ways of dualistic devotion.

The trances were often preceded or accompanied by ecstatic songs and dances joined in by devotees. These had been important features of the secret inner life of plebeian sects (the sole written text of the Kartabhaja, for instance, had been *Bhaver Geet*, a collection of songs).[163] There was nothing secret, however, about Ramakrishna's circle, and not a trace of the ritualized sex central to the hidden life of many Tantric-cum-Sahajiya 'esoteric' cults. Women devotees, in fact, were carefully segregated from the men by Ramakrishna. Unlike mainstream Gaudiya Vaishnavabad, again, which too had abjured esoteric practices while retaining the centrality of song, the singing and dancing in this purely bhadralok cult remained an indoor affair. Chaitanya and his followers had made song (kirtan) the principal mode of mass proselytization, and Keshab Sen tried to revive this mode for Brahmoism in the 1870s. We never hear, however, of Ramakrishna leading *san-kirtan* processions in streets.

The absence of distinctive secret rituals left its mark on Rama-krishna's language. Closer, in its use of everyday images drawn from rural life and labour, to the language of lower-caste sects than to the formal sutra-bhashya format of high-Brahmanical exegesis, its mean-ing always remained single and on the surface. Sandhya-bhasha had been marked by a richness and fluidity of metaphor: the boatmen, river, or caged bird of the Bauls can be understood in many different ways.[164] Metaphor, in contrast, is rare in Ramakrishna: its place is taken by clear-cut analogies or parables, with the intended message

162 During his occasional visits to Kamarpukur, 'the place where the Master was staying was thronged to its utmost capacity with men and women since his ecstacy, resulting in frequent *samadhi* . . . attracted the people'. *Life*, pp. 290-1.

163 Ramakanta Chakrabarti; Debendranath De.

164 Charles H. Capwell, 'The Esoteric Beliefs of the Bauls of Bengal', *Journal of Asian Studies*, XXXIII, 2 February 1974. Asitkumar Bandopadhyay, *Bangla Sahityer Itibritta* III, 2 (Calcutta, 1966, 1981).

often carefully verbalized.[165] Drained of metaphorical excess and iconoclastic content, the rustic turn of phrase and quotidian analogy of the twentieth-century urban guru, god-man or god-woman ends up in banalities. Ramakrishna perhaps represents an early phase of this transition towards an urban consumer-oriented Hinduism.

Ramakrishna, then, did not offer to his devotees any definitive set of rituals or doctrines, the satisfaction of total surrender to a diksha-guru, or promise of miracles. To the middle-aged householders who constituted his principal audience in the *Kathamrita*, his was a broad message of what in bhakti traditions has often been called *grihastha sanyas*.[166] Despite the repeated condemnations of kamini and kanchan, renunciation was not called for. The devotee could remain in the world, while not allowing himself to get immersed totally within it, on the model of the dasi in her master's household. 'You have money and wealth, and yet you call Iswara — that is very good.' A brahmo sub-judge once summed up what might well have been a characteristic audience response when he declared that he was 'filled with peace and happiness on hearing that there . . . [was] no need to leave the world, that Iswara can be attained even while living as a householder.'[167] Thus wealth could still be pursued, though in a non-attached *(nishkama)* manner, and the wife could remain, though sex should be given up after one or two children. The pursuit of bhakti within one's household even had its advantages and was like fighting from inside a fort, for one's minimum material needs would be taken care of.[168] Here, in other words, was a kind of 'this-worldly mysticism' — living in the world, pursuing the normal bhadralok way of life, but inwardly distancing[169] oneself from its travails and frustrations as typified,

[165] I have been helped greatly while formulating this contrast by Kumkum Sangari's distinction between Kabir's reliance on 'the intellectual clarity and "distance" of analogy or allegory' and Mira's 'blurred and displacing realm of metaphor'.

[166] See, for instance, the well-known analysis of Louis Dumont, 'World Renunciation in Indian Religions', *Contributions to Indian Sociology*, IV, 1960.

[167] *KM* IV, p. 31 (16 December 1883); *KM* I, pp. 151-3 (19 October 1884).

[168] *KM* I, p. 153 (19 October 1884).

[169] I am adapting the concept of 'distancing' from the work of the German social historian Alf Ludtke, who has developed the category of *Eigensinn* to analyse a variety of everyday working-class attitudes. These involve a kind of withdrawal or distancing into partially autonomous spaces, and, despite the vast differences in contexts and forms, I find Ludtke helpful in suggesting a way out of the somewhat rigid subordination/resistance binary. Alf Ludtke,

above all, in the chronotype of chakri. Schematically, this can be regarded as the polar opposite of Weberian worldly asceticism. The one allowed householder devotees to pursue wealth in moderation, in obviously traditional, non-innovative ways, with no premium placed upon diligence and economic success — rather its opposite. The other, in its ultimate seventeenth-century Puritan manifestation, had inculcated a work ethic based on new conceptions of time and discipline, where salvation was sought 'primarily through immersion in one's worldly vocation'.[170]

The doctrinal component of grihastha-sanyas came from a blending of selected Vaishnava and Shakta elements: once again, through Ramakrishna, we can watch the processes of continuity-cum-change at work within religious traditions. Ramakrishna disliked the more ritualistic, vaidhi forms of Vaishnava devotion, while rejecting, by implication, also the alternative, more simple and plebeian, emphasis upon formal reiteration of *Hari-nama* alone.[171] Emotional, *raganuga* bhakti, conveyed primarily through songs (kirtans), figure prominently, however, in accounts of Ramakrishna's sessions with his devotees. He was fairly knowledgeable about, but not deeply interested in, the intricacies of Gaudiya Vaishnava scholasticism — with the significant exception of the doctrine of the five bhavas, which enters his conversation very frequently. A link may be suggested here with grihastha sanyas, for, as Dineshchandra Sen perceptively remarked many years ago, the remarkable thing about the Gaudiya Vaishnava theory of bhavas was the relationship established through it between religious sensibility and the emotions of everyday householder life: parental affection, friendship, love (adulterous as well as conjugal), the devotion of servant to master.[172] The dasya-bhava Ramakrishna had come to prefer was expounded by him through a series of homologous parables. Here king and khansama (servant), baralok patron and would-be client, babu and durwan (gatekeeper) have implications which are doctrinal as well as (obviously) social, for they are being used to assert the claims of dualistic bhakti over

---

'The Historiography of Everyday Life: The Personal and the Political', in Samuel and Jones (eds), *Culture, Ideology and Politics: Essays for Eric Hobsbawn* (London, 1982); G. Eley, 'Labour History, Social History, Alltagsgeschichte: Experience, Culture and the Politics of the Everyday — A New Direction for German Social History?' *Journal of Modern History*, 61, ii, June 1989.

170 Max Weber, *Sociology of Religion* (Boston, 1969), pp. 167, 270.

171 *KM* II, p. 18 (11 March 1883).

172 Dineshchandra Sen, *Brihat-Banga*, vol. II (Calcutta, 1935), p. 690.

Vedantic monism. The *samanya jiva* (humble being) should not assume an immediate identity with the Absolute; he needs a prior mediation through devoted service, bhakti expressed through seba:

The king is sitting: if the *khansama* goes and occupies the king's seat, saying, 'King, what you are, I am, too', people will think him mad. But the king himself, pleased by the khansama's service (seba), might tell him one day, 'Why don't you come and sit, next to me — what you are, I am, too'. Then if he sits, that would be all right.[173]

Personalized seba is the opposite of rule- and time-bound chakri governed by the cash nexus, dasya-bhava contrasts with dasatya — and yet the etymological near-identity of dasya and dasatya may not be entirely irrelevant. The servant–master model was not tension-free and demanded constant effort: it remained some distance removed from Ramakrishna's favourite bhakti image of the kitten clinging to its mother in total surrender. Dasya-bhava in Ramakrishna ultimately takes second place to santan-bhava, relating to divinity as child to mother. This had no place in Gaudiya Vaishnava scholastics but came to Ramakrishna from Shakta traditions, as modulated above all through Ramprasad's songs. Santan-bhava, unlike dasya, could be perceived as unmediated, effortless intimacy, made tension-free by complete surrender — and so Ramakrishna ultimately privileged Shakta over Vaishnava, Kali over every other deity.

Shakta–Vaishnava relations had been quite conflict-ridden at times,[174] but a coming together became noticeable from the eighteenth century, with Tantrism often providing the unifying substratum. The Tantric centre of Tarapith, for instance, became a favourite haunt for Vaishnava as well as Shakta sadhus.[175] Formal Shakta doctrine was, and remained, essentially Tantric, but the emergence of a rich tradition of religious poetry and song *(shyamasangit)* from Ramprasad onwards added a vital emotional dimension, absent in the often purely mechanical Tantric practices.[176] Derived in part from Vaishnava imagery, and repeatedly emphasizing the

173 *KM* II, p. 63 (15 June 1883).

174 There was an evident contrast between the Vaishnava emphasis on love and non-violence and Shakta animal sacrifices and blood imagery.

175 Jogendranath Chattopadhyay, *Bamakshepa*, p. 39.

176 Compare, e.g., the 'mechanistic, and even crass', Tantric-Sahajiya text translated by Edward G. Dimock, *The Place of the Hidden Moon* (Chicago, 1966), pp. 235–48, with the richly emotive songs of Ramprasad, or the Shyamasangits incorporated in the audio-cassettes of the twentieth-century singer Pannalal Bhattacharji.

essential identity of Kali and Krishna (and quite often many other forms of devotion), the resultant mix became an extremely powerful compound, richer perhaps in the range of human experience it could incorporate than Gaudiya Vaishnavabad. The aestheticized love-play central to Vaishnava song *(padabali)* had little to say about death or suffering other than *viraha* (separation from the beloved). Shyamasangit (Shakta songs) deliberately embraced sharper polarities: Mother Kali emerged as grotesque, terrible and beautiful — cruel, wayward, and yet somehow endlessly loving.[177] Acceptance of total divine control was combined with a recognition of infinite divine caprice,[178] and the devotee's own response could oscillate across many registers: expression of sheer terror and anguish, deep resentment about the inequities of life, jubilant embracing of contradictions, a sense of triumph over suffering achieved perhaps through Tantric sadhana, the peace of complete child-like surrender to the Divine Mother. Such complexities no doubts appeared more relevant than the endless love-play at Vrindaban in times of trouble, of rapid change beyond comprehension or control — the times, in different ways, of both Ramprasad and Ramakrishna. Kali, again, is related in many ways to conceptions of Kal (time) and Kaliyuga:[179] the Kaliyuga moods we have analysed as crucial for Ramakrishna had perhaps a special affinity for Shakta forms of devotion. It may not be coincidental that a significantly large number of composers of Shyamasangit came from more old-fashioned, often declining, zamindars and zamindari officials of late-eighteenth- and early-nineteenth-century Bengal.[180] Mother goddess cults had flourished also in diverse forms among many plebeian groups. Even in the 1880s Mahendralal Sircar, the doctor treating Ramakrishna during his last illness, could dismiss Kali as 'that Santal bitch'.[181] A major contribution of Ramakrishna, perhaps, was to help make Shakti worship much more respectable and widespread among western-educated middle-class groups.

[177] Sashibhushan Dasgupta, *Bharate Shakti-sadhana O Shakta Sahitya* (Calcutta, 1960), Chapter 8; Asitkumar Bandopadhyay, *Bangla Sahityer Itibritta*, III, 2 (Calcutta, 1966, 1981), Chapter 3.

[178] As for instance in Dewan Ramdulal Nandi of Tripura's *'sakali tomar iccha icchamayee Tara tumi'*.

[179] W.C. Beane, *Myth, Cult and Symbols in Sakta Hinduism* (London, 1977), Chapter 5.

[180] Asitkumar Bandhopadhyay.

[181] *KM* I, p. 235 (26 October 1885).

Shakta worship in Bengal had developed around the two poles of secret Tantric chakras (circles) and public Kali or Durga Pujas, organized often amidst great ostentation by zamindari households or other rich patrons. Ramakrishna, like Ramprasad a hundred years before, shifted the emphasis away from these poles towards a more intimate, yet domesticated and respectable, form of devotion in which Shyamasangit (sung individually, unlike the congregational Vaishnava sankirtan) acquired a central role. Ramakrishna, however, as we have seen, toned down considerably the accents of anguish and resentment which had been very noticeable in Ramprasad. He projected a much less tension-ridden conception of the mother goddess. Ramprasad's Kali was often unjust, cruel, partial towards her rich sons: the poet's ego retained an independent identity and, as in all real-life families, the mother–son relationship was not bereft of tensions and contradictions. Such maturity seems to have been deliberately abandoned by Ramakrishna in an act of total surrender of ego, imagining himself to be a child, or indeed perhaps an infant, in a kind of womb reversion, completely free of problems, because unquestioning.

Ramakrishna went beyond the Ramprasad model also in his insistence that santan-bhava, looking upon all women as emanations of the mother goddess — and so, without exception, as mothers — was the only way one could hope to conquer the lure of kamini. A very strong personal note is evident in Ramakrishna's many passages about the horrors of the feminine body, as well as in his obsessive equation of sex with defecation. Sarada Debi recalled later that dysentery, of which her husband has been a chronic victim, had often made his body an object of disgust for Ramakrishna. There seems to have developed in him a deep fear of matter flowing out of one's body — and the orifices of women appeared enormous and frightening.[182] One might also speculate that the Tantric sexual exercises Bhairabi Brahmani had made Ramakrishna undertake had contributed to a distaste and revulsion for heterosexual intercourse. But once again the personal in Ramakrishna is related also to the social-cum-historical: a very similar theme of overcoming sexuality by conceiving of the temptress as mother is prominent in Nathpanthi legends about Gorakhnath which have circulated for centuries in Bengal's countryside.[183]

Ramakrishna's mother-worship has also a wider dimension going beyond the limits of purely Shakta practices — for it may be related

[182] *KM* IV, p. 68 (2 February 1884); p. 201 (5 October 1884).
[183] Asitkumar Bandopadhyay, II, I (Calcutta, 1966, 1988).

to certain major shifts within bhadralok constructions of woman-hood. For much of the nineteenth century, bhadralok discourses had persistently problematized conjugality, constructing the woman — usually the wife — as victim in need of male reformist succour, epitome of surrender to alien values, or last repository of indigenous virtue in a world otherwise lost to foreign Western domination. The pure woman — again, in late-nineteenth-century plays as wife more often than mother — could also occasionally figure as active agent in a deferentially assertive mode. Ramakrishna, who radically deval-ued all forms of conjugal relationships and presented woman-as-mother as sole counterpoint to the horrors of kamini, was a part of, and contributed to, a decisive shift in the direction of identifying ideal womanhood with an iconic mother figure.

The new, enormously valorized mother–son relationship quickly took on patriotic overtones. Already in the early 1880s, in Bankim-chandra's *Anandamath*, with its 'Bande Mataram hymn', the wild and terrible Kali is the 'Mother as she has become', oppressed and starving — while the resplendent ever-bountiful Durga symbolizes the future liberated 'mother' land. The duty of the sons is an active one — the liberation of the Mother from alien bondage. Durga Puja correspondingly from around the turn of the century started emerg-ing from the households of zamindars to become *sarbajanin* — community-organized — in towns, and Hindu nationalists during the Swadeshi era made many efforts to appropriate Puja rituals and the Shyamasangit form for the patriotic cause.[184]

Ramakrishna himself — for whom Kali was beautiful and ever-loving in her very wildness, in need of no transformation, demanding no activity but only total childlike surrender — remained quite far removed from this Hindu nationalist discourse. And yet the gulf between childlike immersion and activist duty was not unbridgeable, as Vivekananda would soon indicate.

Our focus so far has been primarily on the *Kathamrita*, and it is easy from that to slip into an assumption that Ramakrishna's teachings in the early 1880s constitute a single bloc. But speech is inherently 'dialogic', modulated by contexts and audiences[185] — and Ramakrishna's devotees included many apart from the middle-aged householders who tend to predominate in Mahendranath's text. The *Kathamrita* does not give an equivalent direct access to other groups:

184 For some details, see my *Swadeshi Movement in Bengal 1903–8*, Chapter VI.
185 V.N. Voloshinov, *Marxism and the Philosophy of Language* (Leningrad, 1930; London, 1973).

the very young men who later become sanyasis (they are often present, but not possibly in their more intimate conversations with the saint — for 'M', householder himself, never quite became a member of that inner circle), the wives and widows, the prostitutes-turned-actresses. Ramakrishna's message may well have varied somewhat to suit such distinct audiences, making the range of possible appropriations even wider.

For middle-aged householders, as we have seen, Ramakrishna offered bhakti — embodied in grihastha sanyas — as an 'easy way', soothing many tensions, demanding no learned understanding of doctrine or mastery over ritual, requiring virtually no sacrifice of normal bhadralok careers and lifestyles. These needed only to be carried out in a nishkama, detached manner. In addition, the condemnation of social activism could perhaps be read by such people — some of them reasonably well off — as a denial of the need to spend savings on too much charity or philanthropy.

But it might still be unduly cynical to explain Ramakrishna's appeal, even among this milieu, entirely in terms of his providing a comfortable 'theodicy of good fortune'. The element of playfulness and rejection of some of the inhibitions of normal bhadralok behaviour (becoming emotional in public, dancing in ecstasy) could have been particularly attractive to middle-aged householders in contrast to the dingy formalities of respectable adult life. The lure of a kind of sanctified escape from responsibility, at a time when these tend to crowd upon a man with the onset of middle age, should not be underestimated. Again, middle-aged devotees, even when reasonably successful, must as minor government officials and senior clerks have been frequently subject to the pinpricks of a superior and foreign officialdom. The critique of chakri would not have appeared meaningless here. Through Ramakrishna the householder could perhaps find the solace and comfort of an inner space, distanced from an everyday world dominated increasingly by money and alien power.

The message for the young men and boys was presumably somewhat different, and far more challenging, than that imparted to householders, for it inspired some of them to make a definitive break with kamini and kanchan in the forms of marriage and conventional jobs. Quite often they had to overcome considerable parental hostility even for visiting Ramakrishna, for frequent trips to Dakshineswar could mean neglecting the formal studies which had become the indispensable qualification for respectable professional or clerical careers. Ramakrishna often encouraged such truancy and once made a pun which equated passing examinations with bondage.[186] For these teenagers here was a middle-aged man, revered saint and perhaps avatar, who mixed and talked freely with them in a manner at once serious and yet utterly informal. Such a combination would have been rare with elders in hierarchized homes or with teachers in schools or colleges — the second major site, so far as bhadralok were concerned, of the new discipline of time. This transcending of the barriers of age and youth, work and play, in Ramakrishna's company perhaps had a particular attraction for adolescents engaged in a difficult transition from boyhood to adult responsibility.

We have already explored some of the ways in which chakri, the petty clerical job which was all that most of these young men could have otherwise aspired for, had come to be perceived as quintessentially unattractive. It was also getting more difficult to obtain, as Narendranath, academically the brightest among Ramakrishna's disciples, discovered through bitter personal experience when his father's sudden death in 1884 made him hunt desperately for some time for an office job.[187] Conjugality, the other sacrifice demanded of a sanyasi, apparently had few attractions, too. The Kathamrita is full of hints that the young married men drawn to Ramakrishna were neglecting their wives — with considerable encouragement, at times, from the saint himself. Biographical accounts of devotees mention with some regularity a repugnance for married life, at times preceding the first encounter with Ramakrishna.[188] The prospect, usually, was of marriage by parental arrangement with much younger, uneducated girls, well below the age of puberty.[189] Western education and tastes,

---

[186] Swami Gambhirananda (ed.), *Apostles of Shri Ramakrishna* (Calcutta, 1967), p. 124.

[187] *Life of Swami Vivekananda by his Eastern and Western Disciples* (Almora, 1912, 1963), pp. 88-90.

[188] See, for instance, the accounts of Yogananda (Yogindranath Chaudhuri), Saradananda (Sarat Chakrabarti), Sivananda (Taraknath Ghosh) and Turiyananda (Harinath Chattopadhyay) in Gambhirananda, pp. 148, 171, 202, 305; as well as the biography of a lay devotee, Saratchandra Chakrabarti's *Saadhu Nag Mahasay* (Calcutta, 1912, 1934).

[189] The *garbhadan* ritual demanded intercourse immediately after the first menses, and there was a massive agitation, particularly in Bengal, against the reformist-cum-government proposal to raise the age of consent to twelve years in 1891. Amiya Sen, *Hindu Revivalism in Late Nineteenth Century Bengal* (Delhi, 1993); Tanika Sarkar, 'Rhetoric Against the Age of Consent: Resisting Colonial

confined overwhelmingly so far to males, may have created a new cultural distance within the bhadralok family. More important, however, was the close interconnection between marriage and the sharpened struggle for survival bound up with the travails of chakri. 'Nowadays parents marry their boys too young. By the time they finish their education, they are already fathers of children and have to run hither and thither in search of a job to maintain the family' — Ramakrishna had told Sarat and Sashi Chakrabarti, cousins who later became prominent figures in the Ramakrishna Mission.[190] Life-stories of many disciples indicate more or less independent perceptions of the same crucial association of kamini with a kanchan obtainable, in niggardly amounts, only through chakri.

The skewed family situation, considered from the woman's angle, may go some distance towards explaining what otherwise appears the most puzzling of Ramakrishna's many paradoxes. The man whose conversation was full of extremely negative comments about the lust-filled bodies and luxurious and selfish ways of women still won the devotion of many women.[191] We even have accounts of women casting off inhibitions and parda to go to Dakshineswar in a spirit of almost joyous abandon.[192] Ramakrishna's abhorrence of sex, and his advice to keep off intercourse after one or two children, perhaps struck a chord in married women. Sex may have often seemed a terrible duty for young girls married off to totally unknown men at a tender age, in an era when absence of contraceptives made child-bearing frequent, dangerous and extremely burdensome.[193] Middle-aged or elderly housewives or widows may have found a way of overcoming loneliness and the tedium of household chores by setting themselves up in a maternal role vis-à-vis Ramakrishna. They loved to cook and bring

---

Reason and the Death of a Child-Wife' *Economic and Political Weekly*, 4 September 1993.

[190] Gambhirananda, p. 171.

[191] Thus *KM* II, pp. 161–2 (11 October 1882); *KM* III, pp. 161–2 (9 May 1888), related a story about a guru who convinces a disciple that family affection is illusory, by giving him a medicine that apparently kills him: his mother and wife, though apparently full of sorrow, refuse the guru's offer that he could return to life if they are prepared to die in his place. The story is not directly about the evils of kamini at all — but, significantly, no male relative is put to the same test.

[192] *L* I, *Gurubhava-Purbardha*, pp. 31–6.

[193] A somewhat similar phenomenon has been noticed among early Methodist women: Henry Abelove, 'The Sexual Polities of Early Western Methodism' in Obelkevich, *et al.* (ed.), *Disciplines of Faith* (London, 1987).

food for him, which the holy man eagerly accepted and often asked for.[194] And while little survives of Ramakrishna's conversation with feminine audiences, one must not exclude the possibility that he added an extremely rare, non-personal and (in a limited sense) intellectual content to lives otherwise largely bereft of such mental sustenance.

A startling element was added to the circle of women devotees of Ramakrishna after his visit to Girish Ghosh's play *Chaitanya-Lila* (1884). The holy man blessed Binodini for her performance as the young Chaitanya: the man who normally abhorred feminine contact allowed actresses, recruited from among prostitutes, to touch his feet. Sex in such degraded form was presumably an object of pity and grace, not a threat — and perhaps, for a man who found even sex in marriage intolerable, prostitution was not all that specially repugnant. Ramakrishna's unexpected blessing of theatre women gave a new respectability to a profession despised by many,[195] and assuaged feelings of guilt: he became, in fact, in course of time a kind of patron-saint for the Calcutta public theatre.[196] A wider impact became noticeable also when, in the mid 1890s, prostitutes — and not merely actresses drawn from them — began turning up in large numbers at the annual Ramakrishna birthday festivals at Dakshineswar, much to the horror of many bhadralok.[197] Binodini herself, with some limited encouragement from Girishchandra Ghosh, was emboldened to publish a moving, if somewhat flamboyantly repentant, account of her life as prostitute and actress.[198]

The paradox of the Ramakrishna cult opening up certain spaces for women, in and through highly sexist assumptions and practices, is epitomized in the career of Sarada Debi. The wife who in her husband's lifetime was relegated firmly to household duties, and who could never become a mother thanks to Ramakrishna, blossomed out after Ramakrishna's death into a cult figure in her own right, 'Holy Mother', embodiment of motherhood for Vivekananda and other devotees. Her sayings, taken down and preserved by reverential

---

194 Ibid., p. 33; *L* II, *Gurubhava-Uttarardha*, p. 238.

195 More specifically by Brahmos and those influenced by them.

196 Naliniranjan Chattopadhyay, *Shri Ramakrishna O Banga Rangamancha* (Calcutta, 1978).

197 Vivekananda to Ramakrishnananda, 23 August 1896 — *Patrabali* II (Calcutta, 1949, 1960), pp. 127–8.

198 Asutosh Bhattacharji (ed.), *Nati Binodini Rachana-Sangraha* (Calcutta, 1987).

devotees as Ramakrishna's had been, vividly illuminated this paradox in their autobiographical sections. Life with her husband at Dakshineswar is repeatedly recalled as a tale of bliss *(ananda)* — and yet, without any felt sense of contradiction, we encounter at times in her very next words memories of a tiny, dismal room in an obscure corner of the temple compound with a doorway so low that you often hit your head entering it. Life was an endless round of preparing food, for Ramakrishna as well as for devotees who kept dropping in at all hours, and of waiting for nightfall to relieve herself by the river — for no one had thought of providing a latrine for women. She learnt to read only after overcoming much opposition, particularly from Hriday, the cousin of Ramakrishna who had managed the material side of the saint's life till the early 1880s. There were weeks during which Sarada hardly saw her husband and could only hear him, talking and singing with male devotees, through the chinks of a bamboo curtain. And yet life had been bliss: Ramakrishna had never called her by the contemptuous *tui* and had never beaten her.

The memories of the years after 1886 take on a very different, increasingly self-confident, if still engagingly naive, manner. Ramakrishna, Sarada tells us, appeared in a dream to tell her to start giving diksha, and she also began going into samadhi. We now have passages where she claims to be *jagater ma*, mother of the universe. Her body, precisely because it has endured so much suffering, is *dev-sharir*, divine.[199]

Prostitutes apart, all Ramakrishna's devotees came from the bhadralok — with a solitary exception: Latu, the illiterate Bihari servant the saint had inherited from his early disciple, the well-established north-Calcutta doctor Ramachandra Datta. Latu was given, appropriately, the task of cleaning up by the bhadralok disciples when Ramakrishna during his last days could not go out to defecate. The memoirs of Latu, taken down and published, provide certain fascinating sidelights. Son of a Chapra district shepherd, Latu retained all his life a dignity, independence, even a certain aggressiveness which not everyone liked and which many associated with his passion for wrestling. Serving Ramakrishna became for him a liberation from the burden of naukri in Ramchandra's household. He was fond of retelling Ramakrishna's dasi parable, adding to it a note of plebeian poignancy derived from an immediacy of experience: 'He told me this story so that I could

199 Abhaya Dasgupta (ed.), *Sri Sri Sarada Devi: Atmakatha* (Calcutta, 1980), pp. 12, 15, 18, 30-1, 34, 39, 67-8, 73, 75, 77, 79, 93, 109.

learn how to survive in the house of the manib (master). How else could my sorrows have ended?' Seba to Latu was sharply distinct from flattery — the baralok expect flattery, but not God. But seba, even for Ramakrishna, could be arduous, too — and Latu recalled how he was often scolded, and once was made to walk six miles to bring some special food for Ramakrishna. Sarada could talk freely with him, even in her years of rigorous parda — and Latu's memories about her strike a note utterly different from the standard deification into abstract mother-figure: 'How hard a life she had led. She stayed in that tiny room, for so many years, unnoticed by everyone.'

Revered as one of Ramakrishna's intimate disciples, renamed Adbhutananda, Latu steadfastly refused to stay or even spend a night at the Belur Math founded by Vivekananda. 'We are sadhus — why should we have land, houses, gardens, wealth? I won't stay in such a place.'[200]

IV

Dakshineswar temple, where Ramakrishna had lived for thirty years, and Belur Math, founded by his most illustrious disciple, face each other today on opposite banks of the Bhagirathi, presenting in many ways a vivid study in contrasts, even oppositions. The temple, like any major Hindu sacred site, is thronged with crowds which cut across class divides, noisy, colourful, not over-sensitive to dirt. The holiness of the place permits women to shed inhibitions and bathe in the river ghat alongside menfolk. The approaches are cluttered with shops selling a variety of mementoes, trinkets and eatables, and the atmosphere resembles that of a bazaar or mela. Solemnity reigns to some extent only inside the central shrine of Bhavatarini Kali, and, more evidently, in the corner room where Ramakrishna used to stay: here devotees sit, ponder, or pray. Belur Math is much more of an upper-middle-class devotional-cum-tourist spot: almost aggressively hygienic, it is full of guards and notices warning visitors off from bathing in the river or spoiling the lawns. An image of Ramakrishna, fully clothed in spotless white, constitutes the central shrine. A glass curtain preserves it from physical proximity or the touch of devotees or visitors. Asked where Vivekananda and his associates had themselves stayed, a swamiji points vaguely in the

[200] Chandrasekhar Chattopadhyay, *Sri Sri Latu Maharaj Smriti-Katha* (Calcutta, n.d.), pp. 10, 33, 45, 93, 95, 119-21, 370.

distance. He is much more interested in telling us that the main building had been constructed by Martin Burn in the 1930s, and that Kamala Nehru and Indira Gandhi had been regular visitors. And yet Dakshineswar and Belur remain tied together by indissoluble links, each shedding its lustre on the other: leaving us with the problems of extremely varied worlds which still for some reason require a stable centre in the figure of Ramakrishna. Diverse appropriations of a founding father are of course common and not at all exceptional. While still worth exploration in terms of implications and contexts, the theme most relevant for our present study is the persistence of a need for affiliation with Ramakrishna across decades of sweeping change.

The power and weight of the canonical tradition as established by Vivekananda has somewhat obscured the range of meanings that the image of Ramakrishna has had the capacity to take on or inspire. There has been, for instance, a Tantric Ramakrishna, in considerable discordance with Vivekananda's violent condemnation of Vamachari ways. An acrimonious controversy developed in the 1930s around the precise importance of Bhairabi Brahmani.[201] Ramakrishna's householder devotees, again, had little sympathy initially with Narendranath's band of young sanyasis, and there was even an unseemly quarrel between the two groups over Ramakrishna's ashes.[202] Middle-aged householders, led by Ramachandra Datta, instituted a distinct cult centred at Kankurgachi in east Calcutta, emphasizing a quietistic and highly ritualized devotion to Ramakrishna as an avatar, to the exclusion of social activism. This was, arguably, closer in some ways to the spirit of the Ramakrishna we meet in the *Kathamrita* than the Vivekananda adaptation.[203] The national and international fame of Vivekananda eventually eclipsed the Kankurgachi variant of Ramachandra Datta, but pure ritualized devotion has persisted as a subordinate yet vital

201 Two early biographies emphasized Ramakrishna's Tantric connections: Satyacharan Mitra, *Sri Sri Ramakrishna Paramahansa: Jibani O Upadesh* (Calcutta, 1897), and Bhubanchandra Mukhopadhyay, *Ramakrishna Charitamrita* (Calcutta, 1901). Kalikrishnananda Giri, *Sri Ramakrishner Sri-guru Bhairabi Yogeswari* (Calcutta, 1936) refers to a controversy about the role of Bhairabi in the mid 1930s.

202 *Life of Swami Vivekananda by his Eastern and Western Disciples*, pp. 153–5.

203 Swami Gambhirananda, *History of the Ramakrishna Math and Mission* (Calcutta, 1957), pp. 39–41; Ramachandra Datta, *Sri Sri Ramakrishna Paramahansadever Jivan-Vrittanta* (Calcutta, 1890, 1910); ibid., *Tattva Prakashik* (4th ed., Kankurgachi, 1912). The evils of chakri figure prominently in Ramachandra Dutta's play *Lilamrita* (Calcutta, 1900).

strand even within the canonical Ramakrishna Mission tradition. Sarada Debi is a crucial figure here, with her claim that Ramakrishna had predicted that he would be 'worshipped in every home' after death, and insistence on the importance of diksha, mantra and other rituals.[204] Among the sanyasis, Ramakrishnananda (Sashibhushan Chakrabarti) in particular preferred the ways of ritualized bhakti and puja. The elaborate ceremonies he conducted at the Math were often summarily dismissed by Vivekananda in private letters as useless 'bell-ringing'.[205]

From the mid 1880s Girish Ghosh and his epigoni began projecting yet another, subtly distinct, Ramakrishna through the north Calcutta professional stage, reaching out to an audience considerably wider than the limited range of personal contact or even print. Girish personally was on excellent terms with householder and sanyasi devotees alike, and his representations served ultimately as a kind of bridge between quietistic, though no longer highly ritualized, bhakti and Vivekananda's new turn towards social service. In *Bilvamangal* (June 1886), *Nasiram* (May 1888) and *Kalapahar* (September 1896), Girish introduced the figure of the wandering pagal or 'holy fool', mad to the conventional world but purveyor, really, of divine wisdom, often in words taken straight from Ramakrishna. Wisdom conveyed through wandering folly quickly established itself as a central figure in the Bengali theatre. Aestheticized traces of it persist even in Rabindranath's *thakurda* (grandfather) figures.[206] The pagal of Girish Ghosh appears, at first sight, to embody pure irresponsibility or playfulness, justified on the ground that everything is determined by Hari: 'predestination' here has produced implications diametrically opposed to the puritan work ethic. Only 'Harinama' is needed, else one should behave like a five-year-old child.[207] But pagal figures like

204 *Sarada Devi: Atmakatha*, pp. 67-8, 93, 106.

205 'If you can give up bell-ringing, well and good, otherwise I will not be able to join you . . . The only karma I understand is service to others, everything else is evil karma. Hence I bow to the Buddha. Do you understand? A big gap is emerging between your group and myself . . .' Vivekananda to Sashi (Ramakrishnananda), n.d., 1895 — *Patrabali I* (Calcutta, 1948, 1954), pp. 444, 446. The translation is mine: the official translation, in *Letters of Swami Vivekananda* (Mayavati, 1940; Calcutta, 1970), p. 249, tones down the language considerably.

206 In plays like *Prayaschitta* and *Muktadhara*.

207 'When you were a child, you merrily sucked your mother's breasts, and the mother did all the worrying — now, if you, stop worrying Hari will do the worrying for you.' Nasiram, in the play with that name — Ray and Bhattacharji (ed.), *Girish-Rachanabali*, IV (Calcutta, 1974).

Nasiram, or Chintamani in *Kalapahar,* do in fact preside over and inspire substantial moral change — though action itself is pushed along, significantly, by women: plebeian trickster-figures, or deferentially assertive wives.[208] Inward-turning piety and activism, in other words, do not necessarily remain binaries in the Ramakrishna–Vivekananda tradition. The withdrawal into oneself that Ramakrishna had inspired undercut an activism thought to be based on arrogance, but could serve at times as a prelude, through inner purification, for a higher kind of outgoing action.

In Satischandra Chattopadhyaya's *Annapurna* (1904), Gadadhar himself appears as a 'mad' pujari, alongside a thakurda who distances himself from worldly concerns through dance and devotional song. A clerk sings about his office woes and recalls the happier experiences of Ramprasad with his employer. The heroine, Annapurna, eventually changes the heart of her drunkard husband through endurance and deferential assertion. But Gadadhar himself is now a figure deeply moved by scenes of poverty, and the play ends with a widowed Annapurna erecting a temple where the poor would be fed day and night. Satischandra is clearly writing in the shadow of Vivekananda — who, as we shall see, had exalted the Hindu widow, considered ritually impure by tradition, into the ideal Hindu woman — retaining all the marks of austere widowhood, but immersed in social service. Annapurna, which means bounteous provider of food, is, again, one of Durga's many names — and the Swadeshi movement would soon erect Durga–Annapurna into a central image of the motherland. A minor play thus epitomizes a whole complex transition.

A visitor to Belur Math today is greeted by a signboard that highlights the current philanthropic work of the Ramakrishna Mission. The poor, however, are physically much more distant than at Dakshineswar, and no plebeian bazaar has been allowed to obstruct the spacious entrance to the Math. The contrast points towards a two-way transition. With Vivekananda, sophisticated son of a prominent Calcutta attorney who quickly acquired international and national fame after his Chicago address, the Ramakrishna cult moved from the clerical margins into the centre of high-bhadralok life. Rustic and homely parables, along with the dasatya of chakri theme, dropped out of Vivekananda's discourse, which took the form of lectures (Ramakrishna, incidentally, had detested oratory),[209] and

---

[208] Like Batul in *Srivatsa-Cinta* (1884) or Bhajahari and Prafulla herself in *Prafulla* (1889), ibid.

[209] This in fact was a constant refrain in his conversation. See, for instance,

essays in English or chaste, Sanskritized Bengali. The distancing produced by English education and urban middle-class life was often associated, however, with a deep awareness of the West as, simultaneously, 'stimulus and threat. Among the more sensitive of the nineteenth-century bhadralok, it had led also to repeated efforts to ameliorate the conditions of the underprivileged and oppressed: women, lower castes, the poor.

Vivekananda revived, at the heart of what had begun as inward-turning bhakti, the traditions of such bhadralok activism. First-hand experience of mass poverty, ignorance, and caste oppression, obtained through tours across the subcontinent in 1890-3, added to this revival a distinctive, sharper edge. Ramakrishna, poor himself, had considered poverty a part of natural or divine law, and had displayed a 'peasant' cynicism about do-gooding efforts by rich and learned folk as instances of arrogance and futility: 'You have read a couple of pages in English, and so consider yourself mightily learned . . . [and] . . . think you can do good for the world. Can you end droughts, famines, epidemics?'[210] Vivekananda cultivated contacts with precisely such people — princes, dewans, well-established men — as potential fund-givers throughout his tours of India, and fund-raising remained a major objective of his lectures in America and Europe ('I give them spirituality, and they give me money'[211]). The money he hoped to use for far-reaching plans of elevating the daridra-narayan, God manifested in the poor. Organized philanthropy would be combined with popular education in true high-Hinduism and modern science, via devices like magic lanterns.

Such, Vivekananda visualized, would be the primary tasks of his band of young educated sanyasis, and in practice training this elite came to be foregrounded over the more challenging objective of mass education.[212] What was entailed was a transformation within his own group, which could be achieved only after intense debate. In the words of the official historian of the Ramakrishna Mission, 'the conflicting aims of religion and social service seemed irreconcilable

---

his encounter with Sasadhar Tarakachudamani, the Hindu revivalist orator, in *KM* III, 72ff (30 June 1884).

[210] Gurudas Barmen, *Sri Sri Ramakrishna Charit* (Calcutta, 1910), quoting a conversation with Kristodas Pal, pp. 206-7.

[211] Letter to Sashi, 19 March 1894, *Letters of Swami Vivekananda*, p. 82.

[212] 'I have given up at present my plan for the education of the masses. It will come by degrees. What I now want is a band of fiery missionaries'. Letter to Alasinga, 12 January 1895, ibid., p. 197.

indeed.' Vivekananda's 'greatest triumph lay in re-orientating the outlook of his brother disciples from ideas of personal salvation to a sympathetic comprehensions of the needs of the world'.[213] He had to fight, in a way, against an entire Hindu tradition in which charity might at times be considered a part of the dharma of the king or householder, but where the sanyasi's principal ideal was individual moksha, not improvement of the world.

Basic religious-philosophical concepts, consequently, had to be given new meanings. Karma became, for Vivekananda, not traditional caste-based rituals and obligations determined by previous birth, but non-traditional social service. The jnana of Vedantic monism was sought to be transformed, through a real *tour de force*, into a message of strength and strenuous efforts to help others. The monistic unity of all beings, Vivekananda argued, implied that 'in loving anyone, I am loving myself'.[214] Vedantic jnana was simultaneously exalted in unambiguous fashion over quietistic emotional bhakti, and the Tantric elements in Ramakrishna sought to be suppressed altogether in a firmly structured framework of adhikari-bheda which now defined a clearly demarcated Hindu religion.[215] This was the kind of Hinduism which Vivekananda thought could be projected abroad as intellectually powerful enough to challenge and overcome the arrogant claims of Christian missionaries — claims inseparable, often, from imperialist racism. Through its propagation, Vivekananda emerged as the first major exemplar of that familiar twentieth-century figure, the Indian guru who wins fame and disciples in the west. Adhikari-bheda apexed by Vedanta seemed to have the potential, also, for unifying all Hindus through the incorporation of diversities within a single hierarchy. Nivedita would soon define Vivekananda's achievement at Chicago as the transformation of 'the religious ideas of the Hindus' into

[213] Swami Gambhirananda, *History of the Ramakrishna Math and Mission*, pp. 123, 117–18.

[214] *Vedantism* in *Complete Works of Swami Vivekananda* (9th ed., 1964, henceforward *CW*), III, p. 130.

[215] Two examples, from many; 'I thoroughly appreciate the power and potency of bhakti on men to suit the needs of different times. What we now want in our country, however, is not so much weeping, but a little strength. What a mine of strength is in this Impersonal God . . . That you get alone in the Vedanta — and there alone.' Reply to Jaffna welcome address, 1897 — *CW* III, p. 130. 'All of religion is contained in the Vedanta, that is, in the three stages of the Vedanta philosophy, the Dvaita, Visisthdvaita, and Advaita; one comes after the other.' This he claimed to be 'my discovery'. Letter to Alasinga, 6 May 1895, *Letters*, p. 227.

'Hinduism', for through adhikari-bheda 'there could be no sect, no school, no sincere religious experience of the Indian people . . . that might rightly be excluded from the embrace of Hinduism'.[216] The catholicity of Ramakrishna, modulated and transformed through this construction of a crystallized 'Hindu' identity, thus became for Vivekananda the paradoxical ground for a claim to superior worth: 'Our religion in truer than any other religion, because it never conquered, because it never shed blood'. Vivekananda in the same lecture went on to stress the need for 'iron muscles and nerves of steel', and even visualized 'the conquest of the whole world by the Hindu race . . . [a] conquest of religion and spirituality'.[217]

Vivekananda's rhetoric sounds powerful and self-confident, yet just beneath its surface fissures often lurk, manifesting themselves repeatedly through implicit or explicit contradictions. It is in terms of such tensions, which Vivekananda was too clear-sighted and honest to be able to brush aside, that we can best understand why an apparently wholesale inversion of the ideas of Ramakrishna, accompanied by the entry of themes quite unknown to the master, still remained in need of an ultimate anchorage in the quietistic bhakti of the Dakshineswar saint.

The tensions are clearest in Vivekananda's discourses about women and lower castes. His letters repeatedly associate degradation of women with caste oppression as the two central evils of Hindu society. The contrasts with Ramakrishna in both respects are obvious enough. Awareness of social degradation played no part in Ramakrishna's twin images of women as epitome of danger through sexuality and emblem of maternal purity, and caste had figured rarely in his discourse. Vivekananda had nothing of Ramakrishna's obsessive terrors about the woman's body, and he was careful to substitute kama for kamini, avoiding the implication that lust was somehow peculiarly feminine.[218] Early letters from America enthusiastically acclaimed the free yet responsible and socially committed western women he had met, several of whom had become his ardent disciples: 'free as birds in air', whereas 'look at our girls, becoming mothers below their teens . . . We are horrible sinners, and our degradation is due to our calling women "despicable

216 Nivedita, *Our Master and His Message*, introduction to *CW* I, p. x.
217 *From Colombo to Almora*, *CW* III, pp. 274–5.
218 See, for instance, Vivekananda to Sashi, 24 June 1896, where he explicitly instructed the latter to substitute kama for kamini in the material he was preparing for Max Mueller, *Patrabali*, II, p. 100.

worms", "gateways to hell" and so forth'.[219] The disciple here came
perilously close to a direct criticism of his master. But passages
like these are generally confined to private correspondence. Public
speeches concentrated fire on missionary slanders about Indian
womanhood, and the futility and irrelevance of social reform
movements.[220] Missionary propaganda, arrogant and at times racist,
had the habit of harping on themes like child marriage or the
seclusion of women, and Vivekananda evidently found it demeaning
to national-cum-religious pride to publicly repeat such criticism,
however much he might privately detest many such practices.

The cult of Sarada Debi as 'Divine Mother' which Vivekananda
encouraged was perhaps one way of trying to resolve this tension:
womanhood of one particular kind was being exalted, but through
a markedly traditionalist idiom. The other attempted solution was
ascetic widowhood channelled into social service. Vivekananda,
Nivedita thought, had 'looked, naturally enough, to widows as a
class to provide the first generation of abbess-like educators' — he
had a 'horror' of the 'unfaithful widow', and emphasized 'trustful
and devoted companionship to the husband'.[221] In India, though
not among Western women disciples, several of whom were young,
unmarried, and unconventional, feminine entry into public space
presumably required careful regulation so as not to conflict with
conjugal duty and decorum. The widow who still carried all the
marks of traditional austerity provided the ideal material. The limits,
even here, were revealed by Vivekananda's bitter public quarrel in
the United States with Pandita Ramabai about the condition of
Hindu widows — a quarrel which coincided in time with a gesture
of financial support to Sasipada Banerji's home-cum-school for
widows at Baranagar (April 1895).[222] Setting up widows' homes and
educating their inmates was one thing: a militantly reformist widow
who had turned Christian as a matter of mature voluntary choice
represented a very different proposition.

Vivekananda's comments about caste reveal a similar pattern. His
letters are full of an awareness and anger about caste oppression rare
among the bhadralok intelligentsia of nineteenth-century Bengal,

[219] Letters to Haripada Mitra, 28 December 1893; to Sashi, 19 March 1894,
Letters, pp. 61, 81.
[220] See for example, *From Colombo to Almora*, CW III, pp. 151-3, 198, 207ff.
[221] Nivedita, *The Master As I Saw Him* (Calcutta, 1910, 1963), pp. 142-3, 282-6.
[222] S.N. Dhar, *A Comprehensive Biography of Swami Vivekananda*, vol. I (Madras,
1975), Chapter 9.

where even Brahmo rejection of caste had generally taken the form of token gestures within the bounds of the reformed community.[223] Such awareness, he said, had been brought to him by the 'experience I have had in the south, of the upper classes torturing the lower . . . Do you think our religion is worth the name? Ours is only "Don't touchism". Millions live on *mohua* plants, while *sadhus* and Brahmins "suck the blood of these poor people".'[224] But this new sensitivity towards caste oppression was also bound up with an ideal of a crystallized and unified Hindu society which, too, had been absent in Ramakrishna. Vivekananda's public lectures, in particular, normally situated the need to uplift lower castes in the context of the danger of Christian and Muslim proselytization: an argument that would come to acquire a central place in the discourses of twentieth-century 'Hindutva'.[225] There was also a simultaneous, violent condemnation of the emerging anti-Brahman movements in the south: 'it is no use fighting among the castes . . . The solution is not by bringing down the higher, but by raising the lower up to the level of the higher . . . To the non-Brahman castes I say, be not in a hurry . . . you are suffering from your own fault. Who told you to neglect spirituality and Sanskrit learning?'[226] The hidden interlocutor, once again, must have been the missionary and colonial apologist for whom caste oppression, along with the subordination of women, proved the essential unworthiness and inferiority of Indians.

Bartaman Bharat (Modern India, March 1899),[227] Vivekananda's most famous work in Bengali, provides the supreme example of this radical logic that abruptly turns back on itself as it encounters the rock of patriotic-cum-Hindu faith. It elaborates an interesting conception of history where priestly (Brahman), royal (Kshatriya), and mercantile (Vaishya) power succeeded each other, not just in India but everywhere. All have their merits and deficiencies, but sharpest condemnation is reserved for the eras of priestly domination. Stereotypes of Hindu nationalist historiography are ruthlessly overturned

---

[223] As Brahmoism remained confined to the educated upper-caste bhadralok, inter-marriage and inter-dining remained restricted to the Brahmans, Kayasthas and Vaidyas who had become Brahmos.

[224] Letter to Sashi, 19 March 1894, *Letters*, p. 81.

[225] As in Shraddhanand's activities in the early 1920s, or earlier in Bengal, the 'dying race' theme developed by U.N. Mukherji. Pradip Kumar Datta, 'The "Dying Hindu": Production of Hindu Communal Common-sense in Early Twentieth-century Bengal', *Economic and Political Weekly*, 19 June 1993.

[226] *The Future of India, CW* III, pp. 294–8.

[227] I am using the official English translation in *CW* III.

as Vivekananda indicates a preference for the Buddhist and Islamic
eras, when the decline in Brahman power had enabled the emergence
of powerful empires: Rajput domination, in contrast, is represented
as a virtual dark age. The global British empire obviously embodies
the climax of Vaishya power, after which is predicted a 'rising of
the Shudra class, with their Shudrahood . . . when the Shudras of
every country . . . remaining as Shudras — will gain absolute suprem-
acy in every society . . . Socialism, Anarchism, Nihilism and other
like sects are the vanguard of the social revolution that is to follow'.
('I am a socialist', Vivekananda had proclaimed to Mary Hale in the
course of a letter outlining a similar argument in 1896.[228]) But then,
very abruptly, comes an assertion that in British-ruled India 'the
whole population has virtually come down to the level of the Shudra.'
The only real Brahmans today are foreign professors, the Kshatriyas
are British officials, the Vaishyas the British merchants. The whole
tide of Vivekananda's argument now suddenly reverses itself. What
is branded as blind imitativeness becomes the principal target, and
a whole range of traditional practices and norms is implicitly reval-
orized: the 'Sita-Savitri-Damyanti' model, for instance, as opposed
to the 'unrestricted intermingling of men and women'. 'Westerners
hold caste distinctions to be obnoxious, therefore let all the distinct
castes be jumbled into one.' The rhetoric reaches its climax in the
appeal 'forget not that the lower classes, the ignorant, the poor, the
illiterate, the cobbler, the sweeper, are thy flesh and blood, thy
brothers.' This has often been cited as the pinnacle of Vivekananda's
radicalism, but a retreat has really taken place, from the earlier vision
of Shudra revolution, to the submergence of caste or class differences,
without basic internal transformation, into a nationalist brotherhood. The intended audience ('thy') is clearly the educated, while
the people with 'a rag round their loins' are expected only to proclaim
at the top of their voice: 'The Indian is my brother . . . India's gods
and goddesses are mine'. The concluding pages of *Bartaman Bharat*
have become a standard college or high-school text: the earlier
sections are much less familiar: The authorized *Life of Vivekananda*
'by his Eastern and Western admirers' summarizes much of Vivekananda's writings but omits all reference to *Bartaman Bharat*.

Bartaman Bharat ended with apparently self-confident rhetoric —
but the letter to Mary Hale where Vivekananda called himself a
socialist concluded on a suddenly world-weary tone: 'The sum-total

---

[228] *Letters*, pp. 317–18.

of good and evil in the world remains ever the same . . . Let every dog have his day in this miserable world' — till such time as 'man give up this vanity of a world and governments and all other botherations.'[229] A profound pessimism in fact seems to repeatedly undermine Vivekananda's utopian dreams. The argument that he used, for instance, to appropriate Vedanta for an ethic of social service is in a way deeply cynical, for it assumes that men will help others only if they realize that this is just another form of self-love. Asked by an American woman missionary in 1898 whether he foresaw any hope of eliminating child-marriage and cruelty to widows, Vivekananda sadly replied in the negative. Vivekananda, the missionary reports, seemed to have a 'strange foreboding of ultimate failure' even 'with the Hindu world at his feet' — 'sitting there at twilight, in the large, half-lighted hall, it seemed like listening to a cry'.[230]

Vivekananda's well known oscillation between supremely self-confident activism and inward-turning world-weariness has been sought to be explained in terms of an inner, psychological conflict going back to childhood days.[231] A more contextualized reading, however, is also possible, to supplement — and not necessarily supplant — the psychological analysis. The utopian image of a Bharatvarsha rooted in an ideal Hinduism that Vivekananda passionately tried to adhere to was contradicted repeatedly by the harsh facts of contemporary Hindu society that he was too clear-sighted and honest to be able to ignore. He found no way of resolving these contradictions. What needs to be recognized as tragedy may best be grasped in terms of a grid of alternative action parameters, none of which Vivekananda could adopt without ambiguity or self-doubt.

Vivekananda condemned caste and gender oppression, and found many Hindu practices — including revering the cow as Mother — utterly ridiculous.[232] Yet existing social reform initiatives he considered superficial, with some justice, because confined to the educated elite — and demeaning to national pride. The public condemnation of many evils which he denounced in private was inhibited in him by the fear of strengthening western slanders about a subject race.

Vivekananda, at the same time, could not share the facile nationalist faith that such internal problems were secondary and would

229 Ibid.
230 Lucy E. Guiness, *Across India at the Dawn of the Twentieth Century* (London, 1898), p. 147. (I owe this reference to Tanika Sarkar.)
231 See Ashis Nandy, *The Intimate Enemy* (Delhi, 1983).
232 *Life of Swami Vivekananda*, p. 489.

sort themselves out after the winning of political freedom. His countrywide tours had given an unusual depth of meaning to a patriotism that embraced the entire subcontinent, and found memorable expression in the invocations to 'Bharat' with which *Bartaman Bharat* ends. But Vivekananda had little faith or interest in existing forms of Moderate Congress political activity, repeatedly warned against attaching 'political significance' to his ideas,[233] and seems to have looked upon the British empire, at times, as an opportunity to spread Hinduism abroad (on the analogy of Christianity under the Roman Empire).[234] Deep concern with poverty remained unrelated in Vivekananda to any awareness of colonial exploitation: there is a virtual silence about that already well-established staple of nationalist polemic, the drain of wealth theory.[235] Vivekananda, then, was not quite the 'patriot-prophet' who would soon be revered as patron saint by a whole generation of Swadeshi enthusiasts, revolutionary terrorists, and nationalists in general. Nivedita, who did more than anyone else, perhaps, to promote this image of Vivekananda, herself recognized its partially constructed character: 'Just as Shri Ramakrishna, in fact, without knowing any books, had been a living epitome of the Vedanta, so was Vivekananda of the national life. But of the theory of this he was unconscious.'[236]

Vivekananda the apostle of anti-British nationalism today belongs essentially to the past: what has become ominously relevant is the other, closely related image of the Swami as one of the founders of twentieth-century Hindutva, of a united, muscular and aggressive Hinduism. He had no particular prejudice about Islam,[237] but there is little doubt that like very many Hindu nationalists of his times, or later, the Bharat of Vivekananda's dreams was essentially Hindu. The closing appeal for fraternal embrace in *Bartaman Bharat* somehow forgets to mention Muslims. Much more important is the crucial role of Vivekananda in crystallizing a Hindu identity that is able to play simultaneously on the twin registers of catholicity and

233 Letter to Alasinga, 27 September 1894, *Letters*, p. 148.

234 *Problem of Modern India and Its Solution* (July 1899), *CW*, IV.

235 With one notable exception — a violently anti-British letter to Mary Hale, 30 October 1899, referring to 'blood-sucking' and a 'reign of terror', *Letters*, pp. 394–6. But Vivekananda almost certainly did not consider drain of wealth to be the prime cause of mass poverty.

236 Nivedita, *The Master as I Saw Him*, p. 53.

237 Nivedita recalls his warm admiration about Mughal achievements, ibid., Chapters 3, 5.

aggression: a pattern that has become standard in the discourses of today's RSS–VHP–BJP combine. And yet a gap remains, for Vivekananda could never reconcile himself totally to the harsh realities of caste and gender oppression, of mass poverty for which he refused to affix the responsibility solely on the British, and of 'hundreds of superstitions'. The Triplicane Literary Society Address (1897) which claimed that Hinduism was 'truer than any other religion' simultaneously demanded that such things be 'weeded out'.[238] It was quite impossible for Vivekananda to accept everything in Hindu society in a kind of aestheticized celebration of difference, as multicoloured flowers in a garland.[239]

Faced with such insurmountable tensions, Vivekananda came to perpetually oscillate between exuberant calls to action and moods of introspection, in a pattern that is particularly relevant because it helps us understand why an ultimate anchorage in Ramakrishna remained so indispensable. *Bartaman Bharat* had been preceded by months during which Vivekananda had immersed himself in the songs of Ramprasad, trying 'to saturate his own mind with the conception of himself as a child'. After a mystical experience at Kshir Bhawani in Kashmir, Vivekananda told Nivedita in October 1898: 'It is all "Mother" now! . . . there is no more patriotism. I am only a little child.'[240] This, evidently, was not the Mother of *Anandamath* or Swadeshi nationalism, a patriotic icon calling sons to the path of self-sacrificing action. It was Ramakrishna's Divine Mother, who wants nothing more than childlike surrender, an abjuration of the active responsible adulthood that Vivekananda himself had tried so hard to promote. In some ways, perhaps, it was Ramakrishna himself.

The introspective mood came to dominate the last two years or so of Vivekananda's life, finding expression in words utterly moving and unforgettable:

This is the world, hideous, beastly corpse. Who thinks of helping it is a fool . . . I am only the boy who used to listen with rapt wonderment to the wonderful words of Ramakrishna . . . That is my true nature;

---

[238] *CW*, III, p. 278.

[239] That, roughly, is the dominant outlook of contemporary 'Hindutva' as embodied above all in the Viswa Hindu Parishad. See Tapan Basu, Pradip Dutta, Sumit Sarkar, Tanika Sarkar, Sambudha Sen, *Khaki Shorts and Saffron Flags: A Critique of the Hindu Right* (Delhi, Longman, 1993).

[240] *The Master as I Saw Him*, pp. 124, 128.

works and activities, doing good and so forth are only superimpositions. Now I again hear his voice, the same old voice thrilling my soul . . . I have long given up my place as a leader . . . Behind my work was ambition . . . behind my guidance the thirst for power. Now they are vanishing and I drift. I come! Mother, I come! . . . I come, a spectator, no more an actor. Oh, it is so calm! . . . [241]

Quietistic, inward-turning bhakti, tolerant and non-proselytizing, had thus been transformed, with conflicts but no major rupture, into a crystallized and assertive Hindu identity with activist programmes. But insurmountable contradictions — fundamentally perhaps the limits set to bhadralok idealism by hierarchies of caste, gender and class within a colonial situation — blocked the realization of such programmes, and both the expansion of outlook and the eventual return to origins helped to deepen the appeal of the initial message. Vivekananda's fame preserved and vastly extended the reach of the apparently very different image of Ramakrishna. It is noteworthy, for instance, that Mahendranath brought out four of the five volumes of his Kathamrita between 1902 (the year of Vivekananda's death) and 1910 — years, precisely of Swadeshi nationalist militancy inspired to a considerable extent by Vivekananda's posthumous image as patriot–prophet. A significant number of revolutionary terrorists, it may be added, beginning with two of the accused in the Alipur Bomb Case of 1908, sought shelter within the Ramakrishna Mission in the wake of political frustration or failure. Such recruits provoked occasional government suspicion, but the Mission kept itself determinedly aloof from nationalist politics.[242] It offered space for philanthropic and educational work, but also for quiet devotional piety. Vivekananda's return to Ramakrishna, it seems, had created something like a recurrent pattern.

The Ramakrishna heritage which flourishes today in Bengal incorporates, consequently, an enormous variety of appropriations around a central core of claimed affinity. At one extreme, fleets of cars draw up every evening outside the palatial Institute of Culture of the Ramakrishna Mission in south Calcutta, where learned religious-cum-philosophical discourses provide solace for the rich. The Mission itself carries on valuable educational and philanthropic work, and enough has survived within it of the original catholicity to keep it

---

[241] Letter to Mary Hale, 17 June 1900; to Josephine MacLeod, 18 April 1900, *Letters*, pp. 422-3.

[242] Gambirananda, *History of Ramakrishna Math and Mission*, pp. 88-90, 202-4, 213.

— so far — away from the contemporary politics of aggressive Hindutva typified by the VHP. But little remains of more grandiose dreams of uplifting the daridra-narayan on a countrywide scale, or of a 'Shudra' revolution. Few even of Vivekananda's close associates ever seem to have taken to heart his occasional passionate onslaughts against Brahmanical tyranny and gender oppression.

At another related but somewhat distinct level, crowds of varied social origin throng at Dakshineswar, and portraits of Ramakrishna adorn countless middle- or lower-middle-class homes, an object of deep devotion for many humble men and, perhaps even more, women. The clerical ambience we noted as crucial for Ramakrishna's initial appeal never really disappeared, even though Vivekananda had moved into a higher social world. Of thirty-seven members, for instance, of a Ramakrishna Samiti functioning in Barisal town in 1910 — set up at the initiative of government clerical staff without any affiliation at first with Belur and combining a little philanthropy with collective readings of the *Kathamrita* — twenty-four came from clerical and related professions. At a later stage the clerks tried to 'enlist certain respectable and sympathetic gentlemen of the town', and so a few pleaders and schoolteachers were included in the Executive Committee.[243]

The world of clerks in Bengal, of course, has changed vastly since Ramakrishna's times. Beginning with the Burn Company clerks' strike in October 1905, Bengal's office employees began developing trade union organizations of their own. From the 1950s, the clerical world of Dalhousie Square has been one of the strongest bastions of the Left and trade-union movement in West Bengal. Nor are offices today marked by any stringently enforced discipline of time: symbolically, perhaps, a portrait of Ramakrishna has become a common feature of many offices and banks. But Left political predominance has obviously not been accompanied by any equivalent cultural hegemony, and a depressing and dismal struggle for existence still characterizes much of lower-middle-class life.

Agni-sanket (1984), by the best-selling novelist Sanjib Chattopadhyaya, may provide us with an appropriate concluding note. The context is disillusionment with the Left Front government, the focus, once again, clerical life. Kamini, kanchan and the miseries of lower-middle-class life have come together once more. Drudgery in office

---

243 Government of Bengal, *Home Poll Confidential*, 372/1910 (West Bengal State Archives).

and home remains the lot of the less fortunate, while the successful few climb up by shattering kinship obligations. For both, women and sex are somehow to blame: 'The whole world is turning around the woman's body. On all sides the manholes are open.' Social conservatism has become utterly blatant. Watching girls being 'teased' in crowded buses, the clerk-hero ruminates: 'Where has that veil gone? Where that respect? No leader talks of moral ideals, or of our ancient traditions.' The author presents no real, positive alternatives, neither Vivekananda's patriotic social service nor even Ramakrishna's quiet bhakti and grihastha sanyas. But a good woman changes the heart of the local rowdy, who leaves her as a dying gift a picture of Ramakrishna. The hero dreams about a 'white-belt black-shirt' terror-ist gang to punish evildoers, a taxi-driver blames Kaliyuga for soaring prices, and, in an apocalyptic fantasy ending, the burning body of the clerk goes around destroying symbols of corruption.[244] A deeply depressing, claustrophobic world, where failure and poverty only help to consolidate hierarchies of caste and gender — over which Ramakrishna presides, as an icon that gives perhaps a little comfort, but not hope.

---

[244] Sanjib Chattopadhyay, *Agni Sanket* (Calcutta, 1984), pp. 39, 57, 60, 104 and *passim*.

9

Identity and Difference: Caste in the Formation of the Ideologies of Nationalism and Hindutva

It is not particularly original, in an intellectual climate saturated by Edward Said, to reiterate that identity is usually grounded in difference, and built up through simultaneous constructions of externalized 'Others'. That identities tend to homogenize differences conceived of as being internal to the entities and solidarities that are being forged will also be widely accepted. This second proposition, however, on the whole is often less explicated or explored than the first, and analysis consequently tends to reproduce the ideological elisions of the historical phenomena being investigated. The common-sense or textbook understanding of late-colonial Indian history, for instance, is still in large part grounded on the assumption that the entire meaningful world of political action and discourse can be comprehended through the categories of imperialism, nationalism, and communalism, the interaction among which eventually produced the end result of a coming of freedom that was also the partitioning of the subcontinent. Such an assumption involves an uncritical acceptance of the holistic ideological claims of 'Indian' nationalism and 'Hindu' and 'Muslim' communalism — claims that have sought to homogenize a multitude of differences of region, class, caste, and gender. Radical historiographies have no doubt emphasized the autonomous role of peasant, labour, or subaltern groups, but they have seldom questioned the absolute priority of anti-colonial struggles or attitudes as the ultimate *standard* for evaluating such initiatives.

Ranajit Guha's 'Prose of Counter-Insurgency', it is true, did critique teleological efforts to assimilate peasant rebellions 'to the career of the Raj, the Nation, or the People'. Yet his own programmatic essay inaugurating the project tacitly conflated the 'historiography of colonial India' with that of 'Indian nationalism.'[1] Subsequent developments within *Subaltern Studies* have only strengthened this thrust, for in today's critiques of colonial discourse the principal criterion for valorizing indigenous community has become its degree of cultural autonomy from the modern West. I have argued elsewhere that it has proved difficult to accommodate within this framework sympathetic evaluations of many movements for women's rights and lower-caste protests, for these have often utilized aspects of colonial policies and Western ideologies as resources, and even on occasion presented noticeably 'loyalist' or 'anti-nationalist' images of themselves.[2]

Historiographical elision has been most powerful of all in respect of caste,[3] and yet it is precisely this dimension that has shot into unexpected prominence in recent years, with the lower-caste rally around the Mandal proposals and the Ayodhya Mandir campaign confronting each other, and BJP leader Advani's Rath-yatra of autumn 1990 having an obvious relationship with high-caste hysteria over reservations. Through a case study of late-nineteenth-early-twentieth-century Bengal, I will here attempt a preliminary exploration of the ways in which questions of caste — more precisely, lower-caste aspirations — have been handled in the unificatory projects of Hindutva and Indian nationalism.[4] Even such a limited focus may reveal major

---

[1] Ranajit Guha, 'The Prose of Counter-Insurgency', in Guha (ed.), *Subaltern Studies II* (Delhi, 1983), p. 38; ibid., 'On Some Aspects of the Historiography of Colonial India', *Subaltern Studies I* (Delhi, 1982).

[2] See Chapter 3 in this volume.

[3] My own writings can provide some telling examples. *Modern India* (Delhi, 1983) probably gave more space to caste movements than did most other surveys of late-colonial history. I notice now, however, that I had kept on using phrases like 'false consciousness of caste solidarity' and 'sectional forms' of expressing 'lower-class' discontent even while presenting sympathetic accounts of movements like Phule's Satyashodhak Samaj. I have been going back recently to some early-twentieth-century Bengal material which I must have had a look at while writing my *Swadeshi Movement in Bengal* (New Delhi, 1973). Caste seems now to have been quite a central theme: it had figured only marginally in my doctoral dissertation and subsequent book.

[4] A choice conditioned by linguistic competence, since vernacular data is essential for the kind of questions I am trying to probe. But Bengal, contrary to later developments and contemporary images, was actually fairly crucial in

difficulties of incorporation, and point towards the presence of other histories not neatly encapsulable within the narratives of anti-colonial nationalism or religious communities that have dominated historiography on the whole. Only very recently have a few efforts been made to explore the interrelations between such partially autonomous histories without postulating an a priori normative primacy of the nationalist, or anti-colonial, 'mainstream'.[5]

More specifically, I want to explore the possibility that constructions of Indian nationalism, Hindu unity, and Hindutva in the late-nineteenth-early-twentieth-century may all have been related in part, though in significantly different ways, to efforts to respond to or counter 'pressures from below' in the form of lower-caste aspirations. One needs, perhaps, to recuperate and extend some aspects of the logic of the early *Subaltern Studies*, which has been largely abandoned by many of its present stalwarts.[6]

II

A preliminary question arises at this point. I have already distinguished, in title and argument, between Indian nationalism and Hindutva, but is such a distinction viable at all? The enormous overlaps in personnel, assumptions and symbols are too obvious to need reiteration, and nationalisms grounded in religious identity have been hardly uncommon in history: one thinks of Iran today, Ireland, or even the concept of 'God's Englishmen' in the making of patriotism in Protestant England. Hindutva from its beginnings in the 1920s has rejected any such distinction, and its logic today identifies the RSS–VHP–BJP combine uniquely with the 'Hindu' community, and

---

the early formation of Hindu-nationalist ideologies, and the recent research of historians like Sekhar Bandopadhyay has revealed the considerable importance in the early twentieth century of 'caste politics' in a region now apparently characterized by its virtual absence.

5 I am thinking in particular of the recent work of Gail Omvedt: *Reinventing Revolution: India's New Social Movements* (New York, 1993), and *Dalits and Democratic Revolution: Dr Ambedkar and the Dalit Movement in Colonial India* (New Delhi, 1994).

6 Only a partial and modified recuperation, however: I have emphasized in another essay (Chapter 3) what I now feel to have been the problematic features also of early *Subaltern Studies*. Specifically, studies of lower-caste affirmations, even more perhaps than work on class-oriented movements, will need to avoid romanticizations, not blur distinctions and conflicts within subordinated groups, and steer clear of any assumption of neat binary disjunctions.

then, through a specious majoritarian argument, transforms it into the authentic voice of the nation.[7] From a totally different standpoint, some contemporary anti-secularist critiques of Hindutva also tend towards evacuating such distinctions. Communalism in Indian history becomes a mere labelling exercise which 'secular' nationalists had taken over from 'colonial' knowledge and used to pejoratively brand 'community-identities' which, perhaps, need rather to be valorized as counterpoints to the tyranny of the 'modern nation-state'.[8] Hindutva in such arguments becomes just another, particularly authoritarian, version of the nation-state project: it needs to be rejected, paradoxically, because it is secular and modern.[9]

That both nationalism and communalism are late-colonial constructs, needing for their countrywide reach a degree of communicational, economic, and political integration not attained before the late nineteenth century, may be readily granted. But there can be very many different, and mutually opposed, ways of being modern, and a distinction — if not between nationalism and the inevitably pejorative communalism, at least with reference to 'Indian', 'Hindu', and 'Muslim' nationalisms, seems tenable and helpful in terms of both their preferred 'Others' and constituent premises. In the specific conditions of subcontinental religious, linguistic and cultural diversity, an Indian nationalism distinguished by its anti-colonial stance had to seek a fundamentally territorial grounding, seeking to unite everyone living on the territory of British-dominated India irrespective of religious or other differences. Hindutva and Muslim nationalism, in contrast, tended to subordinate anti-colonial perspectives to the requirements of communal rivalry and conflict. Territoriality remained important for both, but in a significantly different manner. For advocates of Pakistan, it could be located only in the future, as a Muslim homeland to be carved out through bitter communal strife. As for Hindu communalism, its classic foundation

[7] What this majoritarian argument deliberately ignores is the contradiction between the notion of a *permanent* majority (as one based solely on the Census definition of a Hindu would be) and democratic government.

[8] That, perhaps, is at least one possible reading of Gyanendra Pandey's somewhat convoluted arguments in his *The Construction of Communalism in Colonial North India* (Delhi, 1990).

[9] See, particularly, Ashis Nandy, 'The Politics of Secularism and the Recovery of Religious Tolerance', in Veena Das (ed.), *Mirrors of Violence* (Delhi, 1990), and Partha Chatterjee, 'Secularism and Toleration', *Economic and Political Weekly*, 9 July 1994.

text, V.D. Savarkar's *Hindutva/Who is a Hindu?* (1923), began with an emphasis upon *pitribhumi* (fatherland), but immediately equated it with *punyabhumi* (holy land), defining the latter as 'the cradle-land of his religion.' Only Hindus, therefore, could be true patriots, not Indian Muslims or Christians with holy lands in Arabia or Palestine. The edge of this entire, exclusivist argument is clearly directed against them, and not against British colonial rulers who never claimed India to be either pitri or punyabhumi.[10] Savarkar's logic proceeds, as in the entire subsequent discourse of Hindutva, by using authenticity, 'history', and 'culture' as apparently innocent middle terms which are immediately invested with Hindu religious meanings and associations. The RSS leader M.S. Golwalkar spelt out the implications with enviable clarity a generation later with his denunciation of the 'reactionary . . . theories of territorial nationalism . . . which . . . deprived us of the real and positive content of our real Hindu nationhood and made of the freedom movements virtually anti-British movements.' He went on to praise the Nazi 'purging . . . of the semitic races, the Jews' as 'national pride at its highest', and saw in it 'a good lesson for us in Hindustan to learn and profit by.'[11]

It is this quality of hatred and violence, carefully nurtured through generations of pedagogical 'cultural' training through the RSS and its affines, which tends to get ironed out in analysis which sees in majoritarian communalism no more than one more nation-state project aimed at bureaucratic centralization. Behind it lie assumptions of inevitable and overriding conflict with a similarly conceived community-Other. This logically distinguishes developed communalism from the construction, assumption or deployment of more or less homogenized community identities claiming religious basis, or

[10] Savarkar defined the 'Hindu' as 'a person who regards this land of Bharatvarsha from the Indus to the Seas as his *pitribhumi* as well as his *punyabhumi* that is the cradle land of his religion.' (*Hindutva/Who is a Hindu?*, Nagpur, 1923, Poona, 1949, p. iii, 95.) The advantage of claiming to speak for the majority community is that it allows a blurring of lines with Indian nationalism, while Muslim communalism could be branded easily from the same perspective as separatist. Nationalists virtually everywhere have described their country as holy: the key move made by Savarkar lies in the shift to 'cradle-land of religion'.

[11] M.S. Golwalkar, *Bunch of Thoughts* (1966), pp. 142–3; *We or Our Nationhood Defined* (Nagpur, 1938), p. 27. For more details, see Tapan Basu, Pradip Datta, Sumit Sarkar, Tanika Sarkar, Sambuddha Sen, *Khaki Shorts and Saffron Flags* (Delhi, 1993), Chapter II.

even from the 'politicization' of the latter through demands for quotas in jobs or seats or use of religious appeals in election campaigns. A genealogy of Hindu communalism, in other words, would have to think in terms of two transitions, not one: from an inchoate 'Hindu' world without firmly defined boundaries to the late-nineteenth-century constructions, in the context of more integrative colonial communication structures, of ideologies of unified 'Hinduism'; and then a further move in some quarters, roughly dateable to the mid 1920s, towards aggressive Hindutva postulated usually upon an enemy image of a similarly conceived Islam. The ideological thrust of today's Hindutva consists precisely in the effort to elide these distinctions, so that the Sangh Parivar can establish its claim to be the sole authentic representative and embodiment of Hinduism and of being a Hindu.

One needs to add immediately, however, that the Indian nationalist / Hindutva distinction I have been defending can at best claim a certain precision in logic, far less so in practice. It has often seemed important for even the most secular of Indian nationalists to derive sustenance and authenticity from images of subcontinental unity (or at least 'unity-in-diversity') extending back into a supposedly glorious past. As, except for brief periods of 'imperial unity' (often excessively valorized), this is difficult to substantiate at the political level, the tendency has remained strong to assume some kind of cultural or civilizational integration as the ultimate foundation of nationalism. And then it becomes difficult — even for a Nehru writing his *Discovery of India* — to resist the further slide towards assuming that that unity, after all, has been primarily Hindu (and upper-caste, often north-Indian Hindu at that). The slide was made easier by the undeniable fact that the bulk of the leading cadres of the nationalist and even Left movements have come from Hindu upper-caste backgrounds. The harsh words of a contemporary Dalit writer thus indicate an important dimension, exaggerated and unfair though they might sound to many:

The national movement was turned into a form of historical mythological movement and ancestor worship. . . . Those who . . . did not want society to be democratic, started eulogizing history, mythology and ages gone by, because in those mythological and historical ages, they were the supreme victors and leaders. . . . People such as Phule, Agarkar, Gokhale and Ranade who talked about misery and servitude of Shudras and Ati-Shudras, . . . were declared enemies. . . . The intelligentsia won, they succeeded in turning the Indian liberation struggle into a lop-sided fight, and in reducing the other movements to a secondary status.[12]

The blurring of distinctions became qualitatively more powerful after 1947, and most blatant of all after the withering of Nehruvian hopes of sustained independent economic growth, socialistic change and populistic alleviation of poverty. Transformed from inspiration for mass awakening into the official ideology of an increasingly bureaucratized and centralized nation- state, nationalism has become more and more of an icon — with predominantly, though not invariably, Hindu lineaments. The dividing line between 'national' and 'Hindu communal' assumptions and values became increasingly porous, to the great advantage of Hindutva political forces.

III

Indian and Hindu nationalism have thus had significantly varying meanings over time, and it is legitimate to expect questions of caste to have entered into the formations of both also in highly differentiated ways.

We may begin with anti-colonial nationalism, within which it might be helpful to make a (somewhat schematic) threefold distinction, marked, among other things, also by varied articulations with caste. Colonial rule was characterized, particularly in its earlier phases but in some ways throughout, by popular outbreaks that were anti-foreign, yet not imbued with any developed sense of subcontinental unity. Such movements were usually localized, led by tribal chiefs, zamindars or princes, and often backed up by pre-existing solidarities of kinship, neighbourhood, religion and caste. There could at most be some notions of confederal unity, leaving the more-or-less hierarchized internal structures of communities undisturbed.[13] Anti-caste ideologies clearly had little space for development

---

12 Baburao Bagul, quoted in Gail Omvedt (1994), p. 15.

13 The year 1857 was obviously the moment when conceptions of such confederal unity attained their maximal intensity, around a notion of a joint struggle of 'the Hindus and Musalmans of Hindustan' — a shifting amalgam, according to the recent important analysis of Rajat Kanta Ray, of 'race, religion, and realm'. The data presented by Ray includes a fascinating conversation in which a Muslim noble sympathizer of the rebellion described the sepoys as motivated by the fear that 'the Kafirs had determined to take away the castes of all Mohammadans and Hindoos.' Hence they had decided 'that these infidels should not be allowed to remain in India, or there should be no difference

in this milieu, and even the extent of voluntary or autonomous participation of subordinated castes in such movements remains uncertain and little explored. Nor is there evidence of any distinctive role of anti-caste sects which emerged in some profusion during late-medieval times. Most of these were probably absorbed into the local hierarchies as new *jatis* with special beliefs and practices.

The more sophisticated or 'modern' conceptions of Indian unity, as is well known, were confined in the nineteenth century to elite-intellectual, Western-educated circles. They remained for long, mild 'liberal' demands apart, largely disassociated from anti-colonial attitudes. Here, from Rammohan onwards, one does encounter sporadic critiques of Brahmanical domination and caste hierarchy, though on the whole the major social reform initiatives were much more related to gender injustice within the reformers' own middle-class, high-caste milieu. Caste was critiqued in such circles primarily for contributing to disunion, as a hindrance to processes of gradual unification of the Indian people thought to be in progress under a fundamentally 'providential', modernizing British rule. The social injustice argument, while not absent, remained secondary. In a Bengali tract of 1821 Rammohan had criticized *jatibheda* (caste distinction) as 'the root of all disunion', and his much-cited letter of 18 January 1828 argued that caste had 'entirely deprived them [Indians] of patriotic feeling.' A change of religion was required, therefore, 'at least for the sake of their political advantage and social comfort.'[14] Subsequent Brahmo thought and action regarding caste tended to remain tokenistic, confined in practice to giving up the Brahmanical sacred thread and the promotion of intercaste marriages within their own community.[15] The first book-length Brahmo critique came only in 1884, Sibnath Shastri's *Jatibheda*, initially a public lecture given before a gathering of 2000. This included an impressive 'historical' analysis of caste degeneration

---

between Mohammedans and Hindoos.' Anti-foreign unity was necessary precisely to preserve differences of religion and caste. Rajat Kanta Ray, 'Race, Religion and Realm: The Political Theory of "The Reigning Indian Crusade" ', in Mushirul Hasan and Narayani Gupta (eds), *India's Colonial Encounter* (Delhi, 1993). The quote is from p. 142.

14 Quotations from Dilipkumar Biswas's introduction to Sibnath Shastri, *Jatibheda* (Calcutta, 1884; ed., Biswas, 1963), pp. 62–3.

15 For an elaboration of this argument, see my 'The Radicalism of Intellectuals: A Case-Study of Nineteenth-Century Bengal', in *A Critique of Colonial Bengal* (Calcutta, 1985).

compared to early Vedic times, produced by subordination of non-Aryans and, interestingly, the restricted transmission of high culture along hereditary lines due to the absence of print. There was also a moment of passionate indignation, in a chapter making very effective use of Manu's diatribes about Shudras: such passages, along with the sections about history, would be often used in later tracts written by or on behalf of lower castes. Yet the concluding section, listing 'the evils of *jatibheda*', mentioned as the first among them the connection with 'divisiveness and lack of fraternal feeling . . . Bharatvarsha has been easily enslaved by foreigners precisely because of that.' Caste had also encouraged contempt for manual labour, produced intellectual narrowness by forbidding sea voyages among high castes, and was bound up with eugenically harmful rules about marriage. It was, Sibnath concluded, 'a barrier to progress and the enemy of the country.'[16] Caste, then, was still being critiqued as harmful primarily for obstructing national unity and for hindering high-caste improvement: there was little awareness of concrete lower-caste grievances or protests.[17]

The ground for even such limited, reformist critique seemed to get restricted with the rise of nationalist politics. The early Congress excluded caste, along with other allegedly divisive social matters, from its deliberations, and in 1895 Tilak insisted on the expulsion of the Social Conference from the venue of Congress sessions. Extremist efforts at mass recruitment during the Swadeshi years were often remarkably hierarchical, freely using threats of expulsion from caste ('social boycott') to enforce nationalist mandates, and such methods occasionally persisted into Gandhian times.[18] But the logic of peaceful and genuinely mass anti-colonial struggle pointed in a different direction, for Gandhian techniques in particular demanded voluntary and often self-sacrificing participation by very large numbers, many of them inevitably of lower-caste or Dalit origin. Of

[16] *Jatibheda*, pp. 40-9.

[17] The one specific instance of contemporary caste discrimination mentioned by Sibnath Shastri was 'the contempt shown in this city [Calcutta] by Brahmans and Kayasthas towards Subarnabaniks' (a prosperous, fairly educated, mercantile caste with low social status, located therefore on the margins of bhadralok society). *Jatibheda*, p. 40. The pamphlet reveals no awareness of lower-caste movements like that of the Namashudras in the Faridpur region in the early 1870s.

[18] For social boycott, see Sumit Sarkar, *Swadeshi Movement in Bengal*, Chapter VI, and *passim*; and Ranajit Guha, 'Discipline and Mobilize', in Partha Chatterjee and Gyanendra Pandey (eds), *Subaltern Studies VII* (Delhi, 1992).

equal if not greater importance, as I intend to argue shortly, were the growing signs of self-activity of subordinate castes. It was hardly accidental, therefore, that the emergence of Gandhian nationalism roughly coincided with the incorporation of issues of caste discrimination, in however partial and tokenistic a manner, in the Congress agenda. Gandhi, it will be recalled, made the ending of untouchability one of the preconditions for the realization of his 'Swaraj within one year' promise of 1921, and after the confrontation with Ambedkar in 1932 'Harijan welfare' became for some years his principal activity. Nor was there any logical difficulty in incorporating anti-caste, or at least reformist, principles within programmes of anti-colonial nationalism, whether Gandhian, liberal or Left. Gandhi drew on bhakti traditions to critique the extremes of caste oppression, while hereditary caste inequality clearly contradicted both bourgeois-liberal principles of citizenship and socialist ideals of more thorough-going egalitarianism. The characteristic Left programmatic combination of anti-colonial with 'anti-feudal' revolution could incorporate caste among its targets as a presumably feudal relic.

Yet caste, along with gender oppression, all too often became relegated as issues of 'social' reform less immediately relevant than 'basic' questions of political independence or class struggle. They could be postponed, would be more or less automatically resolved with changes in political and economic structures, and might be 'divisive' from the point of view of anti-British struggle. The limitations of orthodox Marxism, on the whole dogmatic and economistic, evidently played a critical role here, blocking theorization from the realities of Left-led mass action in which lower castes and Dalits were often very prominent.

IV

Nationalism, then, could reject caste in principle (or at least, with Gandhi, disown its more obvious abuses, like untouchability and proliferation of jatis), and yet avoid confronting it directly in much of its practice. Caste, in significant contrast, was both more vital, and more embarrassing, for projects of Hindu unity and Hindutva, and so, to some extent, has been gender. For some two thousand years the characteristic high-Hindu dystopia of Kaliyuga, last and most degenerate of eras that is always imagined as the present, has firmly located the sources of evil in the insubordination of Shudras to upper-castes and women to men. It has been next to impossible to think of Hindu society without some form of varna and jati. The votaries of Hindutva have tended to come in the main from high castes quite selfconscious about their status privileges, and yet the conflicts that tended to emerge from hierarchical rigidities needed to be resolved or kept in check if unity was going to be achieved. Evasion through postponement, as an admitted evil which would be remedied in the future, was thus more difficult. There were, rather, uneasy oscillations between volubility and deliberate silencing through diversion, between aggressive assertions of hierarchy, projects of limited, integrative, 'Sanskritizing' reform, and displacements through constructions of powerful enemy-images. The ebb and flow of lower-caste pressures seem to have played a critical role in these variations.

A convenient entry point and focus is provided here by the prominence of the concept of *adhikari-bheda* in mid- and late-nineteenth-century Bengal discourses leading up to the construction of unified notions of Hinduism. Adhikari-bheda (literally, differential rights, claims, or powers) conveyed the notion of each jati and *sampraday* (caste and sect) having its own rituals and beliefs in an unified but hierarchically differentiated structure within which each knew its appropriate place. It represented, in other words, the normative Other of Kaliyuga, and was able to combine, in shifting proportions, catholicity with conservative maintenance of norms appropriate to a group's location within the overall hierarchy. Dumont's structuralist analysis comes very close to this basic Hindu-conservative principle through the much-quoted statement that 'Hinduism hierarchizes and includes.' What needs to be emphasized, however, is that classificatory devices like adhikari-bheda are not just innocent objective descriptions, but projects of specific groups at particular times for acting on social reality: having some relationship with it if they are at all effective, but never of an one-to-one, purely reflexive kind.[19] The historian needs to explore their undersides, as E.P. Thompson did for instance with concepts like paternalism and deference in eighteenth-century England.[20]

Adhikari-bheda in some ways — looked at from below, as it were — gestured towards a relative openness to the emergence and survival of a multitude of practices and beliefs. Such catholicity had been

[19] I have found very helpful here the analysis by George Duby of medieval classificatory strategies in his *Three Orders: Feudal Society Imagined* (Paris, 1978; Chicago, 1980), pp. 8-9.

[20] E.P. Thompson, 'The Patricians and the Plebs', in *Customs in Common* (London, 1991, 1993).

more or less inevitable under pre-modern conditions of undeveloped communicational integration, across a whole subcontinent, in a set of traditions – a Hindu world without firm boundaries, not yet Hinduism – which did not have an unitary textual base, centralized priesthood, inquisition, or consistent state backing. Diversities, in other words, were not necessarily perceived as building-blocks in a Hinduism unified through a single, hierarchically differentiated, order: as is indicated by the difficulties modern observers have faced in classifying the Kabirpanthis or the Bauls, say, as Hindu or Muslim.

Adhikari-bheda as a formal doctrine, in partial contrast, seems to have emerged in the seventeenth–eighteenth centuries as a Brahmanical way of accommodating, and keeping within proper limits, differences in ritual, belief and philosophy.[21] Such adhikari-bheda 'from above', particularly by the late-nineteenth-century, tended to signify not fluidity and openness but neat compartmentalization, the drawing up of definite boundaries and the arrangement of differences in a fixed hierarchy. That, fairly obviously, could be one way of building up a cohesive Hindu community without basically disrupting existing power relations of caste and gender.

. Colonial rule both stimulated such unificatory tendencies and provoked them into existence through its exploitative presence. Communications were qualitatively transformed through print, modern education, and new transport facilities. Orientalist scholarly constructions of Hinduism as grounded essentially in ancient sacred texts like the Vedas and the Upanishads, missionary polemics denigrating Hindus for the absence of such indispensable elements of true religion as unitary texts and uniform rituals, and incipient patriotic sentiments, all contributed in diverse ways towards making unificatory projects appear highly desirable. And, crucially, colonial jurisprudence fostered distinct domains of Hindu and Muslim personal laws within which textualized high-caste and ashraf norms tended to become universalized, while census operations from the 1870s insisted on firm definitions and boundaries. This transition to enumerated communities quickly became productive of acute rivalry between groups now being imagined in increasingly homogenized terms.[22]

It is important, however, to avoid bland, mechanistic depictions of the impact of late-colonial integration or of colonial discourse.

[21] Umeshchandra Bhattacharji, *Bharat-darshan-sara* (Calcutta, 1949), pp. 287–8.

[22] For some discussion of these aspects, see above, Chapter 1, footnote 46 and corresponding text.

These had been the pitfalls of much modernization theory, and one feels at times that the Saidian counterorthodoxy of today has run into similar problems through an inversion of values which retains implicit assumptions of passivity among the colonized. There is need for greater specificity about the precise location, ethos, and strategies of the groups directly involved in the transitions from Hindu towards Hinduism. That they were, overwhelmingly, upper-caste and male would occasion no surprise, for already existing hierarchies of caste and gender played a critical role in determining early access to the new integrative networks. The pre-colonial communicational linkages relevant and necessary for the emergence of notions of adhikari-bheda are likely to have been predominantly Brahmanical,[23] and this high-caste slant of projects of Hindu unity continued on an enhanced scale in the late-colonial era — and beyond.

But let me try to be a bit more specific. My data on late-nineteenth century conceptions of adhikari-bheda comes from three somewhat distinct, though overlapping groups.

There are, first, tracts in the form of religious disputations, written by fairly obscure men, high-caste and predominantly Brahman, that indicate considerable mastery at times of traditional learning. They come from a world of traditional literati and religious specialists that had both gained and lost under colonial rule, in shifting, contradictory ways. The British had for quite some time depended on pandits as native informants in matters of revenue, justice, and the early accumulation of 'Orientalist' knowledge. The influence of Brahmanical sacred texts and of notions of varna hierarchy had been extended and deepened through vastly enhanced dissemination via print and translation, while their everyday importance was simultaneously heightened by the development of

[23] These may have included learned contacts during pilgrimages, the wanderings of ascetics, centres of religious and philosophical discussion like Vrindaban, Varanasi, Nabadwip and some South Indian temples, and courts of princes and zamindars dispensing patronage to Brahman pandits and offering sites for debates on theological matters. Biographical details about nineteenth-century religious leaders offer occasional glimpses of this older world. Thus Dayananda's early years in the Doab were full of acriminous debates with orthodox Brahmans about *shastrartha* (the proper meaning of sacred texts), conducted in Sanskrit and hosted by zamindars, merchants and bankers, while the virtually unlettered Ramakrishna owed his religious training to a succession of holy men passing through Dakshineswar on the way to Gangasagar. J.T.F. Jordens, *Dayanand Saraswati* (Delhi, 1978), Chapter XI. See also Chapter VIII, footnotes 119 and 120.

'Anglo-Hindu' jurisprudence based on high-Hindu texts as interpreted by Brahman experts.[24] Yet there are many indications at the same time, particularly in a region like Bengal where Western education came earliest and had struck fairly deep roots by the late nineteenth century among gentlefolk, of a certain spread of ideas of legal equality and gender justice. There was a corresponding decline in prestige of traditional literati sticking to older ways, and a drying-up of their sources of patronage.[25] Both continued or enhanced influence, and decline in prestige and income, could in different ways stimulate an emphasis upon conservative hierarchized Hindu unity, where Brahman males would once again be firmly on top. This was all the more likely under conditions of an alien rule often suspected of encouraging Christian conversions and Hindu reform.

Plays, farces and prints where the Kaliyuga theme had become central, together with the conversations of Ramakrishna as reported in the *Kathamrita*, have already provided an entry, in several earlier essays, into another milieu where notions of hierarchized distinctions were being implicitly reaffirmed through contrast with the current disintegration of moral norms. The context here was a world of genteel poverty with a markedly clerical ambience. Here, among the less successful of the 'new' educated middle class, Kaliyuga acquired a novel association with *chakri* or the office-job, and bhadralok aspirations without the wherewithal to maintain them could lead to a gendered shifting of guilt and make caste status appear more vital.[26]

Western education, of course, did bring both new ideas and considerable success and upward mobility to some of its recipients. An initial belief that modernizing improvement under British tutelage was both desirable and possible, combined with the self-confidence bred by meritocratic advance at times from fairly humble (though still overwhelmingly Hindu high caste) beginnings, helped to stimulate some direct questionings of notions of adhikari-bheda-

[24] For a brief but helpful discussion, see Robert E. Frykenburg, 'The Emergence of Modern Hinduism as a Concept and as an Institution: A Reappraisal with Special Reference to South India', in Sontheimer and Kulke (eds), *Hinduism Reconsidered* (Delhi, 1991).

[25] Rajnarayan Basu in 1874 listed the plight of the 'Bhattacharji's' (traditional teachers of Sanskrit) as one of the principal evils of contemporary times. *Sekal ar Ekal* (Calcutta, 1874; rpt. Calcutta, 1988), p. 44.

[26] See Chapters 7 and 8.

grounded natural inequality. Rammohan in effect was rejecting adhikari-bheda when he denounced what he called the double standards of Brahmans. They were aware that many sacred texts had valorized the worship of a single, formless Brahma, and yet insisted on 'the rites, ceremonies, and festivals of idolatry' for the populace — for in these lay, he alleged, 'the source of their comforts and fortune'. The 'purer mode of divine worship', he insisted, should be open to ascetic and householder alike.[27] Some sixty years later Vidyasagar, who incidentally had come from a rural poor-Brahman background not dissimilar to that of Ramakrishna,[28] made the saint of Dakshineswar quite angry by suggesting that God could not have been so unfair as to give more powers to some and less to others.[29] But by then the educated young men of Calcutta had started flocking to Ramakrishna rather than to the revered yet isolated and disheartened social reformer. The discourse of inevitable and justifiable inequality was finding increasingly influential adherents. In 1892, to cite just one instance, Bhudev Mukhopadhyay, who had risen as high as any Indian was then allowed to reach within the educational bureaucracy, hailed adhikari-bheda as the supreme example of Indian distinctiveness and superiority in the domain of religious life.[30] The connections between such moods and middle-class disenchantment about British tutelage are obvious enough. And it is of course well known, and hardly in need of restatement, that the crucial ideological and organizational initiatives in the formation of both Hinduism and, later, Hindutva, came primarily from sections of the new middle class produced by colonial education.

[27] Rammohan Roy, Preface to the translation of the Isha Upanishad (Calcutta, 1816), reprinted in *English Works of Rammohan Roy* (Calcutta, 1947), vol. II, pp. 43, 44.

[28] Vidyasagar had been born in a poor, rural Brahman family of traditional pandits, and his father worked as a low-placed clerk in a Calcutta business office: thus once again indicating a link between the struggling literati, old or new, and the world of clerks. Vidyasagar, however, became successful and prosperous through a combination of academic brilliance and business ability: his famous independence was grounded in the printing-publishing firm he had set up in partnership with Madanmohan Tarkalankar in 1847. Asok Sen, *Iswarchandra Vidyasagar and His Elusive Milestones* (Calcutta, 1977), pp. 13–14, 23. See also my essay on Vidyasagar, Chapter 7 within the present volume.

[29] See Chapter 7, epigraph.

[30] Bhudev Mukhopadhyay, *Jatiya bhava*, in *Samajik Prabandha* (Calcutta, 1892), reprinted in Pramatha Bisi (ed.), *Bhudev-Rachanasambhara* (Calcutta, 1962), pp. 7–8.

Elements drawn from traditional religious specialists and literati; a broad, predominantly high-caste, urban or small-town lower middle class; sections of more successful, upwardly-mobile, urbanites: the social lineaments may appear to resemble the contours of today's Hindutva formation quite strikingly. But it seems wiser to avoid drawing such parallels across more than a century of sweeping change. A more helpful focus could be certain discursive and contextual shifts, the changing locations, and therefore implications, of adhikari-bheda within broader arguments. These, I feel, can lead us towards an explanation of the transitions to Hinduism and Hindutva which go beyond the obvious linkages with a generalized disillusionment about alien cultural domination.

In early printed tracts cast in the format of religious disputations adhikari-bheda is not yet part of any project for a more cohesive or homogenized Hinduism, and there are no developed enemy-images: Muslims, for instance, are hardly ever mentioned. Their primary aim is to defend existing, highly varied, Hindu ritual and behavioural norms, occasionally against Christian polemic, but oftener in more internal disputes with Brahmo reformers and alleged *nastikas* (atheists). Variety is indeed the main polemical point. Reformers are branded as intolerant critics of age-old rules and customs, and adhikari-bheda is repeatedly combined with apparently wide notions of catholicity: 'All [forms of worship] are acceptable, to each according to his taste.' 'What is bad is to lose one's *dharma*; the possibility of salvation remains so long as any *dharma* is devoutly followed.'[31] A closer look, however, reveals an obligatory determination of that 'taste' by status. In implicit refutation of the arguments of Rammohan, non-ritualized adoration of the formless Absolute is declared to be legitimate only for ascetics who have forsaken the world. Image-worship and conventional Brahmanical rituals are necessary for householders, and even the renouncer must treat the rules of caste with due respect.[32] Justifications of caste hierarchy often enter this discourse, but it seems usually as means to an end, to provide an additional, if crucial, instance of adhikari-bheda: 'Remember that distinctions of *varna (varna-vivedha)* are indispensable to *mukti* (salvation). Parameswar has given different kinds of powers *(shakti)* to different *jatis* — if one takes up the *dharma* of another, only harm can follow.'[33] Caste inequality

31 Baidyanath Mukherji, *Acara-darpana* (Calcutta, 1845); Lokenath Basu, *Hindu-dharma-marma* (Calcutta, 1856).

32 Nandakishore Kabiratna, *Sandeha-Nirasana* (Calcutta, 1863).

33 *Hindu-dharma-marma*, p. 60.

was asserted still in a remarkably open, indeed matter-of-fact, manner, for the potential readers of such tracts could be assumed to be entirely high caste.

Adhikari-bheda, then, was a bulwark of anti-reformist polemic: but it could also become at times an argument for reconciliation, a plea for the smoothening-over of current rifts within high-caste society. A moderate Brahmo in 1872 used it to argue that image-worship was not sinful, but quite permissible for those with inferior religious understanding: 'All forms of devotion are natural, for they correspond to differences in qualities and powers. . . . Big and small cannot have the same conceptions.'[34] Adhikari-bheda had a similar role, conciliatory rather than polemical, in the conversations of Ramakrishna, even though the ex-*pujari* of Dakshineswar clearly preferred the colour and ceremonial of image-worship to the dry intellectualism of Brahmo sermons. There was a growing tendency, once again manifested notably in Ramakrishna, towards reducing somewhat the starkness of adhikari-bheda through an emphasis upon a devotional piety (bhakti) open to all, in which Shudras and women could even enjoy a paradoxical pre-eminence. The master, moved by the devotion of his servant, might even ask the latter one day to sit beside him for a time. But big and small, as Ramakrishna had reminded Vidyasagar, would always remain fundamentally different, adding variety to the world and leaving space for the *lila* (play) of the gods.

The defence of caste hierarchy remained somewhat marginal in the early adhikari-bheda texts of Bengal, down to roughly the 1890s. The explanation probably is that it was not yet perceived as under serious attack, unlike, say, in Phule's Maharashtra. The central divisive issue in nineteenth-century bhadralok life was much more the question of women's rights, and in earlier essays we have already seen that the explications of Kaliyuga during these decades had likewise focused on insubordinate, Westernized and expensive wives, and not on any threat from Shudras.[35] To move for a moment to a much more exalted intellectual plane: 'discipline' was the central theme of the many essays of Bhudev Mukhopadhyay on social matters in the 1880s and early 1890s, and here once again order within family life was often given pride of place. The head of every Bengali family, he argued in 1882, 'needed to become a Lycurgus, for no royal Lycurgus could be born in Bengal to train Bengalis in

---

[34] Chandrasekhar Basu, *Adhikar-tattva* (Calcutta, 1872).

[35] See above, footnote 37 and corresponding text in Chapter 6, and footnotes 83–84 and corresponding text in Chapter 8.

Spartan virtues.'[36] The argument implicitly postulated the need, as well as the possibility, of a *samaj* or social domain autonomous of foreign control, and simultaneously imparted to it an uncompromisingly aggressive patriarchal tone.[37] Recent research has underlined the ways in which such highly gendered assertions of Hindu hierarchy and discipline reached a point of climax during the 1880s and early 1890s, in the context of the virulent campaign against the Age of Consent Bill of 1891. Discipline was glorified at that moment in an almost sado-masochistic manner, for it was justified precisely in terms of the suffering and pain it often admittedly caused. Thus a pamphlet by the leading conservative writer Chandranath Basu in 1892 categorically located the ultimate virtues and superiority of 'Hindutva' in the 'woman who cooks in her kitchen, all but burnt by the flames, suffocated by the thick smoke. . . .'[38]

Such a note of near-hysteria, however, could not be sustained or be effective for long, and men like Chandranath Basu were soon almost forgotten. Adhikari-bheda, once again, had to be softened through bhakti. Many late-nineteenth-century Bengali plays and farces, we have seen, sought counterpoints to the insubordinate, Anglicized wife in figures of pure women (and, occasionally, good plebeians – devoted domestic servants, even one or two peasants), who act decisively, while always maintaining proper deference, to set right the disturbed moral order. Twentieth-century Hindutva, too, would often oscillate between frank assertions of hierarchical structures, and projections, principally through bhakti, of a softer, more populist, hegemonic face. The greatest success of Hindutva to date has been through the appropriation and development of the image of Ram, central bhakti hero, in whom *udarata* and *krodhita mudra* – benign paternalism and martial prowess – have been classically combined.[39]

Caste, then, had been somewhat marginal in Bengal to bhadralok concerns and discourses, whether reformist or conservative, for much of the nineteenth century. It is my contention that the sudden

---

[36] *Samajik Prabandha* (1882), reprinted in Bhudev Mukhopadhyay, p. 486.

[37] I have explored this important *samaj/rashtra* polarity in Chapter 1.

[38] Chandranath Basu, *Hindutva* (Calcutta, 1892). For the Age of Consent agitation see Amiya Sen, *Hindu Revivalism in Bengal, 1872-1905* (Delhi, 1993), Chapter IV, and Tanika Sarkar, 'Rhetoric against the Age of Consent: Resisting Colonial Reason and the Death of a Child-Wife', *Economic and Political Weekly*, 4 September 1993.

[39] Pradip Kumar Datta, 'VHP's Ram: the Hindutva movement in Ayodhya', in Gyanendra Pandey (ed.), *Hindus and Others* (New Delhi, 1993).

centrality it acquired from around the turn of the century (with Vivekananda providing an obvious landmark) needs to be related to a spate of lower-caste affirmations.

One rough indicator of changing times are the classified catalogues of printed Bengali tracts in the India Office Library. Only 24 entries are listed under the 'Castes and Tribes' heading for the entire period upto 1905; the years from 1905 to 1920, in sharp contrast, include 140 titles, the vast majority of them written by, or in support of, lower-caste claims. What made such claims alarming from bhadralok points of view was that they were being formulated precisely at a time when efforts had begun to take nationalism in Bengal to the masses through the Swadeshi agitation, amidst ample indications that the British would seek to balance any political concessions (like expansion of the sphere of representative government) with safeguards for 'backward' groups: initially Muslim, but capable of extension to lower castes. The role here of British divide-and-rule and classificatory — specifically Census — strategies have been explored often enough, and their relevance remains undeniable. Census Commissioner H.H. Risley's attempt in 1901 to classify jatis according to notions of social precedence prevalent in each region stimulated an enormous quantity of claims and counter-claims whose weight amounted to one-and-a-half maunds by the eve of the 1911 Census.[40] In July 1910 his successor E.A. Gait aroused a storm in high-caste circles, as well as much debate as to the meaning of the term Hindu, by suggesting the omission from that category of those excluded from temples and Brahman services or considered to be polluting by touch or proximity.[41]

Yet any simple impact–response schema remains inadequate, and not just because of the widely divergent ways in which incipient subordinate-caste movements and high-caste advocates of Hindu unity reacted to such colonial moves and discourses. What was frankly accepted quite often as a great opportunity by the first was felt by the second as a threat, almost on par at times with the one posed by what came to be termed 'Muslim separatism'. Efforts to organize lower castes had in some cases begun well before the official

[40] L.S.S. O'Malley, Report on Bengal, Bihar, Orissa and Sikkim, Census 1911, vol. V, part I, p. 440.

[41] Memorandum sent by E.A. Gait, Census Commissioner for India, to Provincial Superintendents of Census Operations, 6 May 1911, citing his earlier note of 12 July 1910, Risley Collection, MSS Eur.E.295/11.

attempt to adjudicate jati hierarchies.[42] Even more significant, though seldom mentioned, is the fact that classification on that basis was quickly given up and indeed was seriously attempted only once, in 1901. Gait in 1911 decided that 'the question of social precedence will not be reopened' and ordered a return to an alphabetical classification.[43] Caste movements and tensions emphatically did not die down, and in fact have flourished now for more than half a century after even questions concerning caste were dropped from the Census agenda. A more adequate explanation would have to look into broader processes. These could include the slow but not insignificant spread of literacy and education among subordinated castes,[44] and, crucially perhaps, economic pressures and opportunities. Transitions to more 'respectable' (usually agricultural) occupations underlay the claims to new identities like Namashudra from Chandal, or Mahishya from Kaibarta, and there is also the possibility that the economic conjuncture of c. 1900-25 was somewhat favourable for 'counter-elite' formations based on a modicum of peasant prosperity and improvement efforts.[45] Certainly lower-caste (as well

[42] Sekhar Bandopadhyay's pioneering research has traced the beginnings of the Namashudra movement back to an agrarian protest in Faridpur in 1872-3, and the formation, possibly even earlier, of the Matua sect. The first 'uplift' conference was organized in 1881. ('Social Mobility in Bengal in the Late-Nineteenth and Early-Twentieth Centuries' — unpublished thesis, Calcutta University, 1985, Chapter v.) Haramohan Barman of Rangpur had started trying to get rulings from Nabadwip pandits to prove the Kshatriya status of Rajbansis from 1890, and raised funds from villages for that purpose (Narendranath Adhikari, *Rajbansiya Kshatriya-Samaj*, Rangpur, 1910, 1911, pp. 25-6.) C.J. O'Donnell's Bengal Census Report of 1891 (p. 268) referred to the 'Rajbansi section of the Koch' as 'dominated by an extreme desire to raise themselves on the social scale of Hindus' by claiming to be Bratya-Kshatriyas. That this was the only reference to a 'caste-movement' in the 1891 report, in sharp contrast to the seven-page section on 'Disputed Points of Social Precedence' ten years later (1901 census, pp. 378-84) is a reminder that the *fin de siecle* still constituted a turning point.

[43] E.A. Gait's Notes of 31 May and 14 June 1911, Risley Collection.

[44] Sekhar Bandopadhyay's thesis includes some interesting data from the 1911 Census Report on this. Ibid., p. 183.

[45] Booming jute prices could have benefited sections of East Bengal Muslim and Namashudra peasants, particularly around 1907-13 and 1922-5 — years marked also by the publication of large numbers of lower-caste and Muslim tracts, often coming out from obscure villages or small towns. Sugata Bose, who highlights these dates, writes also about an early-twentieth-century Mahishya 'new frontier of opportunity', that receded after c. 1920. *Agrarian Bengal: Economy, Social Structure and Politics, 1919-1947* (Cambridge, 1986), pp. 46, 63.

as rural Muslim) tracts of the early twentieth century are remarkably full of themes of improvement through self-help, thrift and economic virtues in general, well summed up by the motto of the Namashudra Matua sect, *hate kam mukhe nam* (concentrating on worldly duties while chanting the holy name).[46] But these are subjects for a different paper: we must return to the question of high-caste reactions to such developments.

These took several different forms. One response seems to have been a more aggressive assertion of hierarchy, and, specifically, of the need for Brahman hegemony, set in a cultural-nationalistic context in which caste was presented as a way of maintaining order and stability in a society that was superior to Western statism, indivi- dualism and class conflict. We have already encountered instances of this approach in the pages of *Dawn* and, briefly, in the writings of Rabindranath during the Swadeshi years.[47] Its clearest expression, however, came from the Hindu-Positivist ideologue Jogendrachandra Ghosh, prominent zamindar, one-time friend of Bankimchandra, and head of the Calcutta Positivist Society, who in 1899 suggested a programme of 'joint political action between Pandits and lawyers'. The orthodox Brahman literati would accept Comte as one of their own *rishis*, with the Positivist intellectuals in return submitting them- selves to the *vyavahar* law of the Hindus as the basis of what Ghosh felt would amount to 'Hindu self-government'. That self-government, Jogendrachandra argued in his *Brahmanism and the Sudra, or The Indian Labour Problem* (*c.* 1900), could be grounded in the already existing 'political dualism of British and Hindu authority', under which the former did not normally interfere in matters of caste governance. Locality-based 'Hindu Samajes' and 'Mahomedan waqfs' under firm Brahman and ulema control could thus evolve into units of 'subor- dinate self-government'. This, Ghosh went on to argue, would be very

---

[46] Early-twentieth-century Mahishya and Rajbansi pamphlets stressed the vir- tues of agricultural work even while claiming a higher, twice-born status that has normally been associated with contempt for manual labour. A Namashudra tract in 1911 emphasized the twin, related virtues of education and economic success through hard work and frugality, and cited the example of Benjamin Franklin. Pandit Bhagabati Charan Pradhan, *Aryaprabha* (Tamluk, 1911); Harakishore Adhikari, *Rajbansi Kulapradip* (Calcutta, 1908); Balaram Sarkar, *Namashudra Jnanabhandar* (Post-office Olpur, district Faridpur, 1911). For the Matua motto, see Sekhar Bandopadhyay, 'Popular Religion and Social Mobility in Colonial Bengal: The Matua Sect and the Namashudras', in Rajat Kanta Ray (ed.), *Mind, Body and Society: Life and Mentality in Colonial Bengal* (Delhi, 1995), p. 169.

[47] See Chapter 1, pp. 27–33.

much preferable to any attempt at importing into India Western notions of 'parliamentary-democratic' government, for there was already a 'possibility of . . . [a] dangerous upheaval from the lower depths of Hindu society'. 'Disruption' of this kind had been avoided so far through the 'discipline effected by the Rishis and Brahmans in the heart and mind of the women and the masses', but there was urgent need now to 'repel all disturbances of Western · origin . . . things like Trade Unions and Socialism . . . strikes, pickets etc. on such Western models would be simply fatal to this country.' 'Let us have freedom at least in the regions of social and historical theory', Jogendrachandra concluded, blissfully unconscious that he had just illuminated the ambiguities of that 'freedom'.[48] Cultural nationalism here has become the means to a higher end, a site for the refurbishing of hegemonies of caste and patriarchy.

Jogendrachandra's book included a condemnation of the 'rhetoric about a Shudra emancipation'[49] — a reference, it would appear, to Vivekananda, whose *Bartaman Bharat*, published in March 1899, had bitterly denounced Brahman priestly oppression, predicted at one point an impending Shudra revolution, and yet ended with a passionate call to embrace Brahman and Pariah equally as brothers, united without basic internal change in a nationalist fraternity against Western cultural domination.[50] Vivekananda's powerful, if

---

[48] Jogendrachandra Ghosh, *Brahmanism and the Sudra, or Hindu Labour Problem* (Calcutta, n.d., but from internal evidence, probably 1900), pp. 1, 11-13, 47-51. Other passages in this collection of essays expressed nostalgia about the importance once enjoyed by pandits in the courts of Warren Hastings, and distinguished Ghosh's current emphasis upon 'Hindu self-government' from fellow-Positivist James Geddes' exposure in 1872-3 of British commercial exploitation: the latter, Ghosh felt, had been marred by a note of 'obtrusive criticism' (pp. 13, 123). There are other near-contemporary instances, too, of such an association of assertion of Brahmanical 'self-government' with the world of Anglo-Hindu jurisprudence. A commentary on Anglo-Hindu case law by a Rajkot lawyer in 1912 described caste as 'any well-defined native Community governed for certain internal purposes by its own rules and regulations' — a 'self-governing body', in other words. L.T. Kilkani, *Caste in Courts, or Rights and Powers of Castes in Social and Religious Matters as Recognised by Indian Courts* (Rajkot, 1912), p. 1. For Jogendrachandra Ghosh and Bengal Positivists generally, see Geraldine Forbes, *Positivism in Bengal* (Calcutta, 1975), and Sabyasachi Bhattacharji, 'Positivism in Nineteenth-Century Bengal', in R.S. Sharma (ed.), *Indian Society: Historical Probings / Essays in Memory of D.D. Kosambi* (New Delhi, 1974).

[49] Ghosh, p. 47.

[50] For an analysis of the tensions within *Bartaman Bharat*, see above, Chapter 8, footnotes 227-230 and corresponding text.

ambiguous, rhetoric pointed towards an alternative approach to problems of caste and Hindu / Indian unity that was reformist and assimilative rather than aggressively hierarchical: one that was to become extremely influential in early-twentieth-century formulations of Indian nationalism, Hinduism, and Hindutva alike.

One element in this new approach, not unexpected in a situation characterized by the growing presence of lower-caste groups both in political life and as members of the vernacular reading public, was that frank assertions of the social implications of adhikari-bheda started becoming less common. Adhikari-bheda remained important, probably more than ever before, as a key argument for basic Hindu unity. But in a move inaugurated once again by Vivekananda, it was given an abstract, philosophical colour and detached from blunt avowals of caste (and gender) inequality. In an argument which to his disciple Nivedita marked the transition from ¡ the religious ideas of the Hindus' to 'Hinduism',[51] Vivekananda at Chicago in 1893 located fundamental Hindu unity in a hierarchy apexed by Vedanta that pertained to philosophy rather than to ritual or social difference.[52] This became crucial particularly in the projection of attractive and impressive images of Hinduism before external audiences. In a reification similar to that made by Vivekananda thirty years earlier, Radhakrishnan for instance in his Oxford Lectures in 1926 on the 'Hindu Way of Life' similarly assumed 'Hinduism' to be unified by an 'absolute . . . Vedanta standard' that has been able to incorporate differences as 'expressions of one and the same force at different levels'.[53]

In social matters, however, adhikari-bheda in this second approach tended to get displaced by a new self-image of upper-caste leadership, formulated in terms of paternalist philanthropy and Sanskritizing reform-from-the-top that would 'uplift' or 'purify' the lower castes — an agenda that was now coming to be recognized as indispensable for building 'Hindu', or 'national', unity. Already in Vivekananda,

---

[51] 'When he [Vivekananda] began to speak [at the Chicago Congress of Religions in 1893], it was of the "religious ideas of the Hindus", but when he ended, Hinduism had been born.' Nivedita's introduction to *Complete Works of Vivekananda* (Mayavati, 1907, 1962), vol. I, p. x.

[52] 'All of religion is contained . . . in the three stages of the Vedanta philosophy, the Dvaita, Visistadvaita, and Advaita: one comes after the other.' This, Vivekananda claimed, was 'my discovery.' Letter to Alasingha, 6 May 1895. *Letters of Swami Vivekananda* (Mayavati, 1940; Calcutta, 1970), p. 227.

[53] Radhakrishnan, *The Hindu View of Life* (Oxford, 1926; London, 1961), p. 24.

passionate denunciations of caste oppression were combined with fear of Christian and Muslim proselytization, and emerging anti-Brahman movements of the South were criticized for being in too much of a hurry and encouraging 'fighting among the castes'.[54] The recent research of Pradip Kumar Datta has established the centrality in the development of this paternalist argument of the 'figure of U.N. Mukherji, the influence of whose *Hindus: A Dying Race* (Calcutta, 1909) provides a convenient case-study of the importance of such hegemonizing strategies . . . as well as of their crucial limits.'[55] Mukherji pressed into service some Bengal Census data and projections from 1891 onwards that seemed to indicate a decline in Hindu numbers relative to Muslims, attributed it to the wretched conditions of the lower castes as contrasted to the supposedly much more virile, energetic, united, and prosperous Muslim peasants, and urged paternalistic upliftment at Brahmanical initiative as a means to Hindu survival, unity, and rejuvenation. Social reform was now firmly focused on caste; in a simultaneous move, it had been annexed to a vision of ineluctable, biological rivalry between Hindus and Muslims: 'At the end of the year they count their gains — we calculate our losses.'[56]

It may be helpful to take a closer look at the specific context in which Mukherji published his *A Dying Race*. Despite the obvious dependence on Census data and predictions, a purely derivative discourse argument is not really tenable even in this most favourable case. Bengal Census Superintendent O'Donnell had started the Hindu decline hare way back in 1891, even predicting that at present comparative rates 'the faith of Muhammad would be universal in Bengal proper in six-and-a-half centuries':[57] there were no marked

---

[54] Vivekananda's denunciations of 'upper classes torturing the lower' and sadhus and Brahmans sucking 'the blood of these poor people' take him much beyond the range of twentieth-century Hindutva, despite recent attempts at appropriation. But he also argued that 'The solution is not by bringing down the higher, but by raising the lower up to the level of the higher. . . . To the non-Brahmans I say, be not in a hurry . . . you are suffering from your own fault. Who told you to neglect spirituality and Sanskrit learning?' Letter to Sashi, 19 March 1894, in *Letters of Swami Vivekananda*, p. 81; *The Future of India*, in *Complete Works of Swami Vivekananda* (9th ed., 1964), pp. 294–8.

[55] Pradip Kumar Datta, 'Dying Hindus: Production of Hindu Communal Common-Sense in Early Twentieth-Century Bengal', *Economic and Political Weekly*, 19 June 1993.

[56] U.N. Mukherji, *A Dying Race* (concluding section), *Bengalee*, 22 June 1909.

[57] 1891 census, vol. III (Bengal), p. 146.

Bengali Hindu reactions for some fifteen years.[58] Nor had any Census report emphasized ill-treatment of lower castes as the key factor in Hindu demographic crisis quite in Mukherji's manner, while the foregrounding of that theme through Gait's Circular came only in July 1910, a year after *A Dying Race*. But acute tensions had started developing in parts of East Bengal around 1907–9 between bhadralok gentry and Muslim and lower-caste (particularly, Namashudra) tenants. Many Namashudras had not only refused to join the boycott movement against the Partition of Bengal but were organizing counter-boycotts of the bhadralok, withdrawing agricultural and menial services. The context was set by resentment about the occasionally high-handed methods of Swadeshi agitators and zamindars, some British encouragement, and peasant efforts during the ongoing Settlement operations in parts of East Bengal to commute produce into cash rents and so benefit from the prevalent high prices.[59] And for once it seems possible to establish a direct link between event and ideological statement. In June 1909, coinciding exactly with the serialization of Mukherji's essay in *Bengalee* (1–22 June), the *Modern Review* carried an article entitled 'What can be done for the Namashudras' by Binod Lal Ghosh, a pleader from Madaripur (Faridpur district). This suggested a series of concrete ways (in which, it was felt, 'our Brahmo friends' could take the lead) of educating and improving the status of the Namashudras, so that they are eventually accorded a treatment by 'high class Hindus . . . in no respect inferior to or more humiliating than what is accorded to Mussalman or Christian, or to those non-Namashudras from whose hands the high-caste Hindu does not drink water.' Such (limited) upliftment was indispensable, the article reminded its readers, specifically because some Namashudras, egged on by 'their

[58] An unsigned article entitled 'Decrease of Hindus' in the *Modern Review* of April 1907 anticipated some of Mukherji's arguments.

[59] The same economic conjuncture made sharecropping and *dhankarari* (fixed produce rents) arrangements attractive particularly for petty bhadralok tenure-holders. The most detailed account of this and other aspects of bhadralok-Namashudra relations during and just after the Swadeshi years is in the unpublished thesis of Sekhar Bandopadhyay, Chapter VI. He mentions also incidents like Dacca Swadeshi youth raiding a Namashudra quarter in a village in October 1907, threatening to strip a woman wearing foreign cloth, a Namashudra deputation to Lieutenant-Governor Hare in the same year which was followed by a few official appointments from that community, and data about anti-bhadralok Namashudra movements in 1907–9 in the Bakargunj-Faridpur-Khulna-Jessore region.

half-educated brethren', had started a 'misguided and suicidal agitation' for cutting off connections with high castes. 'Some of them have gone so far as to cease cultivating the lands of the higher class Hindu landlords as *Burga* tenants. . . . ' This could produce a situation in which the 'limbs' could get paralyzed, making the 'healthy growth of the main trunk' impossible. For 'the high caste Hindus cannot do without' the Namashudras: among other reasons, because they are 'the fighting class among the Hindus'.

The year 1909 in fact was marked by a spurt of suggestions and initiatives for building Hindu unity through high-caste reform from the top, both within and outside Bengal.[60] It would seem a safe guess, however, that most of these suffered from problems similar to those unwittingly indicated by Binod Lal Ghosh through language and specific proposals alike.[61] The key question remained that of 'authority' in Hindu society, as U.N. Mukherji put it with his usual clarity in a pamphlet dated April 1911, urging bhadralok support for the efforts of the Mali community of East Bengal to obtain the services of barbers. The upper castes could legitimize their ebbing authority only through initiating or helping processes of orderly social readjustment, and particularly so because the Muslims with tacit official encouragement from officials were allegedly already trying to convert the Malis.[62]

[60] Sibnath Shastri and his fellow-Brahmo associates set up a Depressed Classes Mission in that year, concentrating mainly on literacy efforts. Shastri had close connections with the Maharashtrian reformer Vithalram Shinde who, along with other Prarthana Samaj activists, helped to constitute a moderate Mahar group that would be marginalized by Ambedkar after *c.* 1920. (Dilip Biswas's introduction to Sibnath Shastri, pp. 89–90; Gail Omvedt, *Dalits and Democratic Revolution*, Chapters 3, 4.) In July 1909, again, the *Modern Review* reprinted an article from the *Punjabee* by Lala Lajpat Rai entitled 'The Depressed Classes' which argued that 'the communal interest of the Hindus' required upper castes to lend a 'helping hand' to subordinated groups, in order to 'avoid the evil consequences of letting the forces of nature to have their own revenge.' Shuddhi efforts by the Arya Samaj under Swami Shraddhanand were also gathering strength around these years.

[61] The latter had included the setting-up of night schools, free dispensaries, gymnasia, and co-operative banks among Namashudras, apart from the (very limited) change in modes of social intercourse mentioned already. There was no reference, it may be noted, to questions of sharecropping or commutation of produce rents, even though the former had been mentioned as a principal source of Namashudra agitation in the first part of the article.

[62] U.N. Mukherji, *The Malis of East Bengal* (Calcutta, April 1911). The pamphlet included an extract from the Bengali weekly *Hitavadi* (25 Kartik

Caste reform geared to projects of Hindu unity was repeatedly
undercut by its persistent high-caste assumptions: conversely, Hindu
unity aims tended to get marginalized, or could disappear altogether, in more determined efforts at caste upliftment and
self-organization. A good example is provided by Digindranarayan
Bhattacharji, who across three decades wrote copiously against
the evils of caste, composed many 'histories' of subordinate jatis,
and was hailed in his lifetime by a lower-caste activist (Manindranath Mandal, a Pod) as comparable to Chaitanya, the Buddha
— and Muhammad.[63] Bhattacharji's *Jati-bheda* (Faridpur, 1912)
carried an introduction by U.N. Mukherji and quoted extensively
from his *Dying Race*. Digindranarayan in later life became active
in the Hindu Mahasabha, and even served as an office-bearer
in its Bengal unit. Yet *Jati-bheda* borrowed heavily also from the
much sharper anti-caste arguments of the identically titled 1884
Brahmo tract of Sibnath Shastri, and in some passages went very
much further than Mukherji in attacking caste oppression and
its justifications in ancient texts like the *Manusmriti*. Significantly,
the tract contained a direct repudiation of adhikari-bheda: God
has given 'the same powers' *(saman shakti)* to all human beings,
just as he has made the same sun for Brahman and Chandal
(untouchable).[64] Digindranarayan maintained this sharp anti-caste
thrust throughout his life and combined it with pleas for improving
the lot of women. He was critical also of narrowly 'Sanskritizing'
movements, through which upwardly-mobile Namashudras or Ma-
hishyas were distinguishing themselves sharply from Chandals or
Kaivartas, and simultaneously imposing tighter restrictions on
their womenfolk in imitation of Brahmanical norms.[65] The theme
of Hindu demographic decline, as contrasted to Muslim growth,
so central for Mukherji's *Dying Race*, was occasionally mentioned

---

1317/1910) full of praise for the Malis for their exemplary devotion and loyalty
towards the bhadralok. The latter, the article declared, should therefore follow
the example of Yudhisthira, who had refused to enter heaven unaccompanied
by his faithful dog.

[63] Manindranath Mandal, *Bange Digindranarayan* (Calcutta, 1927).

[64] Bhattacharji, *Jati-bheda*, pp. 4-5.

[65] Digindranarayan Bhattacharji, *Chaturvarna Bibhaga* (Serajgunj, 1917; Calcutta, 1925), pp. 66-72, is particularly sharp in its critique of 'Sanskritization'
for its divisive and patriarchal implications. See also ibid., *Nipirita Shudrer
Nidrabhanga* (Calcutta, 1926), and *Bidhabar Nirjala Ekadasi* (Calcutta, 1926), the
latter a passionate indictment of the horrors of austere widowhood.

but remained a subsidiary motif for Bhattacharji even in his Hindu Mahasabha days.[66]

Its further marginalization and indeed implicit rejection can be noticed also in tracts directly produced by the Namashudra movement, which in 1905–12 had distanced itself from the bhadralok-dominated Swadeshi agitation against the Partition of Bengal. We may take as examples two pamphlets, published within a month of each other in 1911, but somewhat different in aims and style of argument.[67] *Namashudra-Dwijatattva* deploys 'historical arguments' to establish claims to high-caste status while at the same time making on occasion more radical attacks on caste oppression: untouchability, for instance, is contrasted to the care lavished by the bhadralok on their dogs. *Namashudra-Gyanabhandar* adopts a milder tone and urges self-improvement efforts in education and agriculture. What the two tracts have in common, however, is a firm distancing from all forms of bhadralok politics, a distance that expressed itself at times through loyalist effusions. And while, as Digindranarayan had noted with regret, such lower-caste productions usually raised demands of a limited and sectional 'Sanskritizing' kind rather than attacking caste in principle, there were also occasional organizational initiatives like the Bangiya Jana Sangha of 1923, led by a Pod and a Mali, to achieve cross-caste unity of subordinate groups.

Digindranarayan's critique of narrowly 'Sanskritizing' movements is a reminder that lower-caste assertions have moved along two logically distinct (though in practice at times intermingled) tracks. Movements restricted to claims for higher status are usually confined to particular jatis or their subdivisions, and in effect might strengthen overall hierarchy. (They tend also to confirm and extend gender controls, as Sekhar Bandopadhyay has recently reminded us in a fine essay.[68]) The periodic efforts over the last century to build identities like 'Non-Brahman', 'OBC', or 'Dalit', in contrast, involve efforts at overcoming narrow jati boundaries in the name of new and much wider horizontal solidarities. Fairly often, as under Phule,

---

[66] It was usually combined with pleas for Hindu–Muslim brotherhood, as even in his *Hindur Navajagaran* (Calcutta, 1931), published while Digindra-narayan was Vice-President of the Bengal Hindu Mahasabha.

[67] Kaviraj Sashikumar Bareibiswas, *Namashudra-dwijatattva* (Barisal, April 1911); Balaram Sarkar, *Namashudra-Gyanabhandar* (Faridpur, May 1911).

[68] Sekhar Bandopadhyay, 'Caste, Widow Remarriage, and the Reform of Popular Culture in Bengal', in Bharati Ray (ed.), *From the Seams of History: Essays On Indian Women* (Delhi, 1995).

Periyar or Ambedkar, they have directly attacked caste. On occasion they — or at least some of their leaders — have also been more open to questions of women's rights: a reminder, perhaps, once again that caste and gender domination remain intertwined in structures of adhikari-bheda, and therefore in their rejections.[69] It may be noted in parenthesis that it is movements of the second kind that have often been branded as casteist, notably during the Mandal agitation against the extension of reservations to backward castes. The critics then included several intellectuals who have spent a lifetime writing, in fairly sympathetic terms, about Sanskritization: precisely the kind of caste movement about which that pejorative term could be most meaningfully applied.

If early-twentieth-century Bengal experience indicates some of the difficulties of articulating caste assertions with projects of Hindu unity, the problems must have been far more acute in regions like Maharashtra and many parts of the South. Here many lower-caste and Dalit movements directly rejected Sanskrit-izing claims to higher status within the varna hierarchy, and developed in their place alternative versions of subcontinental history in which upper-caste 'Aryans' figured as alien conquerors — in neat inversions, one might say, of both nationalist and Hindutva arguments of territoriality or pitribhumi. Maharashtra appears particularly relevant in this context, as the land of Phule, Ambedkar — as well as of Savarkar, Hegdewar, and Golwalkar. The crystallization of the ideology and organization of Hindutva in the mid 1920s in Maharashtra, despite the relatively weak presence in that region of the Muslim 'threat' which was its overt justification, may become easier to explain through such a juxtaposition. Nagpur, the birthplace of the RSS in 1925, had also been the site of the All India Depressed Classes Conference of May 1920 where Ambedkar began wresting the leadership of Dalits from more moderate groups associated with Vithalram Shinde's efforts at reform from above under high-caste initiative.[70] And the RSS self-image of its own origins as embodied, for instance, in the official biography of its founder, K.B. Hegdewar, locates lower-caste assertion on par with the Muslim threat as

---

[69] Phule began with a school for girls of lower castes, and later daringly set up an orphanage for the illegitimate children of widows. Periyar is notable for anti-patriarchal statements, and Digindranarayan revived in Bengal a concern about the plight of widows which had largely vanished after Vidyasagar.

[70] Omvedt (1994), pp. 142–7.

the twin dangers that lay behind 'Doctorji's' initiative: 'Conflicts between various communities had started. Brahman-Non-Brahman conflict was nakedly on view.'[71]

The link between demographic decline and the need for lower-caste upliftment, first established by U.N. Mukherji, did play a significant role in the turn towards aggressive Hindutva in the early 1920s. Shraddhanand, who from 1923 had made removal of untouchability and Sanskritization through Shuddhi the major planks in his drive for Hindu *sangathan* (organization, with an openly anti-Muslim thrust), acknowledged his debt to Mukherji through the title of his last tract: *Hindu Sangathan: Saviour of the Dying Race* (1925). Savarkar, too, acquired something of a reputation as a social reformer by his support for moves to bestow the sacred thread and open temples to low castes. But the limits of such reformism were once again revealed when Savarkar advised Mahars to stick to their traditional occupations as village menials, against which they had started agitating under Ambedkar's leadership.[72]

Much more significant, however, is the silence about both lower-caste movements and reform efforts in Savarkar's crucial Hindutva text. This, as well as on the whole the subsequent organizational practice of the RSS, developed yet another strategy for dealing with caste difference, distinct from both aggressive assertions of hierarchy and efforts at controlled paternalistic reform. Savarkar's definition of the Hindu solely in terms of the pitribhumi-punyabhumi equation made differences of caste, along with those of ritual and belief, among Hindus irrelevant: what mattered was not content or status but authentic indigenous origin in 'Bharatvarsha'. Being irrelevant, matters of caste (or gender) inequality became implicitly unimportant, and could be more or less left alone, except when they specifically hindered Hindu unity and mobilization. Difference, in fact, could be celebrated as so many flowers making up the single garland of Hinduism — which was how K.S. Sudarshan, senior official of the RSS, eloquently described the unique wonders of Hinduism in the interview he gave some of us when we were writing the book titled *Khaki Shorts and Saffron Flags*. The new strategy, further, allowed a play across several different registers, ranging from defence of hierarchy to efforts at assimilative reform. Thus adhikari-bheda, too, could be reaffirmed at times, since that, presumably, would be as indigenous and authentic as anything else. Golwalkar did this on

---

71 C.P. Bhishikar, *Keshav Sanghnirmata*, cited in *Khaki Shorts*, p. 14.
72 Dhananjay Keer, *Veer Savarkar* (Bombay, 1950, 1966), pp. 172-97.

occasion, in his more conservative moods.[73] But what the central unificatory thrust of Hindutva ideology did was to make *autonomous* lower-caste assertions appear inevitably divisive. This is made fairly obvious, for instance, by the notes kept by an RSS member attending an 'Officer's Training Camp', which have been reprinted in a generally sympathetic history of the organization: 'In the last thousand years, the bonds that linked society were broken. This led to selfish caste mentality that divided society. . . . The RSS was organized to prevent the further disintegration of Hindu society.'[74]

Another passage in these lecture notes predictably asserted that 'Non-Hindus must be assimilated to the Hindu way of life'. A construction of Hindu unity that evaded rather than sought to eliminate or even significantly ameliorate hierarchy needs for its sustenance the notion of the Muslim as ever-present, existential threat — and one that is actualized and renewed, furthermore, through recurrent communal riots.[75] Mukherji in 1909 had remarked that 'there is nothing excepting religion that is common to two castes'.[76] In 1936 Ambedkar would make a not dissimilar point from a diametrically opposed polemical angle: 'A caste has no feeling that it is affiliated to other castes except when there is a Hindu-Muslim riot.'[77]

V

But how different, it will be asked, was 'Indian' nationalism in its handling of difference, and specifically of lower-caste assertions? Surely all nationalisms, with their projects of constructing modern nation-states, inevitably homogenize and repress internal differences, and surely Hindutva in this respect is no more than a particularly

[73] 'Diversities in the path of devotion did not mean division in society', argued Golwalkar, in an essay that went on to justify varna hierarchy. 'Special concessions' to scheduled castes and tribes, on the other hand, inculcated a 'separatist consciousness'. *The Nation and Its Problems*, in M.S. Golwalkar, *Bunch of Thoughts*, pp. 135, 144.

[74] W.A. Anderson and S.D. Damle, *The Brotherhood in Saffron: The Rashtriya Swyamsevak Sangh and Hindu Revivalism* (New Delhi, 1987), pp. 95-7.

[75] An identical logic has operated, of course, in the production and reproduction of Muslim communalism, with similar consequences in terms of subordinated groups, particularly women.

[76] *A Dying Race*, XI, *Bengalee*, 12 June 1909.

[77] B.R. Ambedkar, *Annihilation of Caste* (1936; reprinted, Jullundur, 1968), p. 42.

aggressive and crude variant of a far more general trend? The sincerity of Gandhi's indictment of untouchability is unquestionable, but his defence of a supposedly original and pure 'varnasrama' against later distortions was unacceptable to E.V.R. Naicker, Ambedkar, and many other lower-caste and Dalit activists.[78] The specific programmes of Harijan welfare and upliftment — opening of wells and temples, village-level constructive work — as well as the term itself, were often rejected as mere paternalism. They were perhaps not all that different in content and quality — minus the anti-Muslim thrust — from the projects of high-caste reform-from-above that we have already considered in brief, and at times encountered similar difficulties. And the record of the non-Gandhian Left — whether Nehruvian, Socialist (the important post-Independence Lohiaite development apart) or Communist — is at first sight even more dismal. The treatment of caste oppression as epiphenomenal to more basic questions of class struggle might even appear to a really harsh critic as not all that different from Hindutva subordination of the same issue to the higher requirements of Hindu unity.

A closer look, however, would indicate some significant differences, and make assessments of the kind I have just outlined less than fair. Crystallized Hindutva after the mid 1920s has on the whole kept away from even paternalistic caste reform, preferring the Savarkar argument of irrelevance and working, as the general RSS practice indicates, overwhelmingly in urban or small-town upper-caste milieus. This did change significantly, through VHP activity in the main, during the height of the Ramjanmabhoomi campaign — but then there can be little doubt that it was the reaction against Prime Minister V.P. Singh's decision to implement the Mandal Commission recommendations which enhanced greatly the appeal of Hindutva among high-caste groups. Lower-caste support in contrast remains highly unstable and problematic, despite opportunistic moves like a short-lived alliance recently with the Bahujan Samaj Party (BSP) in Uttar Pradesh.

Mainstream nationalism, in (partial) contrast and mainly at Gandhi's insistence, refused to consider caste oppression and particularly untouchability to be unimportant or irrelevant, thus moving away to some extent from the earlier Congress separation of political from social matters. Despite many bitter conflicts, a basis for

[78] See, for example, the important debate between Ambedkar and Gandhi in July–August 1936 around the former's *Annihilation of Caste* tract, reprinted in B.R. Ambedkar, *Writings and Speeches* (Bombay, 1989), vol. I, pp. 81–96.

dialogue and compromise with lower-caste and Dalit movements therefore remained. In the 1930s the Maharashtra Congress was able to absorb the bulk of Non-Brahman Satyashodhak activists, and it is surely significant that the murder of Gandhi by a Maharashtrian Brahman was followed by widespread anti-Brahman riots in this region. Gandhi and Ambedkar could, after all, agree in the end to the Poona Pact of 1932, which was bitterly denounced by the more aggressive orthodox Hindu elements within and outside the Congress. Ambedkar had a seminal role in drawing up the Indian Constitution, as well as in preparing the earlier drafts of the Hindu Code Bill, and the post-Independence Congress enjoyed a substantial Harijan electoral base that has been eroded only in recent years. As for the Left, it undoubtedly paid a high price in many regions for its long underestimation of caste as a possible form of subordinate assertion. But it would be quite unhistorical to deny the substantial gains achieved, in terms of human dignity and not just economistic advantages, by lower-caste and Dalit groups in other areas and times under Left leadership and through exploring the mobilizing capacities of class. Caste identity, after all, is not a natural, given, unchanging or hermetically sealed entity — any more than class.

I have emphasized in this essay the importance of caste in the context of its relative neglect in dominant historiographies. It may be appropriate to note in conclusion that, like identities of nation, religious community, class or gender, caste does not emerge automatically, but only through determinate human praxis and discursive projections that select and play upon one or several of the multiple, changing contradictions of social life. The shifting relevance of the language of caste would be an important research theme by itself, particularly in a region like Bengal where, in sharp contrast to adjoining Bihar, its importance seemed to have declined after the 1920s. But that can only be the subject of a different enquiry.